# THE CYPRUS QUESTION
# AND THE TURKISH POSITION IN
# INTERNATIONAL LAW

# The Cyprus Question
# and the Turkish Position in
# International Law

ZAIM M. NECATIGIL

OXFORD

Oxford University Press, Walton Street, Oxford OX2 6DP
Oxford New York Toronto
Delhi Bombay Calcutta Madras Karachi
Petaling Jaya Singapore Hong Kong Tokyo
Nairobi Dar es Salaam Cape Town
Melbourne Auckland
and associated companies in
Berlin Ibadan

Oxford is a trade mark of Oxford University Press

First published 1989
Reprinted 1990

British Library Cataloguing in Publication Data
Necatigil, Zaim M.
The Cyprus question and the Turkish position
in international law.
1. Cyprus. Turkish Cypriot view and
positions of interested parties
I. Title
341.4'2
ISBN 0-19-825225-0

Library of Congress Cataloging in Publication Data
Necatigil, Zaim M.
The Cyprus question and the Turkish position in international law
Zaim M. Necatigil.
Bibliography  Includes index.
1. Cyprus—International status.  2. Turkey—Foreign relations—
Greece.  3. Greece—Foreign relations—Turkey.  4. Cyprus—
Constitutional history. I. Title.
JX4084.C86N43 1989  341.2'9'095645—dc19  88-28943
ISBN 0-19-825225-0

Phototypeset by Cotswold Typesetting Ltd, Gloucester

Printed and bound in
Great Britain by Courier International Ltd
Tiptree, Essex

# Foreword

The history of the island of Cyprus since the negotiated accession to independence of the Republic in 1960 has been a sad and complex sequence of events, in which promises have been broken, the lives of families and communities have been under grievous strain, and the various efforts of third parties to mediate between the two communities have as yet proved unsuccessful. Numerous books and articles have been written on aspects of 'the Cyprus problem' since the violent events of 1963 and, especially, since the Turkish military interventions in 1974. A glance at the select bibliography of Mr Necatigil's present book gives an idea of the attention which the island, its political conflicts, and its international significance have received, quite justifiably.

But all has not yet been said. There is room for a further, detailed exposition and analysis by one who has studied in depth the historical and legal aspects of the Cyprus problem, especially the constitutional evolution of the Turkish Republic of Northern Cyprus, as its Attorney-General. Mr Necatigil has endeavoured to present an accurate and fair account, but he makes no attempt to conceal his own position or that of the government in north Cyprus. Although written by a lawyer with the benefit of his professional skills and his personal knowledge of many of the developments described, this is not a book addressed solely, or even primarily, to lawyers. It may be read with profit by historians of contemporary Europe, by specialists in international relations, whether academic observers or practitioners of the art of diplomacy, by international officials, and by anyone interested in the creation of federal or confederal constitutional arrangements for states comprising more than one national or racial group.

The story is taken up to the early months of 1988. A glimmer of hope shone from the historic meeting of the Greek and Turkish Prime Ministers at Davos, Switzerland, in January 1988. Further negotiations between the Greek Cypriot and Turkish Cypriot authorities themselves await clarification of the position of the Greek Cypriot government following the presidential elections of February in which Mr Vasiliou was elected President in place of Mr Kyprianou, who played a leading and sometimes controversial role in earlier negotiations.

Men and women of good will in many countries, but perhaps particularly those living in the European Community, must hope that not too many more years will elapse before an agreed, fair, and lasting settlement is reached. Mr Necatigil's latest book should contribute greatly to a deeper understanding of the situation by all who read it.

GILLIAN M. WHITE

*University of Manchester*
*July 1988*

# Preface

The aim of this work is to deal with the recent history of Cyprus and to examine the various legal issues that have been raised in connection with various developments.

The events in Cyprus since December 1963 raise a number of interesting issues of international law. International law and institutions have a role to play in decision-making and law has provided a tool of advocacy for policy-makers. Sometimes law has been overshadowed by politics; as is sometimes said, law is the child of politics. It may also be said that, in the long run, law has to keep abreast with developments and not ignore factual situations for ever.

In this work, it has been possible to look, in retrospect, at various events that have taken place in Cyprus. Special consideration has been given to the Treaty of Guarantee and principles of international law relating to statehood and recognition, as well as the principle of self-determination and its application to the situation in Cyprus. I have also dealt with the various stages of intercommunal negotiations under the auspices of the Secretary-General of the United Nations.

Though I am not completely detached from the Cyprus problem, I have taken care to see that the information supplied is accurate and have tried to be as objective as possible and to give a balanced coverage to the views of the interested parties.

I have included a postscript to cover the events from July 1987 to March 1988. It has, however, been possible to prepare a more up-to-date chronology by keeping abreast of developments up to the end of October 1989.

If this work can contribute towards a better understanding of the complex Cyprus problem, my endeavours will not have been in vain.

Z.M.N.

# Contents

# Figures

# Chronology of Events

1571    1 August—Ottoman conquest.

From 1571 to 1878 Cyprus remains under Turkish rule.

1878    Ottoman–British Convention whereby Cyprus is leased to Britain.

1914    Turkey enters the First World War on the side of Germany.

Unilateral annexation of Cyprus by Great Britain.

1915    Britain offers Cyprus to Greece on condition that she comes to the aid of the allies. Greece does not take up the offer which is never renewed.

1923    Treaty of Lausanne. Turkey and Greece recognize the unilateral annexation of Cyprus by Great Britain.

1925    Cyprus becomes a Crown Colony.

1931    Pro-*Enosis* riots in Nicosia; Government House is burnt down; the Legislative Council is abolished.

1947    Colonial government of Cyprus convenes Consultative Assembly to study proposals which provide for constitutional changes and envisage some degree of self-government; proposals rejected by Greek Cypriots who demand complete self-determination (*Enosis*).

1950    Archbishop Makarios II holds plebiscite of Greek Cypriots, which shows 96 per cent in favour of *Enosis*.

Markarios III elected Archbishop.

1954    Further British proposals for a Legislative Council are rejected.

Frustration of first appeal to UN by Greece.

November—Lt. Col. George Grivas arrives secretly to organize the struggle for *Enosis*.

1955    1 April—campaign in favour of *Enosis* started by EOKA (National Organization of Cypriot Fighters) under Grivas, code-named 'Dighenis'.

1956    March—Makarios exiled to the Seychelles.

1957    Radcliffe proposals rejected by Greek Cypriots.

Turkish Cypriots refuse to be colonized by Greece and demand partition.

Makarios released from the Seychelles but banned from Cyprus.

1958    EOKA intensifies activities. Intercommunal violence escalates.

Macmillan Plan, a system of condominium of Cyprus by Britain, Greece, and Turkey. Rejected by Greece and Greek Cypriots.

Cyprus question before the UN. The UN urges the parties to settle their differences through negotiation.

1959    February—the Zurich and London Agreements are signed by Britain, Greece, Turkey, Archbishop Makarios on behalf of Greek Cypriots; and Dr Fazil Kutchuk on behalf of Turkish Cypriots. Under the Agreements Cyprus becomes an independent state; Treaty of Alliance; Treaty of Guarantee; Britain retains 99 square miles as sovereign areas; treaty also provides for a Greek and a Turkish contingent to be stationed in the island.

March—Archbishop Makarios returns to Cyprus.

December—Archbishop Makarios elected President and Dr Fazil Kutchuk Vice-President.

1960    July—General elections to House of Representatives.

16 August—Cyprus becomes an independent republic.

Cyprus joins the United Nations and the Commonwealth.

1961    Cyprus becomes a member of the Council of Europe.

1962    Makarios declares that the Constitution conferred rights on Turkish Cypriots 'beyond what is just' and that he is obliged to disregard or seek revision of those provisions obstructing the state machinery.

1963    Tension between the two communities escalates. The 1960 Constitution not fully applied. Differences of the two communities come to the surface over the question of tax laws and laws relating to municipalities.

Makarios declares that he will not abide by decision of the Supreme Constitutional Court if it upholds that separate Turkish municipalities must be created. The President of the Court resigns.

Each community suspicious of the other. Greek Cypriot Minister of the Interior sets up 'special police'. Turkish Cypriots complain of harassment.

November—Makarios submits proposals for amendment of the Constitution. Turkish Vice-President reject these as being intended to abrogate the fundamental elements of the Constitution and the rights of Turkish Cypriots.

December—Turkey rejects proposals for amendment of the Constitution. Archbishop Makarios says this is unacceptable.

Outbreak of intercommunal violence. Turkish quarter of Nicosia under siege and the Nicosia suburb of Omorphita under heavy firing, as a result of Greek Cypriot armed attacks.

A warning flight of Turkish jet fighters over the island.

Turkish Cypriot Vice-President appeals to all Heads of State to stop Greek Cypriot attacks against his community.

Truce force under British command begins to operate in Nicosia. 'Green Line' dividing the communities is established.

1964 January—Makarios says he wishes to terminate the Cyprus agreements. A conference in London fails to resolve the differences of the two communities.

Co-operation of the two communities in the running of the affairs of the Republic of Cyprus comes to an end due to intercommunal fighting. Greek Cypriot wing of the Republic assumes all the powers and functions of the government of Cyprus.

Turkish Cypriot members of the Executive and the Legislature, as well as Turkish Cypriot public servants, find it impossible to resume their functions in the government.

February—fighting in Limassol.

March—Ktima fighting, the Turkish quarter of the town falls.

Turkey warns that she will intervene.

Security Council resolution (186/1964) in support of Cyprus sovereignty denounces threat of use of force.

The UN Security Council resolves (187/1964) to send a peacekeeping force (UNFICYP) to Cyprus.

Turkish Cypriot leader Rauf Denktash is banned from the island by the Greek Cypriot administration.

May—conscription is introduced on the Greek side.

President Johnson warns Turkish Prime Minister İnönü against invading Cyprus.

June—Grivas returns and assumes command of National Guard.

August—fighting in Kokkina-Mansoura (Tylliria) area. Action by Turkish airforce.

1965 March—Galo Plaza, UN Mediator, publishes report and proposals; rejected by Turkish government and Turkish Cypriots.

UN General Assembly adopts resolution reaffirming the absolute sovereignty of the Republic of Cyprus.

1966 February—joint communiqué signed by the governments of Greece and Cyprus that any solution excluding *Enosis* would be unacceptable.

April—AKRITAS Plan is published by local Greek newspaper *Patris*.

1967 April—military coup in Greece.

June—Greek Cypriot House of Representatives takes a decision to continue the struggle for *Enosis* of the whole of the island.

November—fighting between National Guard under Grivas and Turkish Cypriots in Kophinou area leads to Turkish ultimatum; accepted by Greek junta, which withdraws troops and Grivas from Cyprus.

December—Turkish Cypriots reorganize their administration under the title of Provisional Cyprus Turkish Administration.

1968 January—Makarios declares that he would be seeking a 'feasible', rather than a desirable solution to the Cyprus problem, within the framework of a unified, democratic, sovereign and independent state.

February—presidential elections on the Greek side. Makarios elected President which means renewal of his mandate.

On the Turkish side Dr F. Kutchuk elected as Vice-President.

March–Makarios declares that he is willing to start discussions with Turkish Cypriots and makes proposals to the UN Secretary-General.

June—intercommunal talks are inaugurated between Clerides and Denktash, under the auspices of the UN. Discussions take place with a view to restructuring the Cyprus Constitution.

1969 Greek Cypriot interlocutor emphasizes that the Greek Cypriot side is not prepared to accept under the guise of local government either a federal or a cantonal solution.

1970    Attempt on Makarios's life.
        Parliamentary elections on both sides.

1971    Grivas returns secretly to Cyprus.
        Renewed campaign for *Enosis* by EOKA-B.

        Intercommunal talks enlarged with the participation of Greek
        and Turkish constitutional experts, as well as, the UN
        Secretary-General's special representative in Cyprus, within
        the framework of the Secretary-General's good offices mission.

1973    February—Makarios re-elected President.

1974    January—death of Grivas.
        July—Makarios demands withdrawal of Greek officers.

        15 July—*coup d'état* against Makarios inspired by Greek junta;
        presidential palace destroyed; Nikos Sampson declared President.

        17 July—Turkish Prime Minister Ecevit flies to London for
        talks.

        19 July—Makarios addresses the UN Security Council. He
        says that the coup is an invasion and a flagrant violation of the
        independence and sovereignty of the Republic of Cyprus.

        20 July—start of Turkish military intervention; Turkish troops
        land on Kyrenia coast and take control of a 15-mile corridor
        extending to Nicosia.

        22 July—UN Security Council demands 'the cessation of
        hostilities and the withdrawal of all foreign troops from the
        territory of the Republic of Cyprus' (Resolutions 353/1974 and
        354/1974).

        23 July—democracy is restored in Greece.

        24 July—Glafcos Clerides, President of the Greek Cypriot
        House of Representatives takes over as 'Acting President of the
        Republic of Cyprus'.

        25 July—peace talks between Great Britain, Greece, and
        Turkey open in Geneva.

        30 July—British, Greek, and Turkish Foreign Ministers sign
        Geneva Declaration precluding extension of areas under
        military control of either side and setting up of buffer zones.

        9 August—second phase of the Geneva Conference starts.

        14 August—deadlock in negotiations; Turkey launches second
        phase of military operations.

16 August—Turkish forces reach 'Attila line'; Security Council calls for cease-fire (Resolution 360/1974).

22 August—Cyprus Turkish Administration takes the title of Autonomous Cyprus Turkish Administration.

1975    January—Greek and Turkish Cypriots agree to resume negotiations on the basis of federal government.

February—US imposes arms embargo on Turkey.

13 February—proclamation of the Turkish Federated State of Cyprus.

28 April—intercommunal talks start in Vienna under UN Secretary-General; agreement to set up committee on constitutional matters.

8 June—the Constitution of the Turkish Federated State of Cyprus is approved by a referendum in which 99.4 per cent of the voters say 'yes'.

20 June—elections are held for the 40-seat Legislative Assembly of the Federated State.

July—third round of talks in Vienna; Greek Cypriot negotiator Glafcos Clerides and Turkish Cypriot negotiator Rauf Denktash reach an agreement for voluntary movement (regrouping) of populations, which is implemented under UN supervision.

September—fourth round of talks in New York called off due to lack of formal proposals.

1976    February—fifth round of talks in Vienna; agreement to exchange proposals simultaneously within six weeks.

June—Turkish Cypriots hold presidential and parliamentary elections in the Turkish Federated State of Cyprus.

September—Greek Cypriots hold parliamentary elections in the south.

1977    27 January—first meeting between Makarios and Denktash.

12 February—second Makarios–Denktash meeting; guidelines for a Cyprus settlement agreed.

31 March—sixth round of talks in Vienna; Turkish Cypriot proposals submitted; they envisage a 'weak federation'; Greek Cypriots propose two-region federation leaving about 20 per cent of territory under Turkish Cypriot administration.

21 April—Carter administration seeks partial relaxation of US arms embargo.

3 August—death of Makarios.

Spyros Kyprianou, President of the Greek Cypriot House of Representatives becomes Acting President.

Bishop Chrysostomos of Paphos becomes Archbishop.

1978    January—Kyprianou is elected unopposed President for a five-year term.

April—Turkish Cypriots submit proposals for the settlement of the Cyprus problem; Greek Cypriots reject these as inadequate.

November—United States, Canada, and the United Kingdom submit a peace plan, known as the American Plan, which is rejected by the Greek Cypriots.

1979    January—Greek and Turkish Cypriots accept UN formula for a resumption of negotiations.

19 May—summit meeting between Kyprianou and Denktash in Nicosia in an attempt to resolve differences at a meeting chaired by the UN Secretary-General; they conclude a ten-point agreement for a federal solution.

June—intercommunal talks recessed.

1980    August—intercommunal talks resume with an inaugural address of the UN Secretary-General. The parties affirm their support for a federal solution of the constitutional aspect and a bizonal solution of the territorial aspect.

October—Greek Cypriot side tables its proposals for the solution of the Cyprus problem which constitute a detailed elaboration of its 1977 proposals.

1981    May—elections on the Greek side for House of Representatives under new electoral system (reinforced representational).

June—presidential and parliamentary elections in the north.

August—Turkish Cypriot side tables at the intercommunal talks comprehensive proposals including a map as regards the territorial aspect.

September—Greek Cypriot side tables 'further proposals'.

October—Andreas Papandreou's Panhellenic Socialist Movement (PASOK) party wins an overwhelming victory in Greek general elections. Andreas Papandreou becomes Prime Minister. Papandreou and Kyprianou agree to internationalize the Cyprus problem.

November—the UN Secretary-General, Dr Waldheim presents an 'evaluation document', also referred to as Waldheim 'ideas', or 'guide-lines'.

1982 Greek Prime Minister, Andreas Papandreou, pays official visit to south Cyprus.

1983 February—Kyprianou is re-elected president for a second term.

March—Turkish Cypriot side suggests a 'moratorium' on internationalization. This is rejected by the Greek Cypriot side; internationalization continues.

April—progress of the intercommunal talks is hindered due to forthcoming appeal by Greek Cypriot side to UN General Assembly.

May—UN General Assembly debates the Cyprus question. Resolution of the General Assembly of 13 May 1983 (A/37/253) demands immediate withdrawal of all 'occupation forces' and voluntary return of refugees to their former homes. Turkish Cypriots are especially concerned by the clause which affirms the right of the Republic of Cyprus and its people to full and effective sovereignty and control over the territory of Cyprus.

August—in order to break the deadlock following the debate at the UN, the Secretary-General submits his views under the heading of 'indicators' to promote intercommunal dialogue.

September—Kyprianou's hesitation to accept the 'indicators' causes resignation of his Foreign Minister.

October—Denktash informs the UN Secretary-General that the Turkish Cypriot side is ready to resume the intercommunal negotiating process on existing mutually agreed basis.

15 November—the Turkish Republic of Northern Cyprus is proclaimed by the unanimous vote of the Legislative Assembly of the Turkish Federated State of Cyprus, a democratic representative body of the Turkish people of Cyprus. The declaration emphasizes that this is in fulfilment of the right to self-determination. On the same day Turkey recognizes the new Republic.

18 November—the UN Security Council adopts resolution 541/1983 in which it deplores the 'purported secession', considers the declaration as legally invalid, and calls for its withdrawal.

6 December—establishment of a Constituent Assembly to draft the Constitution of the Turkish Republic of Northern Cyprus.

1984 January—Denktash proposes a series of goodwill measures to settle the outstanding issues between the two communities.

Kyprianou dismisses these proposals as propaganda.

Kyprianou presents to the UN Secretary-General his 'framework' proposals.

March—the UN Secretary-General presents his five-point ideas, called the Secretary-General's 'scenario'. He suggests that there will be no follow-up to the 15 November 1983 declaration by the Turkish Cypriots (freezing the situation) and the Greek Cypriots will refrain from taking further steps to internationalize the Cyprus problem.

May—UN Security Council debates the situation in Cyprus. The Security Council adopts resolution 550/1984 (11 May 1984); reaffirms resolution 541/1983, condemns 'all secessionist actions', including exchange of ambassadors between Turkey and the Turkish Cypriot leadership and declares them 'illegal and invalid'.

August—in pursuit of his mission of good offices, and after consultations with the Greek Cypriot and Turkish Cypriot representatives, the UN Secretary-General presents to the two sides his ideas, described as 'working points' for the resumption of the intercommunal talks. Both sides give 'positive' response to these initiatives.

September—UN Secretary-General convenes the first phase of the 'proximity talks' between Kyprianou and Denktash in New York.

October—second phase of the 'proximity talks' in New York.

November—third phase of the 'proximity talks' in New York.

1985 17 January—summit meeting between Kyprianou and Denktash in New York under the auspices of the UN Secretary-General. The UN Secretary-General submits his 'Agenda for the Proximity Talks', also described as 'Preliminary Draft for a Joint High-Level Agreement' containing elements for a federal solution, worked out during the 'proximity talks'. Proposals are accepted by Denktash, but rejected by Kyprianou.

12 February—AKEL and DISI parties join forces in the Greek Cypriot House of Representatives in securing a resolution censuring Kyprianou for his handling of the Cyprus problem.

March—the Constitution of the Turkish Republic of Northern Cyprus is accepted by the Constituent Assembly.

12 April—UN Secretary-General submits another draft 'Agreement' to each side without having consulted the Turkish Cypriot side. Turkish Cypriots allege that it has no legal effect.

5 May—Constitution of the Turkish Republic of Northern Cyprus is approved by a referendum; 70.16 per cent of the voters say 'yes' to the Constitution.

9 June—Rauf R. Denktash is elected President of the Turkish Republic of Northern Cyprus.

23 June—parliamentary elections are held for 50 seats of the Assembly of the Turkish Republic of Northern Cyprus.

1986    29 March—UN Secretary-General submits to both sides a slightly revised version of his 'Draft Framework Agreement on Cyprus' containing elements for a federal solution, which is accepted by Denktash and rejected by Kyprianou.

1987    July—Report on Cyprus of the Foreign Affairs Committee of the House of Commons is published. It recommends that the UK government should review its aid programme to Cyprus so that both communities can benefit equally; while it rejects official recognition of the Turkish Republic of Northern Cyprus, it recommends that Britain should help to facilitate normal trade and contacts. It suggests that the Greek Cypriot government should lift the economic embargo on the north.

November—Cypriot government's recourse to the UN General Assembly is deferred till March 1988.

December—Greek Cypriot Foreign Minister declares that the UN Secretary-General's 29 March document 'does not exist' in so far as the Cyprus government is concerned.

December—The European Parliament approves the agreement for the second stage of the customs union of Cyprus with the European Economic Community. This agreement is also ratified by the Greek Cypriot House of Representatives by 31 votes to 17 (the Rally and Democratic Party vote in favour, AKEL and socialist EDEK against).

1988    30–1 January—Greek and Turkish premiers, Papandreou and Özal, meet at the Swiss resort of Davos with the aim of starting a dialogue for friendly settlement of disputes between the two countries. They agree to set up a crisis telephone link between their capitals and to hold a summit once a year to avoid disputes.

14 February—presidential elections in the south. None of the candidates receives over 50 per cent of the vote in the first round. Two of the candidates who receive most of the votes are Clerides of the Democratic Rally Party (33 per cent) and Vasiliou, communist-backed independent (30 per cent), respectively. Kyprianou is beaten in the first round.

21 February—second round of the presidential election. Vasiliou receives over 51 per cent of the vote and is elected president in the south.

28 February—Vasiliou is invested by the Greek Cypriot House of Representatives.

3 March—Denktash proposes a package of goodwill measures. He also offers to meet the new Greek Cypriot leader on the basis of equality and 'without any prejudice to the respective positions of the two sides'. Vasiliou turns down Denktash's offer and instead offers to 'receive him at his palace as the President of the Republic of Cyprus'. Vasiliou proposes instead to meet Özal, the Turkish premier.

22 March—Turkish Cypriot authorities change existing practice for the control of persons passing between southern and northern parts of the island through the Ledra Palace crossing point. New practice involves a requirement for stamping of passports of certain categories of Cypriots and foreign nationals. Greek Cypriot side protests at the UN on the ground that the new practice aims at creating an international frontier in Cyprus. The Turkish Cypriot side says that this is in retaliation for Vasiliou's repeated declarations that he is the President of all Cyprus.

27 May—Greek and Turkish foreign ministers, Karolos Papulias and Mesut Yılmaz meet in Athens. They sign a 'memorandum of understanding' for adopting measures for the establishment of confidence between their two countries.

31 May—UN Secretary-General issues his six-month report on UN operation in Cyprus (S/19927). He appeals to the government of Turkey to reduce its troops in Cyprus.

8 June—at a press conference in New York, after having addressed the special session of the UN General Assembly on disarmament, Vasiliou announces that he is ready to meet Denktash to have 'meaningful negotiations' under UN auspices. Such negotiations must start 'without preconditions and all the key issues must be discussed, including the unity of the country'.

13–15 June—The Turkish premier, Özal, pays an official visit to Athens, the first by a Turkish Prime Minister for the last 36 years, upon the invitation of his Greek counterpart, Papandreou. They adopt agreements reached by the joint political and co-operation committees. They also agree to pursue further the possibilities of joint co-operation to help to foster mutual confidence. The joint communiqué does not refer to the Cyprus problem but the two premiers refer to it in their press conferences. There is no breakthrough on the Cyprus problem. Greece still insists on withdrawal of Turkish troops.

18 June—Vasiliou announces after a National Council meeting that he has accepted a meeting with Denktash under UN auspices.

22–4 June—Turkish Foreign Minister, Mesut Yılmaz, pays a three-day official visit to the Turkish Republic of Northern Cyprus. He briefs Turkish Cypriot authorities about Özal's visit to Greece.

26 June—Turkish President Kenan Evren begins an official visit to the United States, the first by a Turkish President for 21 years. The Cyprus question and the withdrawal of Turkish troops from Cyprus are among the issues discussed during this visit.

4–6 July—Denktash pays an official visit to Turkey on the invitation of President Evren. During the visit, the UN Secretary-General's suggestion that the dialogue between the two Cypriot leaders be held on the basis of the 1977 and 1979 accords is discussed. At the conclusion of the visit it is announced that Denktash is ready to meet Vasiliou to discuss the Cyprus problem on an open agenda and without preconditions, under UN auspices. Denktash explains that if the dialogue is to commence it should either be on an open agenda, or it should refer to all the accords reached within the framework of the intercommunal talks, including the 29 March 1986 document presented by the UN Secretary-General. Reference to the 1977 and 1979 accords only would cast doubt as to the validity and binding effect of all other principles accepted during the intercommunal talks. If this problem is settled it is expected that the high-level meeting will take place in September.

12–15 July—President Evren of Turkey pays an official visit to the UK. During this visit, the Cyprus question, Turkey's entry into the EEC and bilateral relations are discussed.

24 August—The leaders of the two Cypriot communities, Vasiliou and Denktash, meet in Geneva at the *Palais des Nations*, European headquarters of the United Nations, under the auspices of the UN Secretary-General. In a statement after the meeting the Secretary-General outlines the common agreement of the two sides to resume the intercommunal talks in Nicosia on 15 September. The two sides also reaffirm their commitment to the high-level agreements of 1977 and 1979 and refer to the 'opening statement' of the Secretary-General of 1980, the 'evaluation document' of 1981 and the 1984 Vienna 'working points'. They declare their readiness to find a solution through negotiation and undertake to co-operate with the Secretary-General in his mission of good offices. They acknowledge that this would require a determined and sustained effort by both sides, as well as the creation of an atmosphere of mutual confidence. They express their determination to attempt to achieve, through negotiation without preconditions, a solution on all aspects of the Cyprus problem by 1 June 1989. The two leaders acknowledge that the success of these talks depend on their personal and continued involvement and agree to meet frequently, beginning with a further meeting between them on 16 September at the residence of the Special Representative of the Secretary-General, Oscar Camilión. They accept the invitation of the Secretary-General to meet him in New York after the first round of meetings in Nicosia, to review the progress achieved during the initial stage. The parties agree to proceed along the lines of the Geneva Accord, that is, to:

(*a*) develop a common understanding of the elements that are central to an overall settlement,

(*b*) identify those components of an overall settlement which are agreed, and concurrently negotiate agreement on those components where disagreement remains or which require further consideration,

(*c*) agree on detailed provisions of all the components of an overall settlement.

15 September—the intercommunal talks are inaugurated at the UN Conference Room at the Ledra Palace Hotel. The two leaders attend with their advisers. Statements are made by the Special Representative of the UN Secretary-General, Oscar Camilión, as well as by Vasiliou and Denktash.

16 September–7 November—first round of the talks. During this round twenty meetings are held in private between the

two leaders in the presence of Camilión at his residence. The talks enable the two leaders to explain to each other their views and concerns about a wide range of issues. The question of 'three freedoms' (the freedoms of movement and settlement and the right to property) feature prominently in the discussions.

22–23 November—the two leaders meet with the UN Secretary-General in New York for an evaluation of the first round of the talks. In a surprise move the Turkish side presents to the UN Secretary-General, as well as to the Greek Cypriot side, six separate papers containing its views on various aspects of the Cyprus problem. At the conclusion of the evaluation meeting the Secretary-General makes a statement saying that in his opinion the first round has proved helpful in building a good working relationship and in clarifying many of the issues and difficulties. It is agreed to begin the second round in Nicosia on 19 December and to devote this round to developing, on a non-committal basis, a wide range of options for each of the issues that must be resolved and to evaluating these options in the light of the interests and concerns of both sides. The Secretary-General invites the two leaders to meet him again during the first half of March 1989 (later postponed to 5 April 1989).

19 December–28 March—second round of the talks. The topics taken up during the previous round are discussed in greater detail. The two leaders discuss federal principles, the powers and functions of the federal government and its units, representation abroad of the federation, the legislative and judicial organs, the boundary between the units or federated states and reserved or residual powers. Later the subjects are postulated as (1) constitutional arrangements—including the 'three freedoms', (2) territorial arrangements and the question of refugees—including 'settlers', and (3) security, de-militarisation and guarantees—including the establishment of balance of forces.

Vasiliou insists that the federal government should be strong in order to represent the unity of the country and that the residue of unspecified powers should be entrusted to the federal government. Denktash insists on a weaker federation so that the federal government will not override the units, and stresses the necessity of effective participation in all organs of the federal state and of equality of the two peoples. Turkish Cypriot side proposes that the presidency of the federal republic should rotate between the two peoples, and seeks equality in the federal council (council of ministers) whose decisions should be taken by consensus. Greek Cypriot side cannot accept rotation of the presidency; it proposes a council of ministers composed of 7 Greek and 3 Turkish ministers. Conceptual differences as regards 'bizonality' and 'bicommunality' persist. Denktash insists on an effective guarantee system that will not exclude Turkey.

Despite differences of view on issues discussed, both leaders agree that the legislature shall be bicameral with equal participation of the two peoples in the upper house. They also agree to submit to the approval of their two communities, in separate referenda, the overall agreement reached within the framework of the intercommunal talks.

1989 9 January—Denktash formally tables the set of six documents which he had presented in New York. These papers deal with issues such as, the 'three freedoms', deconfrontation (balance of forces), guarantees, and federal structure. At the same meeting two new documents are tabled on the Turkish Cypriot approach to the federal constitution as part of an integrated whole, and to the federal executive as part of an integrated whole. In addition, the document entitled 'The Turkish Cypriot position' which was submitted earlier, is formally tabled in an expanded form.

30 January—Denktash tables another document on the Turkish Cypriot approach to the federal legislature as part of an integrated whole. At the same meeting Vasiliou tables a document entitled 'Outline proposals for the establishment of a federal republic and for the solution of the Cyprus problem'.

13 February—Turkish Cypriot side submits its written comments on the Greek Cypriot outline proposals.

19 March—Tension grows as a mob of several hundred Greek Cypriot women violate the boundary and cross over to the Turkish Cypriot controlled area at two points, when they are encountered by angry and resentful Turkish Cypriot women. Turkish Cypriot authorities warn that if further boundary violations occur the culprits will be arrested and legal proceedings brought against them.

5–6 April—evaluation meeting in New York. It is agreed to devote the third round to the preparation of a 'draft outline of an overall agreement' in which the goals to be achieved for each of the elements of the outline will be described.

Vasiliou and Denktash accept the Secretary-General's suggestion that his colleagues (Oscar Camilión, assisted by Gustave Feissel) meet with them, jointly and separately, to prepare the 'draft outline'. It is envisaged that first, on the basis of the headings and topics discussed during the second round of the talks, the elements of an agreement will be outlined and, second, the description of the goals to be achieved for each of the elements of the draft outline will be prepared. Both sides agree to meet with the Secretary-General in June, if necessary to complete the outline, to consider its status and to agree on how to proceed from there.

1 May—in a letter to both sides the Secretary-General elaborates on the procedure to be followed in the preparation of the proposed outline.

5 May-10 June—third round of the intercommunal talks. This round is devoted to the preparation of the 'draft outline of an overall agreement' described by the Secretary-General in his statement of 6 April. In accordance with the Secretary-General's letter of 1 May, the following procedure is followed: The Special Representative and his colleague, Gustave Feissel, prepare a text on the basis of views put forward by the two sides during the second round. In separate discussions each side is asked to critique that text and indicate how it does not adequately meet its interests. The objective of this procedure is to prepare a revised text after taking into account those comments. The discussions throughout this process are to remain non-committal and the status of the 'draft outline' to be produced is to be considered in June, during the evaluation meeting in New York.

. During this round only three direct meetings are held between the two leaders in the presence of the Special Representative of the UN Secretary-General, that is, on 5 and 15 May, and finally, on 10 June.

By the end of the third round a document described as a 'non-paper' is completed but is not presented or discussed at a joint meeting of the two sides.

16 May—UNFICYP succeeds in working out agreement with both sides for the unmanning of military posts in three areas of Nicosia as part of a deconfrontation measure along the Green Line.

31 May—in his report to the Security Council (S/20663) about 'United Nations Operation in Cyprus', in a very

optimistic mood, which does not seem to be justified in view of major differences subsisting between the two sides, the Secretary-General states (para. 39) that the talks have 'progressed to the point where the contours of an overall agreement are discernible'. He continues to say (para. 40) that 'the discussions have brought out a number of specific ideas that could go a long way in resolving major issues.'

9 June—the President of the Security Council issues a Note to the UN Secretary-General saying that the Council expects the Secretary-General to play an active role to help to bring the two sides within effective negotiating range and not merely to act as a recorder of their positions.

10 June—at a meeting of the two leaders in the presence of the Special Representative of the UN Secretary-General, the arrangements for the forthcoming evaluation meeting in New York are discussed. The Special Representative assures Denktash that no paper will be submitted in New York because the 'draft outline' has not yet been prepared by the two sides. He further explains that there would be need for the talks to go on after the target date of June 1989. In view of this there would be a 'split meeting' in New York to give time for the preparation of the outline.

11 June—statement by Clerides appears in Greek Cypriot press to the effect that a 'draft agreement' is to be prepared by the UN Secretariat and presented to the two leaders in New York when they meet the Secretary-General.

18 June—parliamentary elections in Greece. None of the political parties receive an absolute majority. The centre-right New Democracy Party of Constantine Mitsotakis secures 144 seats in the 300-member parliament. Prime Minister Andreas Papandreou's socialist PASOK secures only 125 seats, losing its pre-election majority of 154. Papandreou, beset by political and personal scandals loses his bid to win a third consecutive four-year term.

25 June—Denktash has a meeting in Istanbul with Turkish President Evren and Prime Minister Özal.

28–29 June—evaluation meeting in New York. On 28 June the UN Secretary-General holds separate meetings at UN Headquarters in New York with Vasiliou and Denktash. Denktash suggests 'transparency' in the talks so that each side might understand the approach of the other. He also urges direct talks, rather than 'proximity' talks.

On 29 June the UN Secretary-General has a joint meeting with Vasiliou and Denktash at UN Headquarters. After the meeting, the Secretary-General, recalling, that pursuant to his mandate he is expected to play an active role to bring the parties within effective negotiating range, makes an opening statement putting forward certain ideas to help in the preparation of the 'draft outline'. In this statement he summarizes the ideas that could be included, as an integrated whole, in the outline of an overall agreement which his colleagues had explored on a non-committal basis with the two sides. The Secretary-General notes that both sides had a first discussion with his colleagues (Camilión and Feissel) on the annotations of the headings, and that no joint meetings had yet taken place to consider together the 'draft outline'.

The Secretary-General's opening statement includes the following ideas:

(1) The principles of equality of the two communities and the bicommunal nature of the federation are reflected in the equal role of the communities in the establishment of the federation, in the need for their joint approval in adopting the constitution and in the equality and identical powers of the two federated states.

(2) The bi-zonality of the federation is clearly brought out by the fact that each federated state will be administered by one community which will be guaranteed a clear majority of the population and land ownership in its area.

(3) The additional features of the federation will be the effective participation of both communities in all organs and decisions of the federal government, and the inability of the federal government to encroach upon the powers and functions of the federated states.

(4) The unity of the federation is to be reflected in its single international personality and single citizenship.

(5) All functions not vested in the federal government to be under the jurisdiction of the two federated states, and that each federated state to decide on its own governmental arrangements.

(6) The freedoms of movement and settlement and the right to property will be recognized in the federal constitution and regulated by the federated states in a manner consistent with the federal constitution. Freedom of movement will be exercised as soon as the federal republic is established.

Freedom of settlement and the right to property will be implemented by taking into account the ceilings to be agreed upon concerning the number of persons from one community who may reside in the area administered by the other and the amount of property which persons of one community may own in the federated state administered by the other.

(7) The 1960 Treaties of Guarantee and Alliance will remain a valid framework, but they should be updated.

(8) The criteria for working out territorial adjustment should enable a substantial number of Greek Cypriot displaced persons to return under Greek Cypriot administration, as well as take into account the practical difficulties, particularly those concerning the Turkish Cypriot displaced persons who would be affected.

After summarizing the above ideas the Secretary-General goes on to propose that his colleagues (Camilión, assisted by Feissel) resume their talks with both sides through joint meetings in order to complete the drafting of the 'outline' and invites both sides to meet him in New York in September to consider the completed 'outline' and to launch the negotiations of an overall agreement.

1 July—in Greece, after abortive attempts by individual party leaders, agreement is reached between the conservative New Democracy Party and communist dominated Coalition of the Left and Progress to form the Government, thus ending the political deadlock. The party chiefs agree that the coalition will have a three-month life span and will be limited to the restoration of democratic institutions and a catharsis of Greek political life.

4 July—the Greek Parliament elects Athanasios Tsaldaris, of the New Democracy Party, as the new President of Greece.

9 July—Greek Greek Government obtains a vote of confidence.

19 July—on the eve of the fifteenth anniversary of the Turkish intervention several hundreds of Greek Cypriot women, shouting, jeering and behaving provocatively, under the banner 'Women Return Home' cross the Green Line at Ayios Kassianos quarter of Nicosia, violating the UN controlled buffer zone. They crush the fence erected by UNFICYP to delineate the southern limit of the buffer zone, and they destroy the

UN observation post in the vicinity and the UN flag flying over it. The crowd pushes back the line formed by UNFICYP soldiers, claiming that there are no borders in Cyprus and that the Green Line must be dismantled. Turkish Cypriot side is angered by this violent provocation and violations of its borders. Turkish Cypriot police arrests 108 Greek Cypriots, most of them women, among whom are Bishop Chrysostomos of Larnaca and Archimandrite Papachrysostomou. Greek Cypriot detainees are tried and most of them sentenced to 3 days imprisonment and fined. The accused state they do not recognize the courts of what they describe as the 'pseudo state'.

20 July—UN Secretary-General expresses concern at the violence in the UN controlled buffer zone by the Greek Cypriots, and at the same time says that it is 'unacceptable' that the Turkish Cypriot side allegedly crossed the northern limit of the cease-fire line and made arrests. He requires respect for the integrity of the UN buffer zone and requests the Turkish Cypriot authorities to release without delay the persons that were apprehended. Turkish Cypriot side rejects the Secretary-General's statement as to the place arrests were made; it says that the arrests took place on the Turkish Cypriot side of the border, where a Turkish Cypriot post was 'unmanned' in accordance with the deconfrontation agreement. The border incidents and ensuing escalation of tension and enmity cause damage to the intercommunal dialogue.

24 July—the UN Security Council meets privately on the matter of the arrested persons. The Council's President says that the Council expressed grave concern over the situation and would appeal to both sides for restraint.

Arrested Greek Cypriot women are released on expiration of their terms of imprisonment and in the case of some of them, on payment of fines. Convicted men refuse to pay fines. They are released later.

25 July—amid growing tension on both sides due to buffer zone incidents, the UN Secretary-General's Special Representative in Cyprus, Oscar Camilión, writes to Vasiliou and Denktash presenting a paper containing a set of ideas which the Secretary-General summarized in his opening statement of 29 June. He says that the ideas are not presented as a formal proposal, but are offered to help the task of preparing

an outline of an overall agreement, by providing 'food for thought' and structure for discussions. The UN paper (described as a 'non-paper') is leaked to the press. Compared with the Secretary-General's opening statement of 29 June, the paper now presented contains more detailed ideas, especially on the subject of powers and functions of the federal government, and the structure, composition and functioning of the federal organs, that is, the legislature, the executive and the judiciary. On the question of guarantees, the Secretary-General says that the present guarantee system should continue but it should be up-dated and brought in line with article 52 of the UN Charter.

26 July—on the Turkish side fifty associations and societies petition Denktash urging him not to continue the talks because the Greek Cypriot side cannot be trusted and has no intention of respecting Turkish Cypriot rights. Denktash says that the Greek Cypriots who crossed the buffer zone have put a question mark over the reunification talks.

30 July—Denktash issues a statement saying that it is necessary for him to consult parliament about the UN paper and the future of the intercommunal talks. He says that parliament is recessed for the summer vacation and will be convened on 21 August.

7 August—Nelson C. Ledsky, Special Cyprus Coordinator of US State Department visits Cyprus and has a meeting with Vasiliou.

9 August—Ledsky has a meeting with Denktash. He urges continuation of the talks and preparation of the 'draft outline' by the end of September.

21-25 August—the parliament of the Turkish Republic of Northern Cyprus debates the Cyprus question and the future of the talks. A resolution, taken by majority at the conclusion of the debate, refers to the right of self-determination of the Turkish Cypriot people, requires that no concessions should be made from the Turkish Cypriot position as stated in papers submitted by the Turkish Cypriot side during the process of the intercommunal talks (especially on bi-zonality, political equality, effective guarantee of Turkey, and settlement of respective claims to property), stresses that a solution based on the free will of the two peoples would require recognition of the legal, social, cultural and religious existence of the Turkish Cypriot people by the other side, and notes that no one except the two sides can make proposals, present documents, or put forward any formula.

25 August—in a letter addressed to the UN Secretary-General, Denktash explains his side's attitude towards the Secretary-General's paper and states that he is willing to continue direct talks if Vasiliou will not make it a condition that the paper will be used as the basis of the talks.

26 August—British Foreign Office statement describes the resolution of the Turkish Cypriot parliament as 'unhelpful' because, the Office alleges, it puts forward preconditions for the intercommunal talks. The statement says that Britain continues to support the UN Secretary-General's efforts, and deplores any action which complicates the resumption of the talks.

28 August—Vasiliou states that he will not consent to the withdrawal of the Secretary-General's paper. He says that the paper was presented to be accepted or rejected. Elements of the paper which are accepted should be noted, and that negotiations should continue on those issues on which agreement had yet to be reached.

31 August—Vasiliou briefs his all-party National Council. He says that the likely course his side would be inclined to follow would be to make recourse to the Security Council or to the General Assembly, but the final decision would be taken after the Non-Aligned Conference in Belgrade, due to begin on 4 September.

1 September—the Secretary-General reiterates that his paper is not presented as formal proposals, it is non-committal and contains ideas only as food for thought. He says it is not possible to continue the talks in September. The talks should not be held for the sake of talks and that he would decide about the future course after meeting with Denktash.

4–8 September—in their declaration on Cyprus, heads of state of Non-Aligned countries meeting in Belgrade, express concern for the obstacles placed on the continuation of the talks and call for their removal. They also demand the immediate withdrawal of 'occupation troops' and 'settlers' from Cyprus and the voluntary return of 'refugees' to their homes. They point out that sustained and substantial dialogue in their intercommunal talks are the only way of reaching a just solution to the problem by peaceful means on the basis of the principles of the UN Charter, the Non-Aligned declarations and the high-level agreements. The Non-Aligned heads of state reiterate their solidarity with and support for the 'people' and 'government of Cyprus' and reaffirm their support for the independence, sovereignty, territorial integrity and Non-Aligned status of the Republic of Cyprus. Denktash states that this declaration will encourage Vasiliou to be even more daring in the field of propaganda.

11 September—Greek Cypriot spokesman says that the declared readiness professed by the Turkish Cypriot side to return to the negotiating table is 'plasmatic'. The spokesman accuses the Turkish Cypriot side of paying lip service to the talks and says that Turkish demands such as partnership rights, self-determination and unilateral guarantees are 'impossible conditions for the talks'.

12 September—the UN Secretary-General in his Annual Report states that for the first time in the 25-year history of the problem the leaders of the Greek Cypriot and Turkish Cypriot communities have personally committed themselves to a sustained effort to achieve an overall settlement. In an optimistic mood he expresses the belief that a 'critical juncture' is reached 'where an overall settlement that will safeguard the legitimate interests and meet the concerns of both communities seems possible'.

4 October—the UN Secretary-General meets Vasiliou in New York.

11 October—the UN Secretary-General meets Denktash in New York. They discuss the resumption of the intercommunal dialogue. It is announced that the talks between the two leaders under UN auspices will be resumed in October.

# I

# The Zurich and London Agreements and the Establishment of the Cyprus Republic

## I. INTRODUCTION

Cyprus is the third largest island in the Mediterranean with an area of 3,572 square miles, lying 40 miles south of Turkey, 77 miles west of Syria, 300 miles north of the Arab Republic of Egypt, and approximately 500 miles south-east of the Greek mainland. Its area is about the size of Lebanon or of the English counties of Norfolk and Suffolk combined. According to the census of 1960 the population of Cyprus was 573,566, out of which 441,656 were Greeks, 104,942 were Turks and 26,968 were of other races—Maronites, Armenians, Latins, for example. Thus the ratio of population was 77.0 per cent Greeks, 18.3 per cent Turks, and 4.7 per cent other races. The population of Cyprus is currently estimated to be about 700,000. According to statistical estimates Turkish Cypriots make up about 24 per cent of that population. However, there are no reliable statistical data as no island-wide census of Cyprus has been conducted since 1960. Greek Cypriots belong to the Greek Orthodox Church and speak Greek.[1]

Turkish Cypriots are Moslems and speak Turkish. Unlike their Greek Cypriot compatriots, Turkish Cypriots have long subscribed to the idea that affairs of religion must be separated

[1] Greek Cypriots claim descent from the early Aegean colonists, but this is disputed by archaeologists. The ancient Greeks did not at any time control the whole island even though they set up separate city kingdoms on the island during the fifth century BC, the most important of which was Salamis. Besides the Greeks, Phoenicians from Syria also came to Cyprus and settled on its coasts. Moreover, Greek influence was not exclusive; Cyprus had in fact succumbed to a succession of conquerors, such as the Assyrians, the Egyptians, and the Persians. Turkish Cypriots, on the other hand, are descended from the immigrants who came from southern Anatolia after the Turkish conquest of 1571. Unlike the Greek Cypriots, they were never subjected to foreign rule, except for a brief period of British administration.

from the affairs of state and have given constitutional force to this doctrine.

Each community has its own system of education conducted in its own language, with the exception of a few foreign language schools. Most of the Greek and Turkish schools follow the curricula of their counterparts in Greece and Turkey, respectively, with some variations to cater for local needs. There is no intermarriage between the two communities, who have maintained and jealously guarded their respective cultural and national heritages over four centuries of coexistence.

The fact that members of each of the communities speak of themselves as Greek Cypriots and Turkish Cypriots, and do not have the feeling of belonging to a Cypriot nation, may be the root cause of the problem. This fact, coupled with strong suspicion and distrust, prevents either side from approaching the problems of nation-building in a positive and constructive spirit. However, such a national awareness cannot be implanted from the outside, it has to grow from within the island itself. At present the possibility of creation of such an awareness seems very bleak. However, these facts have to be faced with understanding.

### 2. HISTORICAL BACKGROUND

#### The Anglo-Turkish Convention of 1878

The island of Cyprus was part of the Ottoman Empire from 1571 until 1878. In the latter year, faced with the Tsarist armies at the gates of Istanbul, Britain joined Turkey in a defensive alliance and signed the famous Convention on 4 June 1878 in the Ottoman capital. Under its terms, Turkey agreed to assign Cyprus to Britain to occupy and rule, though not legally to possess it. By an annexe to the Convention (1 July 1878), Cyprus was to be returned to Turkey, and the Convention annulled, if Russia gave back to the Ottoman Empire the eastern provinces of Batum, Ardahan, and Kars, which she had occupied the previous year.

There is no unanimity as to the legal position of Great Britain in respect of Cyprus during the period from its occupation in

1878 till the annexation in 1914. This is due to the provisions of the Convention itself under which Turkey 'assigned' the administration of the island to Great Britain, an expression which denotes transfer of title, whilst at the same time provision is made in the annexe for the eventual return of Cyprus on the fulfilment of certain conditions.[2]

### British rule

After Britain took over Cyprus, the government was headed by a High Commissioner, aided by an appointed Legislative Council, and by the six district officers who administered the areas into which the island had been divided, corresponding to the Turkish *Kazas*. In 1882 the Legislative Council was enlarged by an additional twelve elected members (9 Greek and 3 Turkish) with six appointed by the High Commissioner, who also had the casting vote and right of veto. In short, the Council had very limited powers. It frequently voted along communal lines, with the Greek and Turkish Cypriot members opposed. The Greek Cypriot members regularly began to demand *Enosis* (union with Greece), an end to the annual tribute paid to Turkey (under the terms of the Convention), and proportional representation.

### Local government

In the towns, the British later introduced a system of representational local government in which power lay in the hands of the Greek Cypriots, who were numerically superior. As a result, Turkish Cypriots extended the activities of Evcaf, an Islamic religious, educational, social, and cultural organization[3] to provide essential amenities such as water supplies in a number

[2] An analysis of the nature of the British administration under the Convention was made in the decision of the Anglo-Turkish Mixed Arbitral Tribunal in the case of *Parounak & Bedros Parounakian* v. *The Turkish Government*, Annual Digest 1929–1930, case no. 11. The Tribunal held in that case that the occupation of Cyprus lacked 'juristic precision', but it was analogous to protectorate status in the sense that it fell within the designation of country 'under protection' of Great Britain within the meaning of Article 64 of the Treaty of Lausanne.

[3] As to the administration and status of Evcaf, see Zaim M. Nedjati, *Cyprus Administrative Law* (Nicosia 1970), 92–3.

of towns as well as basic social and educational services, such as the running of Turkish schools. It was therefore a communal organization, performing administrative functions, although not handed over to Turkish Cypriot control until 1956.[4]

## Annexation of Cyprus

Because Britain and the Ottoman Empire were antagonists in the First World War, Britain annexed the island outright on 5 November 1914. However, Turkey did not recognize this until the Treaty of Lausanne in 1923. But the status of Cyprus remained nebulous until 10 March 1925, when it was declared a Crown Colony. In place of the High Commissioner, a governor was appointed who ruled with an Executive and a Legislative Council.[5] However, after the serious disturbances of 1931, when the governor's house was burnt down by Greek Cypriot *Enosis* agitators, the Legislative Council was abolished and never reconstituted.[6]

## Self-government offer

When the Labour government came to power in Britain in 1945, a Consultative Assembly was convened two years later, which aimed to give Cyprus a large measure of self-government, but it had to be dissolved in 1948 when the Greek Cypriots refused anything short of *Enosis*, for which they were campaigning since Britain took over seventy years earlier. Indeed, the campaign could have succeeded in 1880 when Gladstone became Prime Minister, if he had not changed his mind, or in 1915, if Greece had taken up Britain's offer of *Enosis* which was subject to the condition that Greece came to the aid of the allies. Such accidents of history made the Turkish Cypriots apprehensive about Britain's self-government proposals of 1947 with only limited safeguards for them. Greek Cypriots under the lead-

---

[4] Evcaf and Vakfs Law, Cap. 337, whereby the administration of Evcaf was assumed by the High Council of Evcaf.

[5] For the text of the Letters Patent, see the extraordinary issue of the *Cyprus Gazette*, No. 1691 of 1 May 1925.

[6] See the Letters Patent of 12 November 1931, published in the extraordinary issue of the *Cyprus Gazette*, No. 2177 of 16 November 1931.

ership of Archbishop Leontios had already decided that their future aim should continue to be *Enosis* and only *Enosis*, a policy followed by his successors, Archbishops Makarios II and Makarios III, respectively.[7]

## *Enosis* campaign

On 15 January 1950 the Greek Cypriot Orthodox Church held a plebiscite in churches, when an overwhelming majority of Greeks voted in favour of *Enosis*,[8] that is, the colonization of Cyprus by Greece and spiritual expansion, in total disregard of the right to liberty of the Turkish Cypriot community. It was in this atmosphere that Makarios, like his predecessors, was elected Archbishop on the *Enosis* ticket on 20 October 1950. When he was enthroned he took the following oath: 'I take the Holy oath that I shall work for our national aspirations and shall never waver from our policy of annexing Cyprus to mother Greece.'[9]

Greek Cypriot nationalists, under the influence of a right-wing Greek army colonel by the name of George Grivas, who was Cypriot by birth, began organizing for a terrorist fight against Britain. In loyalty to his oath, Archbishop Makarios III, under the patronage of the Greek Orthodox Church, founded the EOKA underground organization, which launched its terrorist activities on 1 April 1955. The foundations of EOKA (Ethniki Organosis Kyprion Agoniston) were laid in Athens in a secret meeting where Archbishop Makarios took the following oath on 7 March 1953: 'I take the oath on the Holy Spirit not to disclose anything I know or I shall hear about the *Enosis* struggle of Cyprus even if it costs me my life or even if I am subjected to

---

[7] This is confirmed by Mr C. Tornaritis in his *Cyprus and its Constitutional and Other Legal Problems* (Nicosia, 1977) at p. 29. A very incisive examination of the *Enosis* story is contained in Miss Nancy Crawshaw's *The Cyprus Revolt* (London, 1978).

[8] The voting took the form of signing one's name under a petition *in public*. If a Greek Cypriot was to 'vote' on this issue at all, it was as embarrassing and risky for him to 'vote' against *Enosis* as to declare in public that he was not 'a true Greek': Zenon Stavrinides, *The Cyprus Conflict: National Identity and Statehood* (Nicosia, 1975), 28.

[9] See *Cyprus: The Paradox of Enosis* (introduction by O. Örek) (Turkish Cypriot PIO, Lefkoşa 1971), 5.

the greatest of tortures. I shall obey all orders given to me without questioning them.'[10]

Colonel Grivas secretly landed in Cyprus and arms and explosives were smuggled to the island. Bombs were set off which wrecked police stations and other public buildings in scattered parts of Cyprus. Thus began a four-year period of terror and repression, arson, murder, and intercommunal clashes which eventually resulted in the London and Zurich Agreements creating an independent Cyprus Republic. The Greek Orthodox Church has, as ever played a major part in the political life of Cyprus. The Holy Synod, a gathering of Greek Orthodox bishops meeting under Archbishop Makarios, held regular meetings to 'chart the course of the Cyprus Problem' and draw up plans for the achievement of *Enosis*.

After EOKA started its destructive activities, the governor of Cyprus was replaced by Field Marshal Sir John Harding (later, Lord Harding), who after arriving in Cyprus started protracted talks with the Ethnarch (National Leader) Archbishop Makarios in order to find a solution to the problem. Due to the support given to the EOKA campaign by the Archbishop and his refusal to condemn violence, he was deported to the Seychelles, with the Bishop of Kyrenia and two others, all of whose complicity in the *Enosis* movement was clearly proved, a fact which was later proudly admitted by them all—including Archbishop Makarios. The Archbishop refused a British proposal to grant him freedom in exchange for a denunciation of violence. But he was released shortly afterwards in March 1957, on the understanding that he could not return to Cyprus. He returned to Cyprus on 1 March 1959.

### Turkish Cypriot reaction to EOKA

Turkish Cypriots adamantly refused to be colonized by Greece. As EOKA's aim was to bring about *Enosis*, Turkish Cypriot leaders expected that sooner or later the campaign of terror would be directed against the Turkish Cypriot community, which stood in the way of the fulfilment of this goal. Being

[10] The oath was taken by Archbishop Makarios, Col. Grivas, and ten others, including a Greek general, Nicolas Papadopullos: See *Memoirs of General Grivas* (London, 1974), 20.

concerned about the safety of their community, the Turkish Cypriot leadership organized an anti-terrorist militia which bore the name of *Volkan*. In 1957 this anti-terrorist movement was reorganized and named *Türk Mukavemet Teşkilâtı* (Turkish Resistance Organization), which became better known by its acronym 'TMT'. Its purposes were:

1. to fill the gap in Turkish Cypriot defences, which was daily becoming more apparent as EOKA was growing in strength;
2. to unify all existing Turkish Cypriot underground forces and co-ordinate their activities;
3. to form ties with sympathizers in Turkey;
4. to inspire confidence among the Turkish Cypriots.[11]

The Turkish Cypriot partisans who belonged to TMT became commonly known as *mücahits*, freedom fighters.

## Constitutional proposals

The British government concentrated on preparing a working plan for self-government for Cyprus and for this purpose entrusted Lord Radcliffe to prepare and submit constitutional proposals for Cyprus. In accordance with his terms of reference, Lord Radcliffe proposed that during the period of the Constitution Cyprus was to remain under British sovereignty. There should be a governor, appointed by Her Majesty, and a deputy governor, appointed by the governor. There would be a Legislative Assembly and a Cabinet of Ministers responsible to that Assembly. The governor should retain power to make ordinances and conduct executive administration in respect of external affairs, defence (including the fulfilment by HMG of their international obligations) and internal security. The constitutional proposals aimed at conferring a wide measure of responsible self-government coupled with reservations, provisions, and guarantees with the aim of protecting the special interests of the various communities. These proposals were turned down by the leaders of the Greek community as they did

[11] S. Bilge, *Le Conflit de Chypre et les Cypriotes turcs* (Ankara, 1961), 174; and Rauf Denktash's article 'TMT' in D. Manizade, *Kıbrıs: dün, bugün, yarın* (Istanbul, 1975), 160–1.

not come up to their expectations—*Enosis* through Greek Cypriot self-determination at the expense of the Turkish Cypriots, who looked upon *Enosis* as a change of colonial masters for the worse.

In the ensuing violence that was unleashed Turkish Cypriots were forced out of thirty-three villages and many lives were lost. In fact EOKA terrorists killed more Greek Cypriots than British soldiers.

EOKA continued its activities and conditions in Cyprus deteriorated culminating in communal strife between the *Enosis*-bound Greek Cypriots and the anti-*Enosis* Turkish Cypriots. Sir John Harding was succeeded as governor by Sir Hugh Foot (now Lord Caradon). It was the new governor's ideas that mainly inspired the Macmillan Plan, which was announced in 1958. Under this Plan a partnership scheme was proposed for Cyprus—partnership between the two communities in the island and also between the governments of the United Kingdom, Greece, and Turkey. Archbishop Makarios declared that the Macmillan Plan was unacceptable. The Turkish Cypriots and Turkey indicated their willingness to accept this Plan as an experiment in political partnership in the evolution of a bi-national independence.

## Towards the 1960 Constitution

The United Nations dealt with the Cyprus problem between 1954–8. In 1954 the Greek Claim for *Enosis*, as a right of self-determination, was turned down because it aimed at a change of sovereignty. During the General Assembly debates of 1957 and 1958 the Greek claim for *Enosis* again created serious difficulties since it could not be easily distinguished from annexation or *Anschlüss*. In the end, the UN General Assembly urged the parties to seek a peaceful, democratic and just solution in accordance with the UN Charter.[12] Despite acrimonious exchanges between the delegates of Greece and Turkey, at the conclusion of the 1958 debate a ray of hope for a negotiated settlement emerged. Consequently, in February 1959 negotiations were held in Zurich

---

[12] UN doc. A/C1/L.172 (XI) and Resolution 1287 (XIII).

between the Greek and the Turkish governments for the purpose of finding a just solution. After consultations with the respective Cypriot leaders an agreement was reached on 11 February 1959 at Zurich between the Greek and the Turkish Prime Ministers for the establishment of an independent state, the Republic of Cyprus. The two Prime Ministers initialled three documents, viz. (*a*) a draft Basic Structure of the Republic of Cyprus; (*b*) a draft Treaty of Guarantee between the Republic of Cyprus on the one part and Greece, Turkey, and the United Kingdom on the other part; and (*c*) a draft Treaty of Alliance between Cyprus, Greece, and Turkey. These became known as the Zurich Agreement.

On the same day, the Ministers for Foreign Affairs of Greece and of Turkey flew to London to consult the Secretary of State for Foreign Affairs of the United Kingdom. It was agreed between them, as a result of these consultations, that certain areas of Cyprus should be retained under the sovereignty of the United Kingdom and that an additional article should be inserted in the draft Treaty of Guarantee, providing for respect for the integrity of these areas as well as the use and enjoyment of various rights in connection thereto to be secured to the United Kingdom. At this stage, the documents initialled at Zurich, together with the British declaration and acceptance by the Ministers for Foreign Affairs of Greece and Turkey, were put before the respective leaders of the two national communities in Cyprus, namely Archbishop Makarios and Dr F. Kutchuk (Küçük).

At a conference held at Lancaster House in London in February 1959 documents setting out the agreed foundations of the final settlement of the problem of Cyprus were adopted and signed, on 19 February 1959, by the Prime Ministers of Great Britain, Greece, and Turkey and the respective leaders of the two national communities in Cyprus.[13] On the same day

---

[13] At the Conference at Lancaster House on 15 Feb. 1959, Archbishop Makarios raised a number of objections and expressed strong misgivings regarding certain provisions of the Agreement arrived at in Zurich. However, he signed the Accords because, as he put it, 'of the grave consequences that would have ensued' if he had rejected them: *Cyprus To-day*, vol. 1, No. 6 (1963). In addressing the Non-aligned Conference as President of Cyprus in Cairo on 9 Oct. 1964, Archbishop Makarios said, 'rejection of the Agreements would have meant denial of independence and increased bloodshed'.

provision was made, and was initialled by the three Foreign Ministers, for the setting up of three committees in order to give final form to what had been agreed upon: (*a*) a Joint Commission for drafting the constitution (with representatives from Greece and Turkey as well as from the Greek and Turkish Cypriots); (*b*) a Transitional Committee for the transfer of authority to the Republic of Cyprus; and (*c*) a Joint Committee for the purpose of preparing the final treaties giving effect to the conclusions of the London Conference.[14]

At this stage the Prime Ministers of the United Kingdom, Greece, and Turkey signed a memorandum by which they adopted, on behalf of their respective governments, the documents as 'the agreed foundation for the final settlement of the problem of Cyprus'.[15]

The Joint Commission completed its work on the draft constitution on 6 April 1960 and the document was signed on that date.[16] It came into force on 16 August[17] upon its signature by the then governor of Cyprus on behalf of the British government, by the representatives of the governments of Greece and Turkey, and by Archbishop Makarios, and Dr Kutchuk, who had been returned as President-elect and Vice-President-elect, respectively, as a result of elections held in December 1959.

The London Joint Committee, after protracted talks in London and Nicosia, completed its work on 1 July 1960.[18]

The Constitution having been signed, as indicated above, and the Treaties of Establishment, of Guarantee, and of Alliance having also been signed by their respective parties,[19] Cyprus was declared to be an independent sovereign Republic on 16 August 1960.[20]

---

[14] *Conference on Cyprus*, HM Stationery Office (1959, Cmnd. 679), 14–15.

[15] Ibid. 4.

[16] *Cyprus*, HM Stationery Office (1960, Cmnd. 1093), 3.

[17] By Order-in-Council SI 1368/1960 made under the Cyprus Act, 1960.

[18] (Cmnd. 1093), 4.

[19] See generally ibid., in which a variety of other arrangements of a legal nature are also set out.

[20] In so far as English constitutional law was concerned, Cyprus became independent as a result of Order-in-Council SI 1368/1960 made under the authority of the Cyprus Act, 1960. Though Cyprus became independent on 16 Aug. 1960, the Council of Ministers, by its decision No. 3222 of 11 July

Generally, constitutions are drawn up by constituent assemblies or by existing legislative assemblies and then referred to a referendum. In the case of the 1960 Constitution of the Republic of Cyprus, however, completely different steps were taken. The basic principles of this Constitution were formulated by Turkey and Greece, in consultation with the Turkish Cypriot and Greek Cypriot communities, through negotiations. Later, a constitutional commission was set up with the participation of Turkey and the Turkish Cypriot community and Greece and the Greek Cypriot community. This commission drew up the Constitution of the Republic of Cyprus on the basis of the framework which had been agreed upon. The Constitution came into effect together with the other international treaties.[21] The way in which the 1960 Constitution was drafted does not only imply a difference in procedure or form, it actually represents documentary evidence proving that the 1960 Constitution was one based upon the agreement of the parties concerned. The 1960 Constitution comprised, on the basis of agreement between the parties concerned, certain solutions and institutions which differed from those contained in other existing constitutions. This Constitution was based on principles agreed upon by the parties concerned rather than on precedent existing in other constitutions. Every article of the Constitution was drawn up after agreement was reached between the sides concerned. The rejection of the 'proportional representation system' provides an example of this approach. The result was that Turkish Cypriots

1963 decided that Independence Day should be celebrated on 1 Oct., instead of 16 Aug. (Suppl. IV, Part 1 of the *Official Gazette* No. 267 of 25 July 1963). The Turkish Vice-President, as well as the Turkish Ministers, objected to this.

[21] The dissatisfaction with the result achieved is reflected in an article in *The Economist* of 13 Aug. 1960. It said: 'Probably no people in history have ever viewed their independence with less enthusiasm than the Cypriots.' In Feb. 1984 Mr Clerides, who was the Minister of Justice of the Transitional Cyprus Government and head of the Cyprus Greek Delegation at the Joint Constitutional Commission which drafted the Constitution, stated that though they were not satisfied with the Zurich and London Agreements, the Greek Cypriot side signed them with the intention of abrogating them in order to achieve *Enosis*. He also said that the circumstances in 1959 forced them to sign the Agreements to prevent partition: Greek Cypriot daily *Alithia* of 2 Feb. 1984.

and Greek Cypriots were represented in the House of Representatives and other public institutions not on the basis of the population ratio but on the basis of an agreed fixed ratio. Article 62 of the Constitution clearly expounds this approach.

At the conference held in London in February 1959, documents setting out the agreed foundation of the settlement were adopted and signed on 19 February not only by the Prime Ministers of Greece, Turkey, and the United Kingdom but also by the respective leaders of the two national communities in Cyprus, namely Archbishop Makarios and Dr F. Kutchuk.

A statement made by the then Foreign Minister of Greece, Mr Evangelos Averoff, at the London Conference clearly shows that the Zurich Agreement was accepted by all the parties concerned and that Archbishop Makarios, who 'was in agreement with these agreements', was considered by Greece 'in all our deliberations as representing the will of the Greeks of Cyprus'.

At the conclusion of the negotiations the Prime Minister of Greece made the following declaration:[22]

From the very outset of these negotiations our main preoccupation was that there should be no victor in them, except the people of Cyprus themselves. I am certain we have achieved this. It is the best solution because its main foundation is co-operation between Greeks and Turks in the island, and in our two countries. And it is the best solution because it leaves to the island's majority the rights enabling it to develop in the most appropriate manner all aspects of its life, while it secures to the minority a splendid opportunity for maintaining its character and institutions, as well as for enjoying their generous share of common authority and responsibilities.

It is interesting to note that over ten years after the signing of the Zurich and London Agreements the Greek Foreign Minister (Mr E. Averoff), in an interview in 1969 with the staff correspondent of the Greek Cypriot newspaper *Makhi*, confirmed that the decisions taken at the time of the Zurich and London Agreements were taken 'in consultation with the Cypriot leadership'.[23]

It is true that the Cyprus Constitution of 1960 was not

[22] Cmnd. 680 (HMSO, 1959).
[23] *Cyprus Mail*, 20 July 1969. See also Necati Ertekün, *The Cyprus Dispute* (Oxford, 1984), 13–14.

submitted to a referendum. The Greek Cypriots have argued therefore that they were faced with an imposed constitution. However, the first election at the end of 1959 under the Zurich and London Agreements for the Greek Cypriot President was contested by Archbishop Makarios and the late John Clerides. The main issue at this election was the settlement under the Zurich and London Agreements and Mr John Clerides was campaigning against the agreements. In his defence of the agreements Archbishop Makarios declared on his nomination as President-elect of the Republic on 13 November 1959, 'For the first time in eight centuries the government of the island passed into Greek hands.'[24] The Archbishop's election as President, with a big majority, by the Greek Cypriots may be considered a Greek Cypriot 'yes' for the Zurich and London Agreements.

### 3. THE 1960 CONSTITUTION

As noted above, the Republic of Cyprus came into being as a result of international agreements. The Republic was set up as a compromise between the claim of Greek Cypriots for *Enosis* and the Turkish Cypriot standpoint that if Great Britain was to give up sovereignty over the island, it should be returned to its former owner, Turkey, and not to Greece.

The bi-communal nature of the Republic is fundamental to the state of affairs created by the 1960 treaties, and from its very inception the Republic of Cyprus has never been a unitary state in which decisions are made solely by one community, except in regard to matters within the jurisdiction of the respective Communal Chambers. The two communities were political equals; not in the sense that each had the same legislative or executive powers, for those accorded to the Greek Cypriots by the Constitution were greater by virtue of their numbers; but in the sense that each existed as a political entity.

The main features of the 1960 Constitution were as follows:[25]

[24] Greek Cypriot press of 14 Nov. 1959.
[25] The terms of the 1960 Constitution and the 1960 Agreements are analysed in some detail in S. Kyriakides, *Cyprus: Constitutionalism and Crisis Government* (Philadelphia, 1968), 53–71.

1. It provided for a presidential regime, the President being Greek Cypriot and the Vice-President being Turkish Cypriot elected on the basis of separate Greek Cypriot and Turkish Cypriot electoral rolls.[26] The President and the Vice-President could not deputize for the President in the latter's absence. The President of the House of Representatives, who could only be Greek, had the right to deputize for him. On the other hand the Vice-President was vested with veto rights with regard to foreign affairs, defence, and security.[27]

other hand the Vice-President was vested with veto rights with regard to foreign affairs, defence, and security.[27]

2. It provided for the participation of the two national communities in the central government, the Legislature, the Judiciary, the Public Service, and the Army. The Council of Ministers was composed of seven Greek Cypriot ministers and three Turkish Cypriot ministers. One of the following ministries, that is to say the Ministry of Foreign Affairs, the Ministry of Defence or the Ministry of Finance, was to be entrusted to a Turkish Cypriot minister.[28]

The House of Representatives was composed of thirty-five Greek and fifteen Turkish members elected on the basis of separate Greek Cypriot and Turkish Cypriot electoral lists.[29]

The Constitution endowed the Republic with two superior courts, the Supreme Constitutional Court and the High Court of Justice. The Supreme Constitutional Court was composed of a neutral judge as president, a Greek Cypriot and a Turkish Cypriot judge as members. On the other hand, the High Court of Justice was composed of a neutral judge as president, two Greek Cypriot judges and one Turkish Cypriot judge.[30] The subordinate courts were the District Courts. In purely Turkish cases, the court had to be composed solely of a Turkish judge or judges, in purely Greek cases of a Greek judge or judges and in mixed cases by mixed courts.[31] The Public Service was to be composed of 70 per cent Greek Cypriots and 30 per cent Turkish Cypriots.[32]

3. Each community exercised autonomy in matters relating to religion, education, culture and teaching, personal status,

---

[26] Art. 1 of the 1960 Constitution.     [27] Arts. 36–60.
[28] Art. 46.     [29] Arts. 62–3.     [30] Arts. 133–64.
[31] Art. 159.     [32] Art. 123.

family affairs, and the like, through their respective Communal Chambers.[33] The Chambers were given legislative as well as executive powers in the above matters.

4. According to article 182 of the Constitution, certain articles set out in annexe III thereto, which were incorporated in the Zurich Agreement of 11 February 1959, were the basic articles of the Constitution and they could not, in any way, be amended. The other provisions in the Constitution could only be amended in the manner prescribed by article 182, paragraph 3.

The 1960 Constitution contained checks and balances in order to ensure the coexistence of the two communities in the island who professed divergent ideologies and philosophies, without one community dominating the other or encroaching upon the rights of the other. The system envisaged by the 1960 Constitution was in effect a functional federation. Communal affairs had been defined by the 1960 Constitution and were given to the Communal Chambers. The Constitution also envisaged separate municipalities which are local government organs, whereas in the central government, the Legislature, and the Judiciary the Constitution envisaged the partnership of the two communities on an agreed basis. The functional federative system was therefore inherent in the Constitution in the way it provided for the partnership and co-founder status of the communities, the bi-communality of the state, and the dichotomy of functions and powers between the state and the communities.

Professor Thomas Ehrlich makes the following comments about the 1960 settlement:

The documents of the 1960 settlement are incredibly detailed, often repetitious, and occasionally ambiguous. Despite substantial weaknesses, the settlement did represent an imaginative resolution of many difficult problems. Given patience and a spirit of compromise on each side, it might have worked. It is not a model of draftsmanship; but, viewing the circumstances, no more could have been expected. There was general agreement, however, that substantial goodwill would be needed on the part of both communities to make the arrangements work.[34]

---

[33] Arts. 86–111.
[34] *International Crises and the Role of Law: Cyprus 1958–1967* (Oxford, 1974) 38.

Under Article 1 of the Treaty concerning the Establishment of the Republic of Cyprus,[35] the Akrotiri and the Dhekelia Sovereign Base Areas remained under the sovereignty of the United Kingdom.

The Treaty of Alliance[36] was concluded between Cyprus, Greece, and Turkey. By this treaty the contracting parties undertook to resist any attack or aggression directed against the independence or territorial integrity of Cyprus. Under the Treaty of Guarantee,[37] the Republic of Cyprus undertook the obligation to maintain the state of affairs so created and the three guarantor powers, Great Britain, Greece, and Turkey, guaranteed the continuation of the existence and maintenance of such order, as well as the independence and territorial integrity of Cyprus. Furthermore, they reserved the right to take steps for the restoration of the status of Cyprus in case of any change in, or disturbance of, such status.[38]

There are many who believe that Archbishop Makarios, the first President of the Republic, accepted independence as a spring-board for achieving *Enosis*. This is supported by later public declarations. Before the ink was dry on the paper, Archbishop Makarios publicly stated that the Agreements were merely 'a bastion and starting point for peaceful' campaigns. That was on 1 April 1960—a year after the main principles of the Constitution had been agreed upon at Zurich and London, but four and a half months before the island became officially independent in August. As the historian H. D. Purcell wrote: 'before the constitution was promulgated, he [Archbishop Makarios] showed he had every intention of amending it'.[39] A Cypriot 'nation' did not in fact exist in Cyprus. The birth of such

---

[35] (Cmnd. 1093), 13–15. Under the 1960 treaties the British government provided £12 million financial aid for the first five years and agreed to review, 'in consultation with the Government of the Republic of the provisions of this part of the agreement' and to 'determine the amount of financial aid to be provided in the following period of five years'. In view of this Mr Kyprianou had been demanding 'rent' for the bases. This has been refused since the bases are British Sovereign Areas and no rent can be considered to be due: *Cyprus Mail*, 22 June 1983.

[36] Cmnd. 1093, 88–90.

[37] Ibid. 86–7.

[38] Arts. I, II, and IV.

[39] *Cyprus* (London, 1969), at 306.

a 'nation' would require time, goodwill, and co-operation between the two communities. The situation was not however conducive to the creation of such a 'nation'. Archbishop Makarios proclaimed that the Agreements had not in fact settled the Cyprus problem, that the 'national aims' of the Greek Cypriots were unalterable, and that the Greek Cypriot 'national aim' was none other than the achievement of *Enosis*.[40]

On 21 September 1960 Cyprus became a member of the United Nations[41] and on 24 May 1961 a member of the Council of Europe upon the application of the two communities, as the State of Cyprus is composed of two communities.[42]

### 4. THE BREAKDOWN OF THE CONSTITUTION

Uneasy years followed the establishment of the Republic because the Greek side did not want to implement certain articles of the Constitution which underlined the partnership

[40] Various speeches of Archbishop Makarios are compiled in a publication of the Turkish Cypriot Information Office, entitled, *Cyprus: The Paradox of Enosis* (Lefkoşa, 1971, reprint 1977). Of particular relevance in this context are the following:

No Greek, who knows me can ever believe that I would wish to work for the creation of a Cypriot national awareness. The Agreements have created a State but not a Nation. (Makarios in a statement published in the *Cyprus Mail* of 28 March 1963.)

The aim of the Cyprus struggle was not the establishment of a Republic. These Agreements only laid the foundations. (From Makarios's statement made on 13 March 1963.)

Union of Cyprus with Greece is an aspiration always cherished within the hearts of all Greek Cypriots. It is impossible to put an end to this aspiration by establishing a Republic. (From Makarios's statement to the correspondent of the London *Times* on 9 April 1963.)

[41] See UN General Assembly Res. No. 1489, 15 UN GAOR, Suppl., 16, at 65 (A/4684) (1960).

[42] The 1960 Constitution provided for power-sharing by the two communities, particularly in matters relating to foreign affairs and defence. Art. 46 provided for a Council of Ministers to be composed of 7 Greek Cypriot and 3 Turkish Cypriot ministers. The President and Vice-President of the Republic, who were Greek Cypriot and Turkish Cypriot respectively, had veto powers, to be exercised conjointly or separately, on matters relating to foreign affairs and defence.

status of the Turkish community and thus reinforced all those provisions which prohibited union of Cyprus with Greece. Archbishop Makarios and many other Greek Cypriots did not like the rights accorded to the Turkish Cypriots in the Constitution which were intended as safeguards against any attempt at Greek Cypriot hegemony. Many of the terms of the Constitution were never implemented. Repeated promises to enforce the 30 per cent Turkish Cypriot participation in the public service were never fulfilled. Although the ambassadors at Bonn and Ankara were Turkish, the appointments to the UN delegation and to embassies were usually made without prior consultation or agreement. Within less than six months of independence, Dr Kutchuk, the Vice-President of the Republic, complained to Archbishop Makarios that he had not been consulted about the two Greek Cypriot representatives sent to the Belgrade Conference of Non-aligned States, nor had the agreement on Turkish Cypriot participation in the UN delegation and the Washington embassy been fulfilled.

It was not simply a numerical question of the 70:30 ratio, but there were far too many EOKA men who were given civil service posts. Even more ominous was the inclusion by Archbishop Makarios in the Council of Ministers of such persons who had been affiliated to the EOKA movement, one of whom was Mr Polycarpos Georghadjis, the late Minister of the Interior. Mr Zenon Rossides, who had been active in the early campaign of 1930–1, was appointed the first Cypriot delegate to the UN. In 1962, when his term of office expired, it was arbitrarily extended by Archbishop Makarios despite protests by the Turkish Cypriot Vice-President.

Controversy also arose over the Cyprus army, which in accordance with the settlement should have numbered 2,000 in a ratio of 60 per cent Greek and 40 per cent Turkish. The Turks wanted separate units and Dr Kutchuk, the Turkish Vice-President, vetoed a law passed by the House for the formation of an integrated unit. As a result Archbishop Makarios announced that he would not establish an army at all.[43]

In December 1961 the Turkish members of the House of Representatives refused to support the enactment of the island's

[43] *The Times* (London), 23 Oct. 1961.

tax law as a reprisal for the Greek failure to fulfil certain obligations affecting Turkish interests in other spheres. The President, however, ordered taxes to be collected under the pre-1960 income tax law, on the ground that the right to a separate vote on tax matters did not include 'the right to use this privilege over other unconnected demands'.[44] As a result, Greek and Turkish Communal Chambers enacted separate laws for levying of personal tax (income tax) on members of their respective communities.[45]

In the wake of these controversies the archbishop gave the first indication that he would not acquiesce in Turkish Cypriot vetoes over the decisions of the majority, even though they were in accordance with the provisions of the Constitution. In January 1962 he charged that the Zurich–London Agreements conferred rights on the Turkish Cypriots 'beyond what is just' to protect them, and 'since the Turkish minority abuses these constitutional rights and creates obstacles to the smooth functioning of the state, I am obliged to disregard, or seek revision of, those provisions which obstruct the state machinery, and which, if abused, endanger the very existence of the state'.[46]

There was also a serious dispute about the municipalities. The 1960 Constitution required that separate municipalities must be set up within six months of independence, but by procrastination their establishment was forestalled. Articles 173–7 of the Constitution provided that separate municipalities for the Greek and Turkish inhabitants should be established for the towns of Nicosia, Limassol, Famagusta, Larnaca, and Paphos and that the administration of such towns must bear certain additional fundamental features which are set out specifically in the said articles. Articles 87 and 89 of the Constitution further envisaged that the laws concerning municipal administration as far as they apply to the five towns in question must be

---

[44] *Observer* (London) 2 Apr. 1961. In Feb. 1963 the Supreme Constitutional Court ruled that the pre-1960 law was no longer in force and that there was therefore no machinery for the assessment or collection of taxes: *Kyriakides* v. *The Republic*, 4 RSCC (1963), 109.

[45] Personal tax was collected by the government and paid to the Communal Chambers after deduction of 5% commission.

[46] *The Times* (London) 5 Jan. 1962.

supplemented by subsidiary legislation and administrative measures of the Communal Chambers.

Separate municipalities had been functioning in Cyprus since the intercommunal violence of 1958. The Zurich Agreement recognized these municipalities and left the door open for reunification within four years if the two sides so desired. All that was needed was to pass legislation to give constitutionality to the existing municipalities. Yet, instead of proceeding to act as envisaged by the Constitution, the Greek Cypriot members of the Council of Ministers declared these municipalities to be non-existent and attempted to convert them into mixed 'improvement areas' for the purposes of the Villages (Administration and Improvement) Law, Cap. 243. Moreover, the Council proceeded to make appointments to the Improvement Boards of such areas, thus destroying a vested right of the Turkish Community.

This order of the Council of Ministers[47] was declared, by majority[48] of the Supreme Constitutional Court, as void *ab initio*.[49]

Non-implementation of Articles 173–7 of the Constitution, which was partly motived by the Greek Cypriot side's dislike of geographical regions for Turkish municipalities despite the mandatory provisions of Article 177, caused dissatisfaction among the Turkish inhabitants of towns, which culminated in a number of references to the Supreme Constitutional Court.[50] Archbishop Makarios himself publicly declared that he would not comply with the decision of the Supreme Constitutional Court to be issued in respect of municipalities.[51] As a result of

[47] Not. Nos. 4 and 5, Suppl. III of the *Official Gazette* of 10 Jan. 1963.

[48] The Supreme Constitutional Court was composed of an independent President Prof. Ernst Forsthoff of Heidelberg University and a Turkish and Greek Cypriot judge, Messrs. M. N. Munir and M. Triantafyllides, respectively.

[49] *The Turkish Communal Chamber* v. *The Council of Ministers*, 5 RSCC 59 *et seq.*

[50] See e.g. *The Turkish Communal Chamber* v. *The Council of Ministers* 5 RSCC 59 and *Celaleddin and Others* v. *The Council of Ministers and Others*, 5 RSCC 102.

[51] On 12 Feb. 1963, while the cases relating to municipalities were pending before the Supreme Constitutional Court, the *Cyprus Mail* reproduced the text of the statement made by Archbishop Makarios to a correspondent of the *Sunday Express*, which was to the following effect: 'Even if the Constitutional Court says that what I am doing (on municipalities) is unconstitutional I will not respect anything of these things.'

this affront the President of the Supreme Constitutional Court, Prof. E. Forsthoff, resigned his post. In his letter of resignation of 21 May 1963, addressed to the President and the Vice-President of the Republic, Prof. Forsthoff referred to their earlier meeting to discuss the internal difficulties of the court and stated that his assistant Regierungsrat Dr Heinze had been shadowed by detectives everywhere on the pretext of offensive insinuations whose perpetrators, for reasons that needed no explanation, intended also to affect the Professor himself. This state of affairs destroyed the possibility of his further co-operation in the court as a result of which he decided to resign *de facto* as from 21 May 1963 and *de jure* as from 15 July 1963 in order to make it possible for the court to keep functioning till the latter date.

The argument of the Greek Cypriot side that the Constitution was unworkable[52] can be interpreted as a pretext for demanding its amendment.[53] The evident desire of the Archbishop by 1963, and even before, was to terminate the entire 1960 settlement and to devise a new arrangement that would eliminate both some Turkish Cypriot power and all authority of the guarantor powers over the island's destiny.[54]

Against this background of mistrust that existed between the two communities, the President of the Republic, Archbishop Makarios, on 30 November 1963 made his famous thirteen-point proposals for amendment of the Constitution, to the Turkish Vice-President, Dr Kutchuk. The thirteen points were:

1. The right to veto to be abandoned.
2. The Vice-President to deputize for the President in case of his temporary absence or incapacity to perform his duties.

[52] Professor Ernst Forsthoff stated in answer to a question put to him by a correspondent of the Associated Press on 5 Jan. 1964 that 'Every constitution can have its peculiar problems. There is no constitution in the world which has not got its particular difficulties and problems. This is primarily a question of goodwill. If there is goodwill a constitution can be implemented and this Constitution is capable of being implemented.'

[53] It seems that during the second round of the Geneva Conference, Mr G. Clerides himself stated on 10 Aug. 1974 that the 1960 Constitution was in existence even though it could be said that it had not been implemented fully or that it was partially implemented: P. G. Polyviou, *Cyprus in Search of a Constitution* (Nicosia, 1976), 335.

[54] Ehrlich, *International Crises and the Role of Law*, 39.

3. The Greek President of the House of Representatives and the Turkish Vice-President to be elected by the House as a whole and not as stipulated in the Constitution.
4. The Vice-President of the House of Representatives to deputize for the President of the House.
5. The constitutional provisions regarding separate majorities to be abolished.
6. Unified municipalities to be established.
7. The administration of justice to be unified.
8. The division of the security forces into police and gendarmerie to be abolished.
9. The numerical strength of the security forces and of the defence forces to be determined by a law.
10. The proportion of participation of Greek Cypriots and Turkish Cypriots in the composition of the public service and the forces of the Republic to be modified in proportion to ratio of the population of Greek and Turkish Cypriots.
11. The number of the members of the Public Service Commission to be reduced from 10 to 5.
12. All decisions of the Public Service Commission to be taken by simple majority.
13. The Communal Chambers should be abolished and a new system should be devised. Should the Turkish Community, however, desire to retain its Chamber, such a course is to be open to it.

A few of the changes, such as authorizing the Vice-President to act for the President in the event of the latter's temporary absence or incapacity, would actually have provided the Turkish Cypriots with more protection than before. But seven revisions would have amended 'unamendable' (basic) articles for which the Turks had fought hard at Zurich and London, including the Vice-President's power to veto, the requirement of separate majorities in the House for passage of important legislation, separate municipalities, a limited security force, and assurance of 30 per cent representation in the public service and 40 per cent in the army.

Such proposals, Vice-President Kutchuk pointed out immediately, were 'of a sweeping nature' and attacked the very roots which gave life to the Republic; their 'ulterior intention was to leave the Turks at the absolute mercy of the Greeks'. Turkey rejected the thirteen-point proposals on 16 December 1963.

It has been argued that the memorandum containing the proposals for amendment of the Constitution was prepared at the instigation of Sir Arthur Clarke, the British High Commissioner, who also made corrections on the text in his own handwriting.[55]

Professor Ehrlich writes that 'The case for revision could not be rooted in classic precepts of international law'. He goes on to say:

The traditional view is that, as a question of law, there is not much to be said upon revision of treaties. The only well-recognized doctrine of direct relevance deals not with modification of treaties but with their termination: *rebus sic stantibus*. And whether under the so-called subjective or objective approach—or some alternative formulation— no persuasive argument could be made for its application in this context. The only change in circumstances between 1960 and 1963 was that the Accords had been tried for three years and found wanting by at least the Greek Cypriots. Their defects from the Greek Cypriot perspective could be characterized as 'fundamental', but this would not, in the traditional view, provide an option to terminate.[56]

A Greek Cypriot author has expressed the view that 'putting forward all 13 proposals simultaneously may have been a mistake and a tactical miscalculation. It would have been preferable, given the climate of distrust, for a gradual process of amendment to have been embarked upon.'[57] This would have been the right approach had the proposals for amendment rested on any legitimate reason. In fact, as seen in the context of the Akritas Plan,[58] the proposals for amendment of the Constitution were merely a pretext for abrogating the whole set of Agreements, the whole essence of which outlawed union of Cyprus with Greece.

[55] See Dimitri S. Bitsios, *Cyprus: The Vulnerable Republic* (Institute for Balkan Studies, Thessaloniki 1975), 121–4.
[56] Ehrlich, *International Crises and the Role of Law*, 53.
[57] G. Polyviou, *Cyprus: The Tragedy and the Challenge* (London, 1975), 39.
[58] See the following section.

## 5. THE AKRITAS PLAN

Turkish Cypriots have consistently claimed that Greek Cypriot proposals for amendment of the 1960 Constitution had been put forward as a first stage of a course of action to abrogate the treaties and clear the way to *Enosis*, and that the procedure for the attainment of these objectives was carried out in accordance with a pre-conceived plan, known as the Akritas Plan.[59]

The Akritas Plan, drawn up in 1963, was first published by a local Greek newspaper, *Patris*, on 21 April 1966, with the professed intention of exposing the mishandling of the Greek Cypriot 'national cause' by Archbishop Makarios. In a series of articles published subsequently in the same paper, it was disclosed that Archbishop Makarios had assumed the responsibility for the implementation of the Plan, and that he had appointed Mr Polycarpos Georghadjis, the then Minister of the Interior, as its head under the *nom de guerre* of 'Chief Akritas', together with other top ranking Greek members of the government as officers of the secret organization.

The Akritas Plan was a conspiracy to dissolve the Republic of Cyprus by a combination of military and political action. The Plan was to be carried out progressively. The first stage was to convince the world that the 1960 Constitution was unworkable; the second, to put forward proposals for amending it, ostensibly to make it workable, but in reality to remove the constraints which it imposed on Greek Cypriot control of the government and of the island's affairs in general. Later stages were to be the neutralization of the Turkish Cypriots (who would be bound to oppose any revision of the Constitution) without provoking Turkish intervention, the abrogation of the treaties, and, finally, the unfettered exercise of 'self-determination' by Greek Cypriots. The presumption was that Turkey would not intervene simply because proposals for revision of the Constitution had been put forward. If the Greek Cypriots could manage to become 'masters of the situation within a day or two, outside intervention would not be possible, probable or justifiable'.

According to this document, the final objective of the

---

[59] See Appendix 1, below.

organization was *Enosis*, but the struggle had to be based on self-determination in order to influence international public opinion.

The events of December 1963 have shown that Greek Cypriots had in fact set up a para-military 'organization' in 1963 under the late Minister of the Interior, Mr Polycarpos Georghadjis. This was due to suspicion that Turkish Cypriots were also being armed, and trained by Turkish mainland officers. The degree of personal involvement of Archbishop Makarios in the preparation and carrying out of the Akritas Plan has been contested.[60] There is the evidence of his own actions, in particular the submission of his thirteen points for amendment of the 1960 Constitution, which sparked off the December crisis in 1963 and the collapse of the Republic.[61] He seemed to have been acting in conformity with the strategy outlined in the Plan. There is evidence of his continued advocacy of *Enosis* after independence (in spite of the clear prohibition of such activity in the Constitution), of his assiduous efforts to convince opinion outside Cyprus that the 1960 Constitution was unworkable, and of his precipitate announcement that the treaties had been abrogated on 1 January 1964. The coincidence between his own actions and the tactics outlined in the Akritas Plan is undeniable.[62]

Although prepared in 1963, the preparations for action of the kind indicated in the Plan had started long before. Indeed, the Greek army general who was the first commander of the Greek Cypriot National Guard established by President Makarios disclosed in the Athens press in 1965[63] that, as early as August 1960, the Archbishop had already decided to train and arm the Greek Cypriots and to revise the 1960 Constitution by doing away with the Turkish Vice-President's power of veto, which was the principal safeguard for the Turkish Cypriots against

[60] e.g. Aristos Katsis, *Phileleftheros* (Greek Cypriot newspaper) 10 Nov. 1979 and John Torode, *The Independent*, 28 Jan. 1979.

[61] See Richard A. Patric, *Political Geography and the Cyprus Conflict, 1963–71* (Waterloo, Ont., 1976), 42.

[62] John Reddaway, *Burdened with Cyprus: The British Connection* (London, 1986), 134 and 147.

[63] Lt. Gen. George Karayannis, 'The Events of December 1963', in *Ethnikos Kiryx* (Athens newspaper), 13 June 1965.

Greek Cypriot domination of the Republic. The same Greek general, referring to the outbreak of violence in December 1963, remarked that 'Archbishop Makarios put his plan into effect and the Greek attack began', but he did not refer to the Akritas Plan.[64] Similarly, a Greek diplomat who served as Greek Consul-General in Nicosia during the EOKA revolt and who was later responsible for Cyprus affairs in the Greek Ministry of Foreign Affairs in Athens records that from 1962 onwards the Archbishop was contemplating 'a new act of power, a new offensive' and that in January 1963 planning exercises were carried out by his staff officers in the presidential palace in Nicosia with the object of neutralizing the Turks.[65]

Although the text of the Akritas Plan has been widely publicized[66] it has never been officially denied or repudiated by the Greek Cypriot government. It has simply been passed over in silence by them. It has, however, been referred to in unofficial Greek Cypriot publications more and more openly and in critical vein. Mr Glafcos Clerides is reported by a Canadian scholar to have confirmed in 1971 that it was genuine.[67] On the other hand, some Greek Cypriot writers have passed over in silence this damaging evidence, even in books written quite recently.[68] Certain articles from the Greek Cypriot press confirm that the authenticity of the Akritas Plan is now widely accepted among Greek Cypriots.[69]

[64] Lt. Gen. George Karayannis, *Ethnikos Kiryx*, 15 June 1965.

[65] Angelos Vlachos, *Deka Khronia Kypriakou* (Ten Years of the Cyprus Problem) (Athens, 1980), 274.

[66] e.g. as UN document A/33/115; S/12722.

[67] Patric, *Cyprus Conflict*, 42. Mr Clerides has included the text of the Akritas Plan in vol. 1 of his book, *Cyprus: My Deposition* (Nicosia, 1989), 212–9. He argues that the Turkish Cypriot leadership also had a plan to be put into effect in case the other side abrogated, or refused to implement, the Zurich and London Agreements. This contingency plan envisaged the establishment of a 'separate Turkish Cypriot state'.

[68] Stavros Panteli, *A New History of Cyprus* (London and the Hague, 1984); Polyviou, *Cyprus: The Tragedy and the Challenge* and *Cyprus in Search of a Constitution*.

[69] Alecos Constantinides, 'A Revision of History', *Alithia*, 14 Nov. 1979; 'Graverobbers and *Coups d'État*', *Alithia*, 14 Dec. 1985, and Aristos Katsis, 'The Akritas Plan', *Phileleftheros*, 10 Nov. 1979. Mr L. Loucaides, Deputy Attorney-General of the Greek Cypriot government has, however, in an address on 22 June 1987 during 409th session of the Committee of Delegates of the Council of Europe, considering application No. 8007/87, denied the existence of the Akritas Plan.

## 6. WHY *Enosis*?

Irredentist nationalism of the nineteenth century gradually gave way during the twentieth to the application of the principle of self-determination as a means of decolonization with the ultimate object of achieving independence. This was not so in the case of Greek Cypriots, who, after the Second World War, began to make claims for union with Greece rather than independence. This was mainly because of the nature of Greek Cypriot ideology, inculcated by Church and educational system alike.

The Greek side's demand for *Enosis* could well be interpreted as part of a wider movement which aimed to unite all Greek-speaking peoples in the region who were, or claimed to be, of Hellenic origin. That, indeed, was how Mr George Papandreou, the then Greek premier, saw it as late as 1964. This, the revival of the Byzantine Empire—or the '*Megali Idea*' as it came to be called—was cherished by Athens from the nineteenth century when the Ottoman decline evoked expansionist policies at Turkish expense.

*Enosis*, therefore, seems part of a much greater dynamism than the union of Cyprus with Greece would suggest. Furthermore, the ideology of *Megali Idea* not only aimed at territorial expansion, but at hellenizing the territories acquired in such a way that there would be little or no room left for non-Greek peoples. The classic example was Crete. Of the 88,000 Turkish inhabitants in 1895, virtually none now remain.

The *Megali Idea* was further boosted in November 1920, when King Constantine returned from exile with plans for the re-establishment of the Byzantine Empire—already well on its way through the Treaty of Sèvres the previous August, which gave the Greeks a free hand in the Izmir (Smyrna) region of mainland Turkey. In the following year they launched their great offensive in the Anatolian heart of Turkey to unite the former Byzantine provinces with Greece, only to be routed by Atatürk and İnönü—a feat which shook the world and changed history. But the new Turkish Republic renounced all territorial ambitions beyond liberating the mainland.

But the *Megali Idea* did not die with the Greek débâcle in

Turkey. Four years after the birth of the Cyprus Republic, the Greek Prime Minister, George Papandreou, explicitly linked the *Enosis* of Cyprus with the *Megali Idea* when he declared that 'Cyprus must become the springboard for the dreams of Alexander the Great in the Orient'.[70] The remark may have sounded more ludicrous than criminal at the time, as the historian H. D. Purcell wrote. But, as he commented: 'It was a definite indication that the *Megali Idea* might be revived when the circumstances were favourable'.[71]

There may still be much conjecture on the ultimate objects of *Enosis*; but certain aspects cannot be questioned. It was never peaceful in method, anti-colonial in conception, nor self-defensive in aim, as the experience of Crete, Anatolia, and Cyprus shows. On the other hand, although Turkish Cypriot affinity with Turkey is as natural as that of Greek Cypriots with Greece (possibly even more so because of geographic proximity and nearer kinship), the motives for seeking help or closer ties are fundamentally different. Turkish Cypriots have never looked to Turkey to join hands in an expansionist revival, or to oppress or drive out Greek Cypriots from Cyprus. *Pan-Turanism*, the movement for uniting all Turkish peoples throughout the world, and the nearest equivalent to the *Megali Idea*, never caught on in Turkey, and is quite foreign to the basic ideas of Atatürk and the Turkish Republic. Nor have Turkish Cypriots campaigned, either peaceably or violently, for union with Turkey.

[70] 27 Oct. 1964, in Salonica. This speech is reported in the main Athens newspapers of the following day.

[71] Purcell, *Cyprus*, 391. '*Megali Idea*, the sole ideology which the Greek people cherished for long years went to pieces after the Cyprus tragedy': Penayotis Lambiras, the Greek government's spokesman, in a statement published in the *New York Times* and reproduced by *Milliyet* newspaper of Istanbul on 31 Aug. 1976. This does not mean, however, that the ideal has been abandoned. It is interesting to note that, after so many years since its inception, the national struggle of Greek Cypriots and EOKA as its organization were recognized by Law No. 48 of 1987 passed by the Greek Cypriot House of Representatives and published in the Greek Cypriot *Official Gazette* of 3 Apr. 1987.

# 2

# The Uneasy Years 1963-1974

I. THE INTERCOMMUNAL HOSTILITIES

Tensions rapidly built up through the summer and autumn of 1963. On 3 December, Archbishop Makarios, the President of the Republic, publicly announced his thirteen-point proposed revisions of the Constitution,[1] which he had submitted to Dr F. Kutchuk, the Turkish Vice-President, a few days earlier. Turkey rejected these proposals on 16 December 1963. The Archbishop refused to accept Turkish rejection. Within days, the fighting began.[2]

As one commentator wrote, on 21 December 1963, 'a trivial incident sparked the outbreak, but the tinder was dry and plenty of fuel lay to hand'. Two Greek Cypriot policemen, according to his report, 'asked some Turkish Cypriots to produce their identity cards. The Turks refused; an argument followed, and a crowd began to gather. The policemen, finding themselves surrounded, drew their guns. Shots were fired, it seems, by both sides. Two Turks were killed and a policeman seriously injured.'[3]

On 23 December the intercommunal fighting began. In an interview published in a major Athens daily, Lieutenant General George Karayannis, the Greek commander of the Cyprus National Guard during the 1963-4 crisis, candidly stated: 'when the Turks objected to the amendment of the Constitution, Archbishop Makarios put his plan into effect and the Greek attack began in December 1963'.[4] The Turkish quarter of Nicosia was under siege on 23 December and the

[1] See previous chapter.
[2] *The Times* (London) 7 Dec. 1963.
[3] Charles Foley, *Legacy of Strife: Cyprus from Rebellion to Civil War* (Baltimore, 1964), 166, 168.
[4] *Ethnikos Kiryx*, 15 June 1965 (quoted in H. D. Purcell, *Cyprus* (London, 1969), 323).

Nicosia suburb of Omorphita (K. Kaimaklı) was under heavy fire.[5]

Dr Fazil Kutchuk, the Vice-President of Cyprus, in a letter addressed to all heads of state in December 1963, described the situation in the following words:

To all Heads of States,

The Greeks of Cyprus, taking advantage of, and abusing their majority strength in the Government and Security Forces of the Republic, have planned and put into execution an organised armed attack by the Greek Police and civilians on the Turks and Turkish property in towns and villages, including my own residence and office, since the night of 20 December 1963.

These attacks continued in a most brutal and barbarous manner until the intervention of the three Guaranteeing Powers. During these attacks Turkish houses in Nicosia and elsewhere have been broken into and many innocent Turks, including women and children, have been murdered in cold blood in their houses or driven away as hostages.

The Greek leaders, who are misrepresenting to the world the true facts have, in complete disregard of our Constitution and Laws, illegally armed with heavy weapons the Greek members of the Security Forces and also thousands of Greek terrorists while Turks holding political posts have been deliberately prevented from exercising their powers and functions and Turkish members of the Security Forces have been disarmed and placed under detention.

At the same time, Turkish citizens have been labelled by Greek leaders as rebels to be shot dead on sight if seen outside their houses or sectors.

Despite the cease-fire agreement, Turkish life and property are still in great and imminent danger in Cyprus.

Even after the cease-fire, Turks have been killed and kidnapped and many Turkish houses have been looted or maliciously set on fire by the Greeks. Turks both in towns and villages are still besieged and all means of communication have been cut off to them. Also, the normal supply of foodstuffs to Turkish citizens is no longer possible.

Reliable reports reaching us indicate that, even now, the Greeks are arming and preparing another onslaught for a general massacre on a larger scale than before. . . .[6]

---

[5] See H. Scott Gibbons, *Peace Without Honour* (Ankara, 1969), 10–15. This work by a British journalist in Cyprus contains the most detailed and reliable account of the 1963–4 crisis. See also Pierre Oberling, *The Road to Bellapais: The Turkish Cypriot Exodus to Northern Cyprus* (New York, 1982), 87–121.

[6] For the full text of this letter, see Rauf R. Denktash, *The Cyprus Triangle* (London, 1988), 226–8.

A 'warning flight' of Turkish jet fighters was ordered over the island on Christmas Day of 1963 when it was apparent that violence was increasing throughout Cyprus. This was meant to be a warning that the fighting must stop. The flight of jet fighters enabled the Turkish army contingent (which was stationed on the island under the Treaty of Alliance)[7] to move safely from its barracks to a new camp on the Nicosia–Kyrenia road. It has been stated that this move was made because the contingent considered it extremely dangerous for its own security to remain in its camp, which was situated in close proximity to the Greek army camp in an area controlled by Greek Cypriots.[8] One observer has claimed that the real reason for the move was to protect the road to several Turkish Cypriot positions.[9]

As a response to the above move, the Greek Cypriot government formally declared that the Treaty of Alliance had been terminated as a result of alleged violations of its terms by Turkey.[10]

On 28 December 1963 the *Daily Express* carried the following report from Cyprus:

We went tonight into the sealed-off Turkish Quarter of Nicosia in which 200 to 300 people have been slaughtered in the last five days. We were the first Western reporters there and we have seen sights too frightful to be described in print. Horror so extreme that the people seemed stunned beyond tears.

Following the events of 1963, the Turkish Cypriots felt that their position was such that they needed to defend themselves. The ensuing situation is described in paragraphs 29 and 30 of the Report of the Secretary-General of the United Nations to the Security Council on the United Nations Operations in Cyprus,[11] in the following words:

29. Following the events in December 1963, the Turkish Cypriot

---

[7] Under article VI of the Treaty of Alliance, Greece was allowed to station on the island a contingent of 950 officers, non-commissioned officers, and men. Under the same article, the Turkish army contingent was composed of 650 officers, non-commissioned officers, and men.

[8] Speech of the Turkish representative at the UN Security Council, 19 UN SCOR, 1136th meeting, 9 (1964).

[9] Foley, *Legacy of Strife*, 170.

[10] e.g. 19 UN SCOR, 1136th meeting para. 38 (1964). For the Turkish response see UN Doc. No. S/5663 (1964).

[11] Doc. S/5950 of 10 Sept. 1964.

fighting elements gathered in areas inhabited by their community and fortified them against possible attacks. Map II in addendum I to the present report gives an indication of the areas now so occupied, the most important of which include a part of the city of Nicosia and its northern suburbs; a narrow area astride the Kyrenia road extending from the northern suburbs of Nicosia up to the southern edge of the town of Kyrenia; the town of Louroujina; an enclave in the Lefka region and two beach-heads of Kokkina and Limnitis.

30. In the defence of the areas they control, the Turkish Cypriots have set up road-blocks, trenches, fortified posts and sandbagged emplacements either on the ground or behind windows or on the roofs of buildings. Around those positions the Government forces have erected their own fortifications and road-blocks. The opposing military positions, manned by determined and well-armed men, and sometimes separated by less than fifty yards, create a situation fraught with constant danger.

This recourse to aggression, in disregard of the Republic's treaty obligations and the international consequences, was aimed at the subjugation of the Nicosia Turks by a swift knockout blow and the consequent surrender of the smaller Turkish populations in the rest of the island. The Turkish Cypriots were largely defenceless, the Turkish police having been disarmed as the result of a ruse on the part of the Greek Cypriot Minister of the Interior, Mr P. Georghadjis, the day before the fighting started. Former EOKA members and other irregulars in groups of a hundred, usually led by the police, took part. The offensive was sanctioned by Archbishop Makarios and the cabinet but, according to the testimony of diplomats in the capital at the time, the Archbishop and some of the ministers were genuinely taken aback by the excesses committed.[12]

As a result of the hostilities, 364 Turkish Cypriots and 174 Greek Cypriots were killed during the 1963–4 crisis, 103 Turkish villages were completely or partially destroyed, and 25,000 Turkish Cypriots were made refugees in their own country.[13] It is again pertinent to quote from the UN Secretary-General's above referred report:

177. As indicated in my report of 15 June 1964, the disturbances of

---

[12] Nancy Crawshaw, *The Cyprus Revolt* (London, 1978), 367–8.
[13] See Oberling, *The Road to Bellapais*, 120.

December 1963 had resulted in the total or partial destruction of many dwellings, a high proportion of them simple homes whose owners would be but slightly able to fend for themselves. In many localities this tended to create or to aggravate a refugee problem, as the owners of these houses and their families fled to safer areas, where many of them lived in temporary camps in precarious conditions.

178. Serious efforts were made by UNFICYP to induce refugees from the Omorphita suburb of Nicosia to return from camps a few miles away to houses which could be at least partially occupied. About half of these refugees would have been ready to do this had they not feared for their personal safety.

179. In refugee camps near Nicosia many hundreds of children living in crowded temporary quarters and exposed during the great heat of the summer months to the risk of dehydration survived without serious illness partly because an UNFICYP architect and military engineers planned and, with local help, built provisional matting roofs to give shelter from the sun, as well as open-air showers.

180. The United Nations Force carried out a detailed survey of all damage to properties throughout the island during the disturbances, including the Tylliria fighting. The survey shows that in 109 (*sic.*) villages, most of them Turkish Cypriot or mixed villages, 527 houses were destroyed while 2,000 others suffered damage from looting. In Ktima 38 houses and shops were destroyed totally and 122 partially. In the Omorphita suburb of Nicosia 50 houses were totally destroyed while a further 240 were partially destroyed there and in adjacent suburbs.

From Omorphita alone 6,000 Turks were made refugees. Mr Nicos Sampson, the owner of *Makhi* newspaper, declared that 'Omorphita has been conquered by Greek arms; conquered lands can never be returned.'[14] The inhabitants of these 103 villages fled to the nearest bigger Turkish villages for safety. Greek Cypriots immediately destroyed all Turkish houses in these villages. The United Nations asked Mr Ortega to prepare a report, which he did. The story is now a sad record of the past with detailed figures. This wanton destruction meant that the inhabitants of these houses were not wanted back. Indeed the Greek press was quite categoric in advising the Turkish

[14] From *Makhi* (Greek Cypriot newspaper) of 17 June 1973.

population to leave Cyprus 'if you do not like to live under the Greek flag'.

The intercommunal strife was not confined to Nicosia, gradually it spread to other towns and villages. This is how the Ayios Vassilios massacre was reported by the *Daily Telegraph* of 14 January 1964:

Silent crowds gathered to-night outside the Red Crescent hospital in the Turkish sector of Nicosia, as the bodies of nine Turks found crudely buried outside the village of Ayios Vassilios, 13 miles away, were brought to the hospital under an escort of the Parachute Regiment. Three more bodies, including one of a woman, were discovered nearby but they could not be moved.

Turks guarded by paratroops are still trying to locate the bodies of 20 more believed to have been buried on the same site. All are believed to have been killed during fighting around the village at Christmas.

It is thought that a family of seven Turks who disappeared from the village may be buried there. Their house was found burnt, and grenades had been dropped through the roof.

Shallow graves had apparently been hurriedly scooped by a bulldozer. The bodies appeared to have been piled in two or three deep. All had been shot.

One man had his arms still tied behind his legs in a crouching position and had been shot through the head. A stomach injury indicated that a grenade may have been thrown into his lap . . .

On 4 February 1964 Greek Cypriots numbering about 1,000 and armed with bazookas, mortars, and heavy machine-guns launched an attack on the Turkish village of Gaziveran on the pretext that the Turks had set up a road-block. The village had been under their siege for a week. The initial phase of this unprovoked attack lasted for five hours and during the intense fighting one Turkish Cypriot was killed, three others were wounded, and many houses were destroyed.

At about 15.20 hrs. on the same day, Greek Cypriot gunmen, in violation of the cease-fire agreement which had been reached at lunch time, renewed their attacks with even heavier arms, killing four more Turkish Cypriots and injuring many women and children. The assailants even fired at about 500 women and children who had taken refuge in the small village school premises and threatened them with the words: 'You either surrender or else we kill you *en masse.*'

The *Daily Sketch* reporting the fighting in Limassol in its issue of 14 February 1964 stated *inter alia* that the Greek Cypriots had with their armed attack murdered the Turkish Cypriot inhabitants of Limassol and had altogether complicated the situation. The paper said Makarios turned a blind eye to the bloodshed and, by flagrantly disregarding this state of affairs, tried to strike a bargain on the conditions of the truce and insisted that the international force should be attached to the Security Council. The paper claimed that Makarios was turning the island into a province of Greece by using the United Nations as a means and that he knew that the utterly complicated composition of a UN force would provide an easy opportunity to this end.

The *Observer* reporting also on the situation in Limassol in its issue of 16 February 1964 said that the atmosphere was tense and that the Greek Cypriots were, as always, claiming that the fighting had been started by the Turks. But this claim was improbable as it was illogical for six thousand Turks, surrounded by a force many times greater than their numerical strength, to have knowingly provoked the Greeks. Nevertheless, the Greek Cypriot attack had been very heavy. Even though the cease-fire agreement had become operative as from Wednesday, the Greek Cypriots were not permitting the British troops to patrol the town. The *Observer* continued to report that, according to General Young, the Greek Cypriot onslaught of the previous morning had taken place contrary to the assurances that no attack of any sort would be launched. According to the statement by a high-ranking British officer, the attack had been pre-planned and launched at dawn, the paper stated.

On 9 March 1964, in spite of the cease-fire agreement, the Greek Cypriot gunmen launched an attack on the Ktima Turks. The Greek Cypriots, who were equipped with heavy arms, prevented the British military fire brigade from entering the Turkish sector of Ktima in order to put out fires at Turkish houses and shops. During the fighting 15 Turks were killed, 22 others were wounded, and the minaret of *Büyük Cami* (the Great Mosque) was blown up by mortar shelling. Damage to Turkish property was estimated at £2 million. The Greeks also opened fire on British armoured vehicles and prevented them from entering the Turkish sector of the town for the evacuation of Turkish women and children to areas of safety.

On 12 March 1964, Turkey threatened military intervention

in Cyprus unless 'all ... assaults ... against the Turkish Community in Cyprus ... [are] stopped ... [and] an immediate cease-fire ... [is] established'.[15] Turkey backed away from this threat, but only under strong Security Council pressure.[16] In June 1964, the Turkish government came to the brink of deciding to make a landing on Cyprus. Again it was dissuaded; this time by an urgent appeal from US President Johnson.[17] Each time Turkey threatened to use force but was unable to do so, the likelihood that she would ever actually intervene seemed to lessen.

## 2. KOKKINA-MANSOURA FIGHTING AND ACTION BY THE TURKISH AIR FORCE

Early in 1964, during the debates at the Security Council, Greek Cypriot representatives maintained that the use of force was neither permitted by the terms of article IV of the Treaty of Guarantee nor consistent with the United Nations Charter. Turkey continued to rely on article IV of the treaty. But the difficulty was that this treaty restricted the situations in which Turkey might intervene. Unilateral action under article IV is limited to re-establishing 'the state of affairs created by the present Treaty' and requires prior consultations with the other guarantor powers.

At the beginning of August 1964, a Greek Cypriot force under the command of General Grivas launched a series of attacks against the Kokkina-Mansoura (Tylliria) areas on the north-western coast, a stretch of seashore held by Turkish Cypriots. The Greek Cypriot government claimed that the area was the landing spot for arms and other supplies from Turkey and that it was a centre for carrying out a plan 'to spread and intensify the rebellion in Cyprus, and resort to warfare'.[18] The Turkish

---

[15] See UN Doc. No. S/5596, annexe, 2 (1964).

[16] See 19 UN SCOR, 1103rd meeting (1964), and the resolution that resulted from that meeting, UN Doc. No. S/5603 (1964).

[17] See the letter to Prime Minister Inonu from President Johnson, dated 5 June 1964, reprinted in Greek Cypriot Public Information Office publication *Cyprus: The Problem in Perspective* (Nicosia 1968), 33–4.

[18] 19 UN SCOR, 1142nd meeting, 18 (1964).

government responded that the Archbishop intended 'to wipe out the inhabitants of the area . . .'[19] In fact the Greek Cypriot attacks violated an express assurance given by Archbishop Makarios to the United Nations force commander.[20] In order to force the Greek Cypriot government to check its military efforts Turkey decided to resort to a limited armed intervention. On 7 and 8 August 1964 Turkish bombers attacked military targets in the area,[21] but reports from United Nations representatives in the field concluded that defenceless people had also been killed and much property destroyed.[22] On 9 August the Security Council denounced the Turkish action and issued an appeal to the government of Turkey to cease instantly the bombardment and the use of military force of any kind against Cyprus.[23]

In his statements to the Security Council after the bombings the Turkish representative stressed the mistreatment of Turkish Cypriots by the Makarios government and the inability of either the United Nations or the guarantor powers acting collectively to protect the Turkish Cypriots. This was the first occasion during the crisis that began in December 1963 that a Turkish representative had publicly referred to self-defence as a basis for limited military action. In the words of the Turkish representative, 'This action undertaken by Turkish aircraft is directed exclusively at military targets and constitutes a limited police action taken in legitimate self-defence.'[24] To put it briefly, Turkey claimed that since the United Nations peacekeeping force could not protect the Turkish Cypriots, bombing was Turkey's only recourse. On the other hand, Archbishop Makarios threatened that he would 'order every Turkish Cypriot village to be attacked, if the Turkish air force did not stop bombing the Greek force around Kokkina'.[25] In fact, it was

---

[19] Ibid. at 10. If the Greek attacks had not been stopped by the Turkish air force the whole garrison of Turkish Cypriot students in the area and the Turkish youth of the village might have been wiped out.

[20] See Secretary-General's Report on the United Nations Operations in Cyprus, UN Doc. No. S/5950, 23 (1964).

[21] See 19 UN SCOR, 1142nd meeting, 12 (1964).

[22] Secretary-General's Report S/5950, 64 (1964).

[23] Security Council res. 193, UN Doc. No. S/5868 (1964).

[24] 19 UN SCOR, 1142nd meeting, 11–12 (1964).

[25] See UN Secretary-General's Report S/5950 of 10 Sept. 1964, 83.

Turkey's action that stopped the fighting in the Kokkina-Mansoura area.

The Turkish claim of self-defence could have been based on article 51 of the United Nations Charter or on customary international law. Such an argument could be put forward as an alternative defence to the one based on article IV of the Treaty of Guarantee. Article 51 of the UN Charter recognizes the right 'of individual or collective defence if an armed attack occurs . . . until the Security Council has taken the measures necessary to maintain international peace and security'. In the circumstances of early August 1964 Turkey could claim that it was responding to a Cypriot armed attack. However, Turkey would have to show that the United Nations troops had been unable to implement 'measures necessary to maintain international peace and security'. The fact that the Greek Cypriot forces had attacked in violation of an express assurance given by Archbishop Makarios to the United Nations force commander would be substantial evidence for the Turkish position.

Turkey could also expect to face at least a conceptual hurdle in describing a military action against Cyprus as self-defence. The use of force to protect a nation's citizens has been justified on the ground that a state is no more than a collectivity of its nationals, and, therefore, that protection of them is protection of the state itself.[26] The ties that bind Turkish Cypriots to Turkey are strong, and, in the eyes of Turkey, their defence was undoubtedly the defence of Turkey. But many in the United Nations could be expected to question whether Turkish Cypriots should be viewed as an extension of Turkey's 'self' since they lack 'a nexus of nationality'.

## 3. ATTACK AT AYIOS THEODOROS

The 1960 Treaty of Alliance stipulates that not more than 950 Greek troops shall be stationed on Cyprus. In the wake of the crisis that began on Christmas Day 1963, however, large numbers of Greek forces as well as arms were brought to the island. By 1967, upwards of 10,000 to 12,000 Greek soldiers—

[26] See D. W. Bowett, *Self-defence in International Law* (Manchester, 1958), 91–4.

estimates vary—were stationed in Cyprus.[27] They were led by General George Grivas, who still openly called for *Enosis*. General Grivas had returned to Cyprus from Greece in 1964 as Supreme Commander of the Cypriot Defence Forces. These forces included the Cypriot National Guard, which was established on the basis of compulsory conscription.[28] The National Guard increased its strength from about 15,000 to an estimated 20,000.[29] Included in this figure were an estimated 5,000 men who arrived in Cyprus from Greece during the month of July 1964 through the port of Limassol.[30]

On 15 November 1967 the National Guard launched a series of attacks against the Turkish Cypriot villages of Kophinou (Geçitkale) and Ayios Theodoros (Boğaziçi). A journalist on the scene concluded that General Grivas ordered the attack with the approval of the Greek government to 'put the Turkish Cypriots in their place'.[31] Whether or not that judgment is accurate, there seems little doubt from the Secretary-General's reports that the Greek forces in Cyprus had carefully planned the move.[32] The instant cause of the attack was the insistence of the Greek Cypriot police that they patrol these areas and the resistance put forward by the Turkish Cypriots. There was a tacit agreement with the UN force that such patrols would not be resumed until the force agreed that tensions had sufficiently eased in the area. However, General Grivas decided to flout UN authority. He said that if the UN force did not protect the patrols, the National Guard would escort them and 'would be prepared to meet whatever consequences resulted'. In fact, the

[27] Some reports indicated that 20,000 Greek troops had come to Cyprus: *NY Times*, 19 Nov. 1967, but most estimates were in the 10,000 to 12,000 range. In his book *Democracy at Gunpoint: The Greek Front* (London, 1970), Mr Andreas Papandreou, former minister in the cabinet of the then premier of Greece, Mr George Papandreou, revealed that an agreement was reached between his father (premier George Papandreou) and Archbishop Makarios for supply of arms and troops to Cyprus in a clandestine way. About 20,000 fully equipped officers and men landed in Cyprus. The UN were barred from the areas of these operations.

[28] UN Secretary-General's Report of 15 June 1964, S/5764.

[29] The enlisted men were mainly Greek Cypriots, but many commissioned and non-commissioned officers were mainland Greeks.

[30] UN Secretary-General's Report of 10 Sept. 1964, S/5950, para. 20.

[31] *The Times* (London) 29 Nov. 1967.

[32] UN Docs. No. S/8248/Add. 1–3 (1967).

National Guard had already begun large-scale military manœuvres in the area. One of these patrols met a road-block, shots were fired, and the National Guard attack was launched with heavy machine-guns, artillery, and mortars. United Nations posts were destroyed by shelling; National Guard troops dismantled the United Nations radio at one key position, and disarmed the United Nations soldiers in another. United Nations efforts to arrange a cease-fire were ignored until the villages had been virtually overrun. A cease-fire, and withdrawal of National Guardsmen, was negotiated on 16 November, after strong United Nations protests to the Greek Cypriot government. *The Economist* reported, 'Rarely has there been a Cypriot crisis in which—in terms solely of its immediate causes—guilt has belonged so much to one side'.[33]

Turkey accused Greece of genocide of the Turkish Cypriot villages of Kophinou and Ayios Theodoros and insisted on the withdrawal of Greek armed forces from Cyprus. The fighting at these villages which brought Turkey and Greece to the brink of war was a matter of concern for the USA; and Mr Cyrus Vance, the former Secretary of State, managed to get an accord between the parties following shuttle diplomacy between Athens, Ankara, and Nicosia. Under this agreement Greece withdrew from Cyprus over 100,000 troops it had clandestinely brought to the island. Archbishop Makarios, however, managed to leave behind 3,000 Greek officers under the pretext that they were on contract to his administration for the training of his army. Grivas also left—only to return in 1971 to organize a reborn EOKA, the so-called EOKA B. A plot pitting the militant pro-*Enosis* forces led by Grivas against the regime of Archbishop Makarios was hatched. EOKA B began its terrorist activities. It was generally thought that, despite official denials, the Greek junta in Athens was behind the anti-Makarios movement.

## 4. INTERCESSION, MEDIATION, AND PEACEKEEPING

On 23 December 1963, the Turkish Foreign Minister announced that 'Turkey decided to use her own right of

[33] 2 Dec. 1967.

unilateral intervention on the basis of Article IV of the Treaty of Guarantee, but she confined her intervention to a single warning flight of jet fighters of the Turkish air force'.[34] In response, the Security Council was convened to consider Greek Cypriot charges that Turkey had committed 'acts of (a) aggression, (b) intervention in the internal affairs of Cyprus'.[35] However, no specific proposals for United Nations measures were made by any Council members.

On Christmas Day, when it was apparent that violence was increasing throughout Cyprus, the three guarantor powers informed the Cypriot government 'of their readiness to assist if invited to do so, in restoring peace and order by means of a joint peace-making force under British command' and composed of British, Greek, and Turkish contingents already present on the island under the Treaty of Establishment and Alliance.[36] In the British view, the guarantor powers would be acting as a 'regional arrangement' established under the Treaty of Guarantee and authorized by Chapter VIII of the United Nations Charter.[37] The Greek Cypriot government agreed to a temporary cease-fire under the supervision of the guarantor powers, but the Archbishop insisted that the four governments jointly request the Secretary-General to appoint a representative 'to observe the progress of the peace-making operation'.[38] From 26 December 1963 until 27 March 1964, the truce force operated in the island, doing police work, under British command. In fact this was an all-British peacekeeping force.

The only power likely to protect the Turkish Cypriots was Turkey, if it could act under the Treaty of Guarantee. On

[34] 19 UN SCOR, 1098th meeting, 15–16 (1964).
[35] See letter from the permanent representative of Cyprus to the President of the Security Council, 26 Dec. 1963, in UN Doc. No. S/5488, 1 (1963); 18 UN SCOR, 1085th meeting (1963).
[36] See UN Doc. NO. S/5508, 2 (1964).
[37] See 688 HC Deb. (5th ser.), 530–1 (1964). Article 52 of the Charter provides that 'Nothing in the present Charter precludes the existence of regional arrangements or agencies for dealing with such matters relating to the maintenance of international peace and security as are appropriate for regional action, provided that such arrangements or agencies and their activities are consistent with the Purposes and Principles of the United Nations.'
[38] UN Doc. No. S/5508, 3 (1964).

1 January 1964 Archbishop Makarios announced his decision to abrogate the Treaties of Alliance and Guarantee.[39] Immediately after the announcement, British representatives convinced Archbishop Makarios that the move was a mistake, and a new statement was issued declaring that the Cypriot government sought no more than 'to secure the termination of these treaties by appropriate means'.[40]

Archbishop Makarios repeatedly tried to use the truce force to further his own political aims. He insisted that it should assist the 'legal state forces', namely Georghadjis's army, in disarming the Turkish Cypriot fighters (*mücahits*) and taking over the Turkish Cypriot enclaves. He accused British troops of fostering partition of the island by putting themselves between the combatants and escorting fleeing Turks from mixed villages to Turkish-held areas.[41] The truce force was also accused of creating the 'Green Line' separating the Greek and Turkish sectors of Nicosia. The Archbishop requested that the British force take no action without approval of the Greek Cypriot government, which would have given the Greek Cypriots veto power over all peacekeeping operations. On 2 January 1964 the *Daily Telegraph* wrote: 'The Greek Cypriot community should not assume that the British military presence can or should secure them against Turkish intervention if they persecute the minority. We must not be a shelter for double-crossers.'

In the meantime both the Greek and Turkish governments had become highly agitated by the Cyprus controversy, which created a rift within NATO. England no longer wished to bear the burden of policing Cyprus, therefore a new peacekeeping force had to be organized. The British government developed a plan with the United States for an enlarged peacekeeping force from NATO nations.[42] Turkey and Greece accepted the plan, but Archbishop Makarios rejected it. US Under-Secretary George Ball tried to change the Archbishop's mind, but when he did not succeed, accused him of trying to make the island 'his private abattoir'.[43] As it soon became clear, the Archbishop

---

[39] *The Times, Daily Telegraph*, 2 Jan. 1964.
[40] Robert Stephens, *Cyprus: A Place of Arms* (London, 1966), 185–6.
[41] *Newsweek*, 9 Mar. 1964, 36.
[42] 689 HC Deb. (5th ser.) 841 (1964), and 19 UN SCOR, 1095th meeting, 10 (1964).          [43] Oberling, *The Road to Bellapais*, 103, 106.

wanted to take his case to the United Nations where he hoped to gain the organization's condemnation of the 1960 Accords.

On 15 January 1964 a conference was held in London to resolve the differences of the two Cypriot communities. It soon became clear that the differences among the parties were too deep for easy resolution. The Archbishop insisted that, in order to enable the machinery of the Cypriot government to function, the 1960 settlement should be altered in a way to allow government by the Greek majority with constitutional guarantees of Turkish Cypriot rights. But Turkey and the Turkish Cypriots would not accept such a scheme. In these circumstances, the Archbishop insisted that the United Nations was the only international forum in which the crisis could be resolved.[44]

Foreign newsmen flocked to Cyprus in 1963–4 and were horrified at what they saw. For a brief period, sympathy lay with the Turks. However, Greek Cypriots were quick to take advantage of international recognition. They had men in the right positions; they had already prepared the ground. Diplomats gave way to the power of the lobbies. In the United Nations, in the Commonwealth, and at the Conference of Non-aligned Nations in Belgrade (1961) and Cairo (1964), Archbishop Makarios won increasing support for the principle of 'self-determination' to be applied to Cyprus which, he claimed, could only be done by getting rid of the 1960 Treaties of Alliance and Guarantee.[45] In order to disguise his plans to subjugate the Turkish Cypriots, Makarios had to present Cyprus as a fledgling republic, formed in the upsurge of national movements but

[44] See Thomas Ehrlich, *International Crises and the Role of Law, Cyprus 1958–1967* (Oxford, 1974), 58–9.

[45] In order to gain more international support for the cause of *Enosis*, under the guise of 'self-determination', the Greek Cypriots set up, in 1964, the Co-ordinating Committee of Cypriot Self-Determination with its headquarters in New York. Their greatest success was at the Cairo Conference of Non-aligned States in October, 1964. The Cairo Declaration not only called upon all states to refrain from the threat or use of force, 'but also to refrain from intervention directed against Cyprus and from any efforts to impose upon Cyprus unjust solutions unacceptable to the people of Cyprus. . . . Cyprus, as an equal member of the United Nations, is entitled to and should enjoy unrestricted and unfettered sovereignty and independence, allowing its people to determine freely, without any foreign intervention or interference, the political future of the country. . . .'

circumscribed by the treaties which he had been reluctantly forced to accept, under the threat of partition by the Turks.

Britain, as one of the guarantor powers, was an easy scapegoat because of her recent colonial past. Turkey, in NATO, was labelled as a reactionary power. Turkish Cypriots were exploited as a 'minority' to appease those Afro-Asian countries which had inherited minority problems. On the other hand, the USA was caught in the dilemma of a possible war between NATO allies. The Greek premier at that time, Mr George Papandreou, thought that it was opportune to broadcast an appeal, on 29 February 1964, for the revision of the Zurich and London Agreements. The US Greek lobby succeeded in winning the support of 37 senators, 36 congressmen, 4 state governors, and the mayor of New York for what the Greek Cypriots were bent on achieving, but the declaration of support kept quiet about *Enosis*.

On 4 March 1964, the Security Council unanimously adopted a resolution[46] which in paragraph 4 recommended the creation, with the consent of the 'Government of Cyprus',[47] of a United Nations peacekeeping force in Cyprus (UNFICYP). Paragraph 5 of this resolution recommended that the force should function in the interests of preserving international peace and security, and 'use its best efforts to prevent a recurrence of fighting and, as necessary, to contribute to the maintenance and restoration of law and order and a return to normal conditions'. Furthermore, the Security Council recommended that the Secretary-General designate a Mediator.[48]

The troops of UNFICYP could not take the initiative in using armed force, which could be used only in self-defence. The

---

[46] S/5575, resolution 186 (1964). The terms of the mandate were further clarified by an *aide-mémoire* of the Secretary-General, (1964) III *International Legal Materials*, No. 3. This was the first time that all five permanent members of the Council unanimously voted to set up a peacekeeping force.

[47] It could be assumed that the reference in the Security Council resolution of 4 Mar. to the 'Government of Cyprus', was to the government established by the 1960 Constitution which should be composed of both Greek and Turkish Cypriot elements. However, the Greek Cypriot wing of the government of Cyprus, which since Dec. 1963 had attempted to overthrow the 1960 Constitution, pretended to be that government.

[48] The Finnish diplomat Sakari Tuomioja was appointed the first Mediator. He was succeeded upon his death by Dr Galo Plaza.

mandate was conceived within Chapter VI of the United Nations Charter and not Chapter VII concerning enforcement action.

The UN Force in Cyprus became operational on 27 March 1964 with the arrival of the Canadian contingent.

The Secretary-General's reports to the Security Council indicate that the Turkish Cypriots and the Greek Cypriots held differing views with regard to the interpretation and implementation of UNFICYP's mandate as embodied in the Security Council resolution of 4 March 1964. The Turkish Cypriots contended that UNFICYP was to reinstate the constitutional order under the 1960 Constitution before the outbreak of hostilities, while the Greek Cypriots stated that UNFICYP should help them in subjugating the Turkish Cypriot 'minority' within a unitary state.[49] Commenting on the Security Council resolution of 4 March 1964, Archbishop Makarios declared: 'We have secured a resolution in the first phase of our struggle in the international field. Turkey cannot in future threaten intervention in Cyprus invoking the Treaty of Guarantee.'[50]

The presence of the United Nations force in Cyprus served to check recourse to armed force, but it only palliated some symptoms of the crisis during 1964 and reached none of its basic causes. The mandate of the force has been renewed at six-month intervals since its creation in 1964, but its numerical strength has been considerably reduced.[51].

Anxious to prevent a conflict between two NATO allies on Russia's doorstep, President Johnson informed the Turkish premier, İsmet İnönü, in June 1964, that America would not

[49] The Secretary-General's report of 14 Sept. 1964 (S/5950) clarified the term 'return to normal conditions' as not being the restoration of the constitutional situation, as interpreted by the Turkish Cypriots. Nor could the force, under the terms of its mandate, act as an instrument of the government in helping it to extend its authority by force over the Turkish Cypriots (S/6228, Report of 11 Mar. 1965). However, the Secretary-General, U Thant, is himself reported to have remarked that the solution of the Cyprus problem was first and foremost a matter for the 'Cypriot Government'. Such attitudes hardened the Greek Cypriot stand and failed to contribute to an agreed settlement of the Cyprus dispute.

[50] *Cyprus Mail*, 5 Mar. 1964.

[51] By June 1964 the strength of UNFICYP was 6,411; by June 1967, 4,627; and by June 1987, 2,328.

tolerate Turkish intervention in Cyprus, and promptly posit-
ioned his 6th Fleet between Turkey and the island. President
Johnson also invited both Mr İnönü and Mr Papandreou to
Washington for talks in the last week of the month. Moreover,
talks were held at Geneva in the summer of 1964 between the
representatives of Greece and Turkey under the aegis of the UN
Mediator and with the participation of Mr Dean Acheson, a
former American Secretary of State. American initiatives
resulted in the putting forward of the Acheson Plan. This plan
called for union of Cyprus with Greece, subject to the following
conditions: that Turkey receive the Greek island of Kastellori-
zon (an isle almost touching the Turkish mainland), that two
Turkish cantons be established in Cyprus, and that a military
base be ceded to Turkey.

The Acheson Plan was biased in favour of Greece in that it
accepted *Enosis*, and anticipated Turkish Cypriot emigration by
proposing compensation to those who left. Turkish Cypriots
who remained, however, were to have 'self-government'. This
Plan was described by the Greek side as proposing in effect a
solution based on *double Enosis* and was denounced by Archbishop Makarios. The aim of the Greek side was to achieve
*Enosis* without giving any concessions to Turkey or to Turkish
Cypriots in return.[52] Such attitudes were reinforced by the
failure of other American initiatives, such as the efforts of Mr
Cyrus Vance in 1967.

Finally, the Graeco-Turkish dialogue which had intermit-
tently continued since May 1966 culminated in a meeting held
in Thrace in September 1967 between the Prime Ministers of
Greece and Turkey. These talks did not yield any result because

---

[52] In a series of articles on the events of 1964 (published almost a year after
the events) in the Athens daily *Ethnikos Kyrix*, it was disclosed, in the issue of
24 June 1965, that at a meeting of the Greek General Staff on 5 July 1964,
attended also by General Grivas and General Karayannis (the commander of
the 'National Guard'), the Greek Defence Minister, Mr Garufalias, said that
no concession of territory was envisaged to Turkey (under the Acheson Plan)
and that efforts would be made to avoid granting even a base to Turkey. This
hopeful forecast of the Greek minister enjoined General Grivas and General
Karayannis to avoid any action that would disturb the peace and upset the
plans for a possible *Enosis* in August, 1964. For Mr Acheson's own account of
his efforts, see Acheson, 'Cyprus: The Anatomy of the Problem', 46 *Chicago B.
Record* 349, 352–3 (1965).

Greece was still making efforts to achieve *Enosis*. Turkey insisted on geographical federation. As a result, the chance of a bipartite settlement without involving the Archbishop appeared further away than ever.[53]

## 5. UN MEDIATOR'S REPORT

The UN Mediator, Dr Galo Plaza, submitted his Report to the Secretary-General on 26 March 1965.[54] The larger part of Dr Plaza's Report is devoted to a factual review of the positions of the parties to the Cyprus issue. Dr Plaza was very critical of the 1960 Constitution, which he described as a 'constitutional oddity'. Certain political circles then interpreted his suggestions in the Report as a rejection of the Zurich and London Agreements, which gave birth to the Republic of Cyprus. However, it was outside the terms of reference of the Mediator so to do. He concluded that any settlement of the Cyprus problem had to take account of, and be based upon the following considerations:

(i) The problem of Cyprus could not be solved by attempting to restore the situation which existed before December, 1963; a new solution had to be found.

(ii) Any settlement, to be viable, had to be 'an agreed one'. It had to be capable of securing the support of all the interested parties identified by the Security Council in its above-referred resolution of 4 March 1964.

(iii) It had to be consistent with the provisions and principles of the UN Charter.

(iv) It had to be in the interest of the well being of the people of Cyprus as a whole.

(v) Finally, it had to be a lasting and durable settlement.

Dr Plaza then proceeded to give his observations and recommendations. He suggested that there had to be 'an independent

---

[53] For reports of the talks, see *NY Times*, 11 Sept. 1967, and 13 Sept. 1967 (editorial).

[54] Galo Plaza Report, UN Security Council Doc. S/6252 of 26 Mar. 1965.

Cyprus with adequate safeguards for the safety and the rights of all its people'. He recommended the Greeks to shelve their demand for *Enosis* so long as the risk of opposition from the Turkish Cypriot community and Turkey persisted. He suggested that establishment of guaranteed independence should be followed by demilitarization of the island. According to the Mediator, establishment of a federal regime required a territorial basis which did not exist. He could not therefore accept the federal schemes proposed by Turkey or any other federal solutions. He was of the view that the Turkish Cypriot community must be protected adequately, but expressed his satisfaction with the assurances which Archbishop Makarios had given concerning such protection. He suggested the appointment of a United Nations commissioner for the protection of Turkish Cypriot minority rights, with a staff of observers and advisers to be present in Cyprus for so long as necessary. Since the Turkish Cypriots had seen the ease with which the Greeks brushed aside the UN's authority, the suggestion that they could be protected by a UN commissioner seemed derisory to them and they refused to accept Galo Plaza as mediator from then on.

In fact Dr Plaza had acted as an arbitrator rather than as a mediator and the suggestions put forward by him meant that even the rights given to the Turkish Cypriots under the existing treaties would have to be curtailed. Instead of suggesting that the international agreements which gave birth to the Republic of Cyprus should form the basis of new discussions, because such agreements cannot unilaterally be abrogated but can only be amended by the consent of the parties concerned, and being highly critical of the 1960 constitutional arrangements, he went on to propose a new constitutional set-up in line with the aspirations of the Greek Cypriot side. This meant acceptance of the *fait accompli* created by the Greek Cypriot side since December 1963. The Turkish government's view was that Dr Plaza had transgressed the limits of his mandate, which was to promote 'a peaceful solution and an *agreed* settlement of the problem confronting Cyprus', by making suggestions which committed him to a certain stand on the substance of the Cyprus problem without the agreement of the parties concerned.

6. EMERGENCE OF A GREEK CYPRIOT ADMINISTRATION

The Greek and Turkish Cypriots hold diametrically opposed views concerning the intercommunal conflict. In 1964 the Greek Cypriots, who controlled the government and 98 per cent of the territory of the Republic,[55] regarded the Turkish Cypriots as rebels and their action as an insurrection against the state.[56] On the other hand, the Turkish Cypriot view is that this community had been ousted from all organs of government, by force of arms, by its Greek Cypriot partner in accordance with a preconceived plan. Turkish Cypriots consider the Greek Cypriot-controlled government illegal and unconstitutional.[57]

After the outbreak of the intercommunal troubles of 21 December 1963, co-operation between the Greek and Turkish Cypriot communities envisaged by the 1960 Constitution in the running of the affairs of the Republic came to an end. Indeed, with the outbreak of communal hostilities the Turkish Vice-President and ministers found it impossible to attend their ministries or the meetings of the Council of Ministers which were being held on the Greek side. Also the Turkish members of the House of Representatives found it impossible to attend the deliberations of the House. The Greek Cypriot government stated that it no longer recognized Dr Kutchuk in his capacity as Vice-President and constitutional provisions as to promulgation of laws by the President and Vice-President were no longer applicable. From this moment onwards the bi-communal system envisaged by the 1960 Constitution came to an end. The very first article of that Constitution provided that the state of Cyprus is an independent and sovereign republic with a presidential regime, the President being Greek and the Vice-President being Turkish, elected by the Greek and the Turkish communities of Cyprus respectively.

[55] UN Secretary-General's Report S/6102 of 12 Dec. 1964, 19.
[56] See Stanley Kyriakides, *Cyprus: Constitutionalism and Crisis Government* (Philadelphia, 1968), 112.
[57] e.g. statement by Mr Rauf R. Denktash, then President of the Turkish Communal Chamber, before the UN Security Council, 19 UN SCOR, 1099th Meeting, 28 Feb. 1964, 8 and 21.

Archbishop Makarios no longer considered binding the
London and Zurich Agreements, the fundamental provisions of
which were incorporated in the 1960 Constitution as 'basic'
articles which could not be amended. On 1 February 1966,
during a commemorative meeting in Athens of the *Enosis*
plebiscite (which had been organized by the Greek Orthodox
Church and held in January 1950), Archbishop Makarios
declared that the Zurich and London Agreements 'today stand
abrogated and buried. Neither Turkey nor any other power can
breathe life into them.'[58] The governments of Greece and
Cyprus also issued a joint communiqué that any solution
excluding *Enosis* would be unacceptable.

The request of the Turkish Cypriot members of the House of
Representatives to return to that House, conveyed by UNFI-
CYP, was encountered by conditions put forward by Mr G.
Clerides, the President of the House, that made the realization of
this impossible. Acceptance of such conditions for the purpose
of returning to the House would have meant surrendering the
constitutional rights of the Turkish Cypriot members and of
their community. They would have to accept, *inter alia*,
statutory changes to the 1960 Constitution as well as the
abrogation of article 78 thereof. It was further stated that the
Turkish Cypriot members had no legal standing in the House.
These events are verified by United Nations Reports.[59]

After these tragic events the Parliament of Cyprus became an
*exclusively* Greek Cypriot body. This body proceeded to enact
'laws' only in the Greek language despite the mandatory
provisions of article 3 of the Constitution which provided that
the official languages of the Republic shall be Greek and
Turkish and that all legislative, executive, and administrative
acts and documents shall be drawn in both official languages.
This Parliament adopted on 26 June 1967 the following
resolution:

Interpreting the age-long aspirations of the Greeks of Cyprus, the
House declares that despite any adverse consequences it would not
suspend the struggle being conducted with the support of all Greeks,
until the struggle ends in success through the *union* of the whole and
undivided Cyprus *with the motherland*, without any intermediary stage.

[58] Greek and Greek Cypriot press of 2 Feb. 1966.
[59] UN Secretary-General's Report S/6569 of 29 July 1965, paras. 7–11.

Moreover, all negotiations on the possible re-employment of the Turkish Cypriot government civil servants in Nicosia and their financial compensation from January 1964 ended in deadlock, as it was considered by the Greek Cypriot government to be a highly political matter linked closely with the final settlement of the Cyprus question.[60]

During the period 1964–74 Greece was responsible for some violations of the treaties. As mentioned earlier, the Centre Union government of Mr George Papandreou, having obtained the agreement of Archbishop Makarios, sent Greek troops clandestinely to Cyprus in 1964, thereby unwittingly paving the way for the Greek junta's *coup d'état* against the Archbishop ten years later.[61]

On the other hand, Turkey refused to accept the changes made to the Constitution of Cyprus and did not recognize the Greek Cypriot government as the government of Cyprus.

Britain, one of the guarantor powers of the Constitution, remained inactive when changes were being made to that Constitution by the Greek Cypriot House of Representatives, except in the case of the 1965 Election Law, which changed the election system of the state.[62]

The world at the time looked on and remained impervious to the state of affairs on this small island, wrongly believing that what was happening was purely an internal matter and of no concern to outsiders.

## 7. VIOLATIONS OF THE 1960 CONSTITUTION AND THE DOCTRINE OF 'NECESSITY'

Generally speaking an independent sovereign state should be able to change its constitution in accordance with the procedure laid down by the constitution itself. This should be considered as part and parcel of the sovereignty of the state, and as an internal

---

[60] UN Secretary-General's Report S/5950 of 10 Sept. 1964, para. 106.

[61] These acts contravened the provisions of the Treaty of Alliance, and the relevant resolutions of the United Nations, particularly that of 4 Mar. 1964 (Res. 186/1964) which, *inter alia*, called upon the 'Government of Cyprus' to take measures to stop violence and bloodshed.

[62] The matter will be examined in more detail under the following section.

matter. In the case of Cyprus, however, that sovereignty is limited by the international treaties (London and Zurich Agreements) which gave birth to the Republic of Cyprus. Cyprus is bound to respect its status as laid down in the treaties and its freedom to change its Constitution is curtailed, as the 'basic articles' are unamendable.[63] Moreover, under the Treaty of Guarantee, the Republic of Cyprus undertook the obligation to maintain the state of affairs so created.

On the Greek Cypriot side, in line with the thirteen-point proposals of Archbishop Makarios, the Greek Cypriot House of Representatives, in the absence of the Turkish members, amended several of the fundamental articles of the 1960 Constitution by ordinary legislation. These laws purported to change the basic articles of the 1960 Constitution and the bi-national character of the Republic.

A list of laws, i.e. statutes enacted by what had become the Greek Cypriot House, which whittled away the 1960 Constitution, is worth looking at:

1. The National Guard Law, 1964 (Law 20 of 1964) as amended, violates article 129 of the 1960 Constitution which limits the strength of the Cyprus army to two thousand men and lays down the proportions of Greek and Turkish Cypriots in its composition. The law introduces compulsory military service. However, article 129(2) of the Constitution provides that compulsory military service shall not be instituted except by common agreement of the President and Vice-President of the Republic. The Vice-President was not consulted on this matter.

2. The Police (Amendment) Law, 1964 (Law 21 of 1964) abolished the proportion of Greeks and Turks in the police and gendarmerie forces and altered the structure of these forces contrary to article 130 of the Constitution. Thus, what was called the Cyprus police was in fact a force of armed men solely composed of Greek Cypriots.

3. The 1960 Constitution endowed the Republic with two superior courts—the Supreme Constitutional Court and the High Court of Justice. However, the Administration of Justice (Miscellaneous Provisions) Law, 1964 (Law 33 of 1964) provides that the jurisdiction and functions of these two superior

---

[63] Art. 182 of the Constitution.

courts shall vest in, and be exercised by, the Supreme Court established under this law. In *Attorney-General* v. *Ibrahim*[64] the Supreme Court of Cyprus held that the doctrine of necessity should be read into the provisions of the written Constitution of Cyprus, thus justifying violations of the Constitution.

4. The Municipal Corporations Law 1964 (Law 64 of 1964), in contravention of article 173 of the Constitution, provides for the establishment of unified municipal corporations instead of the separate municipalities. Thus, the existence of separate Turkish Cypriot municipalities is completely ignored.

5. On 23 July 1965 the Greek members of the House of Representatives passed two laws, one prolonging the term of office of the President of the Republic and of the Greek members of the House and the other amending the electoral law. These are: the President of the Republic and Members of the House of Representatives (Extension of Term of Office) Law, 1965 (Law 38 of 1965), and the Electoral (Transitional Provisions) Law, 1965 (Law 39 of 1965), respectively.

According to article 78 of the Constitution, separate majorities of the representatives from each community taking part in the vote were required for any modification of the electoral law. The Electoral (Transitional Provisions) Law, 1965 purported to amend the existing electoral law, with a view to abolishing separate Greek and Turkish Cypriot electoral rolls. Articles 1 and 32 of the Constitution require that the President of the Republic and the Greek members of the House of Representatives be elected by the Greek community and the Vice-President of the Republic and the Turkish members of the House be elected by the Turkish community.

Law No. 38 of 1965 enacted by the Greek Cypriot Parliament purported to change the electoral system entrenched in the Constitution, by providing for common electoral rolls. This meant that Turkish Cypriots would be deprived of their entrenched right of electing the Vice-President of the Republic and Turkish Cypriot members of Parliament because Greek Cypriots would also be voting for these candidates. The consequence of this would be that those Turkish Cypriot

---

[64] (1964) CLR 195. This case will be dealt with in more detail in the following pages.

candidates favoured by Greek Cypriots (who are in the majority) would be elected.[65] This law, which is in breach particularly of article 62 of the Constitution, has been the subject of protest notes of two of the three guarantor powers, i.e. Great Britain and Turkey.[66]

6. The Greek Communal Chamber (Transfer of Functions) and the Ministry of Education Law 1965 (Law 12 of 1965) provides that the Greek Communal Chamber shall be deemed to have ceased functioning. This law further provides for the creation of a Ministry of Education for Cyprus to exercise administrative power in all educational, teaching, and cultural matters whereas education is within the sphere of each community. Article 46 of the 1960 Constitution provides for a Council of Ministers composed only of seven Greek and three Turkish ministers. A Minister of Education was thus, unconstitutionally, added to the number of ministers. Constitutional provisions as to participation of the two communities in the Council of Ministers according to a 7:3 ratio was abrogated.

7. The Public Service Law 1967 (Law 33 of 1967) provides that the Public Service Commission shall be composed of a chairman and four other members. This law violates articles 124 of the 1960 Constitution which declares that the Public Service Commission shall be composed of seven Greek Cypriot and three Turkish Cypriot members.

The violation of the Cyprus Constitution has been justified by the Cyprus Supreme Court on the 'doctrine of necessity'. It is therefore useful to give some attention to this doctrine.[67] Strictly

---

[65] Reference may also be made to Law No. 124 of 1985, which has raised the number of representatives to 56, despite express provisions of art. 62 of the 1960 Constitution which stipulates that the number of representatives shall be 50, allocated to the two communities on a 70:30 ratio (that is, 35 Greek Cypriot and 15 Turkish Cypriot representatives).

[66] See UN Doc. S/6569 of 5 Aug. 1965. Diplomatic protests were made by both the British and Turkish governments. At a subsequent Security Council meeting the French, Soviet, and United States representatives, as well as those of England and Turkey, were all critical of the Cypriot action (20 UN SCOR, 1235th meeting, (1965) ). Even the Greek representative suggested that 'one might conceivably have some misgivings as to the timing of the legislation' (20 UN SCOR, 1234th meeting, 17 (1965) ).

[67] See also Z. M. Nedjati, *Administrative Law* (Nicosia, 1974), 176–9, and Nedjati and Trice, *English and Continental Systems of Administrative Law* (Amsterdam, 1978), at 98–9.

speaking, the doctrine of necessity is incompatible with the principle of legality when it is invoked to challenge the constitutionality of a statute with the purpose of justifying deviations from constitutional order. The same doctrine is also sometimes invoked for the purpose of justifying an administrative measure which otherwise would be unlawful. The Greek Cypriot judges of the Supreme Court of Cyprus in *The Attorney-General* v. *Ibrahim*,[68] in holding that the doctrine of necessity should be read into the provisions of the written constitution of Cyprus (thus justifying certain acts which otherwise would be unconstitutional), were only tapping a slender stream of authority, particularly academic opinion, to develop an existing doctrine, or rather to create a new spurious doctrine, known as the 'doctrine of necessity'. In this case the respondents were charged under the Cyprus Criminal Code for the offences of endeavouring to overthrow the government by armed force and of engaging in war-like activities. The District Judge of Kyrenia, having first committed the accused for trial at the next assizes, released the accused on bail. The Attorney-General appealed against that release order to the Court of Appeal. A preliminary objection was taken by the respondents against the hearing of that appeal. The respondents argued that the Administration of Justice (Miscellaneous Provisions) Law of 1964, which amalgamated the High Court and the Supreme Constitutional Court of Cyprus, was contrary to the Constitution. In fact the 1960 Constitution of Cyprus had endowed the Republic with two superior courts—the Supreme Constitutional Court and the High Court of Justice and laid down that the provisions creating these superior courts were 'basic articles' of the Constitution which could not in any way be amended by the legislative organ. The 1960 Constitution of Cyprus had envisaged the participation of the Greek Cypriot and Turkish Cypriot communities in the three organs of government, the civil service, and other organs on a specified ratio. The intercommunal troubles of 21 December 1963 had made it impossible for Turkish Cypriots to participate in the running of the affairs of the Republic, but at the time the *Ibrahim* case was decided Turkish Cypriot judges had continued to participate in the

[68] (1964) CLR 195.

judiciary. The respondents argued that the new law was unconstitutional and therefore the courts in Cyprus which were established under that law had no jurisdiction to administer the law of Cyprus.

On the basis of their analysis of the political climate prevailing in the country in 1964, the Supreme Court accepted the Attorney-General's submission that there was necessity for the enactment of the law whose constitutionality was being challenged. Vassiliades J., deriving much authority from a lecture delivered by Dr Glanville Williams[69] at University College, London, concluded that the doctrine of necessity should be read into the provisions of the written constitution of Cyprus and therefore the enactment of the new law was legally justified notwithstanding the provisions of the Constitution. It may be argued however that there was not really a direct relationship between the situation in Cyprus and the amalgamation of the two superior courts.[70] Judges sometimes interpret rules of law in the light of prevailing political trends and philosophies. Moreover, the judges of the Cyprus Supreme Court were sitting in their own cause. If the law in question were unconstitutional, the creation of the 'Supreme Court' would be unconstitutional, with the result that the judges themselves would have no jurisdiction to sit in that court. Furthermore, that court, when hearing the *Ibrahim* case, was composed exclusively of Greek Cypriot judges, even though the Turkish judges were attending the courts at the time.

Here it is significant to make a digression to explain why the

---

[69] *Current Legal Problems* (1953), vi. 216.

[70] Unlike the Supreme Court of Cyprus, the Federal Supreme Court of Nigeria in *Lakanmi and Ola* v. *A.-G. for the Western State of Nigeria and Others* (S.C. 58/59, delivered on 24 Apr. 1970) found no necessity to justify the military government's departure from the Nigerian Constitution of 1963. The civilian government, on 26 Jan. 1966, had recognized the impossibility to govern due to a mutiny in the Nigerian armed forces. On that date the civilian government had invited the army commander to take over the reins of government, and he, in his acceptance speech, had announced the 'suspension of certain parts of the Constitution'. The doctrine of necessity was reassessed by the Pakistan Supreme Court in *Asma Jilani* v. *The Government of West Punjab* (1972) 24 Pakistan Legal Decisions, 139, where the court held that the proclamation of Martial Law did not by itself necessarily give the commander of the armed forces the power to abrogate the constitution.

Turkish Cypriot judges attended the courts at Greek Cypriot-controlled areas for more than two years after the intercommunal troubles. The President of the Supreme Court of the Turkish Federated State of Cyprus, Mr Justice Ulfet Emin, in a statement issued on 13 January 1978 explained the position in the following words:[71]

The Turkish Cypriot judges attended the courts till 2 June 1966, through the efforts of the then neutral President of the High Court Mr Wilson, on the understanding that the provisions of the constitution would be restored and hoping that discrimination against the Turkish community would be prevented. But, to our regret, during the two-year period when Turkish judges attended the courts, not only were the provisions of the Constitution not restored, but the unconstitutional law mentioned above was used as an instrument to persecute the members of the Turkish community. The courts were turned into a 'Star Chamber'. Turkish citizens were arrested, brought before the courts on fictitious charges, such as preparing war-like operations, refused bail, and kept in custody for long periods without being brought to trial. Turkish citizens were sentenced to pay fines £50 to £200 for carrying a genuinely innocent letter from one village to another. We could give many such examples. All these cases were taken before Greek judges in violation of the Constitution although Turkish judges were available. On the other hand the Greeks who attacked or even murdered Turks were not even brought before the courts. Those who were brought for minor charges were let scot-free or treated very leniently on the pretext of being members of the legal forces of the state. . . .
As judges, we shall never forget the day when, on 2nd of June 1966, we were stopped at the check point near the law-courts. Some of us were prevented from attending the courts and one of us, who had managed to get through, was removed from his chambers at gun point and taken back to the check point.

Moreover, little support was given to the doctrine of necessity by

[71] *News Bulletin*, 28 Feb. 1978, No. 3716, vol. 28. He was replying to Mr Justice Triantafyllides, President of the Greek Cypriot Supreme Court, who in a speech had said that he was looking to the days when the Greek and Turkish litigants would use the same courts. The retired President of the Supreme Court of the Turkish Federated State of Cyprus, Mr M. Necati Münir Ertekün also commented on the same speech of Mr Justice Triantafyllides. The Turkish Cypriot judges attended the courts subject to certain reservations of principle (See UN Secretary-General's Report to the Security Council No. S/6102 of 12 Dec. 1964, para 101, 36–7).

the case-law of common-law systems. In *Stratton's* case[72] the lawful governor of Madras was unlawfully put under arrest by certain persons under the plea of alleged necessity. Lord Mansfield said to the jury[73] that in England it could not happen because there is a regular government to which they could apply:

but in India, you may suppose a possible case, but in that case it must be imminent, extreme, necessity; there must be no other remedy to apply to for redress; it must be very imminent, it must be very extreme, and . . . they must appear clearly to do it with a view of preserving the society and themselves.

There is a series of decisions of the Supreme Court of the United States as to the position of the states which attempted to secede during the American Civil War. It was held that during the rebellion the seceding states continued to exist as states, but that, by reason of their having adhered to the Confederacy, members of their legislatures and executives had ceased to have any lawful authority. However, they had continued to make laws and carry out executive functions and the inhabitants of those states could not avoid carrying on their ordinary activities on the footing that these laws and executive acts were invalid.[74] However, the decisions of the US Supreme Court cannot be interpreted as laying down a principle that the doctrine of necessity justifies statutory amendment of constitutional provisions, in a way that is not in accordance with the procedure for constitutional amendment. *A fortiori*, none of the 'basic articles' of the 1960 Constitution of Cyprus could be amended by ordinary legislation.

In general, state necessity cannot be relied on in England to support the existence of a power or duty,[75] or to justify deviations from lawful authority. Necessary acts not authorized by existing law may subsequently be the subject of indemnifying legislation.[76] In *Madzimbamuto* v. *Lardner-Burke*,[77] the critical

---

[72] (1779) 21 State Trials, at 1046.    [73] Ibid. at 1223.

[74] See e.g. *Texas* v. *White* (1868) 7 Wallace 700; *Hanauer* v. *Woodruff* (1872) 15 Wallace 439; and *Horn* v. *Lockhart* (1873) 17 Wallace 570, at 580.

[75] *Halsbury's Laws of England*, 4th edn. (London, 1973), vol. i, para. 2.

[76] See e.g. the Indemnity Act, 1920 and the Town and Country Planning Regulations (London) (Indemnity) Act, 1970.

[77] The decision of the Rhodesian Court of Appeal is reported under the name of *Baron* v. *Ayre* (1968) 2 South Africa Law Reports 284 (R AD). The Privy Council decision is to be found in (1968) 3 All ER 561.

question was whether the Rhodesia Declaration of Independence under the 1965 Constitution was valid. Had the 1961 Constitution been effectively annulled? The Rhodesian Court of Appeal in a 3 : 2 decision held that the 1965 Constitution had not yet acquired *de jure* status and, therefore, the *Grundnorm*[78] had yet to be established. The Privy Council ruled (Lord Pearce dissenting) that the doctrine of necessity or implied mandate could not give effect to the laws of a usurper government such as that of Rhodesia. In *Adams* v. *Adams*[79] Sir Jocelyn Simon, referring to the doctrine of necessity said that this doctrine is intimately connected with concepts of public policy, a sphere in which the courts of law are rightly chary of intrusion. The learned judge saw greater need for the invocation of the doctrine of necessity in countries where legislative powers are constrained by a paramount written constitution.

Relying on the principle enunciated by the Privy Council subsequent to the *Ibrahim* case, it may be argued as a legal theory that the doctrine of necessity could not be relied upon to justify the laws of a government which had itself dismantled the Constitution, violated international agreements, and wrecked the bi-communal set-up, as a result of which an exclusively Greek Cypriot administration came into being.

Never in the modern history of Europe has the doctrine of 'necessity' been effectively invoked (except in the Greek Cypriot part of Cyprus) to justify deviations from written constitutions. The proper method to change a constitutional provision is by amendment of the constitution in accordance with the procedure laid down in the constitutional law of the country concerned. Otherwise there can be no respect for constitutions and the door will be open for racist or oppressive regimes. The jurisprudential value of the 'doctrine of necessity' will always be highly doubtful.

## 8. CYPRUS TURKISH ADMINISTRATION

As a result of the intercommunal hostilities, the Turkish Cypriots were completely disenfranchised, but showed unex-

[78] See ch. 4 s. 3, below.
[79] (1970) 3 All ER 572, at 588. As to the question of validity of acts of officers (including judicial officers) *de facto sed non de jure*, see 588–92 of the Report.

pected fierceness of resistance which enabled them to hold on to certain areas over which they never lost control. The most important was the fifteen-mile corridor between Nicosia and Kyrenia (excluding the harbour town, but including St Hilarion above it), the sole beach-head at Kokkina-Mansoura (Erenköy) near Ayios Theodoros to the west, and the separately administered Turkish quarters in all the towns, save Kyrenia. As stated by the then UN Secretary-General, the writ of the Greek Cypriot government has not run in these Turkish Cypriot-controlled areas since December 1963.[80] The Turkish Cypriots living in these areas were at first administered by a *General Committee*. The day-to-day administration of these areas was undertaken by this committee, decisions of which had the force of law by an *ex post facto* provision in section 5 of the 'Basic Law' of the Cyprus Turkish Administration. The General Committee issued rules and regulations under the laws which were in force. This committee and the Provisional Cyprus Turkish administration which followed were engaged in every aspect of the community's life: the resettlement of over 20,000 refugees; the distribution of aid from Turkey; representations to UNFICYP to try and get essential supplies of food, water, and medicine to isolated enclaves; education; economic affairs; and the payment of £30 a month subsistence allowance to civil servants, all of whom had been deprived of their jobs because of the hostilities and changes in the Constitution.[81]

In addition to the General Committee, the Turkish Communal Chamber continued to function after December 1963 and passed laws and took decisions within the scope of its competence under article 87 of the 1960 Constitution.[82] The Turkish members of the House of Representatives also used to meet separately during the same period.[83]

[80] Report to the Security Council, S/6228 of 11 March 1965.

[81] These payments were at first advanced to civil servants as a loan in the hopeful expectation that they would be able to return to their jobs and receive back pay. Needless to say, that still has not happened.

[82] Between 1965 and 1967 the Chamber took decisions prolonging the term of office of its members (as elections could not take place during the anomalous situation) and passed laws relating to its personnel, legitimation of children, and imposition and collection of personal tax.

[83] The two laws passed by this Assembly are: the 1965 Elections (Vice-President and the Turkish members of the House of Representatives) (Temporary Provisions) Law, and the 1967 Rent Assessment and Control

The *General Committee* was succeeded by the Provisional Cyprus Turkish Administration, the establishment of which was accepted at a meeting convened on the night of 28 December 1967 in the office of the Vice-President of the Republic, consisting of the leading members of the Turkish community who were previously elected to responsible positions under the 1960 Constitution. The Turkish point of view was that several articles of the 1960 Constitution had hitherto been abrogated or disregarded by the Greek Cypriot side, who, in the absence of the Turkish Cypriot members of the House of Representatives, proceeded to pass legislation in contravention of the Constitution. These amendments consisted of statutes enacted by what had become the Greek Cypriot House.

The Basic Law of this administration consisted of 19 sections. Section 1 provided that until all the provisions of the 1960 Constitution were applied, all Turks living in Turkish areas of Cyprus were to be attached to this administration. Section 2 provided for the setting up of a Legislature to enact the necessary legislation for Turkish areas. The Legislative House was to be composed of the Turkish Cypriot members of the House of Representatives and members of the Communal Chamber. Section 7 provided that the Executive power in Turkish areas was to vest in the Executive Council of the administration.

Because of the anomalous situation after 1963, elections could not be held for a number of years, either on the Greek or the Turkish sides, to elect members of the legislatures. On the Turkish side elections for the Vice-Presidency of the Republic were scheduled to be held on 25 February 1968. Dr Fazil Kutchuk, the President of the Provisional Cyprus Turkish Administration, who stood unopposed on the nomination day (15 February 1968), was declared as elected.[84]

(Temporary Provisions) Law. The Assembly also took decisions during the same period extending the terms of office of the Vice-President of the Republic, of the Vice-President of the House of Representatives (a Turkish Cypriot), and of the Turkish members of the House of Representatives, as elections could not be held due to the anomalous situation.

[84] The scheduling of vice-presidential elections on the Turkish side was prompted by the announcement that presidential elections would be held on the Greek side on 25 Feb. 1968. Those elections resulted in the renewal of the mandate of Archbishop Makarios.

The gradual process of political and administrative evolution
continued from the General Committee stage (1963–7) through
the Provisional Cyprus Turkish Administration (1967–74) to
the stage of an Autonomous Cyprus Turkish Administration[85]
(1974–5), the Turkish Federated State of Cyprus, and thence to
the present phase, the Turkish Republic of Northern Cyprus.
These constitutional arrangements, which represent evolutionary organic developments in the field of Cyprus constitutional
law, demonstrate how the Turkish administration took over or
assumed its share of functions under the 1960 Constitution thus
showing its intention to give a constructive hand in reshaping
the 1960 bi-communal partnership.

The 1964–74 decade was the most painful period for the
Turkish Cypriots, who had to bear many tribulations in their
own enclaves whereas the Greek Cypriots became masters in the
political, economic, and military fields. For instance, the New
York *Herald Tribune* reported on 16 September 1964 'degrading
sub-human standards of life' in Cyprus for the Turks,[86] a fact
even more forcefully corroborated by the United Nations
Secretary-General in his report to the Security Council dated
10 September 1964.[87] He said that the economic restriction
being imposed upon the Turkish community in Cyprus was in
some instances so severe as to amount to a 'veritable siege'.

[85] The designation 'Autonomous Cyprus Turkish Administration' was
accepted by the decision of the Council of Ministers, No. 5549 of 3 Sept. 1974.
[86] See also Oberling, *The Road to Bellapais*.
[87] S/5950, para. 222.

# 3

# Intercommunal Negotiations 1968–1974

Until the Kophinou (Geçitkale)–Ayios Theodoros (Boğaziçi) crisis of November–December 1967, the Greek Cypriot side adamantly refused to negotiate with the Turkish Cypriots, whom they called 'rebels'. The attacks at the above-named villages by an army of thousands of men from mainland Greece, under the command of General Grivas, necessitated Turkish intervention. Greece had to withdraw most of the Greek army officers and troops from Cyprus; Greek Cypriots now seemed to be inclined to negotiate with Turkish Cypriots.

In January 1968 Archbishop Makarios issued a statement to the people of Cyprus and in this he stated the following: the Cyprus problem had entered a critical stage. The two main factors which had contributed to this development were the failure of the direct Graeco-Turkish dialogue and the withdrawal from Cyprus of the Greek military forces. These two factors had created circumstances and conditions 'dictating a realistic reappraisal of the handling of the Cyprus problem'. A solution had to be sought 'within the limits of what was *feasible*', which did not always coincide with the limits of what was desirable.

Following presidential elections on the Greek side, which were held on 25 February 1968 and which resulted in the renewal of his mandate, Archbishop Makarios reaffirmed before the Greek Cypriot House of Representatives his willingness to discuss with the Turkish Cypriots ways of ensuring their 'legitimate rights and certain additional privileges', provided that these were kept within the limits of a unitary, democratic, and independent state. With this in mind, on 12 March 1968 he submitted to the Secretary-General, U Thant, his new proposals. The underlying concept was that Cyprus should be a unitary state where Turkish Cypriots should enjoy communal autonomy. The structure of the state and the form of its governmental institutions would be subject to consideration and

discussion, and any proposed constitution should be approved
by the people either directly or indirectly through any
recognized democratic machinery. The Turkish Cypriot community would be proportionately represented in the House of
Representatives, but elections would be on a common electoral
roll. There was to be a Ministry for Turkish Cypriot Affairs
headed by a Turkish Cypriot minister and special provision
would be made for the fair representation of the Turkish
Cypriots in the public service and the judicial organs.

After considerable prodding by the United Nations, intercommunal talks which aimed at restructuring the constitution
of Cyprus began in 1968 between the representatives of the
Greek and Turkish communities under the aegis of the Special
Representative of the Secretary-General of the United Nations.

The conditions under which both sides negotiated within the
framework of the intercommunal talks between the years 1968
and 1974 were different from those prevailing now. Those
negotiations cannot have a bearing and effect on the present
intercommunal talks, which have the aim of reaching a
settlement on the basis of a 'bi-communal federal republic'. For
historical purposes, however, it has been found useful to include
a short assessment of the intercommunal talks that were held
before 1974.

An exploratory first meeting of the representatives of the
Greek and Turkish communities, Messrs Clerides and Denktash, took place in Beirut on 11 June 1968, and there the way
was paved for the opening of substantive negotiations in Cyprus
between the two sides, the first meeting in Nicosia taking place
on 25 June 1968.

At the first phase of the talks the impression was created that
both sides were prepared for a new order and compromise
solution. Between the years 1968 and 1971 the intercommunal
talks comprised three phases, various documents were
exchanged, and various subjects were discussed in depth. Mr
Denktash emphasized that the Turkish political status
entrenched in the 1960 Constitution could not be abandoned
and indicated that a compromise solution would become
possible if certain concessions on Turkish entrenched rights at
government level were exchanged for a degree of local

autonomy. Both sides were therefore prepared to examine the issue of local government. Mr Denktash introduced the idea of the formation of communal groups of villages, but accepted the principle of a unified police. This was rejected by the Greek side for the reason that it conflicted 'with the principle of a unitary state and the accepted forms of local administration'. The Greek government, while supporting the intercommunal talks, because the Greek and the Greek Cypriot sides could not possibly afford to miss another opportunity for the final solution of the Cyprus problem, expressed complete agreement at this stage with the position of the Greek Cypriot side on the issue of local autonomy. Local government areas delineated on geographical and not on communal criteria should be insisted upon, Mr Pipinellis, the Greek Foreign Minister, informed Mr Clerides.

The attitude of the Turkish government at the time towards the talks as communicated to the UN Secretary-General and to the Greek government may be summarized as follows:

(*a*) the intercommunal talks should be encouraged,
(*b*) both *Enosis* and partition should be excluded,
(*c*) the difficulty of the problem should not be underestimated; the discussions were bound to be long and arduous, but they might be the last chance.

During the second phase of the intercommunal talks the two negotiators exchanged concrete proposals on the executive, the police, the legislature, the administration of justice, and local government. On the executive the Greek Cypriot proposals emphasized the presidential character of the regime to be set up. The President of the Republic was to be the head of state and all executive power was to be exercised by him through a Council of Ministers. No reference was made to the office of Vice-President. The President would have no right to veto the laws. The Turkish Cypriot participation in the Council of Ministers would be in proportion to their population.

On the legislature Mr Clerides's proposals provided for a House of Representatives consisting of 60 members, of whom 48 would be Greek Cypriots and 12 Turkish Cypriots elected on the basis of common electoral rolls. The House would have a President and two Vice-Presidents, one of the latter would be a

Turkish Cypriot. All legislative decisions would be taken by majority vote except where the interests of Turkish Cypriots were particularly involved. A two-thirds majority would be required for amendment of constitutional provisions, except those conferring specific rights on the Turkish Cypriots, in which cases a specified number of votes from among the Turkish members would be necessary.

Justice should be administered on judicial and not on ethnic criteria. The President and other judges of the Supreme Court were to be appointed by the President of the Republic out of a panel prepared by the Supreme Council of Judicature. Matters like appointment, promotion, transfer, and disciplinary control over judges of inferior courts would be entrusted to this body. Access to the European Commission of Human Rights would be made possible by recognizing the right of individual recourse to the Commission under Article 25 of the European Convention.

As to the police, a unitary force was suggested in which the Turkish Cypriots would be represented in proportion to their population.

The views and proposals of the Turkish side may be summarized as follows:

1. On the legislature the Turkish side accepted that its participation might be brought down to 20 per cent of the total number of representatives but the number of Turkish representatives should not be less than 15. The House should not be allowed to legislate on matters specifically reserved in the constitution, autonomy being one of them. Greek proposals concerning common electoral rolls could not be accepted.

2. The office of Vice-President must be retained.

3. Turkish and Greek Cypriots should have the constitutional right to have their case tried by a judge of their own language.

The proportion of Greek and Turkish members of the Supreme Court should not be below 3 and 2 respectively unless agreement was reached on the establishment of local administration courts.

4. As for local government, the Turkish side insisted that the grouping of villages should be effected on communal criteria, that each group of villages so constituted should be a local authority area and that each local authority area should elect a representative or representatives who would sit at a central

government authority entrusted with the co-ordination and exercise of local government functions. There would thus be two central authorities, the Turkish local authority council and the Greek local authority council invested with both communal chamber functions and with local governmental powers.

Mr Clerides's answers to a questionnaire submitted by Mr Denktash in May 1969, whereby the Greek Cypriot side emphasized that they were not prepared to accept under the guise of local government either a federal or a cantonal system, signalled the end of the second phase of the negotiations.

The third phase of the talks began in August 1969. The main topic which engaged the interlocutors was the question of local government. On 30 November 1970 the Greek Cypriot side offered a 'package deal' whereby it modified its position particularly as regards the composition of the House of Representatives by accepting that the House could be composed of 60 Greek and 15 Turkish members elected on separate electoral rolls, and by accepting the principle of communal grouping of villages.

The Turkish Cypriot side gave its written reply to the other side on 27 April 1971. The Turkish side proposed the retention of the office of Vice-President of the Republic and his duties and powers as prescribed by the Agreements with the exception of the veto, and the re-establishment of two communal chambers as separate legislative assemblies in charge of communal matters. The powers, duties, and jurisdiction of the local authorities should be embodied in the constitution. There should be central authorities or co-ordinating bodies for local government; they should not be under the District Officer.

The further proposals of Mr Clerides of 26 June 1971 did not help to dispel Turkish Cypriot fears. The latter could not afford to negotiate a settlement in a way or form which did not effectively bar the way to *Enosis*.

EOKA B was now intensifying its activities and political agitation within the Greek Cypriot community did not augur well for the fate of the intercommunal talks. The Turkish side now began to feel that even the Treaty of Guarantee, which barred *Enosis* and which by virtue of article 181 of the Constitution, had constitutional force, was not sufficient for this purpose. In their proposals the Greek Cypriot side was now accepting that Turkish Cypriot participation in the Executive and the police force should be fixed at 20 per cent. The House of Representatives was to consist of 75 members, 60 Greeks and 15 Turks, to be elected on separate electoral rolls. The Vice-President was to be elected by the Turks. The Greek side now accepted that the basic provisions regarding local government should be embodied in the constitution, but the House of Representatives would legislate on local government. The main difference on this issue was that the Greek side could not agree that there should be created a communally based central government authority for local government. The Greek side treated the idea of local autonomy all along as equivalent to limited local government under complete governmental super-vision, whereas the Turkish side treated it as an added autonomous function to the functions of the communal chambers.

In his letters of 9 August and 20 September 1971 Mr Denktash emphasized that there had to be some kind of partnership or functional federation. The Turkish side could not accept the proposed elimination of the 1960 rights of the Vice-President, apart from the veto.

In the autumn of 1971 the talks ended in deadlock.

During the last month of his tenure of office the UN Secretary-General, U Thant, intervened to reactivate the talks. In consequence of his soundings and consultations he submitted an *aide-mémoire* on 18 October 1971 in which he suggested to the governments of Cyprus, Greece, and Turkey that, with a view to facilitating the future conduct of the intercommunal talks, his special representative in Cyprus, Mr B. F. Osorio Tafall, should, in the exercise of the Secretary-General's good offices, take part in the talks between the representatives of the two communities. It was also suggested that the governments of Greece and Turkey should each make available a constitutional expert who would attend the talks in an advisory capacity.[1]

The resumption of the talks was delayed when it was discovered early in February 1972 that Archbishop Makarios had secretly imported a substantial quantity of arms and ammunition of Czech origin into the island.[2]

[1] UN Secretary-General's Report No. S/10401 of 30 Nov. 1971, para. 79.
[2] UN Secretary-General's Report No. S/10664 of 26 May 1972, paras. 30 and 58.

Upon assuming the office of Secretary-General of the UN in January 1972, Dr Kurt Waldheim renewed the efforts for the reactivation of the talks. As a result, the second round of the intercommunal talks, attended now by, in addition to Messrs Clerides and Denktash, the Secretary-General's Special Representative in Cyprus, Mr Tafall, and the Greek and Turkish constitutional experts, Messrs Decleris and Aldikaçti, were inaugurated on 8 June 1972.

While the expanded talks went on, in a spasmodic fashion, Archbishop Makarios continued to make provocative *Enosis* speeches in various parts of the island. The local Greek press ridiculed the Turkish Cypriots' stand on partnership rights and their demand for local autonomy. They urged that the Greek Cypriots' rights to self-determination should never be curtailed for the sake of the Turkish Cypriots, who were free to leave the island if they did not like living under Greek rule.

On 2 April 1974 the Greek Cypriot negotiator, Mr Clerides, walked out of a meeting because the Turkish premier, Mr Ecevit, was reported to have declared that 'a federal system of government was the best solution for Cyprus'. Later Mr Denktash told reporters that the Turkish Cypriot stand on local autonomy in an independent Cyprus was unchanged. Mr Ecevit also confirmed that there was no change in the Turkish position with regard to the intercommunal talks. Eventually, through the efforts of the Turkish side and the perseverance of the UN Secretary-General, the talks were resumed on 11 June 1974.[3]

The activities of EOKA B, the ensuing political agitation, and the differences between Archbishop Makarios and the Greek junta, were now seriously affecting the intercommunal talks in a negative way. The Greek junta, being in favour of *Enosis*, seemed to have been supporting EOKA B. Archbishop Makarios was thus finding himself unable to reach a settlement with the Turkish Cypriot side.

In Turkey, on the other hand, the two-party coalition government of Mr Bülent Ecevit, which was formed in 1973, was, in the beginning of 1974, becoming more and more clearly

---

[3] R. R. Denktash, *The Cyprus Triangle* (London, 1988), 57–8.

in favour of federation as a just and viable solution to the Cyprus problem.

Between the years 1972 and 1974 various views and documents were exchanged and discussions took place on the same subjects at the expanded intercommunal talks. It was eventually found possible to bridge some of the differences but no concrete result or agreement was announced.

It has been argued that, as a result of six years of arduous intercommunal talks, differences of the two sides on the Executive and the Judiciary were narrowed, that complete agreement was reached on the Legislature, and that even on the thorny problem of local government substantial progress was made.[4] The former Greek Cypriot negotiator, Mr G. Clerides, also disclosed in 1976 that a 'near agreement' had been reached during the 1971–2 intercommunal talks, which the Greek Cypriot Council of Ministers vetoed.[5] The reason for this negative stand can be found in the statement of Archbishop Makarios and of Greece that they were not prepared to sign an agreement which bars *Enosis*.[6] Re-establishing the structure of a bi-communal Republic would be treason for leaders like Archbishop Makarios, who had taken the holy oath to unite Cyprus to Greece in 1950[7] and who, in 1970 publicly declared

---

[4] P. G. Polyviou, *Cyprus in Search of a Constitution* (Nicosia, 1976), Part II, Ch. 6, and *Cyprus Conflict and Negotiation 1960–1980* (London, 1980), 105-15.

[5] *Cyprus Mail* of 8 Aug. 1976.

[6] Note e.g. the speech at Yialousa of Archbishop Makarios on 14 Mar. 1971: 'Cyprus is Greek, Cyprus was Greek since the dawn of its history, and will remain Greek. Greek and undivided we have taken it over. Greek and undivided we shall preserve it. Greek and undivided we shall deliver it to Greece.' See *Cyprus: The Paradox of Enosis* (introduction by Osman Örek) (Turkish Cypriot PIO, Lefkoşa, 1977).

Again, in a statement to a French Magazine *Le Point* on 19 Feb. 1973, Archbishop Makarios said: 'I have struggled for union of Cyprus with Greece, and *Enosis* will always by my deep national aspiration, as it is the aspiration of all Greek Cypriots. My national creed has never changed and my career as a national leader has shown no inconsistency or contradiction. . . .'

The Archbishop in an interview given to the Norwegian Newspaper *Degbladet* which was published on 12 Mar. 1977 confessed that 'It is in the name of *Enosis* that Cyprus has been destroyed.'

[7] See ch. 1 n. 9, above.

that all through these years he had not deviated from his oath.[8]
Political agitation within the Greek Cypriot community
impeded the continuation of the talks, which were eventually
overtaken by events, mainly the coup of 15 July 1974.[9]

[8] In an interview with *Eleftheros Kosmos* and *Ta Simerina*, Athens, 19 Aug.
1970, Archbishop Makarios said 'I shall never violate my oath, and I shall
never deviate from my goal. I have desired *Enosis*, and I have never struggled
for anything else other than its achievement.'

[9] In the second volume of his *Cyprus: My Deposition* (Athens and Nicosia,
1989), Greek Cypriot politician Mr G. Clerides has made some revelations
about the intercommunal talks. He says that the period 1964–1970 offered
opportunities for a solution of the Cyprus problem. The one solution could
be *Enosis*, the island's union with Greece, provided a substantial part of
Cyprus territory was ceded to Turkey. The second possible solution was to
reach agreement on an improved version of the 1960 Constitution that would
give Turkish Cypriots autonomy in local government but would reduce their
participation in the executive, the legislature, the civil service and the police
and do away with the veto powers of the Turkish Vice-President. Mr Clerides
blames the Greek Cypriots themselves and their 'destructive characteristics'
for the lost opportunity to achieve an improved solution. He says that, if
during the period 1968–1970, government and opposition had made a realistic evaluation of what constituted a feasible solution, the situation in Cyprus
today would have been different. Mr Clerides says that the Greek Cypriot
side refused to give autonomy to the Turkish Cypriots on local government
on the ground that this constituted a form of 'concealed federation'. But
today, after much pain and suffering, the Greek Cypriot side openly accepts
federation. He continues to say that the Greek Cypriot side did not grasp the
opportunity which was there from 1968–1970, and before the 'catastrophe'
of 1974. The opportunity was lost not only because the Greek Cypriot side
refused to give to the Turkish Cypriot community autonomy in local government, but because Archbishop Makarios continued to hold the view that
the Turkish Cypriots should be reduced, from the position of partners given
them by the Zurich and London Agreements, to that of enjoying only minority rights.

# 4

# Turkish Intervention and its Aftermath

## 1. DISPUTE OVER *Enosis*

The Kophinou disaster had highlighted the folly of working for *Enosis* in the face of Turkey's objections. However, a group of EOKA extremists who supported Grivas and *Enosis* at any price mounted activities which were at first restricted to intimidation and sporadic violence.

The main danger to the survival of Makarios and the independence of the Republic came from the Greek army officers brought by him to Cyprus for the expressed purpose of defence against Turkish 'invasion'. Their barracks habitually displayed the emblems and Hellenic slogans of Greece.[1] *Enosis* propaganda was rife. Early in 1969 a new threat to stability came with the rise of the National Front, an armed organization headed by a former EOKA leader and based in Limassol. The capture of Limassol Central Police Station by one of its branches exceeded in scope and military skill anything ever attempted by EOKA against the British.[2]

The National Front, however, disclaimed responsibility for the attempted assassination of Archbishop Makarios on 8 March 1970 when the helicopter taking him to Makheras Monastery was shot down by gunmen. A week later Polycarpos Georghadjis, the former Minister of the Interior who was dismissed on the Greek junta's orders, was found murdered near Kythrea in mysterious circumstances. Before and after the helicopter incident the local and international communists had widely publicized rumours of a Western plot in which a Greek sponsored coup was about to end the independence of Cyprus as a step towards the establishment of a NATO base.[3]

[1] UN Doc. S/8914, para. 87.

[2] Nancy Crawshaw, 'Cyprus: The Political Background', *Cyprus in Transition, 1960–1985* (Trigraph—London, 1986), 1–19 (7–8).

[3] Digest of the Cyprus Press (BIS, Nicosia, 27 Mar. 1970) and Crawshaw, 'Cyprus: The Political Background', 8.

On 19 March 1970 the Turkish Foreign Minister was quoted as saying 'any attempt to carry out a coup in Cyprus and declare *Enosis* would be opposed by Turkey with all her forces and strength'.[4]

Though the National Democratic party candidate, Dr T. Evdokas, who campaigned for *Enosis*, was not elected to Parliament at the elections of 5 July 1970,[5] Archbishop Makarios continued to be faced with mounting opposition. General Grivas, who had returned to Cyprus in September 1971 and formed EOKA B, was openly campaigning for *Enosis*.

On 26 October 1971, General Grivas issued a proclamation denouncing the Greek Cypriot leadership under Archbishop Makarios as unworthy of the Greek community. He declared that he had come back to fulfil the age-long aspiration of the Greek community to unite Cyprus with Greece.[6] The Archbishop replied three days later, disclosing that he had, from time to time, clearly and categorically told Greek governments that he would unhesitatingly proclaim *Enosis*, if they were prepared to accept such a move and share the responsibilities for the repercussions from such a venture.[7]

At first Archbishop Makarios tried to win Grivas to his side and offered him an important post in his cabinet, but Grivas refused. Later, the Archbishop asked Grivas to join him in forging a new policy for the national struggle. The two men had a secret meeting in Nicosia. They agreed on their common goal, *Enosis*, but disagreed on how it should be achieved. General Grivas wanted an immediate military campaign, while the Archbishop insisted on caution and a low-geared approach.[8]

In February 1972, the Greek ambassador, in a stiff note to the Archbishop, called for the formation of a government of national unity stressing that Athens, not Nicosia, was the

[4] *Cyprus Mail*, 20 Mar. 1970.

[5] The parliamentary seats were distributed as follows: Unified party (Clerides) 15; AKEL (Papaioannou) 9; Progressive Front (Ioannides) 7; Democratic Centre Union (Lyssarides) 2; Independents 2; National Democratic party (Evdokas) nil.

[6] Grivas's proclamation was reported in all Greek Cypriot newspapers the following day.

[7] Archbishop's public statement on the 'Internal Situation in Cyprus', 29 Oct. 1971, reported in Greek Cypriot newspapers the following day.

[8] R. R. Denktash, *The Cyprus Triangle* (London, 1982), 61.

'national centre of Hellenism'. The demand was in due course partly met by the 'resignation' of the Foreign Minister, Mr Spyros Kyprianou, and the reshuffle of the Council of Ministers to include politicians who were less openly hostile to the Greek junta. In March the three Cyprus bishops, of Kition, Paphos, and Kyrenia, accused Archbishop Makarios of abandoning *Enosis* and demanded his resignation as President, claiming that his political role conflicted with his ecclesiastical responsibilities.

On 8 February 1973, Archbishop Makarios was re-elected President unopposed for a third term. The three bishops who had been demanding his resignation were themselves unfrocked by decision of the Synod of Eastern Orthodox Churches, which Archbishop Makarios had convoked.

In November 1973, the Papadopoulos regime in Greece was overthrown by a counter-coup engineered by Brigadier Ioannides, commander of the military police.

On 27 January 1974, General Grivas died in Limassol. Violence nevertheless continued and on 25 April EOKA B was proscribed, but to no effect.

After the death of Geneal Grivas EOKA B came under the direct control of the junta in Athens. Terrorist activities in the Greek sector continued with the assistance and guidance of the Greek army officers. But now Archbishop Makarios began to hit back with his Tactical Reserve Force, which he had established to combat the terrorists. Within the following six months most of the local leaders were apprehended and a considerable quantity of secret documents seized which provided ample evidence proving the complicity of Greek officers in EOKA B activities. The Archbishop finally showed defiance and sent a letter to the President of the Greek Republic, General Phaedon Ghizikis, on 2 July 1974, to ask the junta to withdraw its officers from Cyprus.[9] The text of his letter included the following statements:

. . . You realise, Mr. President, the sad thoughts which have been preoccupying and tormenting me since ascertaining that men of the Greek government are increasingly hatching conspiracies against me and, what is worse, are dividing Greek Cypriot people and pushing

[9] A translation of this letter was published in the *Sunday Times* of 21 July 1974.

them towards catastrophe through civil strife. I have more than once so far felt, and in some cases I have almost touched, a hand invisibly extending from Athens and seeking to liquidate my human existence. For the sake of national expediency, however, I kept silent. . . . But covering things up and keeping silent is not permissible when the entire Greek Cypriot people are suffering, when Greek officers of the National Guard, at the instigation of Athens, support Eoka 'B' in its criminal activity, including political murders and generally aiming at the dissolution of the state.

The Greek government must take great responsibility for this attempt to abolish the state of Cyprus. The Cyprus state could be dissolved only in the event of Enosis. However, as long as Enosis is not feasible it is imperative that Cyprus should be strengthened as a state. By its whole attitude towards the National Guard issue, the Greek government has been following a policy calculated to abolish the Cyprus State.

## 2. THE COUP

In early July 1974 there were reports of a possible coup in Nicosia inspired by Athens. However, the Archbishop's spokesman said that any such attempt would be defeated by strong popular resistance. The Archbishop himself later stated that he had never believed that the junta would do anything that would inevitably provoke a Turkish intervention. However, this warning was not heeded by Athens.

In the morning of 15 July 1974 there took place a *coup d'état*, organized and led by Greek officers of the National Guard.[10] It was engineered and staged by the military junta then ruling Greece. Its aim was to overthrow Archbishop Makarios and set up a government that would unite the island with Greece.

By the use of violent means, directed in particular towards the presidential palace and Archbishop Makarios himself, in the words of the Greek Cypriot Supreme Court, 'the constitutional order was temporarily overthrown'.[11] Within a few hours of the coup the broadcasting station was seized and the presidential palace was ruined by fire and artillery shells, as was the nearby

---

[10] The National Guard was established by Law No. 20 of 1964 of the Greek Cypriot House of Representatives.

[11] *Liasi and Others* v. *The Attorney-General* (1975) 12 JSC 1889, at 1904.

Kykko Monastery where policemen had held out against
National Guard tanks for most of the first day of the coup. A
curfew was imposed and applied in respect of the population of
the island, with the exception of a two hours' break for buying
food, under the threat of execution without any warning of
anyone disobeying the said prohibition until 17 July. It
continued from the afternoon hours to morning hours until and
after the Turkish intervention.

The National Guard announced that they had seized power
to prevent civil war on the island. The announcement said that
Makarios was dead and the National Guard was in complete
control of the situation, except for a few pockets of resistance. By
the afternoon of the first day of the coup Mr. Nicos Sampson,
former EOKA gunman, was installed as 'President'. But
Archbishop Makarios was not dead. The Turkish Cypriot
Bayrak Radio announced at 15.20 hrs. on the day of the coup
that Archbishop Makarios had managed to leave the presidential palace and had taken refuge in a mountain hideout in the
Paphos area, where violent clashes were taking place. The news
broadcast by Bayrak Radio was later confirmed by a broadcast
from the Archbishop himself from his hideout. He urged his
supporters to fight and resist the junta's coup.

There were numerous victims, dead and wounded, as a result
of the coup and the resistance which was offered.[12] Foreign news
reports from Cyprus confirmed Archbishop Makarios's statement to the Security Council that the losses were heavy and that
both Greeks and Turks were suffering. A report in the
*Washington Star News* on 22 July 1974 said that 'bodies littered
the streets and there were mass burials'. On 23 July 1974 *The
Times* of London quoted an eyewitness as saying that many
supporters of Archbishop Makarios had been massacred and
some hundred members of the presidential guard killed. On

---

[12] In Aug. 1976, during the trial of Mr Nicos Sampson, the Deputy
Attorney-General of the Greek Cypriot administration described the situations during the coup in the following words: 'the military operations were
extended on 15 July in the same well-organized manner, with the help of tanks
and other heavy or light weapons, to other towns except Paphos. Most of these
armed attacks ended in blood baths due to the number of injured or killed
among the lawful security forces and civilians. Material damage was
enormous' (*Republic* v. *Sampson* (1977) 2 JSC 108).

25 July, *Combat*, published in Belgium, reported: 'It has been confirmed that during the days following the coup in Nicosia at least 2,000 of Makarios supporters have either been killed in the fighting or executed.'

The *coup d'état* government effected numerous arrests of people (for political reasons) who were let free upon the Turkish intervention and because of it. High-ranking public officers, as well as the holder of the post of Chief of Police, were replaced by others whose names were announced by the radio. The press was under censorship and until 23 July there were published for one day only, that is on 19 July, four out of ten Greek Cypriot daily newspapers.

Archbishop Makarios, having survived the attack on the presidential palace, took refuge at Paphos. He was airlifted from the Paphos bishopric to the British bases and from there was flown to Malta and thence to London. He attended the UN Security Council meeting on 19 July 1974 to tell the Council that the Greek military regime had openly violated the independence of Cyprus and had extended its dictatorship to the island. He claimed that the coup was an *invasion* and a flagrant violation of the independence and sovereignty of the Republic of Cyprus and that it was the work of Greek officers directed by the military government in Athens. About the situation in the island, he said, 'I am afraid that the number of casualties is large and that the material destruction is heavy . . . our primary concern at present is the ending of the tragedy'. He pointed out that the events in Cyprus were not an internal affair for the Greek Cypriots alone, but that the Turkish Cypriots were also affected. Both Greeks and Turks would suffer from the consequences of the junta's invasion.[13]

## 3. THE LEGAL EFFECT OF THE COUP

According to Kelsen's jurisprudential system,[14] a legal system consists of manifold hierarchically arranged norms or legal rules, all of which have one ultimate source, namely, the

[13] Security Council Official Records, S/PV 1780.
[14] See Hans Kelsen, *General Theory of Law and State* (rev. edn., New York, 1960), 117.

*Grundnorm*. A legal system is thus like an inverted collapsible pyramid with the *Grundnorm* as the foundation rock. The *Grundnorm* is the ultimate norm from which all subordinate norms in the legal system derive their validity. If one takes away the *Grundnorm*, then the inverted pyramid collapses for lack of support. Since Kelsen believes that the legal effect of a *coup d'état* is the destruction of the *Grundnorm*, this means that, in his eyes, the legal effect of a *coup d'état* is to remove the bottom rock of the collapsible inverted pyramid and thus to send the whole structure crashing down.

In order to restore the status quo ante, which was disturbed as a result of the *coup d'état*, the Greek Cypriot House of Representatives enacted the 'Coup d'état (Special Provisions) Law 1975' (No. 57 of 1975), which provided that the '*Coup d'état Government*' had no legal basis whatsoever.[15] '*Coup d'état Government*', according to section 2 of the aforesaid law, means 'the person who during the *coup d'état* unconstitutionally and illegally assumed the office of the "President of the Republic" and the Ministers unconstitutionally and illegally appointed by him and the Under-Secretary and it includes every member thereof'. Also, according to section 4, 'any act made by the "*Coup d'état* Government" by invoking its powers or duties is legally non-existent'.

In *Liasi and Others* v. *The Attorney-General*,[16] even though the Greek Cypriot Supreme Court accepted that the 'constitutional order was temporarily overthrown', it ruled that the *coup d'état* had failed to be legalized, because there was no popular acceptance of the situation. It seems that the central issue which the court considered was whether or not the coup was legalized by *subsequent* events. The court said:[17]

According to the case law and legal theories, two are the basic tests whereby a *coup d'état* is legalized. The first, the substantial test, is

[15] Similar measures were adopted in France by the ordinance of 9 Aug. 1944, in relation to the acts of the government of Vichy, and in Greece by the constituent act 58/1945 in relation to the enactments during the time of the enemy occupation and by the constituent acts as from 1 Aug. 1974 to 7 Aug. 1974 and of the fourth resolution of the Fifth Revisional Assembly in relation to the enactments and acts during the time of the dictatorship from 21 Apr. 1967 until 23 July 1974.

[16] (1975) 12 JSC 1889, at 1900 and 1907.

[17] At p. 1905.

popular acceptance, even if a tacit one, of the change and the legal values thereby invoked, and the second, the formal test, is the legalization of the '*Coup d'état Government*' through the recognition of its actions by the next lawful Government.

The court did not refer to the Kelsenian theory. It is submitted that the coup directed by the military government in Athens and spearheaded by Greek army officers in Cyprus was successful even though the life of the *coup d'état* government was a short one due to the Turkish intervention of 20 July 1974, which caused the resignation of Mr Nicos Sampson on 23 July 1974. During its short life the coup had, according to the Kelsenian theory, destroyed the established order, that is, the government of Archbishop Makarios. The Greek Cypriot sector had bowed to the coupists and resistance had ceased. Congratulations were pouring in to the new 'President' by Greek Cypriot organizations and personalities for having saved them from Makarios's dictatorship. Archbishop Makarios had fled the country and there was no one defending his rights or status in Cyprus. It seemed therefore that for a short time the established order was destroyed and its place taken by the *coup d'état* government.

### 4. TURKISH INTERVENTION

The Turkish Premier, Mr Bülent Ecevit, flew to London on 17 July 1974 to seek British cooperation under the Treaty of Guarantee. Mr Ecevit urged joint action whereby the British bases on the island could be used for the purpose of landing troops. It was made clear however that if Britain was unwilling to act Turkey was in a position to intervene on her own. Britain declined the Turkish offer, preferring a solution which would not jeopardize British interests on the island. The USA, deeply concerned over the crisis also offered to mediate. Undersecretary Joseph Sisco visited Athens and Ankara, but Turkey had no alternative but to intervene.

Turkey, acting under the Treaty of Guarantee,[18] intervened

---

[18] The Treaty of Guarantee will be examined fully in ch. 5 below. As to the military aspects of the Turkish intervention see Townsend, 'Vertical Assault: The Proof is in the Doing', *Proceedings of the United States Naval Institute*, Nov. 1977, 119.

militarily in Cyprus on 20 July 1974 when Great Britain refused to act in concert. Turkish intervention was aimed at putting an end to a take-over of Cyprus by Greece and the inevitable destruction of the Turkish community.

As the Turkish 'Peace Operation' proceeded, Prime Minister Ecevit made an impassioned plea for world support. The Turkish armed forces, he declared, 'have started a peace operation in Cyprus this morning to end decades of strife provoked by extremist and irredentist elements'.[19] Turkey as a co-guarantor of the independence and constitutional order of Cyprus was fulfilling her legal responsibility by taking action. He said that this was not an invasion but an act against invasion. It was not aggression but an act to end aggression.

On 20 July the Turkish armed forces launched a sea- and airborne operation. Troops came ashore west of Kyrenia and paratroopers were dropped in the central plain near Geunyeli. The objective was to establish a bridgehead in the Kyrenia area and link up with the large Turkish enclave in Nicosia by a corridor from the sea. Heavy fighting took place on the outskirts of Nicosia for the control of the airport. That evening the Security Council in New York discussed the emergency and adopted resolution No. 353, deploring the outbreak of conflict and continuing bloodshed and expressing concern at the threat to international peace and security and the explosive situation in the Eastern Mediterranean. It called upon all states to respect the sovereignty of Cyprus; upon the belligerents to cease fire; and for the early start of negotiations between Greece and Turkey for the restoration of peace and constitutional government.

The initial Turkish force that landed on the island was too small and met with unexpected resistance. The National Guard, although many units were exhausted after the coup, launched an all out attack against Turkish Cypriot areas in order to thwart Turkey's action. The Greek and Turkish contingents legally stationed in Cyprus under the Treaty of Alliance clashed when the former made an abortive attempt to break through to the Nicosia–Kyrenia road and cut off the Turkish troops before they reached the main Turkish enclave of Nicosia. Only Nicosia

---

[19] *Dış Politika* (Foreign Policy), vol. iv, Nos. 2–3, pp. 226–7.

was adequately defended; elsewhere the Turkish enclaves—Famagusta, Limassol, Paphos, and many small villages—came under National Guard attacks.

Kyrenia did not come under Turkish control until 22 July, the third day of the intervention. The Turks accepted a cease-fire. Fighting, however, continued in the vicinity of the airport. The Turks feared that the Greeks might land troops by air. UNFICYP, strongly reinforced by British troops, took over the control of the airport and immobilized the runways.

During the intervention there was a threat of war between Greece and Turkey. On the day of the intervention the Greek junta ordered general mobilization in Greece. Without air cover it was powerless to send direct aid to Cyprus; in certain quarters the possibility of attacking Turkey across the Evros River was considered, but the Chiefs of Staff advised that the Greek army was in no position to make a counter attack.[20] The threat of war between Greece and Turkey lasted several more days. However, on 22 July the junta ordered a cease-fire in Cyprus and on 23 July Mr Glafcos Clerides, the President of the Greek Cypriot House of Representatives, took over the 'Presidency' from its illegal incumbent, Mr Nicos Sampson.[21] The next day, after a meeting between President Ghizikis and the four heads of the armed forces in Greece, the military junta decided to hand power over to a civilian government. Mr Karamanlis left France for Greece to become Prime Minister after an absence of eleven years. The Turkish intervention not only toppled the *coup d'état* government in Cyprus, it also caused the restoration of democracy in Greece by the overthrow of the military junta.

[20] See, Nancy Crawshaw, *The Cyprus Revolt*, (London, 1978), 390 and M. A. Birand, *30 Hot Days* (Oxford, 1985), 36.

[21] Mr Nicos Sampson himself admitted that he was about to proclaim *Enosis* when he had to quit: *Cyprus Mail*, 17 July 1975. According to the foreign press, there were 20,000 Greek army personnel in the island at the time of the coup. Even though an amnesty was announced by Archbishop Makarios in a public speech on 7 Dec. 1974, Mr Sampson was tried and convicted for offences against the state. His special plea connected with the amnesty was reserved for the opinion of the Greek Cypriot Supreme Court: *Republic* v. *Sampson* (1977) 2 JSC 108. While serving a long gaol term for his part in the coup, Sampson was allowed to leave the island for treatment, but though ordered to return to the island he continues to stay in France.

### 5. THE GENEVA CONFERENCE

In compliance with resolution No. 353 of the Security Council of the United Nations adopted on 20 July 1974,[22] which *inter alia* called upon Greece, Turkey, and the United Kingdom 'to enter into negotiations without delay for the restoration of peace in the area and constitutional Government in Cyprus', and 'having regard to the International Agreements signed at Nicosia on August 16, 1960', the Foreign Ministers of Greece, Turkey, and the United Kingdom held discussions in Geneva from 25–30 July 1974.

The Conference ran into difficulties on the second day owing to conflicting interpretations of the UN resolution. Turkey refused to consider any constitutional plan unless her forces remained in Cyprus. The Turks believed that if their forces were withdrawn the situation would revert to that existing before the coup. Greece took the line that the opposing forces must be withdrawn prior to any constitutional discussions. Despite difficulties a declaration was signed by the three Foreign Ministers on 30 July.[23]

By that declaration, the three Foreign Ministers decreed that, in order to stabilize the situation, the areas controlled by opposing armed forces should not be extended and a security zone should be set up. Furthermore, all Turkish Cypriot enclaves occupied by Greek or Greek Cypriot forces should be immediately evacuated. The three Foreign Ministers also agreed that negotiations should be carried on, to secure the restoration of peace in the area and the re-establishment of constitutional government in Cyprus. As a final observation the ministers noted the existence in practice of two autonomous administrations on the island, that of the Greek Cypriot community and that of the Turkish Cypriot community.

The second round of the Geneva Conference was convened on

---

[22] See Appendix 2, below.
[23] HMSO, Misc. No. 30 (1974), Cmnd. 5712. See Appendix 3, below. At the first round of negotiations at Geneva 25–30 July 1974 Cyprus was not represented. When the second round was convened on 9 Aug., the representatives of the two communities were also present and the representative of the Greek Cypriot community stated that his administration completely subscribed to the Geneva Declaration in question.

9 August 1974. However, the Conference became a stage for mutual recriminations. The Greek representative threatened to walk out unless the Turks withdrew to the cease-fire line of 30 July. The Turkish side demanded new constitutional arrangements which would provide for autonomous areas within a federal state. The Turkish side produced two plans. Mr Rauf Denktash, the President of the then Turkish Cypriot Administration, who was the Turkish Cypriot representative at the Conference, submitted a formula which provided for a bi-zonal federation with the demarcation line running from the west of Lefka in an almost straight line, which would have taken in the Turkish quarters of Nicosia and Famagusta, leaving all the area to the north of the line under Turkish control. The Turkish Foreign Minister, Mr Turan Güneş, submitted a plan for six autonomous Turkish cantons. The Nicosia enclave would have been enlarged to take in all the northern coast from Vivilas to Davlos, part of the Mesaoria, and the Turkish quarters of Nicosia and Famagusta. The Karpass, except for one small Turkish enclave, would have remained under Greek control. Both plans, which would have brought 30 per cent of the island under Turkish control, were strongly objected to by the Greek Cypriot representative, Mr Glafcos Clerides. Nevertheless, the Güneş plan, subject to negotiation, might have formed the basis of a satisfactory settlement.

On 13 August the atmosphere at Geneva was very tense. The Turkish side rejected an adjournment, insisting that its proposals be accepted so that the main outlines of a constitutional settlement could emerge. That side was suspicious of dilatory tactics which might keep a constitutional settlement in abeyance and give the Greek side time for military preparations. The Greek and Greek Cypriot representatives at the Conference, on the other hand, stated that they would not succumb to pressure and would not accept an imposed solution, like that of 1960. The British Foreign Secretary, Mr James Callaghan, would not agree that the guarantors could impose 'any departure' from the 1960 Constitution, though he saw the need for some geographical zone. He stated that the island was the prisoner of the army; but Turkey should not forget, he warned, that 'tomorrow the army might be the prisoner of the island'.[24]

[24] P. G. Polyviou, *Cyprus in Search of a Constitution* (Nicosia, 1976), 358.

The Geneva Conference ended in failure on 14 August and the second round of Turkish military operations began. Greece announced its decision to withdraw from the military wing of NATO on the ground that the Alliance was unable to stop the conflict between the two allies.

### 6. EVENTS LEADING TO THE SECOND ROUND OF MILITARY OPERATIONS

The undertakings at Geneva remained academic. The Greeks and Greek Cypriots continued to lay mines and construct strong points around the Turkish positions and the Turks continued to reinforce their troops and send out patrols. The agreement reached during the first Geneva Conference as to evacuation of Turkish enclaves by the National Guard forces and the provisions as to the establishment of a security zone were not observed. Turkish Cypriots fled from some thirty-three villages and those living in the south were put under an inhuman siege while atrocities were committed against Turkish villages, particularly Maratha (Murataǧa), Sandallar, and Tochni Taşkent), despite the presence in Cyprus of UN troops. All Turkish Cypriots outside the protective umbrella of the Turkish peace force stood in imminent danger of annihilation.

On 22 July 1974 the Turkish Prime Minister called upon the UN to 'stop the genocide of Turkish Cypriots' and declared 'Turkey has accepted a cease-fire, but will not allow Turkish Cypriots to be massacred'.[25] On 23 July the *Washington Post* reported:

In a Greek raid on a small Turkish village near Limassol 36 people out of a population of 200 were killed. The Greeks said that they had been given orders to kill the inhabitants of the Turkish villages before the Turkish forces arrived.[26]

*France soir* reported on 24 July as follows:

The Greeks burned Turkish mosques and set fire to Turkish homes in the villages around Famagusta. Defenceless Turkish villagers who

---

[25] *The Times*, 23 July 1974.
[26] See also *The Times, Guardian*, 23 July 1974.

have no weapons live in an atmosphere of terror and they evacuate their homes and go and live in tents in the forests. The Greeks' actions are a shame to humanity.

On 28 July the *New York Times* reported that fourteen Turkish Cypriot men had been shot in Alaminos.

In the towns of Limassol, Paphos, and Larnaca, Turkish males between the ages of 14 and 60 were separated from their families and held as hostages in open football stadiums.[27] The *Herald Tribune* reported on 25 July 1974:

On the sun-baked dirt floor of the Municipal Soccer Stadium here, about 1,750 men from Limassol's Turkish enclave and the surrounding Turkish villages are penned behind cells of barbed wire.

Their days are spent sheltering under the scorching sun that sends temperatures into high 90s, their nights shivering in the damp breezes that blow from the sea. Greek Cypriot National Guardsmen keep watch on them from machinegun positions in the upper seats of the stadium.

Although the men are dressed in street clothes and claim to be civilians, they are being held as prisoners of war by the Greek Cypriots.

Such treatment meted out to Turkish Cypriots in the south eventually led to the frantic rush of Turkish Cypriots to the safety of Turkish-controlled areas.[28]

The Turkish forces had to move into new military positions and maintain a daily build up of troops, armour, and supplies in the region of the Kyrenia bridgehead. On 31 July they seized Lapithos and Karavas on the north coast. In the meantime, 10,000 Turks had taken refuge in the walled city of Famagusta and 4,000 Turks in Knodhara. From 20 July to 14 August 1974 these refugees lived virtually on water. Greek Cypriot forces encircling these areas would not allow any food to be taken to them while they called for immediate surrender of the Turks.[29]

[27] See Alper F. Genç, *Cyprus Report: From My 1974 Diary* (Lefkoşa, 1978), 110–11.

[28] The story of this plight is told in Pierre Oberling's *The Road to Bellapais: The Turkish Cypriot Exodus to Northern Cyprus* (New York, 1982).

[29] At Geneva Mr Denktash spoke to Mr Clerides on 11 Aug. 1974 in the following terms: 'The situation is very critical. Take immediate steps to normalize the lives of Turks under your control. If I were you I would now phone to Nicosia and order the National Guard to withdraw from Turkish areas . . . I want you to know that as long as you have prisoners in your hands the

The Turkish forces were not secure in their position and could not protect the Turkish Cypriots who were under siege in Famagusta. On 8 August the *Guardian* reported that they had been under sustained mortar attack for twenty days. Accordingly the Turkish army moved out of its bridgehead and advanced upon Famagusta with the object of rescuing the Turkish Cypriot population of Famagusta and of securing a viable defensive position.[30]

The second round of military operations which were carried out as from 14 August 1974, upon the failure of the Geneva Conference, brought about 36 per cent of territory in the north under the control of the Cyprus Turkish Administration. The siege of Famagusta was lifted on 16 August.

In Tochni on 14 August all the Turkish Cypriot men between the ages of 13 and 74, except for eighteen who managed to escape, were taken away and shot. In Zyyi on the same day all the Turkish Cypriot men aged between 19 and 38 were taken away by Greek Cypriot armed elements and were never seen again. *The Times* and *Guardian* of 21 August reported murders of Turkish Cypriot families at the village of Aloa.

Very many innocent people of both communities were killed and went missing in the turmoil of 1974, and in the heat of battle there must have been excesses by individuals on both sides, but the responsibility for this must rest firmly with the Greeks and Greek Cypriots for creating the conditions in which Turkey intervened.[31] The European Commission of Human Rights found that Turkey had committed human-rights violations in Cyprus and was in breach of the European Convention on Human Rights. We shall revert to this subject later on.

Turkish army will move any moment. Under the circumstances you and I have a duty to prevent any further bloodshed.' (Private interview with Mr Denktash.)

[30] The House of Commons Select Committee on Cyprus reported in 1976, 'The second phase of military operations was inevitable in the view of your committee as the position reached by Turkish forces at the time of the first ceasefire was untenable militarily and they needed tanks and armour to consolidate their position and secure Famagusta'.

[31] Michael Stephen, 'Cyprus: Two Nations in One Island', Bow Educational Briefing No. 5, p. 4. See also Bülent Ecevit, *The Cyprus Question* (PIO of the Turkish Republic of Northern Cyprus, Lefkoşa, 1984).

## 7. DEVELOPMENTS ON THE GREEK SIDE

On the Greek side of Cyprus, on 23 July 1974, Mr G. Clerides took over from Mr Nicos Sampson when the latter realized that his continuance at the helm was giving a very unpleasant image of the Greek Cypriots as a whole. However, Mr Clerides did not take the oath of office in accordance with the 1960 Constitution. Article 42 of that Constitution provides that the President and the Vice-President of the Republic be invested before the House of Representatives before which they make an affirmation prescribed by the Constitution. Mr Clerides took the oath of office before a 'renegade' bishop (Yennadios) whom Archbishop Makarios had defrocked.[32] The question may be raised as to how Mr Clerides could be considered the legal 'President' since he did not take the oath of office as provided by the Constitution. Moreover, in his cabinet he retained most of Mr Sampson's men, none of whom had been appointed in accordance with article 46 of the 1960 Constitution. Though under that Constitution Mr Clerides could only act for Archbishop Makarios during the latter's temporary absence, he signed as 'President' and not as the 'Acting President' as required by article 44 of the 1960 Constitution. Under that article he could be so acting for forty-five days, whereas Mr Clerides continued to be 'President' for 5 months, till the return of Archbishop Makarios. When it was realized that Archbishop Makarios would be returning, he assumed the title of 'Acting President'.

In this connection it may be noted that, during the election campaign in May 1981, Mr Kyprianou called the Rally party leader Mr Glafcos Clerides an 'illegal President', a reference to his assumption of power in the interregnum of the post coup period while Archbishop Makarios was away.[33]

[32] See p. 74.
[33] *Cyprus Mail*, 'Local Press', 23 May 1981. See also, *Cyprus Mail*, 'Local Press', 27 Jan. 1983. *Eleftherotypia* (a Greek Cypriot daily) accused Mr Clerides of 'usurping' power by taking the oath of office from a defrocked bishop (Yennadios), expressing appreciation for coupist Nicos Sampson, and declaring that Makarios could be a candidate for presidency when he returned.

Archbishop Makarios stayed in exile after the coup for a period that was not then expected to be temporary; indeed it could not be known that he would be returning at all. No elections for the presidency took place on the Greek side and on his return Archbishop Makarios reassumed the presidency. After the return of the Archbishop in December 1974, the Greek Cypriot attitudes hardened, the opportunity of settling the Cyprus dispute during his absence on the basis of a geographical federation was missed, and the situation froze into a stalemate.

The Greek Cypriot south held its elections for the House of Representatives in September 1976.

With the death of Archbishop Makarios on 3 August 1977, which created a sudden vacuum in the Greek Cypriot leadership, Greek Cypriots were faced with the prospect of two elections.

Article 44 of the 1960 Constitution provides that the President (Speaker) of the House of Representatives must act as the President of the Republic during such vacancy and, furthermore, a by-election must be held within a period not exceeding forty-five days of the occurrence of such vacancy (e.g. death). Mr Spyros Kyprianou, the Speaker of the Greek Cypriot House of Representatives, assumed the office of 'Acting President'. The by-election should have been followed by an election in February 1978 when the term of office of Archbishop Makarios would have expired.[34]

The death of Archbishop Makarios and the question of his successor as the head of the Greek Cypriot administration once again raised the question of representation of Cyprus. The President of the then Turkish Federated State of Cyprus, as well as Turkish Cypriot organizations, declared, in August 1977, that the successor of Archbishop Makarios could not represent Cyprus at its 'President'.

The by-election for the purpose of electing an interim 'President' was held on the Greek side on 10 September 1977. Mr Kyprianou was returned unopposed as 'President' till February 1978.

Bishop Chrisostomos of Paphos was elected ethnarch and archbishop on 12 November 1977. The following day he was

---

[34] Art. 43(2) of the 1960 Constitution.

enthroned at St John's Cathedral in Nicosia. He stated that he would 'continue from where Archbishop Makarios had left'.

On 26 January 1978, Mr Kyprianou was nominated and, as he stood unopposed, Mr Clerides having withdrawn his candidacy following the 'kidnapping' of Kyprianou's son in December 1977, was declared by the returning officer, in accordance with article 39(1) of the 1960 Constitution, as elected. He was sponsored by Mr Afxenthiou, father of an EOKA gunman killed by security forces, who also used to sponsor the late Archbishop Makarios for the office. The significance of the personality of the 'sponsor' and 'seconders' of Mr Kyprianou reflect the 'continuation of the spirit of the EOKA movement and attachment to Greece'.[35]

## 8. EVOLUTIONARY DEVELOPMENTS ON THE TURKISH SIDE

On the Turkish side the Autonomous Cyprus Turkish Administration was succeeded by the Turkish Federated State of Cyprus, which was proclaimed on 13 February 1975. A fifty-member Constituent Assembly was set up to draft its constitution. A democratic constitution was drawn up by the Assembly, approved by a referendum held on 8 June 1975 and published in the *Official Gazette* on 17 June 1975.[36] This was an interim constitution which left the door open for the creation of a federal republic of Cyprus of which the Turkish Federated State would be one of the components.[37]

In Security Council debates which followed the proclamation of the Turkish Federated State of Cyprus, the Turkish Cypriot representative stressed that separation of the two communities

[35] *Cyprus Mail*, 27 Jan. 1978. At a gathering in Limassol on 1 Apr. 1967 on the occasion of the 12th Anniversary of EOKA, Mr Kyprianou had said *inter alia* that 'in spite of a large number of disadvantages, Cyprus is now an independent sovereign state, and, therefore, her struggle for union with Greece is easier and shorter than before'.

[36] The referendum recorded a 99.4% 'yes' in favour of the Constitution. The result was published in Suppl. III of the *Official Gazette* of 17 June 1975.

[37] See Nedjati and Leathes, 'A Study of the Constitution of the Turkish Federated State of Cyprus', *Anglo-American Law Review*, 5 (Jan.–Mar. 1976), 67–92; and Professor Gillian M. White, 'The Turkish Federated State of Cyprus: A Lawyer's View', *The World Today* (Apr. 1981), 135–41.

came about as a result of acts of the Greek Cypriot side and that there could be no return to the 1960 Constitution.[38] Physical separation was vital to the safety of Turkish Cypriots. However, the Security Council members were virtually unanimous in regretting the proclamation of the Turkish Federated State of Cyprus and in declaring continued recognition of the 'Government of Cyprus' under Archbishop Makarios. The British representative was not alone in emphasizing that the proclamation was not a 'Unilateral Declaration of Independence' (UDI) and that it ruled out partition or annexation. The setting up of a legal order which adopted the style and title of the Turkish Federated State of Cyprus was not therefore a break-away from an established constitutional set-up that could be described as UDI. The Security Council adopted resolution No. 376 of 12 March 1975 without vote, regretting the decision to declare 'that a part of the Republic of Cyprus would become a "Federated Turkish State"'. The resolution noted that the proclamation was not intended to prejudge a final settlement. Significantly, this resolution did not call on states to withhold recognition, in marked contrast to resolutions after UDI in Southern Rhodesia in 1965.[39]

On the other hand, the Greek Cypriot administration in the south claimed (and still claims) to be the government of the whole of Cyprus and is treated as such, except by Turkey, even though it has no control or say over areas under Turkish Cypriot control and even though its writ has not run in these areas since December 1963.[40]

In 1975, both sides agreed at the Vienna intercommunal talks, held under the auspices of the Secretary-General of the United Nations, to a voluntary regrouping of populations.[41] This agreement was fully implemented with the assistance of the

---

[38] In fact the 1960 Constitution was not applied after December 1963, and the state of affairs envisaged by that Constitution had ceased to exist. There was not, and is not, in existence a constitutional government of Cyprus but two *de facto* administrations.

[39] SC Res. 277, SCOR 25th year, Resolutions, 5.

[40] Secretary-General's Report S/6228 of 11 Mar. 1965.

[41] The agreement for movement of populations (UN Doc. reference S/11789 dated 5 Aug. 1975) was accepted by the Greek Cypriot Council of Ministers on 5 Aug. 1975. UN Secretary-General's report S/11789/Add. 1,

UN force. The Turkish Cypriot population in the south moved to the north, where by now the Turkish Cypriots had their homogeneous territory. The UN troops moved into the newly established buffer zone dividing the communities and brought about a relatively effective separation of the two. The government of the Turkish Federated State exercised effective administrative control over the north. This control is now exercised by the Turkish Republic of Northern Cyprus.

General elections were held in the north on 20 June 1976 on which date the Constituent Assembly ceased to function and was succeeded by the Legislative Assembly of the Turkish Federated State of Cyprus.

The fact that there was an effectual and established autonomous administration in the north was also recognized by Lord Denning MR in the English Court of Appeal in *Hesperides Hotels and another* v. *Aegean Turkish Holidays and another*.[42] Lord Denning, after reviewing the history of Cyprus since 1960, said, 'There is an effective administration in northern Cyprus which has made laws governing the day to day lives of the people'.[43]

However, the European Commission of Human Rights in *Cyprus* v. *Turkey*[44] ruled that the Turkish Federated State of Cyprus 'cannot be regarded as an entity which exercises "jurisdiction", within the meaning of Article 1 of the Convention, over any part of Cyprus'. Turkey argued, unsuccessfully,

---

dated 10 Sept. 1975, deals with the implementation of this accord. See also ch. 6 n. 3, below.

A considerable number of Greek Cypriots had already fled to the south before the implementation of the above accord for regrouping of populations. However, the number of Greek Cypriot displaced persons cannot be as high as 200,000 as is often alleged. According to Mr Criton Tornaritis, the former Attorney-General of the Greek Cypriot side, the Greek population of the north was 128,563 prior to the events of 1974 (*Legal Aspects of the Problem of Refugees in Cyprus* (Nicosia 1976), 7). The European Commission of Human Rights, in its report of 10 July 1976 in applications Nos. 6780/74 and 6950/75 refers to 'more than 170,000 Greek Cypriot refugees'.

[42] (1977) 3 WLR 656; (1978) 1 All ER 277.

[43] (1978) 1 All ER 277, at 285. See also the author's article, 'Acts of Unrecognised Governments', in the Apr. 1981 issue of the *International and Comparative Law Quarterly*, 388–415.

[44] Decision of the Commission of 10 July 1978 on the admissibility of application No. 8007/77, *Decisions and Reports* No. 13, 85, 150.

that at the material time there were two governments on the island, each of which effectively had jurisdiction only over its own community and its part of the island's territory, and that the area on which the application claimed that the alleged breaches occurred was under the sovereignty of the Turkish Federated State of Cyprus and not under Turkish jurisdiction. The Commission failed to meet the argument that, within a state which is a single party to the Convention, there may be more than one autonomous administration exercising effective control over population and territory and that such an administration can properly be held to exercise 'jurisdiction' within the Convention. Moreover, independently of the question whether the Turkish Federated State of Cyprus was an 'entity' exercising jurisdiction within the meaning of the Convention, the Commission failed to grapple with the issue of the exercise of substantial Turkish Cypriot authority in northern Cyprus under the name of the Turkish Federated State of Cyprus.

As Turkish Cypriots opted for the creation of a 'federated' state in 1975 with the purpose of keeping the door open for a federation of two federated states of Cyprus, in the international field they remained 'stateless' because the Turkish 'Federated' State did not, and could not, ask for international recognition.

## 9. THE EUROPEAN COMMISSION ON HUMAN RIGHTS AND CYPRUS

### Greece v. The United Kingdom

The provisions of the European Convention on Human Rights were invoked by Greece against the United Kingdom in recourses Nos. 176/56 and 299/57 in respect of alleged violations of the Convention in Cyprus. In the *First Cyprus Case* it was alleged that a series of emergency laws and regulations introduced in Cyprus by the United Kingdom were incompatible with the Convention. In the *Second Cyprus Case* the Greek government referred to 49 cases of 'torture or maltreatment amounting to torture' which allegedly took place in Cyprus and for which the British government was allegedly responsible.[45] A political solution was reached during these proceedings as a result of the Zurich and London Agreements and the proceedings were terminated at the joint request of the Greek and the United Kingdom governments.

As long ago as 1959 the European Commission was fully conscious of the intercommunal character of the problem of Cyprus and of the need to approach its solution on a bicommunal basis. In the Commission's Report of 8 July 1959 given in respect of the Second Application by Greece against the United Kingdom (No. 299/57) it said:

. . . the Commission in the conclusion to that Report [its report to the Committee of Ministers on Application No. 176/56] stressed that the full enjoyment of human rights in Cyprus was closely connected with the solution of the political problems relating to the constitutional status of the island.

. . . The Commission need only add that it holds the view as strongly to-day as when it drew up its Report on Application No. 176/56, that the achievement of a final settlement of the political problem is of the highest importance for securing the restoration of full and unfettered enjoyment of human rights and fundamental freedoms in Cyprus.[46]

## The period 1963–1974

Turkish Cypriots and Turkey have consistently argued that basic human rights of Turkish Cypriots were systematically being violated during the years 1963 to 1974 by the Greek Cypriot administration.[47] The reason why Turkey did not file a recourse with the European Commission of Human Rights against Cyprus to raise the issues of violations of human rights of

---

[45] The two Greek applications to the European Commission of Human Rights are described in *Yearbook 2 of the European Convention of Human Rights* (1960), 174–99.

[46] Ibid. 181.

[47] Following the intercommunal hostilities of Dec. 1963, Professor Thomas Buergenthal in an article pub. 1965 observed that, 'in view of the existing civil war in Cyprus and the *de facto* suspension of the Constitution, it is apparent that the Convention is not being applied in Cyprus'. This statement appeared in an article entitled: 'The Effect of the European Convention on Human Rights on the Internal Law of Member States', pub. in *International and Comparative Law Quarterly* Suppl. Publication No. 11 (1965) 79, at 94.

Turkish Cypriots between the years 1963 and 1974 was that
Turkey did not recognize the Greek Cypriot administration as
the lawful Government of Cyprus, and involvement in such
proceedings, particularly during negotiations for a 'friendly
settlement', would have required active contact with the
Greek Cypriot authorities in their capacity as the pretended
Government of Cyprus. Moreover, as the Commission had
previously stated with regard to the *First Cyprus Case* and the
*Second Cyprus Case*,[48] during periods of unrest, full and unfettered
enjoyment of human rights in Cyprus depends on the achievement of a final settlement of the politicl issues, and not on
recourse to the European Commission.

### *Cyprus* v. *Turkey*

After the Turkish intervention of 1974, the Greek Cypriot
administration, purporting to represent the Republic of Cyprus,
lodged on 19 September 1974 application No. 6780/74 and on
21 March 1975 application No. 6950/75 against Turkey.

During the hearing as to the admissibility of these applications, the respondent government argued that the Greek
Cypriot administration was not entitled to bring these applications on behalf of the government of Cyprus, which under the
1960 Constitution composed of the two communities of Cyprus.
Neither of these communities could by itself represent the
Republic of Cyprus. In its decision on admissibility,[49] the
European Commission rejected this argument on the ground
that the applicant government is recognized universally as the
government of Cyprus. The Commission also ruled that the
rights and freedoms guaranteed under the 1960 Constitution
should not be impaired by any 'constitutional defect' of the
applicant government. The Commission however failed to deal
with fundamental constitutional issues that had been raised.
This was not in fact a case of a mere 'constitutional defect'; it was
a case of a party purporting to hold the powers of state
unilaterally and in violation of international agreements, such
as the Treaty of Guarantee whereby the Republic of Cyprus had

[48] See above.
[49] *Decisions and Reports* 2 (Dec. 1975), 125–38.

undertaken to preserve its status quo and not to change the basic elements of its Constitution. The other main issue which confronted the Commission during the admissibility stage was whether the obligation of the respondent government under the European Convention could be invoked in respect of violations which allegedly occurred outside the metropolitan territory of the respondent government. The Commission ruled that the Contracting Parties are bound to secure the rights and freedoms set forth in the Convention to all persons under their actual authority and responsibility, whether that authority is exercised within their territory or abroad, in this case, in Cyprus.

On the basis of the above reasoning the Commission declared applications 6780/74 and 6950/75 admissible. Turkey did not appear before the European Commission at those stages of the applications which followed the decision on admissibility. It has been explained that this was not due to any lack of respect for the Commission. The decision of Turkey not to participate further in the proceedings of the Commission was due to a fundamental consideration—the fact that the government of Turkey does not recognize the Greek Cypriot administration as the legal government of the Republic of Cyprus. Turkey's continued involvement in the proceedings, particularly during the negotiations for a 'friendly settlement', would have required active contact with the Greek Cypriot authorities in their pretended capacity as the Government of Cyprus.

In fact recognition is essential for the implementation of treaties which require direct and active relations between parties. The European Convention of Human Rights requires direct and active relations between the states that are parties to an inter-state application especially because its procedural machinery requires the endeavour to reach a friendly settlement.[50]

The problems confronting the Commission in this case had been essentially political, stemming in the main from the posture of non-recognition assumed by the Turkish government *vis-à-vis* the applicant government in the broad field of general international relations, in consequence of which the respondent government did not participate in the proceedings of the

---

[50] Arts. 28 and 30 of the Convention and Rule 39 of Rules of Procedure.

Commission under article 28. It could be argued that a High Contracting Party can escape from its obligations under the Convention merely by giving some reason for not participating in the proceedings before the Commission, and that it could thus prevent the Commission from fulfilling its functions. The Convention is silent as to the procedure to be followed when the Convention procedures are blocked. One alternative was for the Commission to refer the case, with an interim report, to the Committee of Ministers of the Council of Europe, since such a situation raised a new and complex problem. Instead, the Commission proceeded to prepare its Report in the absence of the respondent government. The Commission argued, in its Report of 10 July 1976, that in such a situation it could, like other judicial organs, such as the European Court of Human Rights and the International Court of Justice, proceed with the investigation of complaints in the absence of the respondent government.[51] It is doubtful as to whether this approach was correct. The Commission is not a court. The express provisions of the relevant texts permit the courts mentioned above to give judgment by default. Unlike the International Court of Justice and the European Court of Human Rights, the Commission is not a judicial tribunal. It acts mainly as an investigating body with quasi-judicial powers.

Another point of importance was that the investigating delegates sent to Cyprus visited only the Greek Cypriot part of the island. The majority of the Commission acknowledged this in paragraph 82 of the Report when they said that 'a full investigation of all the facts has not been possible'. It could not be suggested that any fault for this failure to conduct 'a full investigation of all the facts' could be laid at the door of the Commission or of its Cyprus delegation. The problems confronting the Commission had been essentially political, in consequence of which the respondent government did not see fit to participate in the proceedings.

In the Report which it adopted on 10 July 1976, the Commission found that there had been cases of deprivation of

---

[51] See Report, i. 21. In their separate opinions Mr E. Busuttil and Mr B. Daver were of the opinion that the Commission is not empowered to enter a judgment by default (184 and 189, respectively).

life, contrary to article 2(1) of the Convention; cases of ill-treatment, contrary to article 3; confinement and detention of military personnel and civilians, contrary to article 5; and deprivation of possessions, contrary to article 1 of Protocol No. 1, for which the respondent government was responsible. The Commission also found that the refusal to allow more than 170,000 Greek Cypriot refugees to return to their homes, and consequent separation of families, violated article 8 of the Convention.

It should however be noted that the alleged violations of the Convention occurred in a situation of armed conflict when the respondent government engaged in a military intervention in Cyprus. The respondent government argued that this intervention took place in the wake of a *coup d'état* which put an end to the last remnants of constitutional order in Cyprus, and was based on the Treaty of Guarantee concluded between the United Kingdom, Greece, and Turkey.[52] Article 15 of the Convention provides that, in situations of emergency threatening the life of the nation, a High Contracting Party may take measures derogating from its obligations under the Convention to the extent required by the exigencies of the situation. The respondent government did not formally communicate a notice of derogation to the Secretary-General of the Council of Europe concerning Cyprus. For this reason the majority of the Commission found that, in the absence of some formal and public act of derogation by Turkey, article 15 of the Convention was not applicable in respect of measures taken by Turkey with regard to persons or property in the north of Cyprus.[53] But as stated in the dissenting opinion of Mr G. Sperduti (joined by Mr S. Trechsel) on article 15 of the Convention, 'measures which are in themselves contrary to a provision of the European Convention but which are taken legitimately under the international law applicable to an armed conflict, are to be considered as legitimate measures of derogation from the obligations flowing from the convention'.[54] Under article 32 of

---

[52] The events which led to the Turkish military intervention as well as the Treaty of Guarantee itself will be examined in ch. 5, below.

[53] Report, vol. i, para. 528.

[54] Report, vol. i, para. 171.

the Convention the Commission transmitted its Report to the Committee of Ministers of the Council of Europe.

It should be stressed that the drafters of the Convention laid down that the Commission's role—though important—is only one stage in an extended process established for the protection of human rights. It was recognized that the implementation, or any assessment that there had been a violation of the Convention, would involve a very large political element, either in the achievement of a friendly settlement as a result of negotiation between those directly concerned or in the form of a decision of the Committee of Ministers of the Council of Europe. As the final stage of the above process, the Committee of Ministers took an interim decision on the matter on 21 October 1977; contents of which were leaked in strong criticism by the Greek Cypriot side for not containing an outright condemnation of Turkey for its alleged violations of human rights in Cyprus.[55] It would appear that the Committee of Ministers deplored the violation of human rights in Cyprus without putting the blame on one side only and decided to take up the matter in the future.

On 20 January 1979 the Committee of Deputy Ministers of the Council of Europe decided to remove the case from its agenda and decided further to declassify on 31 August 1979 the documentation relating to this case.[56]

## Application No. 8007/77

In addition to the above proceedings, a fresh application, No. 8007/77 (*Cyprus* v. *Turkey*), was filed with the European Commission of Human Rights and oral submissions of the parties on the admissibility were heard on 5, 6, and 7 July 1978.

By its decision of 10 July 1978 the European Commission declared application No. 8007/77 (*Cyprus* v. *Turkey*) admissible.[57] The Commission has in its 1978 decision followed

[55] See e.g. article, by Greek Prof. G. Siotis, 'Un camouflet pour la Commission Européenne', pub. in *Le Monde*, which alleges that the Committee of Ministers evaded the issue of alleged violations of human rights in Cyprus.

[56] Resolution No. DH(79)1 of the Committee of Ministers of the Council of Europe adopted on 17 Jan. 1979.

[57] *Decisions and Reports* 13, 85 *et seq*. A new aspect of this application is its reference to the question of the so-called 'settlers' from Turkey, coupled with

very closely the reasoning and often the terminology of its 1975 decision.[58]

Since the previous decision of the Commission new developments had taken place in Cyprus during the three-year period that had elapsed and new arguments and evidence were therefore presented to the Commission by the respondent government during the admissibility stage of application No. 8007/77. These related, in the main, to the exercise of substantial authority in the northern part of Cyprus by the then Turkish Federated State of Cyprus, for whose acts, it was alleged, the Republic of Turkey could not be held responsible. However, the Commission evaded the issue of responsibility that was raised as regards the Turkish Federated State of Cyprus, which exercised, at all material times, at least *de facto* exclusive authority in the north of Cyprus. Morever, the Legislative Assembly of the Federated State had enacted laws relating to property rights about which the applicant government was complaining.[59] It was alleged that Turkey could not be held responsible for acts of the Turkish Federated State.

Even though the Commission was aware of the existence of the Geneva Declaration of 30 July 1974 (an international instrument subscribed to by the Foreign Ministers of Greece, Turkey, and the UK, whereby the three signatory Foreign

---

accusations of changing the demographic structure of the island. Greek Cypriot authorities alleged that there were about 50,000 mainland Turkish settlers in northern Cyprus, deliberately implanted in the country in order to 'Turkify' the area. Turkish Cypriot authorities concede that some Turkish seasonal workers and settlers were necessary after 1974 to cultivate the relatively unpopulated lands, but claim that the Turkish Cypriot economy could not absorb the numbers suggested by the other side, and that in any case many of the so-called settlers were people of Turkish Cypriot origin returning from the UK and other countries. Turkish Cypriot authorities say that the number of settlers is about 14,000. The Foreign Affairs Committee of the House of Commons, in their Report of 7 May 1987, say (para. 49) that foreign observers, including the British government, estimate the Turkish settlers in northern Cyprus at about 35,000.

[58] *Decisions and Reports* 2, 125. For a critical examination of the 1978 decision of the Commission, see the author's *The Cyprus Conflict: A Lawyer's View* (Lefkoşa, 1982), 132–140.

[59] The application also referred to alleged looting and robbery of produce and livestock from Greek Cypriot property in the north of Cyprus.

Ministers noted the existence in practice of two autonomous administrations in Cyprus, one, of the Greek Cypriot community and the other, of the Turkish Cypriot community), and even though the Commission was, during the hearing on admissibility, addressed as to the existence of substantial Turkish Cypriot authority in northern Cyprus under the name of the Turkish Federated State of Cyprus, the Commission failed to grapple with the issue raised in holding that the Turkish Federated State 'cannot be regarded as an entity which exercises "jurisdiction", within the meaning of Article 1 of the Convention over any part of Cyprus'.[60]

In its 1978 decision on admissibility the Commission has also held that an inter-state application cannot be declared inadmissible for being substantially the same as a previous application, nor can such an application be rejected as being abusive. Furthermore, the fact that the previous application was pending before the Committee of Ministers of the Council of Europe did not prevent the Commission from examining another application concerning related facts.[61] It is submitted that these broad rulings of the Commission leave the door wide open for repetitive state applications lodged for political propaganda purposes while the matter is substantially before the Council of Ministers.

The report of the Commission, which was adopted on 4 October 1983, is now pending before the Committee of Ministers of the Council of Europe. For this reason the contents of this report are, for the time being, confidential.[62]

[60] *Decisions and Reports* 13, 85, The Law, para. 24, at p. 150. Contrast the attitude of the Commission with that of Lord Denning in the Court of Appeal in England in *Hesperides Hotels and Another* v. *Aegean Turkish Holidays and Another* (1978) 1 All ER 277, at 283-4.

[61] Ibid. The Law, paras. 47-50 and 51-7, pp. 154-6.

[62] Art. 31(2) of the Convention and Rule 17 of Rules of Procedure of the Commission.

# 5

# The Treaty of Guarantee

## I. INTRODUCTION

The Treaty of Guarantee, signed in its final form on 16 August 1960 between the United Kingdom, Greece, Turkey, and the Republic of Cyprus, has four substantive articles.[1] Under article I, the Republic of Cyprus undertook the obligation to maintain its independence, territorial integrity, and security as well as respect for its Constitution. The same article prohibited union with any other state.[2] Under article II, Greece, Turkey, and the United Kingdom guaranteed the independence, territorial integrity, and security of the Republic of Cyprus and also the state of affairs established by the basic articles of the Constitution. Article III contains a pledge on the part of Cyprus, Greece, and Turkey to respect the integrity of the areas retained under United Kingdom sovereignty and not to interfere with the operations of the British sovereign bases. Finally, under article IV the signatories committed themselves to joint consultation and multilateral action in order to enforce the foregoing provisions with the stipulation that failing agreement among the guarantors, any one of them might unilaterally intervene to restore the state of affairs created by this treaty. The text of this article is reproduced hereunder for ease of reference:

In the event of a breach of the provisions of the present Treaty, Greece, Turkey and the United Kingdom undertake to consult together with respect to the representations or measures necessary to ensure observance of those provisions.

In so far as common or concerted action may not prove possible, each of the three guaranteeing Powers reserves the right to take action with the sole aim of re-establishing the state of affairs created by the present Treaty.

---

[1] For text of the treaty, see Cmnd. 1093, 86–7.
[2] The word *Enosis* was not used for reasons of diplomatic prudence.

The *casus interventionis* is established if a breach of the treaty occurs, that is to say, when there has been a breach of the undertaking by Cyprus to maintain its independence, territorial integrity, and security or respect for its Constitution, or when there has been a breach of its undertaking not to participate in any political or economic union with any state.

It may be recalled that the Republic of Cyprus was set up as a compromise between the opposing claims of Greek and Turkish Cypriots. The setting up of the Republic was therefore a manifestation of the two communities of Cyprus, each exercising the right to self-determination, to live together in one state. The substantive aim of the treaty was therefore to prohibit union of Cyprus with any other state and to protect the constitutional rights of both communities.

Article 181 of the Constitution provided that the treaty guaranteeing the independence, territorial integrity, and constitution of the Republic 'shall have constitutional force'. Some of the articles of the Constitution which were incorporated in the Zurich Agreement of 11 February 1959 were 'Basic Articles' that could not, in any way, be amended.[3] The other provisions in the Constitution could only be amended in the manner prescribed by paragraph (3) of article 182.

As already stated in the foregoing pages, Turkey intervened militarily in Cyprus on 20 July 1974, invoking article IV of the Treaty of Guarantee. According to Turkey, the *coup d'état* government of Mr Sampson, who came to power after Archbishop Makarios escaped into exile, was no more than a puppet government under orders from Greece, ready to rule the end of the island's independence and to annex it to Greece. In a Turkish government communiqué of 20 July it was stated that Turkey as one of the guarantor powers had decided to carry out its obligations under article IV(2) of the treaty with a view to safeguarding the security of life and property of the Turkish community and even that of many Greek Cypriots.[4] In the same way, the 14 August intervention purported to protect the Turkish Cypriots as well as to safeguard the independence and

---

[3] Art. 182, para. (1).

[4] For the text of the communiqué see *The Turkish Yearbook of International Relations*, 14 (1974), 125.

territorial integrity of Cyprus. On this occasion too Turkey invoked the Treaty of Guarantee.[5]

## 2. ATTITUDES OF THE PARTIES AS TO THE VALIDITY OF THE TREATY

Soon after the hostilities of 1963 Archbishop Makarios appealed to the guarantor powers to intervene to help to solve the difficulties in the island. Dr Kutchuk, the Turkish Vice-President, joined this appeal. From 26 December 1963 until 27 March 1964 a truce force under British command operated in the island doing police work.[6] The view of the British government was, however, that the peacekeeping operation was by request of the Cypriot government, therefore it would not fall under article IV of the Treaty of Guarantee, which does not contemplate a request of the territorial state.

Speaking to the Security Council in 1964, the representative of Greece, in answer to the Greek Cypriot representative who demanded a declaration from the guarantor states on the question whether the treaty gives the right of military intervention, said: 'Do we—the Greek Government—think that this article gives us the right to intervene militarily and unilaterally without the authorisation of the Security Council? The answer is "no"'.[7] As originally stated before the United Nations in 1964, the Turkish thesis was:

The very preamble of our Charter demands respect for the obligations arising from treaties and other sources of international law. In fact, respect for pledges and commitments embodied in international treaties is the only foundation upon which stability in international relations can be achieved.[8]

In critical debates of 1964 and 1974 on the Cyprus question, representatives of Turkey at the United Nations repeatedly stated that their government's freedom of action derived from

[5] *The Turkish Yearbook of International Relations*, 14 (1974), 130.
[6] See UN Security Council Official Records, (SCOR), 1098th meeting, 27 Feb. 1964, para. 79.
[7] UN SCOR, 1097th meeting, 25 Feb. 1964 (S/PV 1093), para. 168.
[8] UN SCOR, 19th Session, 27 Feb. 1964 (S/PV 1098), para. 40.

the Treaty of Guarantee, whose validity under the doctrine of *pacta sunt servanda* was incontestable.[9]

During the debates at the United Nations in 1964, the British representative's view was that the Treaty of Guarantee did authorize the use of force and that such use would not necessarily be inconsistent with the United Nations Charter. He added that this was a hypothetical question and the best way was to ensure that occasion for intervention never arose.[10] Great Britain did not declare the circumstances in which intervention would be appropriate. It would seem that British officials then had Chapter VIII of the Charter in mind, which does not preclude the setting up of 'regional arrangements' to keep the peace in a particular region.

The UN Security Council passed no 'judgment' on arguments about the validity or effect of the Treaty of Guarantee.[11]

After the Turkish intervention, during the critical debates before the Security Council on 20 July 1974, leading to resolution No. 353 (1974) of the same date, the Greek Cypriot representative put forward his country's view as to the validity of the Treaty of Guarantee. He argued that the coup did not justify Turkey's intervention. Turkey's action contravened the treaty itself, as well as the UN Charter. The treaty recognized the right of the guarantor powers to take action in case of intervention from 'outside' threatening the sovereignty and territorial integrity of Cyprus. The right to take action denotes only the application of peaceful measures and, furthermore, it does not include armed agression, which is forbidden to member states, except in case of self-defence.[12]

During the 1974 crisis the Greek government's attitude was less clear and partly contradicted the 1964 declaration. During

[9]  UN GAOR 29th Session, 23 Sept. 1974 (A/PV 2793), paras. 123–5.

[10]  19 UN SCOR, 1098th meeting, para. 12 (1964).

[11]  See e.g. UN Security Council resolution No. 186 of 4 Mar. 1964. On the other hand, the Parliamentary Assembly of the Council of Europe affirmed by its resolution 573 of 29 July 1974 that the Turkish military intervention was the exercise of a right emanating from an international treaty and the fulfilment of a legal and moral obligation. The resolution was taken after the first round of military intervention. The member states did not maintain this position after the second round of operations.

[12]  UNSC S/PV 1781 (English), 73–5, 92; UN Monthly Chronicle 1974, vol. xi, No. 8, 21–3.

the Security Council debate on 20 July 1974 the Greek representative did not maintain that article IV(2) did not allow a right of intervention. Instead the representative pointed out that for 'unilateral action' to be considered lawful, it would have to take place only after the collapse of negotiations between the three guarantor states and would have to have the sole aim of re-establishing the status quo ante. The Greek representative argued that these prerequisites had not been fulfilled. He proceeded to warn Turkey against attacking the Greek contingent stationed on the island and added that Greece reserved the liberty to take appropriate action as a guarantor state by virtue of the same article of the treaty invoked by Turkey. In his view, Turkish military intervention was aimed at invasion and, in the long run, the partition of the island.[13]

On the other hand, the Turkish representative stressed that the Treaty of Guarantee is valid and that Turkey intervened under this treaty, which gave her the right to take military action. This action was aimed at establishing constitutional administration in the island, as a whole, and protecting the rights of Turkish Cypriots. In every instance where force had to be used there had been a serious threat to the life of the Turkish Cypriot community.[14]

During these debates the United Kingdom did not take up a position over the content of article IV(2) of the Treaty of Guarantee. In the opinion of the British representative, the Cyprus problem can be solved only through the procedure of the

[13] UNSC S/PV 1781, 20 July 1974, 82. It is interesting to note that the Greek Court of Cassation of Athens in its decision No. 2658/79 of 21 Mar. 1979 held that Turkey's intervention as a guarantor power in Cyprus was legitimate as it was justified by the Zurich and London Agreements. Those responsible for the turn of events in Cyprus were the defendant Greek army officers. The court was examining an appeal from the decision of the civil court awarding compensation to the plaintiffs for the death of their son due to the shooting down on 22 July 1974 of a Greek transport aeroplane carrying military personnel to Cyprus. The plane was thought to belong to the Turkish air force and was shot down by Greek anti-aircraft guns. This decision of the Court of Cassation was deemed by the administration to have been against the national interests and was not complied with. But the news was leaked and eventually the judiciary was able to assert its independence and force compliance with its decision.

[14] UNSC S/PV 1781 (English), 87, 97; UN Monthly Chronicle 1974, No. 8, 22–3.

intercommunal talks or through other appropriate procedure.[15]

During the debates of the Security Council on 14–16 August 1974, leading to resolution No. 360 (1974) of 16 August 1974, the Greek Cypriot representative repeated his country's stand as to the Treaty of Guarantee.[16] He proceeded to state that even though it could be assumed that the treaty gave a right to take military action, this right could be resorted to only for the protection of the Constitution. Turkey had refused to return to the 1960 Constitution, subject to certain agreed amendments. The treaty, which had been accepted by the Greek Cypriot community under duress, is null and void under international law, and is therefore no longer binding as it had been contravened by Turkey. Under the circumstances, the United Nations should not remain inactive when the existence of a state that was threatened by a strong power was at stake.[17]

During the same debate the Turkish representative stressed that the Treaty of Guarantee is valid and that it gave Turkey the right of military intervention. Turkey intervened under the treaty because the independence of the island was threatened and the existence of the Turkish community was at stake. Turkey respects the independence, sovereignty, and territorial integrity of Cyprus, as well as the policy of non-alignment which it has freely chosen to follow. These attributes of the Cyprus state have in fact been saved by the existence of the Turkish community on the island. The main reason why a final settlement of the Cyprus dispute was not reached was the unwillingness of the Greek Cypriots to recognize the rights of the Turkish Cypriots. Any status that would recognize the equality and security of the Turkish Cypriots could be considered. However, in view of the experiences of the past fifteen years, the best solution would be a federal one that would secure to each community the possibility of continuing their autonomous administrations in their respective areas.[18]

[15] UNSC S/PV 1781 (English), 13; UN Monthly Chronicle 1974, No. 8, 13.

[16] During this debate the Turkish delegate Mr Olcay argued that Mr Rossides, the Greek Cypriot delegate, could not represent the Turkish Cypriots: S/PV 1792 (English), 61; S/PV 1795 (English), 32.

[17] S/PV 1792 (English), 23–8, 37–47, 71–7; S/PV 1793 (English), 31–42; S/PV 1794 (English), 51, 56.

[18] S/PV 1792 (English), 48–60; S/PV 1793 (English), 71; S/PV 1794 (English), 33–55.

In the opinion of the British representative, after securing a cease-fire, the interested parties should immediately commence discussions with a view to reaching an agreed settlement. The non-implementation of the 1960 Constitution had adversely affected the Turkish community. There is need for an effective settlement. No purpose would, however, be served by a settlement that is unacceptable to the majority of both communities or is reached under duress.[19]

Security Council resolution No. 353 of 20 July 1974 is non-committal. Paragraph 1 calls on all states to respect the sovereignty, independence, and territorial integrity of Cyprus, but the demand, in paragraph 3, for 'an immediate end to foreign military intervention in the Republic of Cyprus' is qualified by the clause 'that is in contravention of operative paragraph 1'. This formulation leaves it to the states to form their own view on the legality of the Greek intervention of 15 July 1974, which caused the coup in Cyprus, and the subsequent Turkish intervention. Paragraph 4 requests the 'withdrawal without delay from the Republic of Cyprus of foreign military personnel present otherwise than under the authority of International Agreements'. The reference to 'foreign military personnel present otherwise than under the authority of International Agreements' begs the question of the legal basis for the presence of Turkish forces. In fact this resolution reinforces the argument for the validity and *authority of International Agreements* such as that of the Treaty of Guarantee.

Security Council resolution No. 360 of 16 August 1974, in recalling its 'formal disapproval of the unilateral military actions undertaken against the Republic of Cyprus', is stronger than the former. However, the resolution refers to 'actions' in the plural, which could cover the Greek as well as the Turkish intervention, and it stops short of actual condemnation, simply recording 'formal disapproval'. Crucially, the resolution is silent as to precisely *which* actions are regarded as being 'against the Republic of Cyprus'.

Even though the British position as to the Treaty of Guarantee was not clearly stated during UN debates in 1974, more light has been shed on this issue during the debates before

---

[19] S/PV 1792 (English), 6–12; S/PV 1793 (English), 46–8; S/PV 1794 (English), 32.

the Houses of Parliament, in particular by a report prepared by the Select Committee appointed to examine the Cyprus situation. In their Report (Session 1975–6), ordered by the House of Commons to be printed on 8 April 1976, the Parliamentary Committee on p. x stated: 'Britain had a legal right to intervene, she had a moral obligation to intervene, she had the military capacity to intervene. She did not intervene for reasons which the Government refuses to give.'

In a more recent debate in the House of Lords on the question of Cyprus, Lord Brockway referred to article IV of the Treaty of Guarantee and said that Great Britain would have had every authority, as a guarantor, for acting at that time.[20] On the same occasion Lord Caradon expressed his feelings in the following words:

Having signed the treaty with the authority of Her Majesty's Government I have naturally watched subsequent events in the island of Cyprus with dismay and with shame that we should have given an undertaking and have failed so shamefully to carry it out.[21]

## 3. THE TREATY OF GUARANTEE AND INTERNATIONAL LAW

It has been argued that the Treaty of Guarantee, in so far as it can be interpreted as authorizing use of force, is contrary to international law and that its provisions are not compatible with the principles and purposes of the UN Charter in that they restrict the sovereignty and the right to self-determination of Cyprus. On the basis of these principles it is claimed that the treaty is void under international law, in view of the provisions of article 103 of the UN Charter which provides that in the event of a conflict between the obligations of the members of the United Nations under the Charter and their obligations under any other international agreement, their obligations under the Charter shall prevail.

In the following pages an attempt is therefore made to deal

[20] 19 Parliamentary Debates (Hansard), House of Lords Official Report, vol. 441, No. 80, 20 Apr. 1983, 618.
[21] Ibid. 620.

with these principles of international law and the arguments put forward by the interested parties.

## Peremptory norms of international law

Article 53 of the Vienna Convention on the Law of Treaties (1969) stipulates that a treaty is void if, at the time of its conclusion, it conflicts with a peremptory norm of general international law (*jus cogens*). For the purposes of the Convention, a peremptory norm of general international law is a norm accepted and recognized by the international community of states as a whole as a norm from which no derogation is permitted and which can be modified only by a subsequent norm of general international law having the same character.

Some authors, like Georg Schwarzenberger and E. D. Brown, representing a traditional view of international law, assert that treaties should not conflict with a peremptory norm of general international law (*jus cogens*), as the principle is expressed in the Vienna Convention on the Law of Treaties, 1969.[22] On the other hand, among Western commentators, Gerhard von Glahn represents the opposing school of thought by denying the applicability of *jus cogens* to international legal problems.[23]

As the Vienna Convention has no retroactive application by virtue of the express provision of article 4 thereof, it has no application to the Treaty of Guarantee, which was concluded in 1960. The Convention is not simply declaratory of general international law, since in part it involves the progressive development of the law. However, particular articles reflect the existing rules or practice. In the following pages, the Treaty of Guarantee will be examined in the light of the provisions of the Vienna Convention, as if the Convention were applicable to the treaty. It will be presumed that the Convention is merely declaratory of the international law or practice.

Under the Convention, as stated above, a treaty is void if it conflicts with a peremptory norm of international law. Not all

[22] Georg Schwarzenberger and E. D. Brown, *A Manual of International Law*, 6th edn. (London, 1976), 139–40.

[23] Gerhard von Glahn, *Law Among Nations: An Introduction to Public International Law*, 3rd edn. (New York, 1976), 455.

norms of international law are peremptory norms. International law is by no means clear as to which of its norms are peremptory. There is some indication in the relevant draft of the International Law Commission[24] that treaties providing for use of force in violation of the principles of the UN Charter, treaties for the commission of acts which constitute crimes under international law, treaties providing for slave trade, piracy *jure gentium*, and genocide, may be cited as examples of treaties that conflict with peremptory norms of general international law.[25]

Article 65 of the Convention relates to the procedure to be followed with respect to invalidity, termination, withdrawal from, or suspension of the operation of a treaty. Article 66 provides rules for the procedure for judicial settlement, arbitration, and conciliation. The Convention, which incorporates the principle of the *jus cogens* into the law of treaties, makes it mandatory to refer the dispute to the International Court of Justice for a decision. Article 66 states that if, under paragraph 3 of article 65, no solution has been reached within a period of 12 months following the date on which the objection was raised, any one of the parties to a dispute concerning the application or the interpretation of articles 53 or 64 may, by a written application, submit it to the International Court of Justice for a decision unless the parties by common consent agree to submit the dispute to arbitration. On this basis, one line of argument that may be put forward is that, in the absence of a ruling of the International Court, a treaty, such as the Treaty of Guarantee, should not be presumed to be invalid as being in conflict with a peremptory norm of international law. In other words, the presumption should be in favour of the validity of a treaty until there is a judicial ruling to the contrary.

An alternative argument may be phrased as follows: if it is asumed that the prohibition of use of force against a member state constitutes a peremptory norm of general international law, before deciding on the validity of a treaty it is still necessary to examine the provisions of that treaty, and the circumstances under which it was concluded. Treaties concluded between two

[24] The Vienna Convention is the outcome of the work of the International Law Commission and two sessions of the United Nations Conference on the Law of Treaties held in 1968 and 1969.

[25] 1966 YILC, ii, 248.

states and authorizing use of force against the territorial integrity or political independence of another state (which is not a signatory to that treaty), may be regarded as void under article 53 of the Convention. However, there is no peremptory rule of international law prohibiting intervention under a treaty to which the subject state is a signatory. In such a case, the signatory has consented to the restriction upon the exercise of its sovereignty. The right of entering into international engagements is itself an attribute of state sovereignty.[26]

### Unequal treaties

The legal position of the Greek Cypriot government, as later articulated in the United Nations, was that the 'Constitution was foisted on Cyprus. ... The combined effect of the Constitution and the Treaty of Guarantee is that a situation has been created whereby the constitutional and political development of the Republic has been arrested in its infancy and the Republic as a sovereign State has been placed in a strait jacket.'[27] The resulting legal conclusion was that to the extent the 1960 Accords precluded amendment of the Constitution, they were 'unequal and inequitable treaties, as a result of which they cannot be regarded as anything but null and void.'[28] According to this argument 'unequal' treaties—agreements imposing burdens on states in substantially unequal bargaining positions—are *per se* void. However, as stated by Ehrlich, Cypriot representatives never pressed this position to its logical conclusion: that the 1960 settlement was void.[29] In part, the reason may have been concern that Turkey and the United Kingdom would respond that if the settlement was invalid then Cyprus was still a British colony. But no one seriously urged that position; the Republic of Cyprus had been a member of the United Nations for over three years and its 'sovereign equality' was recognized by the Charter.

---

[26] *The SS Wimbledon*, Permanent Court of International Justice (1923) ser. A, no. 1 (1 WCR 163).
[27] 19 UN SCOR, 1098th meeting, 20 (1964).
[28] 20 UN SCOR, 1235th meeting, 25 (1964).
[29] *International Crises and the Role of Law, Cyprus 1958–1967* (Oxford, 1974), 48.

Sovereign equality

Article 2(1) of the Charter declares that 'the Organization is based on the principle of sovereign equality of all its members'.

It has been stated that the obligation of the Treaty of Guarantee 'to keep unalterable in perpetuity the constitutional structure and order' purports to deprive Cyprus of one of the 'fundamental requirements of a state as an integral person, internal independence and territorial supremacy'.[30] This point is further elaborated by argument to the effect that article IV of the Treaty of Guarantee conflicts both with customary international law[31] and with article 103 of the Charter of the United Nations for violating the principle of 'sovereign equality' as expressed in article 2(1).[32]

It is true that Cyprus is not entitled to change the 'basic articles' of its Constitution. Absence of power of a state to change its constitution cannot, however, be regarded as affecting its 'sovereign equality'. Furthermore, absence of such power is not incompatible with the concept of independence as a criterion of statehood.[33] This condition did not inhibit other states from recognizing the Republic of Cyprus. It may also be pointed out that Cyprus is not the only example;[34] Canada acquired the power to change her constitution in 1949. The Canadian Constitution is enshrined in an Act of the British Parliament. It was only in April 1982 that the British Parliament relinquished control over the Canadian Constitution.

Moreover, in September 1960 Cyprus was accepted as a

[30] C. G. Tornaritis, *Cyprus and its Constitutional and Other Legal Problems* (Nicosia, 1977), 58–9.

[31] This point has already been taken up under the heading on peremptory rules of international law.

[32] Tornaritis, *Cyprus*, 42, 60. See also, Andreas J. Jacovides, *Treaties Conflicting with Peremptory Norms of International Law and the Zurich–London 'Agreements'* (Nicosia, 1966), 15–28.

[33] Prof. Brownlie's paper entitled: *The Prohibition of the Use of Armed Force for the Solution of International Differences, with particular reference to the affairs of the Republic of Cyprus*, submitted to the International Law Conference on Cyprus, 30 Apr–3 May 1979, at 10, citing Crawford, *British Year Book of International Law*, 48 (1976–7), 93, at 123–4.

[34] R. Higgins, *The Development of International Law Through The Political Organs of the United Nations* (London, 1963), 34.

member of the United Nations *subject* to its special status under the treaties, which status it cannot unilaterally change. This status of Cyprus must be presumed to have been within the knowledge of the member states of the United Nations at the material time. Yet, the questions as to compatibility of this special status of Cyprus with membership of the UN, and its compatibility with the UN Charter, were neither raised nor debated in the Security Council or in the General Assembly, during the acceptance of Cyprus as a member. Therefore, the member states of the UN, by having accepted Cyprus as a 'state' for the purposes of the UN, must be presumed to have waived the right to debate the question of the compatibility of this special status with the UN Charter. During the Security Council debates of February–March 1964, Turkey, as well as Norway, took up this line of argument.[35]

On the other hand, UN membership itself does not affect the restrictions on sovereignty that may have arisen through other legal sources. The UN Organization cannot, by having accepted a country as a member state, be deemed to have automatically effected a change in the legal status of that country. Yet, during the Security Council debates leading to the resolution of 4 March 1964, the Greek, as well as the Greek Cypriot side, tried to extract a resolution that would, on the one hand, affirm the sovereignty, independence, and territorial integrity of the Republic of Cyprus and, on the other, call for abstaining from the use of force against the Republic. Such a resolution would help the Greek side as it would be likely to be interpreted in a way that would raise doubts as to the legal validity of the 1960 treaties. The Soviet Union as well as Czechoslovakia supported this view,[36] whereas Turkey,[37] the UK,[38] the USA,[39] Norway,[40] France,[41] and some other countries maintained that the Security Council is not competent to amend or abrogate a treaty. The

---

[35] UNSC, S/PV 1097 (English), 22; S/PV 1099 (English), 76.
[36] UNSC, S/PV 1096 (English), 2; and S/PV 1097 (English), 22 respectively.
[37] UNSC, S/PV 1095 (English), 78–98; S/PV 1099 (English), 76.
[38] UNSC, S/PV 1095 (English), 42, 44–5.
[39] UNSC, S/PV 1096 (English), 36.
[40] UNSC, S/PV 1097 (English), 22.
[41] UNSC, S/PV 1098 (English), 86.

countries that have adopted the view that the 1960 treaties can be changed only by the consent of the interested parties may be deemed to have accepted, by implication, that there is no incompatibility between the order set up by the treaties and the order envisaged by the UN Charter.

It should also be noted that the right of intervention which the guarantor powers reserved[42] under the treaty, was not a right carved out of an already independent Cyprus Republic in favour of third states. Cyprus accepted being an independent state *subject to* the treaty which prohibited union with any other state and bound it with an obligation to maintain its independence, territorial integrity, and security as well as respect for its constitution. The treaty was not, therefore a derogation from an already existing independence, but a guarantee of independence which came into being as a result of a set of international agreements.

## Self-determination

It may be thought that the Treaty of Guarantee affects the sovereignty of the Republic of Cyprus in that it restricts the right to *self-determination*. One of the purposes of the UN Charter as expressed in article 1(2) thereof is 'to develop friendly relations among nations based on respect for the principle of equal rights and self-determination of peoples, and to take other appropriate measures to strengthen universal peace'. In article 55 of the Charter, reference is again made to 'self-determination' to express the general aims of the United Nations in the fields of social and economic development and respect for human rights. By elaborating these rather cryptic references, the General Assembly has attempted in a very large number of resolutions to define more precisely the content of the principle. Thus, the Colonial Declaration (clause 2) stated that 'All peoples have the right to self-determination; by virtue of that right they freely

---

[42] It seems that the word 'reserved' was used deliberately because the signatories, who had been recognized long ago as interested parties in the Cyprus dispute, already had rights linked to the future of the Cyprus Republic. The Treaty of Lausanne of 1923 had established a political and military balance of power in the area. Union of Cyprus with Greece would upset that balance.

determine their political status and freely pursue their economic, social and cultural development.'[43]

The principle has also been affirmed by the Security Council, for example, by resolution 183 of 11 December 1963, and by the General Assembly, by resolution 2625(XXV) of 24 October 1970. However, the General Assembly has no general law-making capacity. Such resolutions have only recommendatory force and the Assembly has no capacity to impose new customary legal obligations on states.

The principle of 'self-determination' has in fact two quite distinct meanings. It can mean the sovereign equality of existing states, and in particular the right of a state to choose its own form of government without intervention. It can also mean the right of a specific territory (people) to choose its own form of government irrespective of the wishes of the rest of the state of which the territory is a part.[44] However, the scope of the principle of self-determination is not uncontroversial, and furthermore according to the opinion of the International Court in *Namibia*, the principle is not static but is open to change.[45] It seems that judicial reference made to this principle so far has been in the context of territories whose peoples had not attained a full measure of self-government.[46]

Turning once again to the situation in Cyprus, when the country achieved its independence in 1960, the Treaty of Guarantee did not affect its sovereign equality as a state, particularly its right to choose its own form of government without outside intervention.[47] However, the right of self-determination is primarily the right of 'peoples' to determine their destiny.[48] When the stage of affairs envisaged by the 1960 Constitution came to an end with the events of 1963–4, the provisions of the Treaty did not prevent the two peoples of Cyprus from forming their own separate governments. As

[43] GA res. 1514 (XV), 14 Dec. 1960, 'Declaration on the Granting of Independence to Colonial Countries and Peoples'.

[44] J. Crawford, 'The Criteria of Statehood in International Law', *The British Year Book of International Law*, 48 (1975–6), 149–64, at 152.

[45] ICJ Reports, 1971, 16, at 31.

[46] As, for instance, the *Namibia* (referred to above) and the *Western Sahara* (ICJ Reports, 1975, 12, at 33) situations.

[47] See previous section entitled 'sovereign equality'.

[48] See ch. 9.

self-determination is a dynamic right; it is not true to say that once exercised it ceases to exist. The vicissitudes of international life cannot justify such a static view. The right always exists as the basis for the expression of the free will by the two peoples of Cyprus to determine their future and the Treaty does not affect that right.

The right of intervention granted to the three guarantor powers is to ensure the observance of norms which are consistent with the principle of self-determination. The relevant rules are those concerning the basic provisions of the Constitution of Cyprus. However, the object of these provisions is to give Cyprus a 'representative government' which will not make any discrimination between the two communities living on the island and preserve the state of affairs established by the Constitution. As matters stand, not only are the provisions in question far from being inconsistent with the principle of self-determination, but, rather, they act as a way of implementation and are, therefore, consistent with the penultimate paragraph of the principle of self-determination, as embodied in the Declaration on Friendly Relations.[49] The unalterability of the basic provisions of the Cyprus Constitution, which is internationally guaranteed, is what will ensure the 'representative' character of Cyprus, and must not, therefore, be considered inconsistent with the principle in question.[50]

The limitations affecting the exercise of internal and external self-determination contained in the Zurich and London Agreements are a necessary corollary to the history of the island, because 'in a plural society some limitation has to be imposed on the exercise of self-determination by the predominant community in this society if self-determination is to have any meaning for the rest of the communities comprising that society'.[51]

The same is true of the right to intervene. According to Wengler, a treaty providing for a right to intervene against the

[49] This paragraph aims at protecting the territorial integrity of states that are possessed of a government *representing* the people as a whole without any discrimination.

[50] N. Ronzitti, *Rescuing Nationals Abroad Through Military Coercion and Intervention on Grounds of Humanity* (Dordrecht, 1985), 133–4.

[51] A. Rigo Sureda, *The Evolution of the Right to Self-Determination: A Study of United Nations Practice* (Leyden, 1973).

will of a future government of the other state 'is regarded as prohibited by a *jus cogens* rule of general international law . . .'. Nevertheless, this learned writer continues, 'an exception may be valid if intervention is permitted to secure the upholding of an arrangement among different peoples, each one exercising its right of self-determination, to live together in one State . . .'.[52] This observation fits perfectly in the case of Cyprus.[53]

### Prohibition of use of force

Article 2(4) of the United Nations Charter raises a number of difficult issues. That provision requires members to 'refrain in their international relations from the threat or use of force against the territorial integrity or political independence of any state, or in any other manner inconsistent with the Purposes of the United Nations'. The Greek Cypriot government urged that Turkey's obligations under article 2(4) necessarily preclude any armed action under the Treaty of Guarantee.[54]

Turkey maintained that military intervention under article IV of the treaty would not be 'against the territorial integrity and political independence' of Cyprus, since the treaty was designed to 'insure the maintenance of (Cypriot) independence, territorial integrity and security', and action taken thereunder must, in the terms of article IV, be for 'the sole aim of re-establishing the state of affairs created by the . . . Treaty'.[55] This argument had substantial appeal on the issue whether the *first* qualifying phrase in article 2(4) prohibits *all* cases of force under article IV. The question remained, however, whether military intervention under article IV could ever be consistent with the 'Purposes of the United Nations', and if so, under what circumstances and in what manner.

The Charter lists the 'maintenance of peace and security' first among the organization's purposes. Primary responsibility for

[52] W. Wengler, 'Public International Law, Paradoxes of A Legal Order', *Recueil des Cours*, 158 (The Hague, 1977–V), 79 n. 118.
[53] N. Ronzitti, *Rescuing Nationals Abroad*, 133.
[54] See e.g. 19 UN SCOR, 1098th meeting, 18–19 (1964); ibid. 1235th meeting, 63–5 (1964). See also T. Ehrlich, *International Crises and the Role of Law, Cyprus 1958–1967* (Oxford, 1974), 76–7.
[55] 20 UN SCOR, 1234th meeting, 23–4 (1965).

effecting this purpose is assigned to the Security Council by article 24. However, both the General Assembly and regional arrangements[56] are also given express authority to maintain the peace in certain situations.

Reference in article 51 of the Charter to the 'inherent right' of self-defence is the only explicit acknowledgement that nations may separately employ force. On this basis it is generally accepted that all unilateral uses of force, except in self-defence, are prohibited.

However, article 52(1) of the Charter acknowledges that 'Nothing in the present Charter precludes the existence of regional arrangements or agencies for dealing with such matters relating to the maintenance of international peace and security as are appropriate for regional action, provided that such arrangements or agencies and their activities are consistent with the Purposes and Principles of the United Nations.' On the basis of this it can be claimed that the guarantor powers could act as a 'regional arrangement' under Chapter VIII of the Charter. Support for this general proposition can be drawn on the following lines.[57]

Although the negotiating history of the United Nations Charter indicates that its drafters intended to preclude the unilateral use of force except in self-defence, that history must be viewed in terms of peacekeeping schemes projected by the Charter's framers. Analysis of the terms of the Treaty of Guarantee and the intent of the drafters suggests that the treaty provides a mechanism analogous to regional arrangements for the use of force consistent with the Purposes of the United Nations.

The basic aim of the 1960 Accords was to protect the Turkish Cypriot community and to establish conditions for the preservation of peace on an island riven by violence. The Accords provided a carefully conceived structure of guarantees designed to achieve that purpose. The internal guarantees included in the 1960 Constitution were the first line of defence against intercommunal strife, but if these guarantees were not enforced, the mechanism of protection established in the Treaty of

---

[56] See ch. VIII of the Charter, arts. 52–4.
[57] See T. Ehrlich, *International Crises*, 77–82.

Guarantee was to come into operation—collective measures or, if multilateral agreement were not possible, unilateral action. The arrangements contemplated under Chapter VIII concern affairs within a region rather than a single nation. The violation of the Treaty of Guarantee itself could not only lead to a conflict within the state of Cyprus, but could also spread to the Mediterranean region and also involve the United Kingdom with its significant interests in the area.

### 4. ARTICLE 103 OF THE UN CHARTER

Greek Cypriot and Greek governments frequently claimed that Turkish military intervention violated both the 'sovereign equality' accorded to Cyprus under article 2(1) of the Charter and the prohibition against the 'use of force' contained in article 2(4).[58] On this basis, these governments claimed that article IV of the Treaty of Guarantee, to the extent that it authorized forcible action, was void under article 103 of the Charter. This article provides that 'In the event of a conflict between the obligations of the Members of the United Nations under the present Charter and their obligations under any other international agreement, their obligations under the present Charter shall prevail.' It seems, however, that article 103 may be read as restricted to cases in which the conflicting obligations are those of a single country. Thus, for example, a nation's Charter obligations to impose economic sanctions against another state might be inconsistent with its treaty obligations to trade with that state. Under such an interpretation, article 103 could not be applicable to the Cyprus situation, since the alleged conflict is between the Turkish obligations under Charter article 2(1) and 2(4) and the Cypriot obligations to respect Turkey's rights under the Treaty of Guarantee.

Moreover, Cyprus became a member of the United Nations subject to its obligation under the Treaty of Guarantee.[59]

[58] e.g. 19 UN SCOR, 1098th meeting, 16–17 (1964).

[59] However, the drafters of the Charter expressly rejected a provision that would have required states, upon admission to the organization, to procure their release from treaties that were inconsistent with the Charter (Doc. No. 934, IV/2/43, 13 UN Conf. Int. Org. Docs. 701, 706–8 (1945)). Such a

Neither the UN Security Council nor the General Assembly has declared the Treaty of Guarantee void even though the issue was frequently raised at these forums.

Moreover, as stated earlier, during the Security Council debates in 1964 and in 1974 the thesis of the permanent validity of the Treaty of Guarantee prevailed at the United Nations. The basic resolutions of the Security Council on the Cyprus question refer to the treaties signed in 1960, which include the Treaty of Guarantee. Resolution 186 of 4 March 1964 cites the treaties signed at Nicosia on 16 August 1960 in its preamble; resolution 353 of 20 July 1974 states, again in the preamble, 'the necessity to restore the constitutional structure of the Republic of Cyprus *established and guaranteed by international agreements*'.

It may finally be said with a degree of certainty that article 103 of the Charter does not invalidate a treaty that is in conflict with the Charter;[60] such a legal consequence would hardly be possible notwithstanding the existence of article 103. Therefore even if the provisions of a treaty are in conflict with the Charter, the treaty is valid and continues in force; subject to the condition that the obligations under the Charter must prevail.

provision was contained in article 20(2) of the Covenant of the League of Nations and, if it had been adopted at San Francisco during the drafting of the Charter, might have provided a basis for asserting that a nation must either allege at the time of its admission to the United Nations a conflict between the Charter and a treaty or be thereafter held to accept their consistency. However, international relations would be affected in a negative way if states were readily allowed to avoid treaties on the ground of inconsistency with the Charter.

[60] Neither the Security Council nor the General Assembly has ever declared a treaty void under art. 103, although the issue has been raised in both bodies. See e.g. UN SCOR, 22nd meeting, 318–19 (1946) (Anglo-French Agreement of 1945); 7 UN GAOR, 1st Comm. 257 (1952) (Franco-Tunisian treaties of 1881 and 1883). During the General Assembly consideration of the Franco-Tunisian treaties the Australian representative contended that art. 103 'gave no competence to the United Nations and merely stated that the Charter should prevail over agreements . . .': 7 UN GAOR, 1st Comm. 258 (1952). The Indian representative, however, urged that the United Nations could at least 'call the attention of the Member State to that divergence . . .': 8 UN GAOR, 1st Comm. 39 (1953).

## 5. INTERVENTION OR INTERCESSION?

During an International Law Conference held on the Greek side of Nicosia between 30 April and 3 May 1979, the Treaty of Guarantee was fully discussed by a number of international lawyers (among whom were Professor Ian Brownlie and Professor James H. Wolfe). A number of speakers suggested that the Treaty of Guarantee did not give the right of *military intervention* to the guarantor powers, but authorized peaceful representation and intercession only. The argument put forward was that the Treaty of Guarantee could not be interpreted in a way that would sanction use of force against a state. This view leads to the conclusion that, subject to such an interpretation, the treaty is compatible with customary international law and with the principles of the UN Charter.

The interpretation of article IV of the treaty at first sight seems to present some difficulty, but once regard is had to the recent history of Cyprus and the intentions of the parties, its interpretation becomes easier. As stated earlier, Cyprus gained independence after a sanguinary conflict which was not caused by a struggle for independence. This struggle was characterized by fierce communal trouble. Each of the national communities had differing aspirations. The aim of the Greek Cypriots was union with Greece (*Enosis*). The granting of independence was a compromise. It was therefore necessary that strong guarantees should be devised so that the state of affairs established by the Zurich and London Accords and the Constitution of Cyprus could be preserved and that union of Cyprus with any other state or partition of the island be effectively prohibited. Besides, under the Treaty of Alliance, Greece and Turkey had the right to station troops on the island. On the other hand, the United Kingdom maintained its sovereignty over certain military bases. If the use of force should prove necessary, the three guarantor powers could rely on military contingents stationed on the island, and in case of a more serious emergency, mobilize troops from the mainland. These basic considerations suggest that, by drafting article IV, the guarantor states meant to preserve the right to resort to military coercion, as and when the

circumstances required it.[61] On the other hand, since common
or concerted action would not always be possible, each
guarantor state was given the right to take unilateral action
using measures similar to those it would have adopted if acting
in conjunction with the other guarantor states.

It is clear that before the 1974 Turkish intervention every
procedural requirement was fulfilled. Following the Sampson
coup, consultations took place in London on 17 and 18 July,
between the British and Turkish governments; the Foreign and
Commonwealth Secretary James Callaghan met the Turkish
Prime Minister Bülent Ecevit and discussed the action to be
taken following the coup. Greece declared that she would not
attend. The consultations were described by the Foreign and
Commonwealth Office as abortive, but it is cler that Britain
was not willing to intervene jointly with Turkey as a guarantor
power and it is also clear that she recognized the possibility
of military action by Turkey.[62] It can be deduced from the
above that Britain[63] and Turkey did in fact fulfil the obligation
of holding consultations.

Article IV of the Treaty of Guarantee mentions a 'right to
take action'. It is true that the word 'military' has not been used
to qualify the word 'action' and this has led some authors to the
conviction that article IV does not sanction military action but
authorizes intercession only, such as diplomatic representations
and economic counter-measures. In fact the first paragraph
provides for consultation 'with respect to the *representations* or
*measures* necessary to ensure observance' of the provisions that
have been breached. The word 'measures' is also ambiguous; as
articles 41 and 42 of the UN Charter demonstrate, it may mean
actions of a peaceful although coercive nature, as well as those
which involve the use of force. The second paragraph of the
article in question, by providing for concerted *action*, or the right
of any of the guaranteeing powers *to take action*, is stronger in
terms than the first paragraph. If only unilateral intercession
was envisaged, then there was no reason why the second

---

[61] See also N. Ronzitti, *Rescuing Nationals Abroad*, 129.
[62] Report of the House of Commons Select Committee on Cyprus, on p. vii,
s. 9.
[63] Ibid. at p. viii, s. 12.

paragraph should not expressly speak of the right to concerted or unilateral intercession or use words to such effect to indicate that only diplomatic representation or the taking of counter-measures was meant. Moreover, if it was intended to restrict the meaning of the word 'action' to any action other than military, it would be easy for the drafters to do so expressly, or use words of lesser import. In fact it is clear that it was left to the guaranteeing powers, or any one of them to decide what action to take. Otherwise the second paragraph would be a dead letter unable to serve the purpose it was designed to serve.

Article 31(1) of the Vienna Convention on the Law of Treaties stipulates that: 'A Treaty shall be interpreted in good faith in accordance with the ordinary meaning to be given to the terms of the treaty in their context and in the light of its object and purpose.' Taking into consideration the fact that the principal object and purpose of the Treaty of Guarantee was to forbid union of Cyprus with any other state or partition of the island, it is submitted that the guarantors meant to provide effective guarantees in the eventuality of breach of this vital provision. That effective guarantee could be nothing less than military intervention, because it could not be expected that union of Cyprus with any other state (namely Greece) could be effectively prevented by mere diplomatic efforts of intercession. Furthermore, diplomatic representation and intercession can always be resorted to by any state without the sanction of an international treaty. It would not really be necessary to conclude a treaty of guarantee in order to enable a guaranteeing power to intercede by making diplomatic representation or taking other counter-measures. If the Treaty of Guarantee was meant merely to authorize diplomatic intercession, it would have been otiose. In the light of the foregoing, it is submitted that the treaty was concluded with the object of sanctioning military intervention in case of breach of the provisions thereof.

Since 1963 the course of events in Cyprus has shown very clearly that strong guarantees were in fact necessary to preserve the state of affairs established by the 1960 Constitution and the delicate balance between the rights of each of the Cyprus communities.

In view of the foregoing, it is difficult to subscribe to the argument that the Treaty of Guarantee did not authorize military action. There is a case for saying that Turkey was legally justified in acting under article IV when she intervened in Cyprus and her action cannot be described as 'unlawful invasion'[64].

[64] Article IV of the Treaty of Guarantee requires that intervention must be 'with the sole aim of re-establishing the state of affairs created by the present Treaty'. In short, the Treaty excludes the revocability of independence.

After the Turkish intervention of 1974 it was not found possible, or practicable, to return to the 1960 Constitution for the following reasons:

(1) The 1960 Constitution was not applied at least since 1963, and the status quo prior to the intervention of 1974 was not that envisaged under the 1960 Constitution.

(2) Soon after the Turkish intervention of 1974 Mr Glafcos Clerides took over the presidency from Mr Nicos Sampson by taking the oath of office before the bishops instead of the House of Representatives as he was required to do under the 1960 Constitution. The Greek Cypriot side preferred to continue as the recognized government of Cyprus.

In fact the Greek army officers sent by the Greek Junta were in Cyprus at the time and it was impossible to have them withdrawn to clear the way for a political settlement under the Constitution.

(3) Attempts had been continuing since 1968 to find a new status for Cyprus. It was not practicable to restore the 1960 Constitution after a search for a new status had begun. The need to find a new status quo for Cyprus was affirmed in more clear terms by UN resolution 3212 (XXIX) of 1 November 1974. By this resolution (endorsed also by the Security Council by its resolution 365/1974), the UN General Assembly commended the contacts and negotiations taking place on an equal footing, with the good offices of the Secretary-General between the representatives of the two communities and called for their continuation with a view of reaching freely a mutually acceptable political settlement based on their fundamental and legitimate rights.

# 6

# The Intercommunal Negotiations

## I. TOWARDS A 'FEDERAL' STATE

A federation is born when a number of usually separate or autonomous political units, or units with some pretensions of autonomy, mutually agree to merge together to create a state with a single sovereign central government while retaining for themselves some degree of guaranteed regional autonomy.

The forces that make the outward form of federalism necessary are a compromise between centripetal and centrifugal forces that are operative at the same time. A federation is formed when the political units in a region possess some very strong factors of individual identities which create in them a genuine desire to maintain a separate existence, while at the same time there are certain factors of vital importance shared by the units which create a common desire for a strong co-ordinated and united existence. The basic problem is to keep these forces in equilibrium so that the federation will survive.

In a federation there exist two different levels of government—the federal (central) and the unit (federated states, or regional) governments. The legislative and executive powers are divided in a co-ordinated fashion between these two levels each of which acts directly on the people, the central government having jurisdiction over all matters that have a bearing on the development and security of the federation as a whole, and the unit governments exercising jurisdiction on matters of local and more immediate importance to their respective peoples. The central, as well as the regional, powers derive directly from the constitution, which is the supreme law *par excellence*, in the sense that neither the federal institutions nor the component parts of the federation can exercise either unrestricted power in repealing or amending the constitution or unilateral authority in modifying the relationship between the constituent units thereby set up. To ensure that no undue and unauthorized inroads are made by one level of government into the sphere of the other, there is usually a system of judicial review by a supreme court.

Yugoslavia and Czechoslovakia are each examples of federations created after World War II in nation states which came into existence after World War I on the dissolution of the Austro-Hungarian monarchy.

On the other hand, Switzerland, the United States, and Austria are each examples of federations that have arisen out of organic growth, supported by a need for common defence and a desire to exploit economic opportunities. The factors which brought about the need for federation have contributed to the success of this system of government in the said countries. Mere artificial creations are unlikely to be held together by constitutional glue, and in the long run to survive basic disunity. Sometimes even generous constitutional arrangements do not create unity where there are competing cultures. Thus, after a century of federation in which French Canadian culture has been protected by dual language rights, by provincial control of education, by recognition for the Roman Catholic church, and by virtually complete autonomy for Quebec, there have been demands for secession from Canada and for formation of an independent state for Quebec. In recent years, however, the movement for secession has stopped.

In some federations fear of domination by a large ethnic state within the federation has caused instability. For instance, in the Nigerian federation northern domination was feared, which necessitated a restructuring of the federation by dividing existing states into a larger number of units. Constitutional change to this effect has so far successfully met such fears. On the other hand, in Yugoslavia fear of Serb domination has been met by constitutional change in 1978 which enhanced the units at the expense of the centre.

Constitutions have been classified in terms of the balance between centralizing and decentralizing forces as manifested in the state structure. If the powers of government are organized under a single central authority, while whatever powers possessed by local units are held at the sufferance of the central government, the constitution is described as 'unitary'. If the powers of government are distributed between central and local government and the central authority is limited by the powers secured to the territorial units, the state is, generally speaking, 'federal'.

A federation differs from a 'confederation' in that in the latter the central government is subordinate to the unit governments in the sense that it functions at the will of the regional governments, but in a federation neither level of government is at the mercy of the other. In a confederation there is no direct contact between the peoples of the constituent units and the central authority. In a federation, by contrast, there is a direct relationship between the central government and the people. In a confederation the member states retain their sovereignty, whereas in a federation both the constituent units and the centre retain some sovereignty as the former are only autonomous in certain limited spheres. However, the terms 'federation' and 'confederation' are sometimes used rather loosely without regard to the fine distinction indicated above.

When one examines the process of the Cyprus intercommunal talks between the years 1968 and 1974, it can be noticed that the task of the interlocutors during the period under review, was to restructure the 1960 Constitution. With that in mind, the talks were focused on local autonomy for Turkish Cypriots, which, as the Greek Cypriot side put it, should not come into conflict with principles of a 'unitary' state.[1] It was after 1974 that the basis and scope of the intercommunal talks changed and the search for a 'federal' solution of the Cyprus problem began. But, as will be seen in the following pages, the interested parties hold different views on issues relating to a 'federal' solution and give different interpretations to the words 'federation' and 'confederation'.

## 2. THE PERIOD 1975–1977

After Turkey intervened militarily on 20 July 1974, it was agreed by the parties concerned that fresh attempts should be made to solve the Cyprus problem by means of a new series of talks between the two communities on an equal footing under

[1] Ch. 3, above.

the auspices of the UN Secretary-General. The Security Council resolution No. 367 of 12 March 1975, which expressed regret about the proclamation of the Turkish Federated State of Cyprus, called for new efforts to assist the resumption of negotiations. It asked the Secretary-General to undertake a new mission of good offices and to convene the representatives of the two communities under his auspices. The talks called by the Security Council began on 28 April 1975.

The first round of these talks took place at Vienna from 28 April to 3 May 1975 and was followed by two other rounds at Vienna from 5 to 7 June 1975 and from 31 July to 2 August 1975. A short fourth round was held in New York from 8 to 10 September 1975. On 10 September Dr Waldheim adjourned the talks for want of concrete proposals. Negotiations were resumed in February 1976 on the basis of the Brussels Declaration signed by Greece and Turkey.[2]

It is significant to note that at the third round of Cyprus intercommunal talks held at Vienna between 31 July and 2 August 1975, both sides reached an agreement for the transfer to the Turkish area, with UNFICYP's help, of Turkish Cypriots wishing to leave the south and of Greek Cypriots wishing to leave the north to go to the south. This was a welcome arrangement for Turkish Cypriots in the south, thousands of whom had made their way to the north, often at great risk.[3]

On the initiative of Mr Denktash, President of the Turkish

---

[2] For an account of these talks see Necati Ertekün's *The Cyprus Dispute and the Birth of the Turkish Republic of Northern Cyprus* (Oxford, 1984), particularly, 25–44.

[3] UN doc. S/11568, para. 48. See also Pierre Oberling, *The Road to Bellapais: The Turkish Cypriot Exodus to Northern Cyprus* (New York, 1982). In January 1975 the British government allowed 9,390 Turkish Cypriot refugees, who had been camping in the Episkopi base, to be evacuated to Turkey from Akrotiri airfield for resettlement in north Cyprus. The action, taken for humanitarian and security reasons, precipitated anti-British demonstrations in Greece and Cyprus.

The agreement for relocation of populations was fully implemented on a voluntary basis, under the auspices of the UN. By the end of 1975, 8,033 Turkish Cypriots had moved under the arrangement (UN doc. S/11900, para. 49). Only 130 Turkish Cypriots remained in the south. The Greek Cypriots who chose to remain in the north numbered 1,850.

In May 1987, the Greek Cypriot population in the north was 678 (UN doc. S/18880 of 29 May 1987) and the number of Maronites, 327.

Federated State of Cyprus, a meeting was held between him and Archbishop Makarios on 27 January 1977, followed by a second meeting on 12 February 1977 at which the Secretary-General of the United Nations was also present. At the meeting of 12 February the following four guide-lines were agreed upon by the two leaders on the basis of which the negotiations between the representatives of the two communities would be resumed:[4]

1. We are seeking an independent, non-aligned, bi-communal, Federal Republic.
2. The territory under the administration of each community should be discussed in the light of economic viability or productivity and land ownership.
3. Questions of principles like freedom of movement, freedom of settlement, the right of property and other specific matters, are open for discussion taking into consideration the fundamental basis of a bi-communal federal system and certain practical difficulties which may arise for the Turkish Cypriot community.
4. The powers and functions of the central federal government will be such as to safeguard the unity of the country, having regard to the bi-communal character of the State.

It seems that Archbishop Makarios retracted from the above stated principles soon after they were formulated.[5]

## Turkish Cypriot proposals of 1977

Following the second meeting of the two leaders on 12 February 1977 it was eventually agreed that the intercommunal talks should be resumed in Vienna on 31 March 1977 under the auspices of the Secretary-General of the United Nations, Dr Kurt Waldheim, and should continue till 7 April 1977. The sixth round of the Vienna talks were held as scheduled above. At this round of the talks the Turkish Cypriot side submitted proposals for a federal solution of the Cyprus problem on the basis of a partnership in power between two equal political

---

[4] UN Doc. S/12323.

[5] In Mr Likavgi's article in the Greek Cypriot daily *Phileleftheros* of 6 Aug. 1977, Archbishop Makarios is reported to have said: 'The signature in red ink will never be put under an agreement that will give even a piece of stone to the Turks.' As the head of the autocephalous Greek Cypriot Orthodox Church, Archbishop Makarios used to sign in red ink.

entities joining their resources in a central federal administration on a basis of equality, working together at first in a
comparatively limited field, but at the same time co-operating
in many spheres of administration.[6] The functions of the federal
government would be of a purely advisory nature initially, but
might grow into exclusive federal powers as confidence and
the spirit of co-operation between the two communities were
established. These proposals enumerated the powers and
functions of the central federal government and provided that
the residue of power should be vested in the federated states. The
concept contained in these proposals was for the federation to
develop by evolution. Taking into consideration the past history
of hostilities between the two partner communities, the Turkish
Cypriot side thought that this was the kind of federation which
was best suited to the realities of Cyprus.

### Greek Cypriot proposals of 1977

Within the context of the same talks the Greek Cypriot side also
submitted its proposals regarding the principles for the solution
of the Cyprus problem and basic principles which should govern
the constitutional structure of the federal republic of Cyprus,
which included the lists of powers of the federal government and
of regional administration.[7] These proposals envisaged the
establishment of a bi-communal federal state (which should be a
federation and not a confederation) that would preserve the
sovereignty, independence, and territorial integrity of the
Republic of Cyprus, ensure that the federal Republic of Cyprus
would be the sole subject of international law to the exclusion of
the constituent parts, and preserve the unity of the country. The
proposals provided for the setting up of a strong central
government and were based on the assumption that a unitary
'Government of Cyprus' existed at the time and that the Greek
Cypriot administration was that unitary 'Government'. Significantly, however, the Greek Cypriot proposals provided that a
defined area of northern Cyprus (about 20 per cent) should

---

[6] For the text of the proposals, see this author's *The Cyprus Conflict: A
Lawyer's View*, 2nd edn. (Lefkoşa, 1982), 213–17.

[7] For the text of the proposals, see ibid. 219–28.

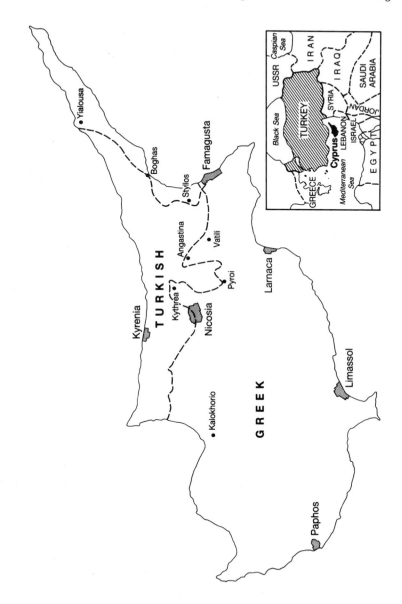

**Fig. 1.** Greek Cypriot territorial proposals put forward at Vienna, March–April 1977.

remain in Turkish Cypriot hands as one part of the proposed bi-communal federal state, namely, the federal republic of Cyprus.

## Death of Archbishop Makarios

After the death of Archbishop Makarios on 3 August 1977 the intercommunal talks were stalled for some time due to the vacuum in the Greek Cypriot leadership. On 26 January 1978 Mr Kyprianou was declared the elected President of the Greek Cypriot administration. After his election, the Greek Cypriot attitude towards the settlement of the Cyprus conflict on the basis of a geographical federation hardened and a public discussion on the issue as to whether the Greek Cypriot side had accepted a 'bi-zonal', in contrast with a 'bi-regional', federation was set in motion. Mr Tassos Papadopoulos, the Greek Cypriot negotiator at the sixth Vienna talks, who had submitted a map showing officially that a defined area of northern Cyprus should remain in Turkish hands as one part of the proposed bi-communal federal state, came under a barrage of criticism as a result of which he resigned from his post. The Greek Cypriot side showed vacillation on this point and raised doubts as to whether the map submitted by the Greek Cypriot side envisaged any boundary for the proposed Turkish Cypriot region. Moreover, there was an attempt to take the Cyprus conflict away from the framework of intercommunal negotiations and to internationalize it.

### 3. TURKISH CYPRIOT PROPOSALS OF 1978

In January 1978 the UN Secretary-General, Dr Kurt Waldheim, made a three-day visit to Cyprus and during his stay met Mr Kyprianou as well as Mr Denktash. The most important achievement of the UN Secretary-General was his success in arranging a meeting between the leaders of the Greek Cypriot and Turkish Cypriot communities on 14 January. At a press conference before his departure on 15 January, Dr Waldheim said that he had found the opportunity to have extensive talks about the situation and especially the negotiating process in the light of new developments. He expressed gratification about the meeting between Mr Denktash and Mr Kyprianou. On the procedure to be followed Dr Waldheim said it was agreed that the proposals which would be put forward should first be given to the Secretary-General of the UN, who would then consult with the parties concerned in order to clarify the situation and to decide, in consultation with the parties, on further procedure, especially the date of the resumption of the intercommunal talks, which could take place in the not distant future.

It was in accordance with the above procedure suggested by the UN Secretary-General that the Turkish Cypriot side put forward comprehensive proposals for the settlement of the Cyprus problem which were presented to the Secretary-General in Vienna on 13 April 1978, which the Secretary-General found to be 'concrete and substantial'.[8] However, the Greek Cypriot side rejected the same proposals. One reason for rejecting the Turkish Cypriot proposals with such haste, without examining their merits, seems to be the fear that any visible progress in the intercommunal negotiations, such as willingness to examine and discuss the Turkish Cypriot proposals, might help towards the lifting of the American arms embargo on Turkey, which issue was about to be considered by the US Congress at the time.

The 1978 proposals of the Turkish Cypriot side envisaged the creation, by the free will and agreement of the two communities, of a bi-communal and bi-zonal federal state to be composed of the Turkish Cypriot and Greek Cypriot federated states. Federal executive power of the proposed republic should be vested in the federal executive under the joint direction of the two Presidents of the federated states. Federal legislative power should be exercised by the legislative assemblies of the two federated states and the federal Assembly. All powers and functions not specifically given to the federal Executive should be vested in the federated states.

As for the territorial aspect, these proposals provided for readjusting the *de facto* boundary line between the Turkish and Greek Cypriot zones. The map attached to the proposals delineated the areas falling between the 'Forward Defence Lines' of the two sides which were to be included in the readjustment. The area between south of Maraş (Varosha) and

---

[8] These proposals are set out ibid. 229–41.

Dherinia was also included in the boundary readjustment scheme.


### 4. THE AMERICAN PLAN

During the period when the intercommunal negotiations were stalled, the United States, Canada, and the United Kingdom took the initiative to submit a peace plan for Cyprus. Though the Plan was supposed to be 'top secret' it was leaked to the press.[9] The twelve-clause Plan was communicated to the UN Secretary-General, Dr Waldheim, and to the Greek and Turkish governments as well as to the Greek and Turkish Cypriot leaders. This initiative attempted to build upon the points agreed to by Archbishop Makarios and Mr Denktash in their February 1977 meeting. It was not a detailed plan for settlement of the problems. Rather, it was an attempt, within the parameters already agreed to by the leaders, to outline the form of an eventual government. The proposal also made suggestions concerning settlement of the refugee problem and the establishment of an economic *modus vivendi* in a future bi-communal state. This plan was not accepted by either side as a basis for restarting the intercommunal process.[10]


### 5. DENKTASH–KYPRIANOU SUMMIT

The deadlock ensuing from the Greek Cypriot rejection of the Turkish Cypriot proposals was eventually broken by the second summit meeting which was held between Mr Denktash and Mr Kyprianou in the presence of the UN Secretary-General

---

[9] See the *Cyprus Mail* of 19 Nov. 1978 reporting on the details of the plan taken from an exclusive report in the Turkish mainland paper *Hürriyet*.

[10] The Plan was presented to the Greek Cypriot delegation in New York in December 1978. The Soviet *Tass* news agency expressed opposition to the American Plan. The Cyprus communist AKEL party issued a statement in Dec. 1978 rejecting the plan as introducing a 'Camp David' process and intervention of the 'imperialist factor' in the internal affairs of Cyprus.

on 18 and 19 May 1979 at which the following ten-point Agreement was concluded:[11]

1. It was agreed to resume the intercommunal talks on 15 June 1979.
2. The basis for the talks will be the Makarios–Denktash guidelines of 12 February 1977 and the UN resolutions relevant to the Cyprus question.
3. There should be respect for human rights and fundamental freedoms of all citizens of the Republic.
4. The talks will deal with all territorial and constitutional aspects.
5. Priority will be given to reaching agreement on the resettlement of Varosha under UN auspices simultaneously with the beginning of the consideration by the interlocutors of the constitutional and territorial aspects of a comprehensive settlement. After agreement on Varosha has been reached it will be implemented without awaiting the outcome of the discussion on other aspects of the Cyprus problem.
6. It was agreed to abstain from any action which might jeopardize the outcome of the talks, and special importance will be given to initial practical measures by both sides to promote good-will, mutual confidence and the return to normal conditions.
7. The demilitarization of the Republic of Cyprus is envisaged, all matters relating thereto will be discussed.
8. The independence, sovereignty, territorial integrity and non-alignment of the Republic should be adequately guaranteed against union in whole or in part with any other country and against any form of partition or secession.
9. The intercommunal talks will be carried out in a continuing and sustained manner, avoiding any delay.
10. The intercommunal talks will take place in Nicosia.

After the ten-point framework agreement, the Greek Cypriot side intensified their efforts to internationalize the Cyprus problem by resorting to international forums. As part and parcel of this campaign, they had made recourse to the UN General Assembly, thereby disrupting the atmosphere of the talks.[12]

[11] UN Doc. S/13369.
[12] Resolution No. 34/30 adopted by the UN General Assembly on 20 Nov. 1979, *inter alia*, demanded the immediate withdrawal of all foreign forces from the Republic of Cyprus; called for measures for the voluntary return of refugees to their homes; and authorized the appointment of an *Ad Hoc* Committee composed of no more than seven member states.

## 6. OPENING STATEMENT OF THE
### UN SECRETARY-GENERAL

The intercommunal talks, which had been recessed since June 1979, were resumed with an inaugural address read at the opening session of the United Nations Conference Room on the Green Line of Nicosia (Ledra Palace) on 9 August 1980. The message of the UN Secretary-General outlined the 'common ground that was worked out', as follows:[13]

(a) Both parties have reaffirmed the validity of the high level agreements of 12 February 1977 and 19 May 1979;

(b) Both parties have reaffirmed their support for a federal solution of the constitutional aspect and a bizonal solution of the territorial aspect of the Cyprus problem;

(c) Both parties have indicated that the matter of security can be raised and discussed in the intercommunal talks. It is understood that this matter will be discussed, having regard to certain practical difficulties which may arise for the Turkish Cypriot community, as well as to the security of Cyprus as a whole;

(d) Both parties have appealed to the Secretary-General for the continuation of the intercommunal talks.

Between 15 September 1980 and 7 January 1981 there had been four rounds of the talks during which the following items on the agenda were taken up in rotation and discussed: (1) Varosha;[14] (2) abstention from any action which might jeopardize the outcome of the talks and attachment of special importance to initial practical measures by both sides to promote goodwill, mutual confidence, and the return of normal conditions; (3) constitutional aspects; and (4) territory.

---

[13] UN Doc. A/35/385-S/14100.

[14] Varosha (Maraş) is the new city of Famagusta, which was deserted by its inhabitants during the Turkish intervention. The exodus of Greek Cypriots from north to south was triggered off by the Greek Cypriot radio broadcasts of the time which described the terrible things the Turkish soldiers would do to the Greeks. This scaremongering was intended to make the Greek Cypriots fight more vigorously against the Turkish troops, but instead it created panic among the Greeks, who left their homes before the Turkish troops arrived: See Denktash, *The Cyprus Triangle* (London, 1982), 96–7.

## 7. TURKISH CYPRIOT PROPOSALS OF AUGUST 1981

Owing to the holding of elections in the island, both sides agreed to a short recess of the intercommunal talks in late May and June 1981.[15] In the meantime package proposals on a new constitution, on territory, and on the question of security were drawn up by the Turkish Cypriot side.

On 5 August 1981 the Turkish Cypriot side presented at the intercommunal talks their comprehensive proposals which included a map on territory.[16] The constitutional proposals, which were negotiable subject to the two summit agreements, were submitted in the form of a draft constitution. The constitutional proposals included the following fundamental principles:

(a) The proposed federal republic shall be bi-communal and bi-zonal. However, the union of two federated states to form a federal state cannot result in the establishment of a unitary state. Moreover, each federated state must have its territory (land, sea and air space), people and government.

(b) Within this bi-communal, bi-zonal federal republic the equal co-founder partnership status of the Turkish Cypriot community shall be maintained. The representation of the Turkish Cypriot community in the legislature and other public institutions should be on the basis of 50:50 ratio.

[15] Greek Cypriots in the south went to the polls on 24 May 1981 to elect 35 members of the Greek Cypriot House of Representatives that would hold office for five years. After the final count of the poll, AKEL (communists) and the Rally party of veteran politician Mr Glafcos Clerides were allocated 12 seats each in the 35-seat Greek Cypriot House (even though AKEL led the poll with a narrow margin), while Mr Kyprianou's Democratic party secured 8 and Dr Lysarides' socialist EDEK party 3 seats.

On 28 June 1981 the Turkish Cypriots in the north went to the polls to elect for the next five years their President and 40 members of the Legislative Assembly. Mr Denktash was re-elected President of the Turkish Federated State of Cyprus. In the elections for the 40 seats of the Legislative Assembly none of the political parties gained an overall majority.

[16] For a detailed examination of these proposals, see this author's *Cyprus Conflict*, 165–74.

(c) The federal or central government shall not be vested with excessive powers *vis-à-vis* powers of the component federated states.

(d) Freedom of movement, freedom of settlement, and the right of property shall be subject to certain restrictions to be regulated in accordance with the principles laid down in paragraph (3) of the Denktash–Makarios guidelines of 12 February 1977.

The Turkish Cypriot draft constitution listed the following as 'federal matters':

1. Foreign affairs.
2. Federal financial affairs.
3. Tourism and information.
4. Posts and telecommunications.
5. Federal health and veterinary services.
6. Standards of weights and measures, patents, copyrights, and trade marks.

All powers and functions not provided in the draft constitution as federal matters would rest with the federated states.

The draft constitution envisaged a bi-communal federal Parliament comprising a federal Senate and a federal House of Representatives. Both houses would be composed of equal numbers of Turkish Cypriot and Greek Cypriot members. The executive power of the federal republic of Cyprus would be exercised by a federal Council composed of three Turkish Cypriot and three Greek Cypriot ministers.

On the territorial aspect, the Turkish side submitted two different maps, one defining the proposed boundary line between the two federated states (components of the Federal Republic), and one showing the Maraş (Varosha) area in particular. These proposals would be valid only subject to final agreement being reached on the constitutional aspect and on the question of security arrangements. The Turkish side concluded that any further reduction in size of its proposed territory as defined on the attached map, would gravely undermine the concepts of economic viability, productivity, land ownership, and security, which constituted the basis of

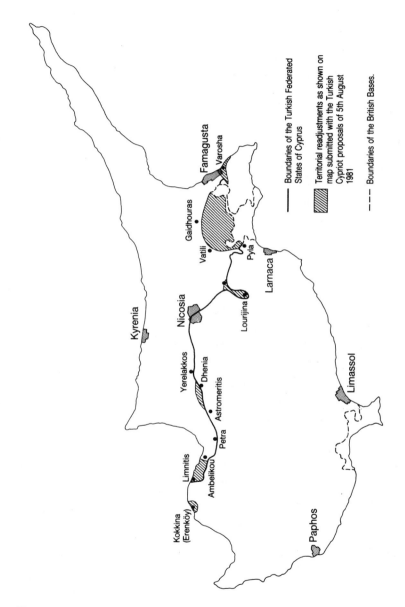

**Fig. 2.** Map submitted with the Turkish Cypriot proposals of 5 August 1981.

the Turkish Cypriot community's concrete proposals on the question of territory.[17]

## 8. GREEK CYPRIOT PROPOSALS OF 1980–1981

The Greek Cypriot side submitted proposals on 1 October 1980 for the solution of the Cyprus problem, which constituted a detailed elaboration of the proposals they submitted at the opening of the 6th Vienna talks on 31 March 1977.[18]

The basic principles of the proposed federal republic were formulated as follows:

1. The federal republic of Cyprus should be an independent, sovereign, non-aligned, bi-communal, federal republic consisting of the Greek Cypriot province and the Turkish Cypriot province.

2. The territory of the federal republic must constitute a single and indivisible whole and consist of the territories of the provinces. The people of the federal republic will comprise the people of the provinces.

3. The federal republic must be the sole subject of international law to the exclusion of the provinces.

4. There will be one sole citizenship for the whole of the federal republic and passports must be issued by federal authorities.

5. Fundamental rights and liberties safeguarded by Part II of the 1960 Constitution, as well as by the European Convention and by the UN International Covenants of Human Rights are to continue to apply throughout the territory of the federal republic, including freedom of movement, freedom of settlement, and the right to property.

6. The federal Legislature and Executive must be vested with such powers as to ensure that Cyprus is reintegrated to

[17] According to a Report submitted to the Committee on Foreign Relations of the United States Senate entitled *Nato Today: The Alliance in Evolution*, which was released on 17 April 1982, if effected, the Turkish Cypriot territorial proposals would leave about 33 per cent of Cyprus territory under the Turkish Federated State.

[18] For details, see this author's *Cyprus Conflict*, 174–9.

form a single economic unit, and to enable coherent development and the consistent application of economic policy.

On the Executive the Greek Cypriot side proposed that the form of government should be presidential with a President and Vice-President. The executive powers of the republic would be exercised by the President, who for this purpose would have a Council of Ministers. The Council of Ministers must be composed of 10 members of whom 8 (80 per cent) should be Greek and 2 (20 per cent) Turkish Cypriots. However, in their 'Further Proposals' of 9 September 1981, the Greek Cypriot side suggested that the composition of the Council of Ministers should be modified so as to be 70 per cent Greek Cypriot ministers and 30 per cent Turkish Cypriot ministers.

The Greek Cypriot side suggested in their 1980 proposals that the federal Legislature should be composed of the federal Council (the upper house) and the federal House of Representatives (the lower house). The representation of the two communities in each house of the legislature should be 80 per cent Greek Cypriot and 20 per cent Turkish Cypriot. In their 'Further Proposals' of 9 September the Greek side stated that it would be prepared to consider an increased participation of the Turkish Cypriot community in the upper house on the basis of a 70:30 ratio, if certain mechanisms for resolving deadlock between the two houses could be found.

The Greek Cypriot side submitted two separate lists of powers, one for the federal Legislature and the other for the provincial Legislatures. The latter would have powers particularly related to local government and municipalities. These were defined exhaustively. On the other hand, the federal Legislature would exercise all the powers enumerated in the list of federal powers, as well as the residue of power not specifically assigned to the provincial Legislatures.

In its 'Further Proposals' of 9 September 1981 the Greek Cypriot side stated that it was prepared to consider certain reasonable adjustments of the federal legislative list and the provincial list, and also the possibility of the introduction of a new *Concurrent List*, if deemed necessary.

The Greek Cypriot side, who for the first time had submitted a map with their proposals at the Sixth Vienna Talks on

31 March 1977, showing that an area of territory in north Cyprus[19] should remain under Turkish Cypriot control, again presented the same map with their proposals of 8 October 1980.

In its 'Further Proposals' of 9 September 1981 the Greek Cypriot side indicated that although it considered that its Territorial Proposals (8 October 1980) provided a proper basis for agreement on the territorial aspects of the Cyprus problem, yet there would be margin for negotiation in relation to the territorial aspects of its proposals, provided that any territorial arrangements did not result in the 'exclusion from the Greek Cypriot Province of large population centres containing the homes of considerable numbers of Greek Cypriot refugees and to which they should be able to return under Greek Cypriot administration'.

The Greek Cypriot side stressed that its proposals were made subject to priority being accorded to the resettlement of Varosha in accordance with Point 5 of the 19 May 1979 high-level agreement.

### 9. WALDHEIM IDEAS

About two months after the Turkish Cypriot proposals were presented, Dr Waldheim, the UN Secretary-General, took the initiative to put forward his ideas to give a new momentum to the intercommunal talks.[20] As it would not be right for the Secretary-General himself to make 'proposals', his evaluations were described as 'ideas' or 'guide-lines'. These ideas were conveyed unofficially to the leaders of the two communities on 22 October and officially to the interlocutors (Mr Onan and Mr Ioannides) on 18 November 1981.[21]

The intercommunal talks were resumed on 18 November 1981. At this meeting the Waldheim 'ideas' were tabled as

---

[19] About 20% of Cyprus territory.

[20] The Waldheim guide-lines are usually referred to as the 'Waldheim evaluation paper' and bear reference as UN Doc. A/36/702.

[21] The most important provisions of the Waldheim guide-lines were published in the *Cyprus Weekly* in its 6–12 Nov. 1981 issue. See also the Report of April 1982 entitled *Nato Today: The Alliance in Evolution*, submitted to the US Senate Committee on Foreign Relations and released on 17 Apr. 1982.

agreed, and both sides expressed their views thereon. More considered opinion on them would be given in the course of further meetings.

The objective of the evaluation was to provide a method for negotiation, an itinerary for discussion, this being the outcome of the comparative study of the constitutional proposals of both sides.

The evaluation mentions, on the one hand, 'points of coincidence', where the views of the two sides, as expressed in the intercommunal talks, approximate to coincidence; and, on the other, 'points of equidistance' between these views. The 'points of equidistance' aspire to locate median positions, or to afford possible bridges between previously divergent standpoints.

Dr Waldheim made it clear in an introduction to his 'guidelines' that his evaluation was in no way final, or exhaustive. Some vacuums should be filled through negotiation.

The points of coincidence listed by the evaluation cover the following:

1. The establishment of a federal republic consisting of two provinces and a federal district that will be the seat of government. The division of the northern province into two administrative districts and the southern into four.[22]

2. The exclusion of 'secession, integration or union of the Republic in whole or in part with any other state'.

3. 'The state shall have an international personality and the federal government shall exercise sovereignty in respect of all the territory.'

4. Single citizenship regulated by federal law.

5. Agreement to be reached by the two provinces for 'a neutral federal flag and national anthem. Each province to create its own flag, using as far as possible elements of the federal flag.'

---

[22] At the meeting of 18 Nov. 1981, when the Waldheim ideas were officially tabled, the Greek Cypriot side expressed the view *inter alia* that there were some instances in the evaluation where 'points of coincidence' were listed, whereas the parties had not as yet reached agreement on such issues. As examples of such instances, reference was made to the concept of administrative districts, their allocation between north and south, a federal district, the fundamental human-rights provisions, the official languages, and the Independent Officers.

Dr Waldheim's evaluation envisaged the establishment of a federal, independent, sovereign, non-aligned republic made up of separate Greek and Turkish Cypriot 'provinces' and a 'federal district' that would be the seat of government.

The evaluation stated that 'the Executive Authority of the Republic shall be exercised by a federal Council composed of six members, one from each administrative district (2 from the Northern Province and 4 from the Southern Province)'. These six members of the federal Council should be appointed. Dr Waldheim suggested that the method of appointment of the members of the federal Council and the election of President as well as the Vice-President should be matters open to discussion during the intercommunal talks.

The federal government or Council would have six ministerial portfolios:

1. Foreign affairs.
2. Defence, citizenship, immigration, etc.
3. Justice and higher education.
4. Co-ordination of international trade and tourism, postal and telecommunication services, and international navigation.
5. Federal finance, central bank, currency, customs, weights, measures, and patents.
6. Co-ordination of environmental matters, natural resources, and health, labour, and social services.

Other powers of the federal Council should include the promulgation of federal statutes and decisions and laws passed by both chambers, allocating the federal budget and setting out the policies of the federal government.

The other ideas put forward by Dr Waldheim cover the following:

1. That the two provinces of the Republic 'shall draft their own Constitutions in conformity with the Federal Constitution'.
2. 'The Federal Legislative power' shall comprise two chambers: The Chamber of Provinces, giving the Greek and Turkish Cypriot communities equal representation of ten members each, and a Popular Chamber composed of

Representatives of the people of Cyprus on a ratio of one member for each 10,000 of the total population.

3. In addition, each province shall elect its own provincial chamber 'whose responsibilities shall include approval of the necessary provincial legislation'.

4. Each province shall establish its own administration of justice and will control the provincial police, but will have no jurisdiction in federal matters.

The area of competence of each province would cover matters other than those allocated to the six-member federal Council.

As to the territorial aspect, the UN Secretary-General suggested a segregation on the basis of a 70:30 ratio, so that the area under Greek Cypriot jurisdiction would be at least 70 per cent, including the buffer zone which is the minimum for the resettlement of a substantial number of refugees. The Secretary-General suggested that a fund for development of the north should be established 'to deal with the socio-economic consequences of the territorial adjustment and, at the same time, would represent an important element of the basis for a vigorous economy and ensure a balanced development in the Republic'.

The Secretary-General suggested that the question of international guarantees in relation to the status of the federal republic of Cyprus would be discussed at the appropriate level after agreement on all other aspects had been reached.

# 7

# An Evaluation of the Intercommunal Talks

## I. CONCEPTUAL DIFFERENCES

In his reports to the Security Council about his mission of good offices, the UN Secretary-General has many times expressed the conviction that the intercommunal talks present the best available means for achieving an agreed, just, and lasting settlement of the Cyprus problem.[1] However, the intercommunal talks have encountered a number of difficulties and stumbling blocks.

All through the process of the intercommunal talks conducted under the auspices of the United Nations since 1975, the Greek Cypriot side assumed that a unitary 'Government of Cyprus' still existed and that the Greek Cypriot administration was that 'Government'. This attitude has been a dominant factor *vis-à-vis* the constitutional aspects of the problem and the matter of practical measures that should be considered by both sides to promote goodwill, mutual confidence, and a return to normal conditions. In fact, the intercommunal talks are being conducted between the representatives of the two communities on an equal footing. The resolutions of the UN Security Council as well as of the General Assembly are explicit on this matter.[2] In view of this, the Greek Cypriot representative at the intercommunal talks is regarded as a spokesman for his community and not for the 'Government of Cyprus'. These resolutions also implicitly accept the bi-communality of the state.

During the arduous negotiations carried out within the

[1] See e.g. the Secretary-General's Reports to the Security Council about UN operation in Cyprus, S/14778 of 1 Dec. 1981, para. 56 and S/15182 of 1 June 1983, paras. 60, 61, and 63.

[2] See e.g. Security Council resolution 367 of 12 Mar. 1975 and General Assembly resolutions 33/15 of 9 Nov. 1978 and 34/30 of 20 Nov. 1979, respectively.

context of the intercommunal talks, important conceptual differences appeared between the two sides. Each side had been arguing that its proposals were made in accordance with the two high-level agreements, but their interpretations of the relevant paragraphs of these agreements had been, generally speaking, diametrically opposite. The question arose whether the proposed federal republic would be 'bi-zonal' and whether there would be a boundary line between the two components of the federal republic. The Greek side argued that 'bi-zonality' meant partition and was unacceptable. The 'unity' of the country would have to be preserved. In view of this, the Greek Cypriot side rejected any notion that there could be two 'federated states'.

In a public statement on the intercommunal talks, the Greek Cypriot leader Mr Kyprianou was reported to have said, *inter alia*, that the Greek Cypriot side had accepted a bi-regional federation but not two states. He continued to say, 'we want a united state and united people',[3] an allusion to a 'unitary state' which is incompatible with the principle of federation.

In the Greek Cypriot view, the proposed federal state

(a) should have 'unity', that is, must be a single entity, a state with a single international personality;

(b) must have unity of people, i.e. all the people inhabiting the state are to be recognized as citizens of the state;

(c) must have unity of territory. In other words, the federation may consist of two or more areas or provinces and provincial or regional administrations but the territory of the state should be accepted as one. The people of the state should be able to move freely throughout the state and settle wherever they may wish, under the superintendence of federal courts applying federal law.

The Greek Cypriot side tried to reinforce the above argument by reference to guide-line 4 of the 12 February 1977 Agreement and point 8 of the 19 May 1979 Agreement which speak respectively of 'unity of the country' and of 'territorial integrity'.

On the other hand, the Turkish Cypriot side contended that 'bi-zonality' simply meant two areas or two states, but that it did

---

[3] *Cyprus Mail*, 16 Dec. 1980.

not imply partition. This side stressed that the concept of 'bi-zonality' was not a neologism; it was agreed upon between the late Archbishop Makarios and President Denktash in the presence of Dr Kurt Waldheim, the then UN Secretary-General, during their summit meeting when the four guide-lines of 12 February 1977 were being formulated.

The Turkish side stressed that the high-level Agreements could not be interpreted as envisaging the creation of a unitary state, because it would be impossible to conceive a 'unitary federation'. Moreover, under guide-line 2 of the 12 February 1977 Agreement it was agreed that the two communities should have 'territory' under their own administration. The word 'territory' has a different meaning from the word 'land', which is used in private law. This word here implies land, sea, and air space under the administration of each component unit of the proposed federation, and therefore 'boundaries'.

Even though there was agreement on the 'federal solution of the constitutional aspect and a bizonal solution of the territorial aspect' as outlined in the inaugural address of the UN Secretary-General, which was read at the opening session of the resumed intercommunal talks on 9 August 1980, the problem as to whether the federation should have 'state boundaries' persisted. The Greek Cypriot side stated that it would not accept such boundaries. This statement was repeated early in February 1982. The 'tyranny of words'[4] continued to prevail.

The Turkish view has been that the federation must be built from the basis of the existing two *de facto* administrations and that Cyprus should be a 'decentralized', or 'weak', or 'loose', federation, with provisions for slow and long-term progress to a customs union and centralized fiscal and economic policy-making; and migration should be limited between the units, in order to preserve the homogeneity of the units as well as for reasons of security of the Turkish community. On the other hand, the Greek Cypriot side has in its proposals suggested that Cyprus should be a 'centralized', a 'strong', or a 'tight' federation. According to the Greek Cypriot side, the desire for interregional free trade and economic development under a

---

[4] This expression was used in Apr. 1980 by the Lord Privy Seal, Sir Ian Gilmour, during his visit to Cyprus.

system of integrated economy necessitates a strong federal government. On this point the Turkish view is that whilst an integrated economy would be preferable for the island in the long run, initially and until the economic gap between the two Cypriot communities, caused by past and present politically motivated actions of the Greek Cypriot side, is removed and confidence is restored between them, each federated state should be responsible for its own economy, but an 'Economic Co-ordination Board' with an equal number of expert members from both communities should be appointed to co-ordinate and develop the two economies under a federal system, with a view to gradual economic integration.

According to the Greek Cypriot side, the Turkish Cypriot proposals did not provide for the setting up of a genuine 'federal' state, but of a *sui generis* association of two states. These proposals were therefore at the confederal end of the spectrum of federations. The Turkish Cypriot side reciprocated by saying that the Greek Cypriot side had in fact proposed a 'unitary state' and not a genuine 'federation', because the strong central government would have powers to override the units.

As there is *de facto* territorial separation between the two peoples of Cyprus and as the 1960 Republic has been replaced by two autonomous administrations with the result that all the functions of the Republic are exercised by two separate administrations, the argument that the sovereignty of the future federal republic should derive from the existing administrations gains persuasive force. This is not a case of devolution of powers from an existing unitary state.

Especially in a 'bi-national' country, federation means a mutually accepted voluntary link between two different national communities, each exercising on an equal footing the right to self-determination. Some federations have clearly enshrined these principles in their constitutions. For instance, article 1 of the preamble of the Constitutional Act, No. 143 of 27 October 1968 concerning the Czechoslovak federation,[5] is explicit on the sovereignty and the equal right to self-determination of the two national communities (the Czechs and

---

[5] Obris Press Agency, Prague, 1978, 2nd edn., trans. from the Czech by Ivo Dvorak, p. 43.

the Slovaks) constituting the federation. Czechoslovakia is, like Cyprus, a bi-national country. Likewise, the former constitution of the Socialist Federal Republic of Yugoslavia, as well as the new constitution which was promulgated on 21 February 1974, contains principles concerning the sovereignty, the equality, and the right to self-determination of the component federated units.[6]

For Turkish Cypriots the basic issue is security. They cannot tolerate a 'strong' federal government until prolonged and happy experience with cohabitation under a weaker one has changed the climate in the island. Taking into consideration the differences of economic and social circumstances as well as the differences of outlook of the Greek and Turkish Cypriot communities, the creation of a 'strong' central government at the outset, at the expense of the autonomy of the component units, could create the risk of emphasizing these differences and of encouraging the centrifugal forces. Moreover, a 'strong' central government would entail the prospect of domination over the Turkish Cypriot unit and of consequent friction between the two units of the federation.

The Turkish Cypriot view, regarding a weak federation with a proviso that more powers may devolve upon the central government as confidence grows, is supported by the Swiss example. Under the Swiss constitution of 1848 the central government's powers were mainly those generally considered an initial necessity in a federation: foreign affairs, defence, and foreign commerce.[7] The Swiss constitution of 1848, which is still in force today, granted additional powers to the federation regarding the armed forces, currency, and commercial and industrial legislation. As confidence grew, more and more powers were transferred to the federation. From 1874 to 1975, 86 revisions of the federal constitution were adopted, and at least a third of these revisions concerned the transfer of powers from the cantons to the federal government. This shows that the Swiss state was not artificially centralized, but built up from below.

[6] *The Constitution of the Socialist Federal Republic of Yugoslavia*, prepared under the chief editorship of Dragoljub Durovic by seven Yugoslav jurists, and trans. into English by Marko Pavicic (Belgrade, 1974), 43, 53, 54, 55, and 307.

[7] George A. Codding, *The Federal Government of Switzerland* (Boston, 1965), 24.

The principle of *equality* is in all cases an important and fundamental element of federalism. Particularly in federations based on an agreement between different national and ethnic communities, this principle assumes a much greater and vital importance. The size of the population of each component part of a federation is immaterial as far as the fundamental basis of equal representation (at least in the upper house) is concerned. For example, the population of California is fifty times as big as that of Alaska or that of Wyoming, but all these states enjoy equal representation in the powerful US Senate.[8] The population of the canton of Zurich is thirty-two times as large as that of the canton of Uri, but all the Swiss cantons have equal representation in the Council of States (*Conseil des États*).[9]

At the root of all their differences lies the disagreement of the two ethnic peoples of Cyprus as to the sovereignty of the future federation. Will the sovereignty of the future federation derive from the sovereign peoples of the two communities previously organized in states of their own or will that sovereignty be derived from a single central government? In other words, will the government of a future federal republic of Cyprus be the successor of the two communal administrations that now exist *de facto* on the island, or of the Greek Cypriot regime which is wearing the mantle of 'the Government of Cyprus'? It is submitted that there can be no genuine equality of status for the two communities in negotiating a settlement as co-founders of the Cyprus Republic, or as co-founders of the future federal republic, so long as the Greek Cypriot regime in Nicosia regards itself and is regarded internationally as the 'Government of Cyprus' and, ignoring the Cyprus realities, insists that sovereignty of the future federal republic of Cyprus will derive from itself.

## 2. CONFIDENCE-BUILDING MEASURES

Point 6 of the high-level agreement of 19 May 1979 stipulates that special importance will be given to the consideration of

[8] According to the 1980 census, the population of California was 22,294,000, that of Alaska 403,000, and that of Wyoming 468,909.

[9] The population of the canton of Zurich is 1,112,800, whereas that of Uri is 34,200.

initial practical measures by both sides to promote goodwill, mutual confidence, and the return to normal conditions.

The search for a peaceful settlement of the Cyprus conflict necessitates the existence of a 'political truce' between the two communities, the cessation of political propaganda, as well as the lifting of the economic embargo on the Turkish Cypriot community, in other words, the campaign of economic attrition. Such campaigns remove all the vestiges of trust. However, by means of a complex web of measures, the Greek Cypriot side tries methodically to prohibit and prevent the Turkish Cypriots from exporting and importing, from using port facilities in north Cyprus, and from receiving their share of international aid.

The Greek Cypriot administration has declared Famagusta and other ports in north Cyprus as 'illegal'. Foreign captains who use these ports are imprisoned and fined if they subsequently enter a port in the Greek Cypriot zone. Steps have also been taken to hinder communications and trade with the north.[10] The Greek Cypriot side has also obtained a resolution at the Universal Postal Union Congress held in Rio de Janeiro in 1979 purporting to declare 'illegal and of no validity' postage stamps issued by the Turkish Cypriot Postal Administration.[11]

During the intercommunal discussions that took place, on the agenda item of 'initial practical measures' the attitude of the Greek Cypriot side had been that such measures should not prejudge the issues involved or pre-empt the outcome of the final political settlement or the basis agreed at the two high-level meetings. The subjects discussed under this heading include: the modalities for the payment of old age pensions to eligible Turkish Cypriots out of the social insurance fund; passports for Turkish Cypriots; the balance of Turkish Cypriot banks maintained with the Central Bank of the Greek Cypriot administration; ports and airports within the boundaries of the Turkish Federated State; Nicosia sewage scheme; the lifting of

[10] For further details about the economic embargo, see this author's *The Cyprus Conflict: A Lawyer's View*, 2nd edn. (Lefkoşa, 1982), 66, 109–14, and *Three Chapters on Cyprus: Chapter 1*, issued by the Turkish Cypriot Human Rights Committee in 1983, 84–92.

[11] The denial of postal and telecommunication facilities to Turkish Cypriots as early as 1963 led to the establishment of these services, including the issue of postage stamps by the Turkish Cypriot authorities.

the economic embargo on Turkish Cypriots; issues relating to Greek Cypriots living in the north; and the fostering of contacts between members of the two communities.

On the question of passports, the Greek Cypriot side would not accept the validity of travel documents issued by the Turkish Cypriot community because this would amount to recognition of this community as a separate international entity. On its part the Turkish Cypriot side would not accept that applications by Turkish Cypriots be lodged with the Greek Cypriot authorities because this would amount to recognition of the Greek Cypriot administration as the government of Cyprus.

The balances of Turkish Banks with the Central Bank amounting to about two million Cyprus pounds consisted almost entirely of the minimum reserve accounts under the Central Bank Law, and in the view of the Greek Cypriot side the abandonment of the minimum reserve requirement might entail serious consequences for the depositors and might hinder the return to normal conditions.

As regards the ports and airports, their operation, according to the Greek Cypriot view, is governed by law and the recognition of facilities adopted and controlled under 'the present *de facto* situation' would promote division. The Greek Cypriot side was ignoring the fact that division exists, a division that was brought about by the Greek Cypriots themselves. The Turkish side insisted that at least the blacklisting of ships and their captains and the campaign of economic attrition should cease.

The Greek Cypriot view has been that the present state of Cyprus will be reshaped into a federation in accordance with the principles agreed for the settlement of the Cyprus question. The contrary position would lead to the dissolution of the country and of the 'Government of Cyprus' and its separation into two components. The initial practical measures should alleviate hardship for both sides and facilitate the return to normal conditions. This, in turn, necessitates resettlement leading to the unification of the country as a whole and to the establishment of federation.

On the other hand the Turkish Cypriot concept, its philosophy, is that there exist two *de facto* administrations which will be legalized with the agreed solution of the Cyprus problem.

The initial practical measures will not pre-empt the constitutional issues involved. Moreover, these measures, such as the Nicosia sewage scheme, can be implemented through the United Nations Development Programme.

The attitude of the Greek Cypriot side on these matters gave the impression that the intercommunal talks were being carried out between the 'Government of Cyprus' on the one hand, and the Turkish Cypriot community, on the other. As each side did not recognize the other, very little progress was made on these issues and nothing was done to lift the economic and political embargo on the north.

### 3. INTERNATIONALIZATION OF THE CYPRUS PROBLEM

Point 6 of the Denktash–Kyprianou accord stated that both sides would abstain from any action which might jeopardize the outcome of the talks. The Greek Cypriot attitude towards the intercommunal talks has not, however, been consistent. While the talks were going on, they continued to have recourse to international forums.

One positive result of point 6 of the high-level agreement was that at the General Assembly of the UN in its 35th session in 1980, after consultation with all concerned, the Cyprus item was deferred and no resolution adopted in view of the fact that under the Secretary-General's auspices the intercommunal talks were under way. The Greek Cypriot side was dissuaded from raising the Cyprus question at the UN General Assembly during 1981 and 1982. However, they brought the question of Cyprus to the commemorative meeting of the Foreign Ministers of the non-aligned countries in New Delhi in February 1981. In the declaration adopted at New Delhi the concept of the 'Government of Cyprus' was the dominant theme, and the reference made to 'the non-aligned decisions and declarations' was apt to create the false impression that these decisions and declarations were among the criteria which form the basis of the intercommunal talks.

After the coming to power of Mr Andreas Papandreou's socialist PASOK party in Greece in October 1981, there was a sharp deterioration in Graeco-Turkish relations. The Cyprus issue became a priority in Greek foreign policy and a stick with which to beat the Turks. Openly sceptical about the usefulness of the intercommunal talks, Mr Papandreou advocated the mobilization of world opinion against Turkey with the object of securing the withdrawal of all Turkish troops from Cyprus prior to a negotiated settlement.

The Kyprianou government's internationalization campaign, already under way, gathered momentum after Mr Papandreou's historic visit to Cyprus in February 1982. On arrival, Mr Papandreou reiterated what had already been agreed with Mr Kyprianou in Athens a week earlier, that is, to launch a crusade to internationalize the Cyprus problem and to strive for the staging of an international conference, an idea advanced by the Soviet Union in 1974. During his stay he spelt out his views about the intercommunal talks and said that he was not optimistic about the outcome; for this reason it would not be necessary to wait for the talks to fail before embarking upon the internationalization course.

The Greek Cypriot side had been taking the line that intercommunal talks concern the internal aspects of the Cyprus problem and that an international conference could take up the external aspects, including the question of guarantees, a move strongly opposed by the Turkish Cypriot side. It is a fact, however, that acrimonious debate in New York and elsewhere undermines the search for a settlement through quiet diplomacy in Cyprus.

In 1983 the Greek Cypriot side, in its effort to internationalize the Cyprus problem further, brought the question of Cyprus first to the 7th Non-aligned Summit Conference in New Delhi and then to the General Assembly of the United Nations. The talks were recessed at the request of the Greek Cypriot side to enable them to appeal to the UN General Assembly. The last meeting of the intercommunal talks was held on 14 April 1983 and the dialogue could not be resumed till 15 September 1988.

# 8

# Towards Declaration of Statehood

## I. GRAECO-TURKISH RELATIONS

On 18 October 1981, Mr A. Papandreou, the new Greek premier, was quick to declare that his government would give stronger support to the 'Republic of Cyprus'. He said that the current talks between Greek Cypriots and Turkish Cypriots, under United Nations auspices, were of little value. The Greek Cypriot side was in effect negotiating with Turkey, whose 'forces occupy the northern part of the island', rather than with the Turkish Cypriots themselves.

Mr Papandreou met Mr Kyprianou, President of the Greek Cypriot administration, in Athens on 22–7 October 1981 to consider together the 'strategy to be followed for the national struggle'. Both men said a 'new chapter' had now opened in the Cyprus issue.[1] Apart from stronger diplomatic support and military aid, Mr Papandreou announced a doubling of Greece's economic assistance to Cyprus. He thought that the Greek Cypriot side had been making too many concessions.

In his foreign-policy statement on 23 November 1981 in Parliament, Mr Papandreou reiterated that 'the dialogue was not between Mr Kyprianou and Mr Denktash, but between the former and the Ankara Government'. Then, there were alarming reports of a big build-up of Greek men and arms in south Cyprus.[2]

As stated (ch. 7, s. 3, above), Mr Papandreou no longer regarded the intercommunal negotiations as the best way to solve the Cyprus problem. He suggested instead that an international conference should be convened.

[1] *The Cyprus Weekly*, 30 Oct.–5 Nov. 1981.
[2] It should be noted in this respect that it was the Greek army officers of the National Guard, backed by Greece, that had organized and staged the coup of 15 July 1974 against the government of Archbishop Makarios. The Turkish Cypriot leaders warned that similar adventurous Greek policies over Cyprus were liable to hurt the Greek Cypriots themselves in the future.

Graeco-Turkish relations were further strained early in 1982 over the Aegean dispute due to the announcement by the Greek government that it saw no use in continuing the dialogue with Turkey over this issue.[3]

## 2. THE INTERCOMMUNAL TALKS DURING THE YEARS 1982–1983

On assumption of office, the new UN Secretary-General, Mr Javier Perez de Cuellar, in a message read by his Special Representative in Cyprus to the press before the meeting of the intercommunal talks on 7 January 1982, expressed his support for the Waldheim evaluations. He reassured the people of Cyprus of both communities, with whom he spent two years of his life as a former Special Representative of the Secretary-General, that he would make every possible effort to reach a fair and just solution of the Cyprus problem.[4]

The UN Secretary-General met Mr Kyprianou in Rome on 4 April 1982 where the Cyprus problem was reviewed. Mr Kyprianou expressed his disappointment about the intercom-munal talks[5] and said that his side would exhaust all margins of the dialogue but at the same time would intensify international mobilization. He also intimated that recourse would be made to the United Nations. In his view an essential prerequisite for the solution of the Cyprus problem was the withdrawal of Turkish troops.

The Secretary-General also met Mr Denktash in Geneva on 9 April 1982. Mr Denktash pointed out the difficulties on the way to a settlement. The Greek Cypriot side had assailed the intercommunal partnership state in 1963 and maintained the

[3] However, the UN Security Council had called upon the two countries to solve their differences through talks (res. No. 395 of 25 Aug. 1976). Both countries had also signed an agreement in Berne on 11 Nov. 1976 agreeing to solve their differences through dialogue.

[4] UNFICYP Press Release: CYP/82/2, Nicosia, 7 Jan. 1982.

[5] The UN Secretary-General's view was that the intercommunal talks represent the best available means of pursuing a concrete and effective negotiating process with the object of achieving a just and lasting settlement of the Cyprus problem: Secretary-General's report S/15502, para. 58 of 1 Dec. 1982.

assault until 1974. So, in his view, the problem was one of re-establishing this partnership in accordance with the Denktash–Makarios guide-lines of 1977 and Denktash–Kyprianou summit agreement of 19 May 1979.

After the meetings of the leaders of the two communities with the UN Secretary-General it was decided, *inter alia*, to speed up the intercommunal talks. On 26 April 1982 Mr George Ioannides, the Greek Cypriot negotiator, resigned in disagreement with Mr Kyprianou over matters of policy and was succeeded by Mr Andreas Mavrommatis. On 1 December 1982 the UN Secretary-General, Mr Perez de Cuellar, submitted his half-yearly Report on Cyprus to the Security Council.[6] In the report the Secretary-General reviewed the progress made in the peacekeeping operations of UNFICYP and in the parallel, humanitarian assistance programmes. He also reported that the intercommunal negotiations continued to focus on the Wald-heim 'evaluation' paper. According to the Secretary-General, this approach was the best means available to provide a 'structured, substantive' method of discussing the differences. He stated further that the discussions remained 'cooperative and constructive' and that the interlocutors, having essentially completed the discussion of the constitutional issues, would then focus on territorial matters. He observed that the task of developing 'an overall package deal' should be undertaken in the near future and that he was confident that, 'with the political will' on both sides, such a package could be accomplished.

Early in 1983 there was little progress in the intercommunal negotiations, which were softpedalling and were being held on an 'open agenda', due to the presidential elections in south Cyprus.

The three contestants in the presidential elections were: incumbent Mr Spyros Kyprianou, right-wing Rally party leader Mr Glafcos Clerides and socialist EDEK party leader Dr Vassos Lyssarides. Mr Kyprianou was supported by the communist AKEL party, as agreement had been reached with that party for an election collaboration based on the so-called

[6] S/14778. Subsequent to the Secretary-General's Report on 14 Dec. 1982 the Security Council voted unanimously to extend the mandate of the UN forces in Cyprus until 15 June 1983 S/PV/2405 of 14 Dec. 1982.

'minimum programme'. The elections were held on 13 February and Mr Kyprianou was returned to office for a second five-year term. With AKEL backing he received 56.54 per cent of the votes. Mr Clerides received 33.93 per cent and Dr Lyssarides, who had the support of the reformist PAME party, received 9.53 per cent of the votes.

At his investiture before the Greek Cypriot House of Representatives on 28 February 1983, Mr Kyprianou pledged consultations with the Greek premier, Mr Papandreou, for the promotion of the cause of Cyprus, stated that the intercommunal talks had not been substantive, and added that parallel to the intensification of efforts for the withdrawal of 'Attila' (Turkish troops), he would give his full support for the well-known proposal of the Greek premier for their replacement by UN troops[7] so that the talks could become more fruitful.[8]

Athens in order to carry out the internationalization programme in concert with Greek leaders.[9] He paid a visit to Athens on 3 March on his way to the New Delhi Non-aligned Summit meeting. A spokesman for the Greek Cypriot government expressed the principle that would guide the joint policy in relation to the Cyprus problem in the following words: 'Cyprus decides and Greece supports'. The spokesman made it clear that this did not imply barring Greece from having a say in the formulation of Nicosia decisions. On the contrary, 'the formulation of policy and the handling of the national issue are always the result of consultations and close collaboration with Greece as the mainstay of our struggle.'[10]

Following the presidential elections in the south, the Special Representative of the UN Secretary-General, Ambassador Hugo Gobbi, reconvened the talks on 8 March 1983. That

---

[7] This could hardly give any security for the Turkish Cypriots. During the decade preceding 1974, the Greek Cypriots simply ignored the UN troops as they chose and the Turkish Cypriots remained as vulnerable as ever. Since the Turkish intervention of 1974, there have been no major border incidents and no intercommunal troubles.

[8] *Cyprus Mail*, 1 Mar. 1983.

[9] See e.g. *Cyprus Mail* of 3 Mar. 1983, 'Kyprianou's new international campaign'.

[10] *Cyprus Mail*, 27 Feb. 1983. However, later developments showed that Athens took the main responsibility for decision-making

meeting was described as cordial by the participants. He agreed, however, that there were 'stumbling blocks' which they were trying to overcome.

### 3. THE NON-ALIGNED CONFERENCE

Following the discussions on 8 March 1983 there was an additional recess of the intercommunal talks, to allow for the meeting of the Non-aligned Movement in New Delhi. In the Final Declaration adopted on 12 March the 7th Non-aligned Conference reiterated, *inter alia*, its full solidarity with and support for the people and 'Government of the Republic of Cyprus' and reaffirmed its respect for that country's independence, sovereignty, territorial integrity, unity, and non-alignment.

The heads of state or government also expressed their deep concern over the fact that part of the Republic of Cyprus continues to remain under foreign occupation forces, the withdrawal of whom is an essential basis for the solution of the Cyprus problem.

The Conference also stressed the urgent need for the voluntary return of the refugees[11] to their homes in safety and respect for the human rights and fundamental freedoms of all Cypriots, and condemned all efforts or actions aimed at altering the demographic structure of Cyprus. It considered that the *de facto* situation created by force of arms and unilateral actions should not in any way affect the solution of the problem.

### 4. THE BREAKDOWN OF THE TALKS

In March 1983 the Turkish Cypriot negotiator at the intercommunal talks suggested a 'moratorium' on internationalization, that is, avoidance of internationalization for six or twelve months. This was turned down.[12]

[11] As to the question of refugees in general, and agreement for voluntary movement of populations, in particular, see ch. 4 n. 41 and ch. 6 n. 3, above.
[12] The Greek Cypriot papers, both pro- and anti-government, were unanimous in their comments that this was a 'trap' and could not be accepted: press summary of the *Cyprus Mail* of 20 Mar. 1983.

There were reports early in April 1983 that the UN Secretary-General would be ready to undertake new initiatives to help the intercommunal talks but only after he had been given the 'green light' from the parties concerned. The Greek Cypriot side retained its ambivalent attitude towards the talks.

The talks continued on an 'open agenda' and there was general exchange of views at the meetings of the interlocutors held on 7 and 14 April, but progress was again hindered due to the pending appeal to the UN General Assembly. The intermission was requested by the Greek Cypriot side. The President of the then Turkish Federated State of Cyprus, Mr Denktash, said that this amounted to 'putting dynamite at the foundation of the intercommunal talks' and added, 'we are determined not to come under the yoke of the Greek Cypriots in Cyprus'.[13]

In April 1983 Mr Kyprianou visited Athens. The Greek Cypriot daily *Simerini* of 20 April 1983 gave the gist of what he told party leaders, or at least the Rally leader Mr Clerides, about the Athens accord during his talks with the Greek government. The two sides, it said, decided (1) that intercommunal talks should be pursued but will not be continued if they become sterile, (2) to continue efforts for pressure on Turkey to withdraw troops from Cyprus, and (3) to encourage the UN Secretary-General to take initiatives.

After the Athens meeting Mr Kyprianou, together with his Foreign Minister, Mr Rolandis, met the UN Secretary-General in Paris during the last week in April. The Secretary-General told Mr Kyprianou of his intention to make new personal efforts and to undertake new initiatives, after sounding all parties for promoting a solution to the Cyprus problem.[14] It appeared that the Secretary-General was encouraged by the Greek Cypriot side and by the Greek government to launch his new initiative. At the same time the Papandreou and Kyprianou governments intensified their two-pronged campaign for the withdrawal of Turkish troops from Cyprus and the cutting of US military aid to Turkey. When the US Assistant Secretary of State, Richard Burt, made remarks in Ankara allegedly defending increased aid to Turkey, his planned visit to Athens was cancelled.

[13] As reported in the *Cyprus Mail* of 8 Apr. 1983.
[14] *Cyprus Mail* of 26 Apr. 1983.

## 5. UNITED NATIONS DEBATE AND RESOLUTION 37/253

At the United Nations Turkey proposed the holding of the debate in the Assembly's Special Political Committee instead of a full session where only representatives of states are normally allowed to speak and where the Turkish Cypriot people would have no voice. The Greek Cypriot side[15] argued that the matter should be dealt with directly by the full body. It said the crux of the problem was Turkey's occupation of part of its territory rather than relations between the island's two communities. Finally the steering committee voted to allocate the question of Cyprus to the full Assembly rather than to the Committee. In a letter to the President of the General Assembly, Mr Imre Hollai of Hungary, the New York representative of the Turkish Federated State of Cyprus said that, since his community was barred from participating in the debate, it rejected in advance any association with a resulting resolution.

A draft resolution before the General Assembly was sponsored by Algeria, Cuba, Guyana, India, Mali, Sri Lanka, and Yugoslavia.[16]

The Greek Cypriot Foreign Minister, Mr Rolandis, addressed the resumed session of the UN General Assembly on 10 May. The Turkish delegation walked out as he opened the debate. He appealed for support to revive the flagging intercommunal talks on the future of Cyprus. He said that the 'Cyprus government' had refrained from going to the UN General Assembly in the last two years 'in order to allow the two communities to proceed with negotiations in a quiet and constructive atmosphere', but the results had fallen short of their expectations. On balance, the intercommunal talks should not be abandoned, but the process must rid itself of shortcomings and be put on the right track. He explained the aims of the recourse as (1) correct orientation of the intercommunal process and (2) boosting of the status of the Republic of Cyprus and the

[15] The Greek Cypriot delegation included leaders of all the parties in the Greek Cypriot House of Representatives to lobby support for their case.

[16] A/37/ 63 of 10 May 1983. The Turkish Cypriot view was that the contact group which prepared the draft had only rephrased a Greek Cypriot text.

coating of its political shield with a protective layer of international support.[17]

During the debates at the UN General Assembly the British delegate reaffirmed Britain's support for the intercommunal talks and urged the Assembly to avoid propaganda points which soured the atmosphere. Canada's delegate indicated the need for strict impartiality when it came to the vote by the countries which maintain troops in the United Nations Force in Cyprus (UNFICYP). Malaysia's delegate dismissed the draft resolution as 'lopsided and partial'. Nevertheless, the motion was adopted without amendment by 103 votes to 5, with 20 abstentions. Most of the NATO powers and four Arab states abstained.[18] Votes against the motion were cast by Bangladesh, Malaysia, Pakistan, Somalia, and Turkey. More than two-thirds of the nations which voted in favour of the resolution were members of either the Soviet Bloc or the Non-aligned Movement. Among the EEC members, France voted with Greece in favour of the motion. Portugal and Spain, candidates for EEC membership, did likewise. Some cohesion and unity of purpose might have been expected from the nations which contribute troops to UNFICYP. However, Australia, Austria, Ireland, Finland, and Sweden all voted for the motion, thereby undermining UNFICYP's reputation for evenhandedness, the prerequisite for effective peacekeeping.

The resolution of 13 May 1983[19] included the perennial demand for the immediate withdrawal of all the 'occupation forces'[20] and the voluntary return of the refugees in safety to their former homes. More recent proposals for an international conference on Cyprus and the demilitarization of the whole island were renewed, thereby reflecting the aims of the Soviet Union and some of the Arab states. It was again suggested that

[17] A/37/PV 116. The Greek Cypriot newspaper *Kyrikas* of 11 May 1983 criticized this inconsistency of foreign policy. The Foreign Minister had spoken about resolutions being 'cheques that cannot be cashed' and now he was speaking about the 'need to coat our shield' with international resolutions and support.

[18] Jordan, Morocco, Saudi Arabia, and Tunisia.          [19] A/37/253.

[20] The Turkish Cypriot view is that the Turkish forces which intervened legally under the Treaty of Guarantee should not withdraw unless a solution to the Cyprus problem is found, or unless the security of Turkish Cypriots is guaranteed first.

the Security Council should examine within a set time-limit the question of the implementation of various UN resolutions on Cyprus.

The Turkish Cypriots were especially concerned by paragraph 2 which affirmed 'the right of the Republic of Cyprus and its people to full and effective sovereignty and control over the territory of Cyprus and its natural and other resources' and called upon all states to support and help the 'Government of the Republic of Cyprus' to exercise these rights. The resolution in fact advocated Greek Cypriot 'sovereignty' over the Turkish Cypriots. For those who give credence to the interpretation that the Greek Cypriot government is the 'Government of Cyprus' and represents the Republic of Cyprus, its meaning is to call upon all states to support and help the Greek Cypriots to reoccupy the lands inhabited by the Turkish Cypriot community and to dominate and subjugate them again. This approach was imaginary and unrealistic, because if such an attempt were to succeed, the situation would revert to the pre-July 1974 position, and in such an event it would no longer be necessary to try to find a solution through the intercommunal talks.[21]

Paragraph 5 of the General Assembly resolution expressed support for the high-level agreements of 12 February 1977 and 19 May 1979. This paragraph, though positive, was incomplete. These were not the only elements on the basis of which the intercommunal talks were being held. In fact the mutually agreed framework of the talks comprised, at the time, the high-level agreements of 1977 and 1979, *as well as* the opening statement of the UN Secretary-General read at the resumed intercommunal talks at 9 August 1980[22] and the UN evaluation document, that is, the Waldheim ideas which were tabled at the intercommunal talks on 18 November 1981.[23]

The UN resolution as a whole, and particularly paragraph 5

[21] Speech of Ambassador Kırca, Permanent Representative of Turkey, before the UN General Assembly on 17 May 1983, A/37/PV 120.

[22] UN Doc. A/35/385. This statement provided, *inter alia*, for a federal solution of the constitutional aspect and a bi-zonal solution of the territorial aspect of the Cyprus problem.

[23] UN Doc. A/36/702. The UN Secretary-General had observed that while the intercommunal talks represent the best available method for pursuing the negotiating process, the evaluation paper constituted a determined effort to lend structures and substance to it: Secretary-General's Report to the Security Council, S/14778 of 1 Dec. 1981.

thereof, was formulated in such a way that it could be interpreted as having changed the character of the talks and the basis on which they were being held. Moreover, many paragraphs of the operative part were inconsistent with the provisions of the high-level agreements. Paragraph 4, which welcomed the proposal of Mr Kyprianou about demilitarization, was a case in point. There was in the high-level agreements clear provision concerning demilitarization. By the same token, paragraph 11, which called for respect for certain human rights and freedoms, was incompatible with and disregarded point 3 of the Denktash–Makarios agreement of 1977 which stipulated:

3. Questions of principle, like freedom of movement, freedom of settlement, the right of property and other specific matters, are open for discussion taking into consideration the fundamental basis of a bicommunal system and certain practical difficulties which may arise for the Turkish Cypriot community.[24]

The resolution laid down principles that should guide the intercommunal talks, even though these principles were not agreed upon by the parties concerned. For instance, it stipulated that the *de facto* situation should not be allowed to influence or affect the solution of the problem,[25] required immediate and effective implementation of UN resolutions on Cyprus, and failed to refer to ideas and modalities already accepted.

Finally the resolution contained provisions which made the reaching of a settlement more difficult. The Cyprus problem can be solved neither by the condemnation nor the victimization of the Turkish side; nor can it be solved by giving purely verbal satisfaction to the Greek side. The only way to solve the Cyprus problem is by serious and realistic negotiations on the basis and within the framework of the documents containing accepted guide-lines for the intercommunal talks.

### 6. THE AFTER-EFFECTS OF THE UN RESOLUTION

The Greek Cypriot representative said that the purpose of the resolution was to reorientate the intercommunal talks. The

[24] UN Doc. S/12323, para. 5.
[25] There was agreement already on a federal solution of the constitutional aspect and a bi-zonal solution of the territorial aspect of the problem, which agreement was doubtless reached as a result of the *de facto* situation.

effect was to encourage false hopes among Greek Cypriots and contribute to the disruption of the atmosphere of the intercommunal talks.[26] This Pyrrhic victory for Greek Cypriots accentuated the awareness of Turkish Cypriots that they were being relegated to the status of a 'minority'. By virtue of the resolution of the General Assembly, before which they had no right of address, their negotiating status was being eroded.

Soon after the UN debate, Mr Denktash was reported to have told the London Times that on his return to Cyprus he would propose that the Legislative Assembly consider the issue of declaring an independent state in the north that should be able to seek international recognition. He said the General Assembly resolution was the 'last drop' which caused the Turks to reassert their partnership rights. On 19 May 1983, the Kyprianou government made representations to the five permanent members of the Security Council—USA, Soviet Union, Britain, France, and China—about this intended move.

The dust had not yet settled after the debate, for the intercommunal talks to be held on 31 May as previously scheduled. Instead, the UN Special Representative, Mr Gobbi, had separate meetings with the Greek and Turkish negotiators and said that he might be going back to New York for new consultations about reactivating the talks. Mr Denktash invited Mr Kyprianou to declare publicly that he accepted the partnership status of the Turkish Cypriots and the establishment of a bi-communal federal republic. He referred to the population exchange agreement reached under the framework of the intercommunal talks at Vienna in 1975. He also called for the lifting of the economic embargo against the Turkish Cypriots and a 'moratorium'[27] on internationalization and raising the Cyprus problem in international forums during the talks. He underlined, however, that the Turkish Cypriots had not abandoned the intercommunal talks and that the best way for a solution was through negotiation.[28]

The damage done by the debate was emphasized a few weeks

[26]  UN Doc. A/37/PV/116, para. 12.

[27]  Mr Kyprianou, addressing a mass rally at *Eleftheria* square in Nicosia on 15 July 1983, to mark the anniversary of the *coup* and the Turkish intervention, rejected the proposal for a 'moratorium'.

[28]  As reported in the *Cyprus Mail* of 3 and 4 June 1983.

later when the then President of the General Assembly, Mr Imre Hollai, came to Cyprus as the guest of the Kyprianou government. A Hungarian diplomat and former ambassador to Greece and Cyprus, Mr Hollai refused invitations to visit the Turkish side. The Turkish side took exception, especially to his remarks at a dinner given in his honour by Mr Kyprianou on 8 June 1983, where he stated that the General Assembly resolution on Cyprus contained all the necessary elements to tackle the problem of Cyprus in its entirety and to find a solution. He went on to say that in the General Assembly the absolute majority of the international community was with those who want to find a solution to the Cyprus problem.

By its resolution of 15 June 1983,[29] the UN Security Council unanimously approved the extension of UNFICYP's mandate for another six months, ending 15 December 1983. The resolution made no reference to the recent General Assembly resolution. In his address to the Security Council,[30] the New York representative of the Turkish Federated State of Cyprus, objected to reference being made to the Greek Cypriot government as 'the Government of Cyprus'.[31] He also requested the Council to review the mandate of the force, which was drawn up in 1964, so as to bring it more in line with the prevailing conditions in Cyprus.[32]

As a first reaction to the UN resolution the Legislative Assembly of the Turkish Federated State of Cyprus on 17 June 1983 adopted a motion affirming the right of Turkish Cypriots to self-determination.[33] The resolution declared that the Turkish Cypriot people of Cyprus have equal rights and status in an independent and sovereign Cyprus. The basis of this proposition is that when the colonial regime ended in the island,

---

[29] No. 534 (1983).

[30] S/PV/2453. The New York representative of the Turkish Cypriots is allowed to address the Council as an expert in accordance with rule 39 of the Council's provisional rules of procedure.

[31] This has been a perennial objection.

[32] This request has been constantly made during the last few years.

[33] *Official Gazette* No. 48 of 21 June 1983, Suppl. IV, Part II. The resolution was adopted by 33 votes to 6. The Turkish Cypriot leaders had on previous occasions intimated that they would establish an independent state in north Cyprus: See e.g. *News Bulletin* of 29 Nov. 1978, No. 3899, vol. 30, and ibid. of 28 Dec. 1979, No. 4266, vol. 32.

sovereignty was not transferred exclusively to one of the two communities but to both of them conjointly as co-founder partners of the Republic. Moreover, the Greek Cypriot administrators who have not been elected by the Turkish people of Cyprus and do not represent them, cannot impose on them any resolution adopted in their absence and against their will. The date of the implementation of self-determination was left open.

As a first reaction to the decision of the Turkish Cypriot Legislative Assembly the Kyprianou government, in a statement on 20 June 1983, rejected the offer of Mr Denktash for a high-level meeting under the auspices of the UN Secretary-General.[34]

## 7. THE UN SECRETARY-GENERAL'S 'INDICATORS'

In his Report to the Security Council of 1 June 1983 on the United Nations operation in Cyprus, the Secretary-General repeated his conviction that the intercommunal talks represent the best available means for achieving an agreed, just, and lasting settlement of the Cyprus problem and stated that in an endeavour to arrest the continuing process of erosion, he had undertaken to strengthen his personal involvement within the framework of his mission of good offices.[35] He appealed to all concerned to show the utmost restraint and to assist him in his efforts.

The Secretary-General's meeting with Mr Denktash in Geneva on 4 July 1983 focused on the Secretary-General's proposed initiative to be undertaken later that year. Mr Denktash said afterwards that he would withhold the bill for a referendum about separate independence in the north until the situation was assessed on resuming the intercommunal talks on an equal basis.[36] Mr Denktash, while still in Strasburg, said he had asked the UN Secretary-General to clarify the Greek

[34] This statement was featured in all Greek Cypriot papers of 21 June 1983. *Agon* and *Eleftherotypia* endorsed the rejection in view of the resolution of the Turkish Cypriot Legislative Assembly for separate self-determination.

[35] S/15182, paras. 60, 61, and 63.

[36] A referendum bill was submitted to the Legislative Assembly of the Turkish Federated State of Cyprus in Oct. 1983, not by the government but by an independent deputy.

Cypriot views on two points: (1) whether they would restore partnership and (2) whether they would continue to see themselves as the 'people of Cyprus' and regard the Turkish Cypriots as a 'minority'.

In order to break the deadlock following the debate in the UN General Assembly, the Secretary-General, Mr Perez de Cuellar, acting within his good offices role mandated by the Security Council, and requested in the latest General Assembly resolution on Cyprus, submitted his *aide-mémoire* and 'soundings' to the two Cypriot leaders on 8 August 1983. By this initiative he attempted tentatively to suggest some subjects for discussion with a view to promoting the resumption of the intercommunal dialogue which had been suspended since May 1983. The two parties were asked to look both at methodology[37] and at the substance of three 'indicators' in the form of the Executive, the Legislature, and Territorial division. The Secretary-General was, in fact, suggesting that, instead of negotiating from their present positions, which presented a big gap, the parties should give consideration to the method of restricting the negotiations within the limits of the indicators. In other words, the Secretary-General was seeking to know whether the two sides were prepared to start moving in the direction that he suggested, which would bring them nearer to a common ground.

According to newspaper leaks,[38] the indicators covered major

---

[37] The Secretary-General took on the task of outlining parameters of key issues within which the two sides could negotiate.

[38] See e.g. *Cyprus Mail* of 16 Aug. 1983, referring to a report from Turkish mainland daily *Cumhuriyet*, and *Cyprus Mail* of 18 Aug. 1983, which included the 'text' of the *aide-mémoire* as published in the Greek Cypriot daily *Phileleftheros* of 17 Aug. 1983.

According to the journalist Mario Modiano, writing in *The Times* of 21 Nov. 1981, 'United Nations experts see a possible breakthrough in reviving the "step pyramid" proposal'. This approach envisages a two-phased deal starting with a loose federation of two provinces, with limited central authority at first. This would be broadened progressively. A key feature of the first step would be the withdrawal of military forces from the dividing line to create a 25-mile-wide demilitarized zone and the making of substantial territorial adjustments. The federal President would be Greek Cypriot and the Vice-President Turkish Cypriot, while the legislature would include a parliament elected proportionately and a Senate divided on an equal basis.

Five years later the Legislature would be asked to start implementing the plan's final phase providing for complete demilitarization and more tightly knit federal structure.

issues that were not resolved in the Waldheim evaluation paper and were outlined in the form of alternative suggestions. On the executive, two possible government structures were proposed. One envisaged a Greek Cypriot President and a Turkish Cypriot Vice-President, who would be the elected head of the southern province and of the northern province respectively. In this eventuality the members of the two provinces should be represented in the federal executive in a proportion of 60:40, respectively. The other envisaged the presidency and prime ministership alternating between the communities. This meant that the elected heads of the southern and northern provinces would be appointed head of state and government respectively on a rotation basis. In this case, the members of the provinces would be represented in the federal executive in the proportion of 70 per cent (Greek Cypriot) and 30 per cent (Turkish Cypriot).

As regards the legislature, the Secretary-General proposed that the federal republic should have a bi-cameral system. The Lower Chamber should have its members elected according to the principle of proportional representation, *or* should be composed of members elected by the Turkish Cypriot community in the proportion of 30 per cent and by the Greek Cypriot community in the proportion of 70 per cent. Both provinces should be equally represented in the Upper Chamber.

The Secretary-General proposed that the territory of the northern province should be a maximum of 30 per cent and minimum of 23 per cent of the island, presumably depending on how much power the Turkish side was prepared to cede on the central government issue.

It was pointed out in the *aide-mémoire* that if the parties agreed to the above indicators the negotiations could proceed under the good offices of the Special Representative of the Secretary-General within the limits defined thereby. The Secretary-General invited the parties to inform him of their reactions by 15 September 1983.[39]

The *aide-mémoire* was studied on both sides of the 'Green Line'.

---

[39] The Secretary-General later extended this deadline by 15 days as his proposed meeting with Mr Kyprianou could not be fixed earlier than 15 Sept., due to other commitments.

Mr Kyprianou chaired a meeting of his cabinet while the then Turkish Foreign Minister, Mr Türkmen, arrived in the north for a three-day visit.

The communist AKEL party in a statement called for a 'positive approach' to the UN Secretary-General's 'soundings'. The right-wing Rally party of Mr Glafcos Clerides made a similar call, but the socialist EDEK party said it added nothing new to the Waldheim evaluation. Archbishop Chrisostomos spoke against the Perez de Cuellar plan. Some Greek Cypriot papers suggested a 'no acceptance, no rejection' course.

Mr Kyprianou also had talks with the President of the Greek Republic and conferred with the Prime Minister and the government of Greece. He returned amid reports that the Greek government held a 'reserved attitude' towards the UN Secretary-General's plan.

Protracted vacillation by Mr Kyprianou caused the resignation on 20 September 1983 of his Foreign Minister, Mr Rolandis, who had advocated acceptance of the initiative. According to Mr Rolandis,[40] Mr Kyprianou, who had avoided making comments, was not in favour of negotiations within the limits of the indicators. Therefore, at a meeting on 14 September 1983, the Secretary-General was compelled to adopt a new approach, which, in the words of Mr Rolandis, far from offering any chance of success, was fraught with danger.

his letter of resignation, Mr Kyprianou made an announcement on the evening of 19 September, saying: 'I wish to state today that we accept the UN Secretary-General's personal effort and his method of approach which aims at leading, through successive phases and soundings, to the formulation of a framework for an overall solution of the Cyprus problem'. He went on to state that the Greek Cypriot side would submit to the

---

[40] His letter of resignation was released on 21 Sept. 1983. The AKEL leader Mr E. Papaioannou was also in favour of accepting the Secretary-General's indicators: *Cyprus Mail* of 15 Mar. 1984, reporting about a lecture at the Nicosia Cultural Centre. Mr Kyprianou's request for clarifications, in the view of Mr Denktash, as he stated in his press conference in the *Palais de l'Europe* in Strasburg on 12 Oct. 1983, emptied the initiative of substance. In Strasburg the Secretary-General of the Council of Europe, as well as the President of the Council, had earlier refused to see Mr Denktash.

Secretary-General its 'remarks, comments and views on the text of his soundings, and also on other points and aspects of the Cyprus problem'. This statement was couched in such phraseology as made it unclear what was accepted. On 30 September 1983 Mr Kyprianou met the UN Secretary-General and handed to him the Greek Cypriot community's response to the soundings. The text has not been disclosed.

Not long after the submission of the Greek Cypriot response to the UN Secretary-General, the Greek Ambassador to Cyprus, Mr Zacharakis, in a speech in October 1983 castigated the preachers of concession by saying that further concessions by the Greek Cypriot side would be 'counter-productive' and hinted that the Greek Cypriot proposals might be withdrawn from the table should the Turks declare independence. He went on to say 'the Greek Cypriot proposals should not be considered as Turkish Cypriot acquired right'.[41] On or about the same day the Greek premier, Mr Papandreou, in a message to the nation on the occasion of 'Okhi' day (symbol of resistance in the Second World War), referred to Cyprus as 'part of our national soil' which was under 'occupation'.[42]

As for the reaction of the Turkish Cypriot side, Mr Denktash informed the Secretary-General in New York on 1 October 1983 that the Turkish Cypriot side was ready to resume the intercommunal negotiating process on the existing mutually agreed basis. The Turkish Cypriot side was inclined to the view that the existing framework of the talks (which included the UN evaluation document) should not be superseded by the Secretary-General's indicators in a fashion that would show him playing the role of a 'mediator', incompatible with the 'good offices' mandate given him by the Security Council resolution 367 (1975). Mr Denktash also suggested that a summit meeting between himself and Mr Kyprianou be arranged under the auspices of the Secretary-General in order to identify the genuine intentions of the two sides for a federal solution through direct negotiations.

[41] The speech was made at the annual general meeting of the Employers Federation. As for the controversy over the speech, see the press summary of the *Cyprus Mail* of 29 Oct. 1983.

[42] The text was later amended by the Athens news agency to read 'national area', instead of 'national soil': See *Fileleftheros* of 28 Oct. 1983.

In his Report to the Security Council about the United Nations Operation in Cyprus of 1 December 1983 the Secretary-General, referring to the responses of both sides to his soundings, said in para. 53 that both sides accepted his personal involvement in the exercise of his mission of good offices, including the furnishing, in consultation with the parties, of concepts and ideas to facilitate the negotiating process.[43] He went on to say that both sides declared their readiness to resume the intercommunal negotiations on the existing agreed basis.[44]

Referring to the suggestion of Mr Denktash about a high-level meeting, which he had discussed with Mr Kyprianou on 6 October, the Secretary-General said, in para. 54 of his Report, that he would be happy to lend his good offices to arrange such a meeting provided it was well prepared and both sides co-operated in ensuring its success. In this respect the UN Secretary-General stated that Mr Kyprianou informed him of his willingness to attend a high-level meeting on that basis.[45] The Secretary-General went on to say that he decided to invite consultations with the parties concerned and, on 14 November, Mr Gobbi returned to Cyprus with his instructions to commence that process on his behalf and to consult with both sides about the agenda for the high-level meeting. Mr Gobbi carried letters to Mr Kyprianou and Mr Denktash, which could not arrive at their destinations before the proclamation of the Turkish Republic of Northern Cyprus.

[43] The report bears reference No. S/16192.

[44] The Secretary-General's statement in his Report is far from being clear as to whether his 'indicators' had been accepted. Acceptance of his 'personal involvement' and the parties' readiness to resume the intercommunal negotiations on the 'existing agreed basis', cannot necessarily be taken as acceptance of his 'indicators'.

[45] Mr Kyprianou's reported willingness to attend a high-level meeting under the auspices of the UN Secretary-General contradicts his statement made at a press conference in New York, shortly before he saw the Secretary-General. It was reported in the *Cyprus Mail* of 5 Oct. 1983 that Mr Kyprianou rejected such a proposal. He also explained why he was in principle against such a meeting. He said, there had been two top level meetings in 1977 and in 1979 'but unfortunately no progress was achieved'. It would not be wise to have a meeting for the sake of a meeting that would fail. Without a radical change in Turkey's attitude no prospect of progress could be expected. However, he would be ready to meet the Turkish leader, General Evren, anytime, anywhere for a dialogue.

## 8. DECLARATION OF STATEHOOD

On 15 November 1983 the Turkish Republic of Northern Cyprus was proclaimed by the unanimous vote of the Legislative Assembly of the hitherto Turkish Federated State of Cyprus, which is a democratic representative body of the Turkish people of Cyprus.[46] The proclamation stressed that the Republic would adhere to all treaties and agreements binding on it, including the Treaty of Guarantee, would follow a policy of non-alignment, would remain faithful to the principles of the United Nations Charter, and would endeavour to facilitate the establishment of a bi-zonal, bi-communal federal republic where Turkish Cypriots and Greek Cypriots could co-operate in peace and harmony. The proclamation emphasized, *inter alia*, that the founding of the Turkish Republic of Northern Cyprus is a manifestation of the right of self-determination of the Turkish Cypriot people of Cyprus.[47] The declaration also stipulated that the newly created entity would not unite with any other state, except with the southern unit to form a federal republic of Cyprus.

When the Secretary-General's Special Representative in Cyprus, Mr Gobbi, met Mr Denktash on 15 November, the latter handed to him a letter addressed to the Secretary-General, explaining to him why the Turkish Cypriot people had been 'left with no other alternative but to take this vital step based on our equal co-founder partnership status in the independence and sovereignty of Cyprus'.[48] The letter expressed

[46] The proclamation of statehood was timed to take place during the interim period before the newly elected government in Turkey took office. In this way the Turkish Cypriots hoped to avoid compromising the newly elected government of Turkey. After the army takeover of Sept. 1980, elections were held in Turkey for the first time under its new constitution on 6 Nov. 1983. The text of the declaration of statehood is included in UN Doc. A/38/586-S/16148 of 16 Nov. 1983.

[47] For a detailed study of the principle of 'self-determination' see ch. 9, below.

[48] The letter, to which the text of the declaration of statehood was appended, was circulated as a document of the General Assembly and the Security Council at the request of the Permanent Representative of Turkey: A/38/586-S/16148.

the disappointment arising out of Greek Cypriot attitudes towards the intercommunal talks, stressed the belief that a genuine federation can only be established between equal partners having the same political status, and affirmed that, having waited for twenty years under an uncertain political status, the Turkish Cypriot people had taken a legitimate step for redefining their political status in the form of an independent and non-aligned republic by exercising their natural right to self-determination. In the same letter, Mr Denktash, drawing attention to the provisions of the Declaration, expressed his desire for the continuation of the Secretary-General's mission of good offices and his readiness to resume the negotiations under the Secretary-General's auspices at any time. He also stated that his proposal for a high-level meeting remained in effect.

The aim of the Turkish Cypriots in declaring, on 15 November 1983, an independent state, i.e. the Turkish Republic of Northern Cyprus, is to assert their status as co-founders of the future federal republic of Cyprus and to ensure that the sovereignty of that republic will derive from the existing two states joining together as equals to form the future federal republic.

The declaration of statehood was supported by 87,928 signatures. On the same day, Turkey recognized the new Republic.[49]

[49] The reasons for recognition are to be found in the statement by the Foreign Minister of Turkey of 15 Nov. 1983, which was circulated as a UN Document under reference number A/38/602 of 23 Nov. 1983.

# 9

# Self-determination

One of the purposes of the UN Charter as expressed in article
1(2) thereof is 'to develop friendly relations among nations
based on respect for the principle of equal rights and self-
determination of peoples, and to take other appropriate
measures to strengthen universal peace'. In article 55 of the
Charter, reference is again made to 'self-determination' to
express the general aims of the United Nations in the fields of
social and economic development and respect for human rights.
By elaborating these rather cryptic references, the General
Assembly has attempted in a very large number of resolutions to
define more precisely the content of the principle. Thus, the
Colonial Declaration (clause 2) states that 'All peoples have the
right to self-determination; by virtue of that right they freely
determine their political status and freely pursue their economic, social, and cultural development.'[1]

The International Covenant on Civil and Political Rights, as
well as the International Covenant on Economic, Social and
Cultural Rights, which were proclaimed by the General
Assembly of the United Nations on 16 December 1966, have
adopted, in their identical article 1(1), clause 2 of the *Colonial
Declaration*. The principle has also been affirmed by the Security
Council, for example, in resolution 183 of 11 December 1963,
and by the General Assembly, in resolution 2625 (XXV) of
24 October 1970. The latter instrument is known as the
Declaration of Principles of International Law Concerning
Friendly Relations and Co-operation Among States in Accord-

---

[1] General Assembly resolution 1514 (XV) of 14 Dec. 1960, 'Declaration on
the Granting of Independence to Colonial Countries and Peoples'.

ance with the Charter of the United Nations.[2] In its Declaration of Principles annexed to this resolution, the Assembly dealt in the following terms with 'The Principle of Equal Rights and Self-Determination of Peoples':

(1) By virtue of the principle of equal rights and self-determination of peoples enshrined in the Charter . . . all peoples have the right freely to determine, without external interference, their political status and to pursue their economic, social and cultural development, and every State has the duty to respect this right in accordance with the provisions of the Charter . . .

(6) The territory of a colony or other non-selfgoverning territory has, under the Charter, a status separate and distinct from the territory of the State administrating it; and such separate and distinct status under the Charter shall exist until the people of the colony or non-selfgoverning territory have exercised their right of self-determination in accordance with the Charter . . .

(8) Every State shall refrain from any action aimed at the partial or total disruption of the national unity or territorial integrity of any other State or country.

By its resolution 3382 (XXX) of 10 November 1975 the General Assembly reaffirmed the importance of the universal realization of the right of peoples to self-determination, national sovereignty, and territorial integrity, and of the speedy granting of independence to colonial countries and peoples as imperatives for the enjoyment of human rights, and it further reaffirmed the legitimacy of the peoples' struggle for independence, territorial integrity, and liberation from colonial and foreign domination by all available means, including armed struggle.[3]

At the thirty-second session of the Commission on Human Rights in 1976, in the course of the debate on the question, it was

[2] Hereafter to be referred to in this chapter as the 'Declaration of Friendly Relations'. The issue of secessionist self-determination provoked prolonged discussions at the Special Committee. Some members, notably the communist bloc, favoured explicit recognition of a right to secession. On the other hand, the UK's oft-repeated belief was that self-determination is a political principle and not a legal right. The majority of the members said that they did not recognize secession as a legitimate form of self-determination: See Lee C. Buchheit, *Secession: The Legitimacy of Self-determination* (New Haven, 1978), 89–90.

[3] See *Official Records of the General Assembly*, Thirtieth Session, Annexes, Agenda Item 77, Doc. A/10309.

said that the right to self-determination, an essential prerequisite for the enjoyment of other human rights, had become a basic rule of international law.[4]

## 2. SCOPE OF SELF-DETERMINATION

The meaning and scope of the principle of self-determination are by no means uncontroversial.

A suggested draft proposed by Third World powers during the debates which led to the formulation of the Declaration of Friendly Relations would have limited the principle, by implication, to cases of colonialism.[5] On the other extreme, a proposal submitted by Czechoslovakia, Poland, Romania, and the Soviet Union broadened the principle to encompass a right of secession: 'Each people has the right to determine freely their political status including the right to establish an independent national State.'[6] The Declaration rejects both of these polar views in favour of a description which states in paragraph 1 that, by virtue of the principle, 'all peoples have the right freely to determine, without external interference, their political status and to pursue their economic, social and cultural development . . .'

The Declaration also attempts a clarification of the relationship between human rights and self-determination. Paragraph 2 implies that the concepts are separable by saying that the subjection of peoples to alien subjugation, domination, and exploitation constitutes a violation of the principle of equal rights and self-determination of peoples *as well as* a denial of human rights. Paragraph 3 reaffirms the duty of every state to promote the respect for, and observance of, human rights and fundamental freedoms.

Paragraph 4 of the Declaration states that 'the establishment of a sovereign and independent state, the free association or

[4] *Official Records of the Economic and Social Council*, Sixtieth Session, Suppl. No. 3 (E/5768), paras. 36–43, and E/CN 4SR 1342–5.

[5] UN Doc. A/AC 125/L 48 (1967); Report of the Special Committee, 24 UN GAOR 1, p. 52, para. 143.

[6] UN Doc. A/AC 125/L 74 (1969), Report of the Special Committee, 24 UN GAOR, p. 53, para. 145.

integration with an independent state or the emergence into any other political status freely determined by a people' constitute modes of implementing the right of self-determination by that people. Buchheit remarks that 'the implementing provision is addressed to the peoples themselves, rather than to states, thus implying a right of self-implementation'.[7]

The first suggestion of a legal impact of the Declaration on claims for self-determination was given by the International Commission of Jurists in its 1972 study entitled *The Events in East Pakistan, 1971*.[8] The jurists' report characterized the 1970 Declaration of Friendly Relations as 'the most authoritative statement of the principle of international law relevant to the questions of self-determination and territorial integrity'.[9] The Commission perceived the principle of self-determination as essentially conflicting with that of territorial integrity. The report noted:

the free determination by a people of the form of their political status . . . constitutes the exercise of the right to self-determination; a decision freely taken automatically leads to the acquisition of a status, and it becomes an infringement of international law for any state to attempt to deprive them of that status by forcible action, and if any state does so, other states should give support to the people asserting their right of self-determination.[10]

The principle of self-determination has in fact two quite distinct meanings. It can mean the sovereign equality of existing states, and in particular the right of a state to choose its own form of government without intervention. It can also mean the right of a specific territory (people) to choose its own form of government irrespective of the wishes of the rest of the state of which the territory is a part.[11]

It has recently become popular to speak of the concept of self-determination as having two component parts: (1) a principle of *external* self-determination whereby a group of people are entitled to pursue their political, cultural and economic wishes

[7] Buchheit, *Secesion*, 92.

[8] Secretariat of the International Commission of Jurists, *The Events in East Pakistan, 1971* (1972).

[9] Ibid. 67.

[10] Ibid. 68.

[11] J. Crawford, *The Creation of States in International Law* (Oxford, 1979), 90.

without interference or coercion by outside states, and (2) a principle of *internal* self-determination which encompasses the right of all segments of a population to influence the constitutional and political structure of the system under which they live.[12]

According to the opinion of the International Court in *Namibia*, the principle is not static but is open to change.[13] It seems that judicial reference made to this principle so far has been in the context of territories whose peoples had not attained a full measure of self-government. This right has been expressly recognized, for instance, for the peoples of the former Portuguese territories, such as Angola, Mozambique, and Guinea-Bissau.[14] The legal nature of the principle in the colonial sphere has been confirmed by an advisory opinion of the International Court of Justice in *Namibia*.[15] Referring to the developments of international law in respect of non-self-governing territories, the court mentions the principle of self-determination and cites the Declaration 1514(XV) of 1960 on the granting of independence to colonial peoples. Even in the relatively narrow field of decolonization, however, the advisory opinion of the International Court in the *Western Sahara* case recognized that 'the right of self-determination leaves the General Assembly a measure of discretion with respect to the forms and procedures by which that right is to be realized'.[16]

Self-determination derives its strength from an innate urge to self-government coupled with a sense of moral objection to alien domination, resulting in exploitation, humiliation, and deprivation of human rights. As appealingly characterized by Judge Fouad Ammoin in his Separate Opinion in the *Barcelona Traction* case, self-determination is one of those norms 'profoundly imbued with the sense of natural justice, morality and humane ideals'.[17]

In addition to its scope in the colonial context, the principle of self-determination has also acquired legal status in respect of an

---

[12] Buchheit, *Secession*, 14.
[13] ICJ Reports, 1971, 16, 31.
[14] S/PV 1639, 67 (1972). See further UN Doc. A/C 6/SR 1179, 6.
[15] See n. 13 above.
[16] ICJ Reports, 1975, 12, 36.
[17] *Case Concerning the Barcelona Traction, Light and Power Company Limited*, Second Phase, 5 Feb. 1970, ICJ Reports, 1970, 3, 310, 311.

independent state when its government exercises racial discrimination such as, for example, racial segregation or apartheid, on a large scale. Such exercise, when viewed as state activity, is regarded as contrary to international law because it constitutes a flagrant violation of human rights and particularly of the principle of self-determination sanctioned by article 1 of the International Covenant on Economic, Social, and Cultural Rights.[18] The condemnation of apartheid is to be found in numerous resolutions passed by the UN General Assembly and the Security Council[19] and in certain conventional instruments.[20] The International Court of Justice has recognized that rules and principles concerning racial discrimination pertain to general international law.[21]

History is punctuated by secessionist attempts, such as those in the Congo (1960), Biafra (1967), and Bangladesh (1971). These undertakings sought justification in the principle of self-determination. According to some jurists, international reaction to a situation like Bangladesh (and to a lesser extent Biafra) confirms the belief that the world community has accepted the legitimacy of secession as a self-help remedy in cases of extreme oppression.[22] However, probably the prevailing tendency among most international jurists is to test the legitimacy of a claim to self-determination by the degree of success that attends the claimant's undertaking.[23]

In the Congo, the attempted secession of Katanga, which also engaged the UN forces in heavy fighting, failed in the end. In 1967, when the Ibo tribe of Eastern Nigeria made a secessionist attempt from the Federation of Nigeria, and sought to establish a sovereign, independent state called the Republic of Biafra, five

[18] N. Ronzitti, 'Resort to Force in Wars of National Liberation', in A. Cassesse (ed.), *Current Problems of International Law: Essays on U.N. Law of Armed Conflicts* (Milan, 1975).

[19] See e.g. General Assembly resolutions: A/Res. 2646-XXV, 3057-XXVIII, 3324E-XXIX, and Security Council resolutions: S/Res. 282 (1970), and 311 (1972).

[20] See e.g. International Convention on the Elimination of All Forms of Racial Discrimination, 1966, and International Convention on the Suppression and Punishment of the Crime of Apartheid, 1973.

[21] See note 17 above, p. 32, paras. 33–4.

[22] Buchheit, *Secession*, 221–2.

[23] Ibid. 45.

states chose to recognize Biafra during the period when it was able to oppose the unionist desire of the Nigerian federal government.[24] As a result of the military success of the Nigerian government early in 1970 and the surrender to representatives of the Nigerian federal government of the Biafran army's chief of staff, the Republic of Biafra ceased to exist. This removed the need for further inquiry into the legitimacy of secession of Biafra.[25]

The case of Bangladesh, on the other hand, is unique among the separatist movements for the reason that it is an example of a successful secession and is likely to have a precedential effect on future claims. East Pakistan lay more than one thousand miles away from west Pakistan, on the other side of India. Although both regions of Pakistan shared the common bond of Islam, they had ethnographic dissimilarities, as well as economic disparity. The east was more densely populated but its per caput income was lower than that of the west. In March 1971, when violence erupted in east Pakistan followed by civil disobedience, the armed forces of west Pakistan commenced a brutal campaign to suppress the secessionist tendencies in the east. As a result of this, the provisional government of Bangladesh in exile (in India) reaffirmed in April 1971 their leader Sheikh Mujib's declaration of independence 'in due fulfilment of the right of self-determination'.[26] An open war between India and Pakistan, which broke out in December 1971, secured Bangladesh's independence from Pakistan. In the debates before the Security

---

[24] The first to do so was Tanzania on 13 Apr. 1968, followed by Gabon, the Ivory Coast, Zambia, and Haiti. Most of the declarations announcing the granting of recognition stressed the ferocity of the Nigerian/Biafra conflict and saw little basis for a future political unity of the country: Ijalaye, 'Was "Biafra" at Any Time a State in International Law?', 65 *American Journal of International Law* (1971), 551, 553–4.

[25] According to Ijalaye, 'it is difficult to establish that Biafra attained statehood in international law' (ibid. at 559). Another commentator has interpreted the same set of circumstances as justifying the belief that the 'factual conditions constituting the basis of independence and sovereignty . . . were present in Biafra'. (C. Okeke, *The Expansion of New Subjects of Contemporary International Law Through Their Treaty-making Capacity* (Rotterdam, 1973), 165).

For a comparison of effects of Katanga and Biafra secessions, see Buchheit, *Secession*, 173–6.

[26] Documents: Civil War In Pakistan, 4 *NYU J. of International Law and Politics* (1971), 524, 559.

Council, the Indian representative expressed the belief that, where a mother state has irrevocably lost the allegiance of such a large section of its people as represented by Bangladesh and cannot bring them under its sway, international law recognizes that conditions are suitable for that section to come into being as a separate state.[27] Bangladesh is now widely recognized by members of the world community and occupies a seat in the United Nations.

### 3. IS SELF-DETERMINATION A LEGAL RIGHT OR A POLITICAL PRINCIPLE?

To say that self-determination is a political principle implies that individual states ought to recognize it within their internal management and, at most, that the international community can use pressure of its opinion to move states in this direction. On the other hand, to say that self-determination is a legal right invests the beneficiaries (peoples) with a right independent of their governing states, which can indeed be exercised in opposition to those states. In this context, self-determination, like individual human rights, warrants continuing international protection. The present task of the international community, under this latter view, is to be more specific regarding the kind of 'peoples' who can legitimately invoke this right.

The use of the word 'right' instead of 'principle' in resolutions arising out of the organs of the United Nations is not the only criterion to justify characterization of self-determination as a legal right. This is due to the sometimes indiscriminate and interchangeable use of the words 'right' and 'principle'. One can also notice an amalgamation of these words in some phraseology. Brownlie has combined the phrases 'political principle' and 'legal right' to give his opinion that self-determination is at present a 'legal principle'.[28]

---

[27] UN SCOR, 1611th meeting (1971), 13, para. 124. At the same meeting the Pakistan representative, feeling bitter about Indian support for the secession, said: 'There will not be a Bangladesh only in Pakistan. There will be a Bangladesh everywhere. We will see to it that it is not only in Pakistan.' Ibid. at 21, para. 192.

[28] *Principles of Public International Law*, 2nd edn. (Oxford, 1973), 577.

In the first instance, the 'principle/right' dispute arose over the meaning of the United Nations Charter's use of 'self-determination', especially in article 1, paragraph 2. The English text refers to the 'principle of equal rights and self-determination of peoples', whereas the French text speaks of respect for the 'principe de l'égalité de droits des peuples et leur droit à disposer d'eux-mêmes' (literally, the principle of equal rights of peoples and their right to self-determination). With an ambiguity thus apparently enshrined in the Charter, the field was left open for the inevitable combat of juristic commentators. Some argue that self-determination is not a legal right but a political one.[29]

On the other hand, a growing number of jurists have accepted the status of self-determination as a right within the law of the United Nations. In addition to the large number of resolutions emanating from the United Nations which employ the 'right' terminology, the International covenants on human rights and the 1960 Declaration on the Granting of Independence to Colonial Countries and Peoples can be seen as supporting this viewpoint, even though the parameters of the right are not as yet clearly defined. Rosalyn Higgins, for example, concludes from her study of the United Nations practice that it 'seems inescapable that self-determination has developed into an international legal right'. Nevertheless, she is quick to point out that the extent and scope of the right is still open to some debate.[30] Lee C. Buchheit, after examining the debates in the Special Committee of Friendly Relations and the Sixth Committee of the General Assembly which produced the Declaration of Friendly Relations, states:

The United States and the United Kingdom recommended terminology stressing the 'principle of equal rights and self-determination of peoples' which was countered by a joint draft submitted by ten Third World nations which spoke of 'the inalienable right to self-determination'. The phraseology adopted in the declaration in paragraph 1

---

[29] See e.g. J. H. W. Verzijl, *International Law in Historical Perspective* (Leyden, 1968), 324; R. Emerson, *From Empire to Nation* (Boston, 1970), 307, and *Self-Determination Revisited in the Era of Decolonization, Occasional Papers in International Affairs No. 9* (Cambridge, Mass., 1964); and L. C. Green, *International Law Association Report of the 47th Conference* (London, 1956), 58.

[30] R. Higgins, *The Development of International Law Through the Political Organs of the United Nations* (Oxford, 1969), 103.

clearly favours the view that self-determination is in fact a right and not merely a political principle.[31]

## 4. APPLICATION OF THE PRINCIPLE TO 'PEOPLES'

The most important aspect of the principle of self-determination is its application to the 'people' of a specific territory. In this context, self-determination implies the right of such people to choose their own political organization. Such a right, in view of its close connection with fundamental human rights, is to be exercised by the people of the relevant unit without coercion and on the basis of equality.[32] In this connection self-determination can result either in the independence of the self-determining unit as a separate state, or in its incorporation into or association with another state on a basis of political equality for the people of the unit.[33]

To characterize self-determination as a collective right possessed by peoples raises awkward theoretical problems because of the difficulty of defining the concept of a 'people' and drawing a clear distinction between that and other similar concepts. Self-determination is a right of 'peoples', in other words, of a specific type of human *community* sharing a common desire to establish an entity capable of functioning to ensure a common future. It is 'peoples' as such which are entitled to self-determination. Under contemporary international law, minorities do not have that right. 'People' and 'nation' are two closely related concepts; they may be one and the same, but they are not necessarily synonymous. Modern international law has deliberately attributed the right to 'peoples', and not to 'nations' or 'states'. However, when 'people' and the 'nation' are one and the same, and when a 'people' has established itself as a

---

[31] *Secession*, 90–1.

[32] J. Crawford, *Creation of States*, 102–3.

[33] Ibid. 103. Cf. Principle VI of Annex to General Assembly res. 1542 (XV), cited with approval in the *Western Sahara* opinion, ICJ Reports 1975, 12, and 32. This principle is also inherent in para. 4 of the Declaration of Friendly Relations, which provides that the establishment of a sovereign independent state, the free association or integration with an independent state or the emergence into any other political status constitute modes of implementing the right of self-determination.

'state', clearly that 'nation' and that 'state' are, as forms or manifestations of the same 'people', impliedly entitled to the right to self-determination.[34] This means that the principle of self-determination can be invoked by a sovereign state to justify its union or integration with another state provided that the self-determining unit can be characterized as a 'people'.[35]

Before a community may legitimately claim to be a 'self' and therefore be entitled to the process of 'determination', there are some criteria which it should possess. One of these is a group identity and distinctness from the ambient population.[36] The criteria of 'selfness' could include elements of a religious, historic, geographic, ethnologic, economic, and linguistic character. As a convenient example, the Permanent Court of International Justice in the *Greco-Bulgarian 'Communities'* case identified a 'community' as an object possessing both objective and subjective distinctness. A community they thought, is 'a group of persons living in a given country or locality, having a race, religion, language and traditions of their own, and united by the identity of such race, religion, language and traditions in a sentiment of solidarity'.[37] Lee C. Buchheit states that a simple satisfaction of such conditions is not enough. Such an empirical approach to the problem tends to ignore the immeasurable factors that together constitute the psychopolitical realities in a given situation that must influence a decision regarding

---

[34] Study prepared by Hector Gros Espiell, *The Right of Self-determination: Implementation of United Nations Resolutions*, E/CN.4/Sub.2/405/Rev.1 (1977), 9, para. 56.

[35] The question arises whether a state which is made up of two distinct 'peoples' can integrate with another state against the wishes of the other 'people' within the self-determining state, or whether, in such a situation each 'people' should exercise the right separately.

Dr Galo Plaza, one time UN Mediator in Cyprus, in para. 143 of his Report submitted to the Secretary-General on 26 Mar. 1965 (S/6252) evaded the above issue over the Cyprus problem. According to Dr Plaza, if Cyprus should become 'fully independent' by being freed from the 1960 treaty limitations it would automatically acquire at the same time the right of self-determination. He acknowledged in para. 135 of the Report that the Greek Cypriots had coupled their aspiration for 'unfettered independence' with the demand for the right of self-determination, the purpose and result of the exercise of which would be to realize union (*Enosis*) with Greece.

[36] Buchheit, *Secession*, 10–11, and 229.

[37] 1920 PCIJ ser. B. No. 17, 33.

legitimacy of the exercise of self-determination.[38] The author also states that in a claim for secessionist self-determination, it seems inescapable that the claimant group must occupy a distinct territory which is likely to be a viable independent entity.[39] However, these requirements for the exercise of self-determination are not necessarily identical with those traditionally needed for statehood.[40]

## 5. INTEGRITY OF STATES AND SELF-DETERMINATION

Paragraph 7 of the Declaration of Friendly Relations, in spelling out the principle of self-determination, reaffirms the need to preserve the territorial integrity of sovereign and independent states, but ties this concept to the requirement that the state must be 'possessed of a government representing the whole people belonging to the territory without distinction as to race, creed or colour'.

The principle of self-determination cannot be construed as authorizing or encouraging any action which would dismember or impair, totally or in part, the territorial integrity or political unity of sovereign and independent states.[41] However, the same paragraph implies that not all states will enjoy this inviolability of their territorial integrity, but only those 'conducting themselves in compliance with the principle of equal rights and self-determination of peoples as described above and thus possessed of a government representing the whole people belonging to the territory'. Furthermore, the territorial integrity that is to be respected must be real and not merely a legal fiction.[42]

The principle prohibiting secession from the territory of a sovereign state is subject to the condition that there must be a

---

[38] *Secession*, 11.          [39] Ibid. 229.

[40] Ibid. 230. The criteria of statehood are usually defined as: people, territory, government, and capacity to enter into international relations: see, *Texas* v. *White* (1868) 74 US (7 Wall.) 700, and article 1 of the Montevideo Convention of 1933, League of Nations Treaty Series, vol. 165, 19.

[41] This clause reaffirms para. 6 of the Declaration on the Granting of Independence to Colonial Peoples: GA res. 1514, 15 UN GAOR, Suppl. 16, 66; UN Doc. A/4684 (1960).

[42] Report referred to in n. 34 above, 6, para. 44.

representative government of that state, representing the whole of the people belonging to the territory.

Lee C. Buchheit states that paragraph 7 of the declaration seems to recognize, for the first time in an international document of this kind, the legitimacy of secession under certain circumstances.[43]

The clause safeguarding the integrity of states subject to their having a representative government is a direct descendant of the belief repeatedly expressed in the writings of Locke, Jefferson, and Wilson that the legitimacy of government derives from the consent of the governed, and furthermore that consent cannot be forthcoming without the enfranchisement of all segments of the population.[44] One of the main themes developed in the writings of John Locke was that when sovereign power had been unlawfully exceeded, or where the legislative power assumed tyrannical character, then by virtue of 'a law antecedent and paramount to all positive Laws of men', an individual or a body of a people has a natural right of resistance.[45]

Thomas Jefferson, the principal draftsman of the American Declaration of Independence, believed in the dignity and wisdom of the average man and the inherent right of men to resist overreaching sovereigns. 'Every man', Jefferson wrote, 'and every body of men on earth possess the right to self-government. They receive it with their being from the hand of nature.'[46]

As the end of World War I came into sight, United States President Wilson began to propagate his image of a world order that would regulate the peacetime conduct of nations and prevent the outbreak of future wars. The first step in this process would be the establishment of a just peace, a peace without retribution and founded on a universal respect for the principle of self-determination.[47]

[43] *Secession*, 92.

[44] Ibid. 93.

[45] *Two Treatises of Government, The Second Treatise* (P. Laslett edn., Cambridge, 1960), paras. 133, 168, 255. For a discussion of Locke's thinking on the right to rebellion, see generally, J. Dunn, *The Political Thought of John Locke* (London, 1969), 165–86 .

[46] *The Writings of Thomas Jefferson* (A. Bergh edn., Washington, 1905).

[47] *The Messages and Papers of Woodrow Wilson* (A. Shaw edn., New York, 1924), 475.

Turning once again to secession and integrity of states, concepts which stand in contradiction to one another, the various shades of juristic opinion are studied in Lee C. Buchheit's work.[48] Rosalyn Higgins, despite her belief in the legal nature of the right to self-determination, nevertheless thinks, at the present stage of international law and relations, that 'self-determination refers to the right of a majority within a generally accepted political unit to the exercise of power. In other words, it is necessary to start with stable boundaries and to permit political change within them.'[49]

On the other hand, U. Umozurike argues that secession can be legitimated in some circumstances, primarily as a method of redress for the violation of human rights. He says:

There is no rule of international law that condemns all secession under all circumstances. The principle of fundamental human rights is as important, or perhaps more so, as that of territorial integrity. Neither a majority nor a minority has the legal right to secede, without more, since secession may jeopardize the legitimate interests of the other part. . . . [A] majority or minority accorded its normal democratic rights cannot legally request the international community to help it to secede.[50]

It seems that at present international jurists lack even the rudimentary consensus required to decide the legitimacy of secession and that the problems are rarely susceptible to juridical solutions.

## 6. DIFFERING VIEWS AS TO THE APPLICATION OF THE PRINCIPLE IN CYPRUS

The Greek and Turkish Cypriots hold completely opposite views on practically all issues relating to the application of the principle of self-determination in Cyprus.

[48] *Secession*, 131–7.
[49] *The Development of International Law Through the Political Organs of the United Nations* (Oxford, 1969), 104.
[50] *Self-determination in International Law* (Hamden, Conn., 1972), 199. Cf. I. Delupis, *International Law and the Independent State* (Epping, 1974), 17: 'A right to secession must be enjoyed before independence is reached. The right to secede must therefore be enjoyed only by certain fairly consolidated groups of people, which to themselves and to the world appear to be emerging "nations".'

The Turkish view is that the right to self-determination was exercised in 1960 jointly by the two communities which were recognized as co-founders of the bi-communal Republic of Cyprus.[51] This argument stems from the fact that independence was not granted as a mere unilateral act on the part of the United Kingdom, but was the consequence of the conclusion of a number of treaties between Cyprus, the United Kingdom, Turkey, and Greece. The representatives of the two communities signed the relevant documents so that sovereignty derived from both of the communities conjointly, irrespective of their numerical size.

The purpose of the 1963 Greek Cypriot coup against the Constitution of Cyprus was to give the Greek Cypriots a monopoly of political power, and to relegate the Turkish Cypriot community, equal co-founders of the Cypriot state, to the status of a mere minority.[52]

As the Republic of Cyprus had undertaken by treaty not to amend the basic articles of its Constitution, the unilateral amendment of these provisions[53] in 1963 and during the following years was not simply an internal matter of the Republic of Cyprus, but was a matter of international law stemming from the Treaty of Guarantee. In such a situation it was the duty of the guarantor powers (Great Britain, Greece, and Turkey) to refuse to recognize the *de facto* situation created as a result of that violation.[54] In view of this, Turkey refused to recognize the Greek Cypriot government as the government of the Republic of Cyprus[55] while the two other guarantor powers, as well as other states, did so.

As a result of the intercommunal hostilities of 1963 the 'state of affairs' envisaged by the treaties of Establishment, Guarantee, and Alliance which gave birth to the Republic, came to an end. However, the treaties themselves remained in force and the

[51]  Speech of Ambassador Coşkun Kırca, the Permanent Representative of Turkey, to the UN Security Council, S/PV 2498 of 17 Nov. 1983, 27.

[52]  Ibid.

[53]  Art. 182 of the Constitution provides that the basic articles thereof, set out in Annexe III thereto, which have been incorporated from the Zurich Agreement of 11 Feb. 1959, cannot be amended, whether by way of variation, addition, or repeal.

[54]  Ambassador Kırca's speech (n. 51 above), 26.

[55]  Ibid. 27–8 and 36.

Republic of Cyprus as a legal entity continued to exist. Turkey, as well as the Turkish Cypriots, recognize the existence of the Republic of Cyprus, but they recognize no existing organ as legally or legitimately representing this state in international relations. In the view of Turkey and the Turkish Cypriots, the administration of the Greek Cypriots, which presents itself as the government of Cyprus, represents only the Greek community. The affairs of the Turkish Cypriot community are managed by their own administration and only Turkish Cypriot leaders are competent to represent this community.[56]

Only the two communities together are competent to bring about a negotiated solution which will lead to the regeneration and restructuring of the institutions of the Republic of Cyprus. There are references to the two 'communities' in a number of United Nations resolutions. The General Assembly has always encouraged the continuation of the talks between the two communities in the search for a solution of the Cyprus problem. For instance, the General Assembly resolution 33/15 of 9 November 1978 calls for urgent resumption in a meaningful and constructive manner of the negotiations under the auspices of the Secretary-General between the two communities and for these 'to be conducted freely on an equal footing'. The Secretary-General has many times expressed the conviction that the intercommunal talks present the best available means for achieving an agreed, just, and lasting settlement of the Cyprus problem.[57] Since in Cyprus there are two national communities which agreed in 1960 to found an independent republic, and which must negotiate together for the purpose of rebuilding and rehabilitation, one of these communities cannot enjoy the privilege of forming a government and exercising the right of self-determination to the exclusion of the other.[58] The intercommunal negotiations have been conducted on the basis that they are not to prejudice the claims of the two sides. Consequently

[56] Ambassador Kırca's speech before the UN General Assembly, A/37/PV 120 of 17 May 1983, 43. The two communities hold their elections separately on separate electoral rolls.
[57] See e.g. Secretary-General's Reports to the Security Council about UN operation in Cyprus, S/14778 of 1 Dec. 1981 para. 56 and S/15182 of 1 June 1983 paras. 60, 61, and 63.
[58] Mr Kırca's speech referred to in n. 51 above, 36.

this process does not of itself imply the recognition of the political status of one side by the other, but it does indicate that the sovereignty of the future federal republic of Cyprus will derive from the communities, who by joining the federal republic, will be exercising the right to self-determination.

The recognized Greek Cypriot government, not unnaturally, opposes all the above views. In its view, the argument that the Turkish Cypriot community in the area can exercise the right to self-determination is doubly fallacious. 'First', says Mr Moushoutas, the Greek Cypriot Permanent Representative of Cyprus to the United Nations, 'it is a distortion of this lofty principle, embodied in General Assembly resolution 1514 (XV), which is to be exercised by a people as a whole, and not on the basis of factional, religious, communal, or ethnic criteria'. The second leg of the argument is that the Turkish Cypriots cannot exercise such a right on a part of the territory of Cyprus, on which they have all along been but a small minority, while the large majority—80 per cent—has been expelled and supplanted by 'the Turkish military occupying forces'.[59] He goes on to say that in Cyprus, as in so many other countries, there are people of more than one ethnic background. If the right to self-determination could be applied to a community within a state, 'it would dismember every state and nation on the face of this earth, including Turkey'.[60]

A recent publication by the Greek Cypriot Press and Information Office, entitled *Self-determination and the Turkish Cypriot Minority*, elaborates further the Greek Cypriot view on the matter. It says the Turkish Cypriots are a 'minority' whose rights have not been denied. The independence Constitution of 1960 remains in force and there is a 'standing offer to the Turkish Cypriot community that they return to their rights under that Constitution'. The publication repeats the argument that the present situation on the ground is the result of 'illegal use of force by Turkey' and that because of the 'Turkish invasion', no 'lawful or adequate expression of political will can take place in that area'.[61]

[59] Security Council, S/PV 2503 of 15 Dec. 1983, 12.
[60] Security Council, S/PV 2454 of 15 June 1983, 10.
[61] Pp. 4–5.

The argument that the Turkish Cypriots are a 'minority' and not a 'people' implies the existence of a nation.[62] In Cyprus no Cypriot nation exists, as stated by the first President of the Republic, Archbishop Makarios—namely that 'the Cyprus Agreements of 1960 established a state but not a nation'.[63] As a corollary to this, both of the co-founders described as 'communities', are to be treated as 'peoples'. If one of the 'communities' qualifies as a 'people', so must the other.

On this point Ambassador Kırca says:

The Turkish community of Cyprus is not an ethnic minority. It is an organized political community, and the Constitution of 1960 acknowledged the right of equal participation in the state machinery of decision-making. . . . In any given country there can be citizens of different racial and ethnic origins. That is indeed the case in most modern states. These citizens must be satisfied with enjoying human rights on an equal footing, or else, for special reasons, certain rights of certain ethnic categories of citizens may be guaranteed by means of a minority status.

In Cyprus the model chosen was none of these, but a different model. That of co-founding communities of the state. That particular model is not for export. But other states, concerned with their own problems, need not seek to export to and impose on Cyprus their own model by becoming the advocates of a usurping Greek Cypriot administration.[64]

The fact that there is no single representative government in Cyprus but two exclusive administrations, as recognized by section 5 of the Geneva Declaration of 30 July 1974 issued jointly on behalf of the governments of Greece, Turkey, and the United Kingdom,[65] adds force to the Turkish view. After the disruption in 1963 of the constitutional order, virtually all the ties of government and administration between the two

---

[62] Letter of Mr Rauf R. Denktash, President of the Turkish Republic of Northern Cyprus, which appeared in the *Washington Post* of 2 Dec. 1983.

[63] Statement published in the *Cyprus Mail* of 28 Mar. 1963.

[64] UN Security Council, S/PV 2498 of 17 Nov. 1983, 37–8.

[65] HMSO, Misc. No. 30 (1974), Cmnd. 5712. At the first round of negotiations at Geneva 25–30 July 1974 Cyprus was not represented. When the second round was convened on 9 Aug., the representatives of the two communities were also present and the representative of the Greek Cypriot community stated that his administration completely subscribed to the Geneva Declaration in question.

communities became severed, the resistence of the Turkish Cypriots assumed the characteristics of a national liberation movement and two separate and self-governing entities emerged.

As regards the allegation of 'occupation', Turkey and the Turkish Cypriots say that Turkey intervened under the Treaty of Guarantee[66] when there was a *coup d'état* in Cyprus in 1974 against the government of Archbishop Makarios, which was inspired by Athens and spearheaded by the Greek army officers in Cyprus. 'It was not the Turkish Army that invaded Cyprus in 1974,' says Ambassador Kırca, 'it was the Greek army that did so.'[67] He quotes from the address of Archbishop Makarios before the UN Security Council on 19 July 1974, describing the effects of the coup: 'the events in Cyprus do not constitute an internal matter of the Greeks of Cyprus. The Turks of Cyprus are also affected. The *coup* of the Greek junta is an invasion, and from its consequences the whole people of Cyprus suffers, both Greeks and Turks.'[68]

In the view of Turkey and Turkish Cypriots, the question of Cyprus did not begin in 1974 but in 1963. Turkey's action in 1974 did not create the problem of Cyprus but was designed to help to solve it according to the terms of those international arrangements that originally gave birth to the Republic of Cyprus as an independent state.[69]

As to expulsion and displacement of the Greek Cypriot population by the 'Turkish military occupying forces', Turkey refers to the agreement for regrouping of populations (1975) which was fully implemented on a voluntary basis, under United Nations auspices.[70]

Voting at the organs of the United Nations tends to be influenced by considerations of expediency rather than the

[66] A Parliamentary Select Committee of the United Kingdom House of Commons, in its report published on 8 Apr. 1976, did not accept the argument that the Treaty of Guarantee was a dead letter. It reported that Britain had an obligation to intervene, had the military capacity so to do, but did not intervene for reasons which the government refused to give.

[67] General Assembly, A/37/PV 120 of 17 May 1983, 46.

[68] S/PV 1780, 21.

[69] Ambassador Kırca's speech before the UN General Assembly, A/37/PV 120 of 17 May 1983, 46.

[70] See ch. 4, n. 41, above.

merits of any given dispute[71] and the above problems are rarely susceptible to juridical solutions.

## 7. CONCLUSIONS

There is a growing realization that self-determination is going through a process towards acquiring legal status as a principle that can be invoked to secure decolonization of peoples under foreign domination. This is because the world community has generally accepted the undesirability of colonization. Outside the sphere of colonization and apartheid, self-determination can be construed as a principle of international social ethics only, with some legal and political overtones. But, the Declaration of Friendly Relations conceives the principle in universal terms. It requires every state, be it colonial and racist or neither, to conform to the principle and it designates any people (whether under colonial domination or not) as the beneficiary.

There seems to be a reluctance to accommodate claims to separatist (secessionist) self-determination, due to fear on the part of most independent states that such a principle would constitute an unmanageable threat to the internal order of states and consequently have an adverse effect upon the stability of the international system. Therefore, the internal merits of a separatist attempt have to be balanced against the justifiable concern of the international community before a decision can be reached as to legitimacy. Secessionist attempts are usually viewed with suspicion by states which have ethnic populations within their territories and their reactions to such attempts are to some extent influenced by domestic factors. However, as a

---

[71] Nancy Crawshaw, 'Cyprus: A Failure in Western Diplomacy', in *The World Today*, Feb. 1984, 73–8, 78. Miss Crawshaw's view is that the Western powers must bear some responsibility for the consolidation of partition. Had they treated the Greek and Turkish administrations as integral components of one state, in the spirit of the bi-communal provisions of the 1959 Zurich Agreement, the trend towards separation could have been contained and the chances of a settlement based on eventual reunification facilitated. Instead they followed the procedure adopted by the UN in 1964 in recognizing the Greek Cypriot administration as the only government representing Cyprus, thus pushing the Turkish Cypriots into isolation, as a result of which a *de facto* separate state evolved by passage of time.

result of developments in conventional law and stands taken on
the occasion of the secession of Bangladesh (and, to a lesser
extent, Biafra) and in view of the recent resolutions of the UN
General Assembly which attribute the right of self-determination to the Palestinian people, it can be said that, under certain
circumstances, the international principle of self-determination
can be invoked as the basis for legitimate secession.

A balance has to be struck between the principle of integrity
of states on the one hand, and the merits of a claim to self-
determination on the other. It may be reasonable neither to
uphold the integrity of a state when it no longer satisfies the
fundamental purposes of a political association, nor to sanction
parochialism for the sake of parochialism.

In examining the implications of the declaration of statehood
by the Turkish Cypriots in November 1983, which was
supported by 87,928 signatures of the adult population, one is
faced with a *sui generis* situation. The developments recounted in
Chapter 4, section 8, indicate that at the time of the
proclamation Turkish Cypriots were already organized as a
'federated state' in their territory in north Cyprus. The
government of the federated state exercised *de facto* sovereignty
and control over its people to the exclusion of the recognized
'Government of Cyprus', that is, the Greek Cypriot government. There was, and still is, a *de facto* line dividing the north and
south sections of Cyprus. The federated state looked forward to
the creation of a federal republic of Cyprus to be composed of
the Greek Cypriot and the Turkish Cypriot regions. But until
such time the federated state exercised full control and
sovereignty over its people. Negotiations had been going on
between the two sides on and off since 1975, under the auspices
of the UN Secretary-General, for the creation of a federal
republic of Cyprus. The two sides had reached agreement for a
federal solution of the constitutional aspect and a bi-zonal
solution of the territorial aspect of the problem.[72] Under the
circumstances, declaration of statehood meant that the Turkish
Cypriots were making a choice as to their political organization,
which would now be in a position to ask for international

[72] UN Secretary-General's opening statement at the resumed session of the
intercommunal talks on 9 Aug. 1980 (UN Doc. A/35/385-S/14100).

recognition. This was an important step in the process of political and administrative evolution, but not a 'secession', or 'unilateral declaration of independence', in the true sense of the words. Such terms imply a breakaway from an omnipotent exclusive government that exercises effective control over the whole territory under its sovereignty. In Cyprus, at the material time, with the geographical separation of the two ethnic peoples and their respective governments, there was not a single exclusive government. Moreover, the declaration states that the Turkish Cypriot community considers itself bound by the treaties which gave birth to the Republic of Cyprus and stipulates that the newly created entity will not unite with any other state, except with the southern unit to form a federal republic of Cyprus.[73]

The overriding principle of respect for territorial integrity of states is subject to their being possessed of representative governments. Furthermore, the territorial integrity that is to be respected must be real and not merely a legal fiction. The Republic of Cyprus, as envisaged by the 1960 Constitution, had ceased to be a political association of the two communities.[74]

Another interesting aspect of the declaration of statehood in north Cyprus is that this move does not purport to be a final political solution of the Cyprus problem. The instrument of statehood clearly says that the Turkish Republic of Northern Cyprus looks forward to, and even aims at facilitating, the establishment of a federal republic of Cyprus on the basis of equality and double-sovereignty. The Turkish Cypriot point of view is that a federation can be formed by the voluntary will of two equal self-governing units, and that the declaration of statehood attempts to elevate the negotiating status of the Turkish Cypriot unit to that of the Greek Cypriot.[75] With this in mind, the proclamation of statehood, a manifestation of the right to self-determination, reserves for the Turkish Cypriot

[73] The text of the declaration of statehood is included in UN Doc. A/38/586-S/16148 of 16 Nov. 1983.

[74] See ch. 2, above.

[75] The need for equality of the units of a federation is underlined in a UN study, dated 16 Jan. 1968, which contained a suggestion in para. 56 that the Turkish Cypriot administration, as it then was, declare its independence for a pledged duration of 24 hours prior to joining a bi-communal federation.

people the right to exercise it once more, this time in favour of creating a federal republic of Cyprus.[76] In other words, statehood is not attained as a final exercise of self-determination. It may be exercised again in favour of a federal republic to be established by mutual agreement.[77]

[76] Especially in a bi-communal country, federation means a mutually accepted voluntary link between two different national communities, each exercising on an equal footing the right to self-determination.

[77] Self-determination is not a static right. The vicissitudes of international life justify the taking of such a view. It is dynamic also in the sense that it always exists as the basis for the expression of free will by a sovereign people determining at any moment its internal or external political status and deciding how to pursue its economic, social and cultural development. More to the point in this regard is the wording of the text of the eights principle of the decalogue of principles of the Helsinki Final Act of 1975.

# 10

# Statehood and After

## I. REACTIONS TO DECLARATION OF STATEHOOD

### The United Nations

At the request of the United Kingdom, Cyprus, and Greece, the Security Council considered the situation in Cyprus during four meetings held on 17 and 18 November 1983.

Mr Denktash, the President of the Turkish Republic of Northern Cyprus, went to New York to explain to the Security Council why the Turkish Cypriot people, in the exercise of their right to 'self-determination', had decided to put 'a roof of statehood' over themselves.[1]

During the meeting of the Security Council on 17 November, the UN Secretary-General stated before the Council that the move by the Turkish Cypriot side was, in his view, 'contrary to the resolutions of the Security Council on Cyprus and at variance with the high-level agreements of 1977 and 1979'. He added that such a move would adversely affect the situation in the island and complicate his efforts aimed at promoting an agreed, just, and lasting settlement. He reiterated, however, his determination to continue such efforts and he appealed to the

---

[1] United Nations press conference on 17 Nov. 1983 and his speeches at the Security Council, S/PV 2498 of 17 Nov. 1983, 3–22 and S/PV 2500 of 18 Nov. 1983, 52–63. In order to show that he was still prepared to discuss some practical measures, Mr Denktash made an offer, on 17 Nov. 1983, relating to Varosha and the Nicosia international airport. (A/38/594 of 21 Nov. 1983). The Turkish Cypriot side declared its readiness to engage immediately in negotiations with the Greek Cypriot side within the framework of the good-offices mission of the UN Secretary-General on the following subjects:

    (a) The establishment of an interim administration in Varosha under the auspices of the United Nations.

    (b) The reopening of Nicosia international airport for civilian traffic under an interim United Nations administration.

parties to exercise restraint and to refrain from any action that might further aggravate the situation.[2]

On 18 November, the Council adopted resolution 541 (1983),[3] in which it deplored the declaration of the Turkish Cypriot authorities for the 'purported secession' of part of the Republic of Cyprus, considered that declaration as legally invalid and called for its withdrawal; called for the urgent and effective implementation of its resolutions 365 (1974) and 367 (1975); requested the Secretary-General to pursue his mission of good offices in order to achieve the earliest possible progress towards a just and lasting settlement in Cyprus; called upon the parties to co-operate fully with the Secretary-General in his mission of good offices; called upon all states to respect the sovereignty, independence, territorial integrity, and non-alignment of the Republic of Cyprus; called upon all states not to recognize any Cypriot state other than the Republic of Cyprus; called upon all states and the two communities in Cyprus to refrain from any action which might exacerbate the situation; and requested the Secretary-General to keep the Security Council fully informed.

The Turkish view about the Security Council resolution was expressed by Ambassador Kırca. The proclamation of statehood could not be regarded as null and void. That decision was taken in accordance with the principle of self-determination in order to re-establish the state of affairs laid down in the basic provisions of the Constitution as envisaged in the Treaty of Guarantee, and as a means of remedying the continuous usurpation by the Greek community of the title 'Government of the Republic of Cyprus'. In his view, the Council would have done better to recognize the legal truth and declare null and void the illegal amendments made unilaterally by the Greek Cypriot community to the basic and unalterable provisions of the 1960 Constitution, in violation of that Constitution and of the Treaty of Guarantee. Therefore Turkey had to reject the relevant paragraph of the draft resolution. He said emphatically, 'since there can be no question of the Turkish community's revoking its proclamation of independence, it would be

---

[2] S/PV 2497.

[3] See Appendix 4. The resolution was passed by a vote of 13 in favour and 1 against (Pakistan), with 1 abstention (Jordan).

absolutely unthinkable for Turkey to withdraw recognition of the Turkish Republic of Northern Cyprus'.[4]

Commenting on the relevant paragraph of the draft resolution which considered the Turkish Republic of Northern Cyprus to be 'invalid', Mr Denktash said, 'it [the Security Council] considered China non-existent for 30 years and East Germany non-existent for 25 years. It does not matter; they are now here among us, and I greet them with respect.'[5] He continued to say,

We are not seceding from the independent island of Cyprus, from the Republic of Cyprus, or will not do so if the chance is given to us to re-establish a bizonal federal system. But if the robbers of my rights continue to insist that they are the legitimate Government of Cyprus, we shall be as legitimate as they, as non-aligned as they, as sovereign as they in the northern State of Cyprus, but we shall keep the door wide open to re-establishing unity under a federal system.[6]

The UN Secretary-General had meetings with Mr Kyprianou on 18 and 22 November, with Mr Denktash on 19 November, and with Foreign Minister Türkmen of Turkey also on 19 November to discuss the Cyprus situation. On 17 November, the Secretary-General had had a meeting with Foreign Minister Haralambopoulos of Greece and further discussions with the Permanent Mission of Greece on 21 November. In all these contacts the Secretary-General strongly urged all concerned to observe the provisions of resolution 541 (1983) in all its aspects. On his part, the Secretary-General expressed his determination to pursue his mission of good offices and he drew the attention of the parties to the provision of the resolution by which the Council called upon them to co-operate fully with the Secretary-General in that mission.[7]

However, the main criticism that can be made about the

---

[4] S/PV 2500 of 18 Nov. 1983, 31. Turkey recognized the new republic on the same day it was proclaimed. The reasons for recognition are to be found in the statement of the Turkish Foreign Ministry of 15 Nov. 1983, which was circulated as UN Doc. A/36/602 of 23 Nov. 1983.

[5] S/PV 2500 of 18 Nov. 1988, 61.

[6] Ibid. 61–2.

[7] Secretary-General's Report to the Security Council of 1 Dec. 1983 on the United Nations operation in Cyprus: S/16192, para. 57.

Security Council resolution 541 (1983) is that even though it expressed support for the intercommunal talks[8] it could be interpreted as having at the same time laid down a condition for their resumption, namely the withdrawal by the Turkish authorities of the declaration of statehood.

The United Kingdom representative said that the draft resolution, which reflected the views of his government, was directed at the deplorable action of the Turkish Cypriots, but it did not purport to deal with the whole problem of Cyprus. 'We all know', he said, 'that the present action by the Turkish Cypriot authorities is not the only wrong of one kind or another that has been done since the Treaties were signed in 1960.' In his view, it was just as necessary as before to make every effort to bring the two sides together.[9]

The author's view is that Security Council resolution 541 (1983) wrongly treats the declaration of statehood as 'secession' and wrongly assumes that there is a representative government in Cyprus and that that government is the Greek Cypriot administration. Moreover, it may be argued that the Security Council, by declaring that it considered the creation of statehood as 'legally invalid', acted as a court of law, in spite of the provisions of article 36(3) of the UN Charter that legal disputes are, as a general rule, to be referred to the International Court of Justice.

### The guarantor powers

Greek and Greek Cypriot leaders condemned the Turkish move and said that they would make every effort to neutralize the action and to see that it was revoked. Mr Kyprianou was quoted by the *New York Times* of 17 November 1983 as having said that while Mr Denktash wanted a bi-zonal federation, a unitary state was what Cyprus needed. Mr Kyprianou was thereafter involved in extended diplomatic efforts around the world to gather international support for his government's position.

---

[8] By requesting the Secretary-General to pursue his mission of good offices in order to achieve a just and lasting settlement and by calling for the urgent and effective implementation of its resolutions 365 (1974) and 367 (1975).

[9] S/PV 2500 of 18 Nov. 1983, 39–40.

Greek anger at the declaration of independence is reflected by a resolution adopted on 17 November, addressed to the Council of Europe as well as to the European Parliament and the United Nations, appealing to 'all states to refuse any support or recognition for the international existence of this pseudo-republic, to denounce this act of provocation and to exert pressure to force its annulment'.

The Athens daily *Ethnos* of 24 November 1983 reported the following statement by the premier of Greece, Mr Andreas Papandreou:

> Our Cyprus policy can be summarized as follows: we can only negotiate for a unitary Cyprus. For us neither federation nor confederation is an acceptable solution.[10] So, what do we propose? Our proposal is for the establishment of a unitary state. We can negotiate on this after the departure of the Turkish soldiers.

On the other hand, Turkey's initial official statements expressed surprise at the declaration of statehood. Coming only days after the first Turkish parliamentary elections since the military took power in 1980, the move occurred when Turkey was in an unusual interregnum between the rule of President Evren and the shared power of Evren and the new Prime Minister.

In the statement of Turkish recognition of the Turkish Republic of Northern Cyprus,[11] Foreign Minister Türkmen said his government would have preferred a solution through the intercommunal process. Nevertheless, the Turkish Cypriot side could not be held responsible for the fact that the negotiations, which had already lasted nine years, had failed to bring about a solution. In view of the elements which had formed the basis for the setting up of the Cypriot state in 1960 and of the principles enshrined in the Charter of the United Nations, it was incontestable that the Turkish Cypriot people enjoyed the right

---

[10] This supports the argument of the Turkish Cypriot side that non-progress at the intercommunal talks was due to a lack of political will of the Greek Cypriot side for reaching a federal solution as envisaged by the high-level agreements and underlined by the UN Secretary-General in his opening statement of 1980 and the Waldheim evaluation paper of 1981. (See letter dated 9 Dec. 1983 of Mr Denktash to the UN Secretary-General, UN Doc. A/38/765-S/16227).

[11] Issued on 15 Nov. 1983 and circulated as UN Doc. A/36/602 of 23 Nov. 1983.

of self-determination as much as the Greek Cypriots. The fact that the holding of negotiations between the two communities had been approved by the international community was an important element confirming the validity of this point. The statement also mentioned that the Turkish government had taken particular note of the peaceful and conciliatory stand of the Turkish Cypriots, who had stated that independence does not necessarily mean that the island will remain divided forever and that they are determined not to unite with any state, unless it be in a federation with the Greek Cypriots.

As for the reaction of Great Britain, one of the other guarantor powers of the Constitution of Cyprus, the British Foreign Secretary said in Parliament that his government deplored the action taken by the Turkish Cypriot community. The British representative at the United Nations stated before the Security Council that the Council should forthwith adopt a clear and measured resolution. He went on to say:

We recognize only one Cypriot State, the Republic of Cyprus under the Government of President Kyprianou. The Turkish action is incompatible with the state of affairs brought about by the Treaties governing the establishment of the Republic of Cyprus. My Government has treaty obligations in this respect which we share with the Governments of Greece and Turkey. It is not only our position in the context of the Treaties of 1960 which specially involves Britain in this problem. We are also concerned because of our long historical links with Cyprus, continuing into the present with our mutual membership of the Commonwealth and with the settlement in Britain of many Cypriots from both communities.[12]

The United Kingdom, sponsor of the UN Security Council resolution, also proposed a 'tripartite' meeting of the three guarantor powers (UK, Greece, and Turkey) to try to defuse the tension. Turkey welcomed this proposal while emphasizing that it would have been better if the UK had followed this procedure

[12] S/PV 2500 of 18 Nov. 1983, 38. The above view is based on the assumption that the 'state of affairs' created by the Treaty of Establishment and guaranteed by the Treaty of Guarantee still exists. The author's view is that the treaties themselves are valid, but the 'state of affairs' which they envisaged, that is, the bi-communal Republic, came to an end in Dec. 1963 when the Turkish Cypriot co-founder partner was ousted from the organs of the Republic, as a prelude to amending the 1960 Constitution by unconstitutional means and to establishing a purely Greek Cypriot administration.

in the first place, instead of resorting to the Security Council. A spokesman for the Greek Cypriot government stated that Cyprus was concerned with the effective functioning of the Treaty of Guarantee,[13] but it was clear that there was an open disagreement between Mr Kyprianou and the Greek premier, Mr Papandreou, on the question of a tripartite conference.[14] The latter preferred a 'bipartite' system of consultations with Great Britain who would carry on parallel consultations with Turkey. A rift developed between the two leaders which necessitated the intervention of the Greek President, Mr Karamanlis.

Meanwhile, the Cyprus communist AKEL party's political bureau, in a statement before the divergence erupted, said that AKEL opposes any 'tripartite or five party or any other conference outside the UN framework'. The socialist EDEK party leader, Dr Lyssarides, also expressed himself against a tripartite conference and said that there should be a 'repositioning' of the Cyprus problem with stress on the demand for withdrawal of Turkish troops.[15] On the other hand, the *Simerini* newspaper criticized Mr Papandreou for not responding to the British suggestion for such a conference.

The London *Times* of 7 December 1983 reported that at the Athens European Community Summit Mrs Thatcher and Mr Papandreou 'were too tired and too concerned to discuss in detail Britain's proposal for tripartite consultations'.

The suggested conference never succeeded in getting off the ground.

### Commonwealth Conference

Shortly after the UN Security Council resolution, the Commonwealth Summit Conference (of 48 heads of state or government)

---

[13] Soon after the 1963 hostilities Archbishop Makarios declared that the Agreements were dead and buried. The Greek Cypriot Attorney-General also stated in a publication of 1977 that the obligation of the Treaty of Guarantee 'to keep unalterable in perpetuity the constitutional structure and order' purports to deprive Cyprus of one of the 'fundamental requirements of a state as an integral person, internal independence and territorial supremacy'. He elaborated this point by saying that art. IV of the treaty conflicts with customary international law and with art. 103 of the UN Charter.

[14] *Cyprus Mail* of 27 Nov. 1983: 'Reports Confirmed'.          [15] Ibid.

held in New Delhi endorsed, on 29 November 1983, the UN Security Council resolution calling upon the Turkish Cypriots to withdraw their declaration, and requested all countries to withhold recognition. The Commonwealth leaders also set up a five-nation group to work with the United Nations to try to solve the crisis.

## The Council of Europe

The Parliamentary Assembly of the Council of Europe, by its Recommendation 974 of 23 November 1983, rejected the 'unilateral declaration of independence of the northern part of Cyprus' and demanded the immediate withdrawal of the 'occupying Turkish troops' as an indispensable condition for the final solution of the Cyprus crisis.

The 73rd session of the Committee of Ministers held on 24 November 1983, to which the above Recommendation 974 was addressed, anticipated the débâcle of the Athens Summit (European Council) of the Ten to the extent that, for the first time, no final communiqué was issued. A resolution on Cyprus was, however, adopted, but, in the absence of unanimity, it could not be made public or even communicated to the Assembly. According to press reports, an amendment proposed by Switzerland, which, like Recommendation 974, called for an independent Council of Europe effort, to complement (and not to contradict) the initiative of the United Nations Secretary-General, failed because of abstentions to secure the absolute majority (11 votes) needed for adoption. Six countries voted against.

The Baumel report about the situation in Cyprus,[16] which was unanimously adopted by the Political Affairs Committee on 10 January 1984, could not be considered by the Parliamentary Assembly in its February 1984 session but was instead adopted by the Standing Committee on 21 March 1984, acting on behalf of the Assembly.[17] The resolution deplored the 'illegal declaration' by the leaders of the Turkish Cypriot community, described it as a secession of a part of the Republic of Cyprus,

---

[16] Doc. 5165 of 13 Jan. 1984.
[17] Resolution 816.

stressed that the Council of Europe as such cannot disinterest itself from this crisis, and decided to give effect without further delay to the intention, already expressed in Recommendation 974, to make contact, through its Bureau and the competent committees, with leaders of the states and communities concerned in order to do all in their power to promote a reconciliation and the necessary search for a just and lasting solution.[18]

In May 1984 the Parliamentary Assembly of the Council of Europe ratified the credentials of two Greek Cypriot parliamentarians (one Representative and one Substitute) to represent the Parliament of Cyprus at the Parliamentary Assembly, even though this would not be entirely satisfactory, for one of the two communities which constitute the state of Cyprus would not be represented.[19] The decision was taken upon the recommendation of the Committee on Rules of Procedure.[20] One Representative's seat and one Substitute's seat are still reserved for the Turkish Cypriot community. By this resolution the Assembly

[18] The Baumel report concedes in para. 15 that, in the words of Recommendation 974, 'the Constitution of 1960 has "unfortunately been imperfectly applied for 20 years" '. This paragraph concludes as follows: 'The prospects for the Turkish minority in the island, in their own eyes and in those of many impartial observers, was that of permanent second class citizenship. In the words of Mr. Denktash in his statement before the U.N. Security Council: "In a hellenistic paradise no Turkish birds are asked to sing" '.

[19] Since Cyprus joined the Council of Europe in 1961, the Cypriot delegation to the Assembly had comprised two Representatives and two Substitutes appointed by the Greek Cypriot MPs and one Representative and a Substitute appointed by the Turkish Cypriot MPs.

After the events of 1963/64, when the Parliamentary Assembly met on 20 April 1964, it was presented with credentials for three Greek Cypriot Representatives and three Greek Cypriot Substitutes, which gave rise to objections on the ground of unconstitutionality. Reference was made to art. 73(4) of the Cyprus Constitution, which provided that parliamentary committees had to be constituted in the same proportions as Parliament itself with regard to reprsentation of the Greek and Turkish communities, namely 70%:30%. Cyprus was not represented at the Parliamentary Assembly till 1984, because the Assembly refused to accept a parliamentary delegation representing only one of the two communities of Cyprus. Such a partial representation would be incompatible with the principle of the 'rule of law' embodied in art. 3 of the Statute of the Council of Europe and with the principles laid down in the preamble thereof.

[20] Butty Report, Doc. 5215 of 7 May 1984.

changed its long-established democratic practice of not accepting an 'incomplete' or 'partial' representation from Cyprus. In
fact, there had been no 'common' or 'representative' Parliament
in Cyprus since 1964 and the situation had not changed in 1984
to justify such a change of practice. The 'reserved' or 'vacant
seat' formula is also open to criticism because it allows an
'unrepresentative' Parliament to represent its country at the
Parliamentary Assembly. This device also raises legal complications because only Parliaments of member states can be
represented at the Assembly and not Parliaments of national
communities which constitute the population of a particular
state. By keeping 'vacant' the seat of the Turkish community of
Cyprus the Assembly is deemed to have tacitly acknowledged
that the Greek Cypriot representative taking his seat in the
Assembly represents only his community and not the Turkish
Cypriot community.

After the parliamentary elections in south Cyprus which were
held on 8 December 1985, in a letter of 25 February 1986
addressed to the President of the Parliamentary Assembly, the
Representative of the Turkish Cypriot community in Brussels
objected to a one-sided representation of Cyprus at the
Assembly because the newly elected Greek Cypriot House of
Representatives could not represent the whole of Cyprus and
because it was not the House of the bi-national Republic of
Cyprus as envisaged by the 1960 Constitution. The validity of
the credentials of the Greek Cypriot Representative was also
contested by some members of the Parliamentary Assembly, as a
result of which the final decision on the matter was deferred. In
the mean time some parliamentarians signed a petition urging
the Council of Europe to study urgently the practical possibilities of elected representatives of both communities attending
plenary sessions and relevant committees of the Assembly to
'enable a genuine dialogue to take place within the only
democratic, international forum embracing all countries of
Western Europe'.[21]

However, the Assembly did, during its 38th ordinary session,
adopt, on 28 January 1987, the report of the Committee on
Rules of Procedure[22] suggesting validation of the credentials of

[21] Doc. 5609 of 22 July 1986.
[22] Doc. 5675 of 16 Jan. 1987, as amended on 27 Jan. 1987.

the 'Cyprus delegation' (a Greek Cypriot Representative and a Greek Cypriot Substitute) for the remainder of the 38th session, that is, up to 4 May 1987.[23] In spite of the outcome, the objection to the credentials has once more drawn attention to the unsatisfactory nature of provisional formulae as to representation of Cyprus before a mutually agreed settlement of the Cyprus problem has been reached. These proceedings have also shown that the Greek Cypriots may not be able to rest on their laurels for good.

## 2. DENKTASH PROPOSALS

On 2 January 1984 Mr Denktash, the President of the Turkish Republic of Northern Cyprus, announced a series of goodwill measures designed to settle some of the outstanding issues between the two communities.[24] Included among these were proposals to turn over a defined sector of the city of Varosha and the Nicosia international airport to an interim United Nations supervision and administration. The Turkish side made it clear that holding of negotiations on these issues would be without prejudice to the respective positions of the two sides with regard to each other's political status.

As regards Varosha, the Turkish Cypriot side proposed to place under United Nations administration the sector to the east of Dherinia road and extending in the south up to the Greek Cypriot forward defence line of the Varosha area as defined in the Turkish Cypriot map of 5 August 1981. The question of Greek Cypriot resettlement in the area defined should be considered, as stipulated in point 5 of the 1979 Denktash–Kyprianou summit agreement, simultaneously with the beginning of negotiations for a comprehensive settlement without awaiting the outcome of the discussions on other aspects of the Cyprus question.

On the question of the Nicosia international airport, the Turkish Cypriot side reiterated its proposal as to the reopening

[23] Doc. AS(38)CR 20. On 5 May 1987 the Assembly validated the credentials of the Greek Cypriot delegation.

[24] The text of the proposals was circulated as a UN Doc. under reference No. A/38/770-S/16246.

of the airport to civilian traffic under an interim United Nations administration for the benefit of the two sides, without insisting that the airport be administered by the parties themselves on the basis of equality.

In order to finalize the humanitarian issue of missing Turkish and Greek Cypriots, the Turkish side proposed that the Committee on Missing Persons, set up in 1981, be reactivated in accordance with the 'terms of reference' agreed to between the two sides.[25] These proposals also included a framework of principles that should guide the relations of the two sides and the common ground on which their actions should be based in order to facilitate progress towards a final settlement of the problem.

The framework included a series of confidence-building measures. The two sides should refrain from hampering each other's interests in the fields of trade, tourism, and communications, both sides should benefit equally from all economic assistance provided for Cyprus, and an economic and technical commission should be set up to study the question of co-operation between the two sides in the areas of trade, tourism, municipal problems, water supply, etc. It was also proposed that the two sides should consider joint endeavours in the cultural field to promote a better understanding between the younger generations, in particular to promote the teaching of Turkish and Greek as a second language respectively, to co-

---

[25] After these proposals were submitted, the Committee's first working session began on 2 May and further meetings were held on 7, 10, and 14 May. The Committee is composed of a Greek Cypriot member, a Turkish Cypriot member, and a third member designated by the International Committee of the Red Cross and appointed by the Secretary-General with the agreement of both sides.

The number of Turkish Cypriot missing persons is 800 (600 cases were added after 1974). The number of Greek Cypriot missing persons cases stands at 1,600.

When the Committee resumed its work in 1985, 168 cases had been submitted to it, 60 of which were Turkish. These cases are at different stages of investigation. The basic reason for the deadlock in the Committee's work is the difference of approach. The Turkish Cypriot side, basing itself on the 1950 Chicago Convention, is inclined to accept a person to be dead if there is no proof of that person being alive for five years after his disappearance. The Greek Cypriot side does not regard the case as closed until the circumstances of a person's disappearance have been established. Another difficulty is that the people who witnessed these tragic events are not inclined to give evidence.

operate in higher education, to study the feasibility of setting up a joint university, and to organize scientific and cultural joint meetings. Furthermore, both sides should agree to refrain from all kinds of provocation and undertake to refrain from the threat or the use of force; they should agree that their respective leaders meet under the auspices of the United Nations Secretary-General to discuss the process of steadily moving towards federal arrangements, and call upon Turkey and Greece to encourage and assist their efforts in search of a negotiated settlement on the basis of the 1977 Denktash–Makarios agreement, the 1979 Denktash–Kyprianou agreement, the 1980 'opening statement' of the UN Secretary-General, and the 1981 UN 'evaluation document'.[26]

The United States administration welcomed these proposals as a 'movement' in the right direction.[27] On the same day the proposals were made, the government of Turkey announced its intention to withdraw 1,500 Turkish troops from Cyprus.

On 6 January the Greek Cypriot government dismissed the overtures of Mr Denktash as propaganda aimed at misleading international opinion.[28]

### 3. KYPRIANOU 'FRAMEWORK'

Five days after rejecting the proposals of Mr Denktash, that is, on 11 January 1984, Mr Kyprianou presented to the United Nations Secretary-General a document containing a 'framework' of proposals for the comprehensive settlement of the Cyprus problem.

According to newspaper leaks,[29] the document comprised six

[26] See ch. 6, s. 2, s. 5, s. 6 and s. 9, above.
[27] President Reagan's periodic report to Congress on Cyprus, which was released by the Office of the White House Press Secretary on 24 Jan. 1984.
[28] Mr Kyprianou presented to the UN Secretary-General on 11 Jan. 1984 written observations setting out the reasons for his government's rejection of the Turkish Cypriot proposals: *Cyprus Mail* of 13 Jan. 1984.
[29] Mr Kyprianou discussed the 'framework' with American officials and Western leaders including British Prime Minister Mrs Thatcher and the main points thereof appeared in the London *Guardian* in Jan. The Athens paper *Nea*, in its issue of 26 Jan., gave the full text of the document. The Greek Cypriot government disclosed the text of the 'framework' officially on 4 May 1984.

sections in the following order:

1. Demilitarization: the 'framework' proposed complete demilitarization of the island and withdrawal of all troops and disbanding of all security forces including the National Guard and the Turkish Cypriot forces.

2. An international force under UN auspices with troops from countries not involved, to supervise peace and security.

3. International guarantees with interested countries barred from the guarantee treaty.

4. A genuine federal republic.

5. Territory: Mr Kyprianou had already told Mr Perez de Cuellar on 30 September that the Greek Cypriots could agree to Turks retaining 23 per cent of the land but, for the sake of helping things, that could be raised to 25 per cent, provided Famagusta and Morphou (previously inhabited mostly by Greeks), reverted to Greek Cypriot control and administration.

6. Constitution: such as not to lead to deadlock.

(a) Executive authority: maintenance of the presidential system of the 1960 Constitution with a Greek Cypriot President, a Turkish Cypriot Vice-President, and a Council of Ministers comprising 70:30 representation of Greeks and Turks.[30]

(b) Legislature: one single chamber is preferable. Alternatively a lower chamber with the two communities represented according to population and an upper chamber in which representation would depend on the powers and functions of the chamber.

(c) Justice: equal representation of the two communities in the federal Supreme Court.

(d) Power of federal government and the government of the constituent parts: the federal government to have authority over external affairs, passports, external communities, international communications, natural resources, etc.

(e) Human rights including freedom of movement, settlement, and ownership to be safeguarded.

(f) Finances: the federal government to have powers to ensure equal opportunities and living standards for all the population.

[30] No number of ministers is mentioned.

Mr Kyprianou made it clear, however, that there could be no direct negotiations unless the Turkish Cypriots first withdrew the declaration of statehood,[31] a condition which the Turkish Cypriots could not, and cannot, accept. Putting forward such a condition did not augur well for the future of the intercommunal talks and cast doubts on the practicality, or even the sincerity, of such conditional proposals.[32]

The Greek Cypriot daily *Simerini* of 21 January described Mr Kyprianou's proposals for international guarantees to replace the present treaty guarantees as 'naive' and 'nonsensical'. The paper said the proposals introduced the Soviet Union into the scene and this was bound to tie the hands of the Americans whose assistance was sought. It also said that a UN Force as a guarantee for the security of the Turks was not practical in the eyes of many because they were either against the dispatch of such forces, or would only accept them for a limited period. Another Greek Cypriot paper *Agon* of the same date argued that the idea concerning the revision of guarantees had not pleased the UN Secretary-General either, and that the 'framework', instead of getting things out of stagnation, might well lead to worse developments. In an editorial commentary, the same paper referred to the comment of the London *Guardian* of 19 January to the effect that the Kyprianou 'framework' was very similar to the American Plan of 1978. According to the commentator, if this was so the Greek Cypriots deserved 'commiseration' because the five years since the American Plan was presented had been lost in vain.

[31] Press releases of 6 and 12 Jan. 1984, issued by the Cyprus High Commission in London, and *Cyprus Mail* of 20 Jan. 1984.

[32] Greek Cypriot daily *Simerini* of 14 Jan. 1984 in its editorial, said that the 'President and the government' again acted in an amateurish way, putting 'the horse behind the cart' by demanding that the 'framework of settlement' be conditional on the revocation of the Turkish Cypriot declaration of independence. See also the *Cyprus Mail* of 26 Feb. 1984: 'Attitude unchanged'. The Greek Cypriot government reiterated that it stood by its decision that any top-level meeting between the two Cypriot leaders must be preceded by the revocation of separate independence. The communist AKEL party, in a statement, said that the resumption of talks or a top-level meeting could not imply recognition of 'secessionist proclamation in the north'. The AKEL party's paper *Haravgi*, in its editorial of 7 Mar. 1984, said that the Greek Cypriot side had everything to lose and nothing to gain by making revocation a condition for the resumption of the intercommunal talks.

Speaking before the Security Council on 3 May 1984, Mr Denktash said that the UN Secretary-General gave him only the gist of the 'framework' when they met on 16 January at the IVth Islamic Summit Conference in Casablanca, but the proposals could not be given to him in full.[33] When he asked the Secretary-General why he was not given the full text the answer was, 'I know that you would reject it totally, and it is not my purpose to give parties what they will reject; I try to find something that they could accept. That is why I did not give it to you.'[34]

### 4. MAKING THE CONSTITUTION OF THE NEW STATE

After the declaration of statehood on 15 November 1983,[35] the Legislative Assembly was convened on 2 December and heard an address by Mr Denktash, the President of the Turkish Republic of Northern Cyprus. At that session the Assembly decided by a majority vote of 26 to 14 to set up a Constituent Assembly,[36] composed of 40 members of the Legislative Assembly of the Turkish Federated State of Cyprus, 19 representatives of unions, professional bodies, and some small

[33] S/PV 2531, 53.

[34] In his report to the Security Council of 1 May 1984 (S/16519, 3) the Secretary-General says that when he met Mr Denktash in Casablanca he provided him with a summary of the Greek Cypriot 'framework', on which subject they had a discussion.

[35] The declaration was published in Suppl. IV, Part II of the *Official Gazette* No. 88 of 15 Nov. 1983.

[36] Although the Assembly had adopted its resolution of 15 Nov. by unanimous vote, the resolution setting up the Constituent Assembly was taken by a majority. The move to set up the Constituent Assembly was criticized by the Communal Liberation Party (11 seats) and the Republican Turkish Party (6 seats). These two political parties believed that the then existing Assembly was competent to prepare the constitution of the new state. The Communal Liberation Party filed at the Supreme Constitutional Court a petition for annulment of the said resolution (Constitutional Court appl. No. 34/83), which was rejected by decision of the court on 27 February 1984 mainly on the ground that the resolution which was being challenged for unconstitutionality was itself of constitutional force having precedence over ordinary legislation. Moreover, deputies belonging to the applicant political party had themselves already taken the oath of office and accepted without reserve to work as members of the Constituent Assembly.

political parties that had no representation in the Assembly, one person to be appointed by the former Vice-President of the Republic of Cyprus (Dr Fazil Kutchuk), and 10 persons to be appointed by the President.[37]

The task of the Constituent Assembly would be to draft the constitution of the new republic and also to function as a legislative assembly until general elections were held, but it was not tied down to a programme. The resolution setting up the Constituent Assembly provided that the Constitution of the Turkish Federated State of Cyprus should remain in force subject to the provisions of the instrument of statehood. References to the 'Turkish Federated State of Cyprus' in that constitution should be read as references to the 'Turkish Republic of Northern Cyprus'. Mr Denktash said that the projected constitution would retain the parliamentary system, but he believed that the President should be given more power.[38]

The Constituent Assembly held its first meeting on 6 December 1983, during which members were sworn in.

The first government of the new republic under Prime Minister Nejat Konuk took office on 13 December.[39]

A Constitutional Commission composed of a chairman and 14 members was set up by a decision of the Constituent Assembly taken at its meeting of 23 December 1983. The Commission began its work on the constitution as from its first meeting, held on 31 January 1984.

It is interesting to note that a large number of members of the Constituent Assembly belonged to political parties or groups.

It was announced on 11 April that the tentative date for a referendum on the Constitution to be drawn up by the Constituent Assembly would be 19 August and that general elections were planned to be held on 4 November. By its resolution of 17 April 1984 the Constituent Assembly called

[37] The decision providing for the composition of the Constituent Assembly and certain other related issues was published in Suppl. IV, Part II of the *Official Gazette* No. 98 of 3 Dec. 1983.

[38] Local papers and the *New York Times* of 3 Dec. 1983.

[39] To pave the way for the work of the Constituent Assembly, Mr Mustafa Çagatay, the Prime Minister of the Turkish Federated State, resigned on 29 Nov. 1983 but the ministers continued in a caretaker role until the interim government was formed.

upon its President to make all the necessary arrangements to enable the holding of general elections on 4 November 1984, as previously announced.[40]

The Constitutional Commission prepared the draft constitution which was published in the *Official Gazette* of 8 June 1984 for public notification.[41] The public were invited to communicate their views and suggestions on the draft within a certain time limit which expired on 16 July 1984.

The Turkish Cypriot side, however, showed goodwill in delaying the making of its constitution, the holding of a referendum thereon, and the holding of general elections till after the failure of the 'proximity talks'.[42] The Constitution of the Turkish Republic of Northern Cyprus will be considered elsewhere.[43]

## 5. ESCALATION OF TENSION

At a speech at Iannina on 21 February 1984, the Greek premier said that Athens would not tolerate any 'further advances by the Turkish army'.[44] This was followed by reports of a Greek military build-up in southern Cyprus. Some reports said that Greece would dispatch a division of 15,000 men to Cyprus if Mr Kyprianou so requested.[45] According to the *Cyprus Mail* of 8 March 1984, informed sources in Nicosia said that the Greek Cypriot government admitted strengthening its defences, but described this as a normal defensive posture constituting no threat to Turkish Cypriots in the north.[46] As the tension grew, Mr Kyprianou went to Athens for talks with the Greek premier which covered a full review of the policy so far followed and the reinforcements of the island's defences. The joint communiqué

[40] Suppl. IV, Part II of the *Official Gazette* No. 40 of 20 Apr. 1984.
[41] *Gazette* No. 57, Suppl. I, Part II.
[42] See ch. 11, below.
[43] See ch. 12, below.
[44] ANA news agency report of 22 Feb.
[45] The first reports appeared in the twice-monthly *Enimerosis* of 3 Mar. and the weekly *Kyrikas* of 4 Mar. 1984. These were picked up by the Greek and Turkish Cypriot press: See e.g. the Greek Cypriot press summary of the *Cyprus Mail* of 9 Mar. 1984.
[46] 'Island Crisis Deepens'.

issued at the end of the talks on 10 March 1984 stated that the two men reached conclusions on 'a series of actions and measures', but did not specify what these were.[47] The *Turkish Daily News*[48] reported that the *Vima* and *Eleftherotipia* newspapers of Greece had confirmed published reports that Greece and Greek Cypriot leaders 'have signed a defense agreement' which the papers called 'a continuation of the 1960 Guarantee Agreements'.

In the atmosphere of mounting tension Mr Denktash proposed a non-aggression pact between his government and the Greek Cypriot side. The Greek Cypriot government described this as a 'ploy' for recognition. The spokesman said that Denktash's suggestion in itself presupposes the existence of two states.[49]

An incident of 7 March 1984 in the Aegean, when Turkish warships on exercise allegedly fired against a Greek destroyer, grew into a short-lived crisis with the recall of the Greek ambassador from Ankara. Athens accused Ankara of deliberately firing at one of its destroyers. The crisis subsided when Greece reversed her decision to recall her ambassador following a satisfactory Turkish explanation. Turkey denied that ships engaged on aerial gunnery practice had fired on a Greek vessel.

Turkey's Parliament debated the reported build-up of Greek troops in the southern part of Cyprus. The parliamentary resolution of 8 March declared that Turkey wanted to live in peace with Greece but she was determined to take all necessary measures against attempts to jeopardize the region's security, to upset the balance of power in Cyprus, or to threaten the security of Turkish Cypriots.

The Constituent Assembly of the Turkish Republic of Northern Cyprus also debated the question of the military build-up in south Cyprus and the Aegean crisis. The Assembly passed a resolution on 13 March 1984 calling for resumption of talks 'without conditions' between the two peoples of Cyprus, stressing that no disturbance of the balance of power in Cyprus can be tolerated. The resolution also stressed that peace in Cyprus and a just and viable solution to the Cyprus problem can

[47] *Cyprus Mail* of 11 Mar. 1984.
[48] 9–15 Mar. 1984.
[49] *Cyprus Mail* of 29 Feb. 1984.

only be found through the intercommunal talks by the
establishment of a bi-zonal federation based on the partnership
of the two equal communities.[50]

On 6 March 1984 a subcommittee of the US Congress voted
to cut the 1985 military aid to Turkey by 39 million dollars
despite the Reagan administration's warning that the move
could jeopardize talks to resolve the Cyprus crisis. The US
Senate Foreign Relations Committee voted on 29 March 1984
to withhold 215 million dollars of military aid to Turkey until
Ankara agreed to place the Varosha sector of Famagusta under
UN auspices.[51] In Athens the suspension of the aid to Turkey
was seen as easing the superficial tension between Athens and
Washington on the eve of extensive talks between US Defence
Secretary Caspar Weinberger and Greece's socialist leader. A
Greek spokesman hailed the Senate Committee decision as a
'clear political message to Turkey'.[52]

On the other hand Mr Denktash sharply criticized the
decision as 'fundamentally undermining' the peace initiative of
the UN Secretary-General and said there could be no
connection between American aid to Turkey and the question of
Famagusta. He also said that the Turkish side had no property
for sale.[53] In Washington, Turkey's ambassador criticized
moves by Congress to cut aid to his country because of the
Cyprus dispute, saying Greek American lobbyists were trying to
'turn Congress into an anti-Turkish propaganda arena'. He
went on to say: 'this ill-conceived approach will hamper, not
strengthen, current initiatives under way to start negotiations'.
Referring to the decision of the Committee, the Turkish Prime
Minister Turgut Özal said: 'If they have tied the aid to
concessions on Cyprus, then they are dreaming.'[54]

On 17 April 1984, there took place an exchange of
ambassadors between Turkey and the Turkish Republic of
Northern Cyprus, as already planned. The Turkish ambassador
in Nicosia presented his credentials to President Denktash, and

---

[50] *Official Gazette* No. 29 of 15 Mar. 1984, Suppl. IV, Part II.
[51] However, the Senate Appropriations Committee did not include a
similar condition in its decision of 26 June 1984 concerning aid to Turkey.
[52] As reported in the *Cyprus Mail* of 30 Mar.
[53] Turkish Cypriot newspapers of 3 Apr.
[54] As reported in the *Cyprus Mail* of 31 Mar.

at the same time the representative of the Turkish Republic of Northern Cyprus in Ankara presented his credentials to President Kenan Evren. Official announcements said that this was a normal diplomatic event which followed Turkey's recognition of the Turkish Republic of Northern Cyprus.

The announcement of a referendum on the Constitution and general elections later in the year, as well as the exchange of ambassadors, in themselves not very serious events, provided a pretext for the Greek Cypriot side, in consultations with Athens,[55] to have recourse to the UN Security Council. At the same time, the Greek Cypriot side announced that it was postponing indefinitely the intercommunal talks and withdrawing its interlocutor, Mr Mavrommatis, who would be returning to his former post of Director-General of the Foreign Ministry. Mr Moushoutas, the Greek Cypriot Permanent Representative at the UN, submitted his government's request on 30 April 1984 for a session of the Security Council. Mr Moushoutas said that the recent actions of the Turkish side 'worsen the crisis already existing on the island, and pose a most serious threat to international peace and security in the region.'[56] He asked for 'urgent and effective measures in accordance with the relevant provisions of the Charter, for the full and effective implementation of its resolutions in all their aspects'. Not surprisingly, the debate was acrimonious when the Security Council met early in May.

## 6. NEW RECOURSE TO THE UN

The United Nations Security Council debated the situation in Cyprus at its meetings held on 3, 4, 7, 9, 10, and 11 May 1984.

Mr Kyprianou appealed to the Security Council urgently to put an end to the situation. He said the Council must do whatever it can. There was danger to Cyprus and to its very existence. He warned the Security Council not to allow the gradual disappearance of Cyprus as an independent country. In his view, the implementation of its resolutions was the only way

---

[55] Within the previous 4 months Mr Kyprianou had visited Athens 14 times for consultations with the Greek premier, Mr Papandreou.
[56] S/16514.

to ensure a process towards a peaceful evolution that would, in turn, ensure the independence, unity, territorial integrity, and sovereignty of Cyprus, its non-alignment and its continuation as a member of the UN. Mr Kyprianou also stressed that he saw no purpose in meeting Mr Denktash unless the declaration was reversed.[57]

On the other hand, Mr Denktash, whom the Security Council under its rules of procedure had invited to take part in its meetings, stressed that the problem of Cyprus did not start in 1974. The sovereignty, independence, and territorial integrity of the country was attacked by the Greek Cypriot leadership in order to destroy the bi-national character of the state, with a view to annexing it to Greece.[58] Greece was behind this conspiracy. Mr Kyprianou had demanded from the Council the right of the Greek Cypriot majority to decide the destiny of Cyprus. This, naturally, had created a stalemate, and the Turkish Cypriots had declared statehood to break this impasse. Reversal of the present position, by dismantling the Turkish Republic of Northern Cyprus, would mean destroying a living political body, Mr Denktash declared. Why should Greek Cypriots come to the table and talk with Turkish Cypriots when they are treated as rulers of the whole island? Mr Denktash also said that the decision of statehood was not his and that he could not himself reverse it. It was the decision of his people. The making of the constitution and holding of a referendum were all decided on the day independence was declared. He complained that 'each time we establish a missing link of our statehood, we shall be brought here'. In his view, the negotiating process had not been successful because the Security Council continued to treat one of the parties to the problem as the legitimate government of Cyprus even though that party lacked all the

---

[57] S/PV 2531 of 3 May 1984, 6–25.

[58] In a letter addressed to the UN Secretary-General on 26 Oct. 1983 by the Greek representative at the United Nations, which was circulated as Doc. S/16079, it was stated that even though in the 1950s the people of Cyprus were struggling for self-determination, the realization of which might have led to union with Greece, and that Greece supported that anti-colonial struggle, the people and the democratic governments of Greece were now genuinely supporting the independence, sovereignty, unity, and territorial integrity of Cyprus.

fundamentals of legitimate government. He stressed that his side was not destroying anything but trying to prevent the destruction of one of the peoples of Cyprus.[59]

The Security Council adopted resolution 550/84 on 11 May 1984 by thirteen votes to one against (Pakistan), with one abstention (United States of America).[60] Reaffirming its resolution 541 (1983) the Council condemned all 'secessionist actions', including the 'purported exchange of ambassadors' between Turkey and the Turkish Cypriot leadership, declared them 'illegal and invalid' and called for their immediate withdrawal. The resolution reiterated a call upon states 'not to recognize the purported State of the Turkish Republic of Northern Cyprus' and called upon all states to respect the 'sovereignty, independence, territorial integrity, unity and non-alignment of the Republic of Cyprus'. It considered attempts to settle any part of Varosha by people other than its inhabitants as inadmissible and considered any attempts to interfere with the status or deployment of the UN peacekeeping force in Cyprus as contrary to the resolutions of the United Nations. By this resolution the Council also reaffirmed the mandate of good offices given to the Secretary-General and called upon all parties to co-operate with him in his mission of good offices. It also decided to remain seized of the situation with a view to taking, in the event of non-implementation of its resolution 541 (1983) and the present resolution, 'urgent and appropriate measures'.

The Pakistan delegate criticized the draft resolution for not making reference to the resumption of intercommunal talks or to the high-level agreements of 1977 and 1979 which were fundamental to any search for a just settlement of the Cyprus problem. In his judgment it was likely to become yet another obstacle rather than a milestone of progress on the difficult path to intercommunal reconciliation.[61]

Speaking after the vote was taken, the United Kingdom representative said that although he voted for the resolution he did not regard it as ideal; it had several drawbacks.[62] He

[59] S/PV 2531, 26–58.
[60] S/PV 2539.
[61] S/PV 2539 of 11 May 1984, 13.
[62] Ibid. 16.

expressed concern that misinterpretation of it might worsen the situation. He said,

I have voted in favour of the resolution on the understanding derived from the co-sponsors that operative paragraph 8,[63] means that the Secretary-General's mandate set out in Security Council resolution 367 (1975) remains wholly valid. It is our understanding that the Secretary-General has a free hand. He will of course take account of the principles of the Charter and of relevant resolutions, but that is all. The Secretary-General is as free after this resolution as he has always been in the past.[64]

The United States representative said that though his country condemned the exchange of ambassadors between Turkey and the Turkish Cypriot leadership, as well as other announced actions which seek to reinforce the declaration by the Turkish Cypriot authorities of 15 November 1983, they had abstained because 'we also recognize that strong feelings exist among the parties to this issue, and in view of this we seek to avoid any possible exacerbation, even if unintended, of the conflict.'[65]

Mr Denktash, speaking on behalf of the Turkish Cypriot community, said that resolution 541 (1983) was counter-productive from the point of view of peace and could not be accepted. The Council had based the present resolution on it; therefore he could not accept the present resolution.[66]

The Turkish representative said that Turkey had been obliged once again to reject a Security Council resolution on the question of Cyprus. The text of the resolution by no means satisfied the criteria of impartiality, historical objectivity, and a desire to uphold the supremacy of the rule of law. The resolution did not serve the cause of reconciliation and understanding between the two communities of Cyprus. It was based on a fundamentally erroneous concept. It recognized as the govern-

---

[63] Operative para. 8 requested the Secretary-General to undertake new efforts to attain an overall solution of the Cyprus problem 'in conformity with the principle of the Charter of the United Nations and the provisions for such a settlement laid down in the pertinent United Nations resolutions, including Security Council resolution 541 (1983) and the present resolution'. The drawback was that the resolution did not refer to the high-level agreements, the 1980 'opening statement' of the Secretary-General and the Waldheim 'evaluation document' which were fundamental to any search for a settlement.

[64] Ibid. 17.          [65] Ibid. 14–15.          [66] Ibid. 22.

ment of the Republic of Cyprus a team of usurpers who could claim only to represent the Greek Cypriot community.[67]

In short, the Security Council resolution did not give full satisfaction to any of the interested parties. It condemned the 'secessionist actions' and thus displeased Turkey and Turkish Cypriots, but did not go far enough to impose sanctions on Turkey or the Turkish Republic of Northern Cyprus, as had been demanded by the Greek Cypriots.

## 7. THE SECRETARY-GENERAL'S MISSION OF GOOD OFFICES

Within the framework of his good-offices mission entrusted to him by the Security Council in its resolution 367 (1975), and in an endeavour to bring the two sides together, the UN Secretary-General Mr Perez de Cuellar had a meeting in New York with Mr Denktash on 16 March 1984 during which all aspects of the Cyprus problem were discussed. The Secretary-General also met the Greek Cypriot Foreign Minister, Mr George Iacovou, on 19 and 20 March. According to press leaks[68] the Secretary-General pressed Mr Denktash to refrain from asking for recognition of the new republic and not to take steps to consolidate separate independence (that is, to 'freeze' the issue of independence) and requested the handing over of Varosha as a condition to restarting the intercommunal talks.[69] Speaking to reporters at Ercan State Airport on 20 March upon his return to the island, Mr Denktash said that it was the Greek Cypriot side who had left the conference table and that concessions were now being demanded from the Turkish Cypriots to induce the other side to return to the table.

Some sources disclosed that the Secretary-General had in

[67] Ibid. 27.

[68] Greek Cypriot press summary of the *Cyprus Mail* in its issues of 15 and 18 Mar. 1984.

[69] Even before Mr Denktash met the UN Secretary-General, the *Cyprus Mail* reported in its issue of 8 Mar. 1984 that the US Assistant Secretary of State, Richard Burt, had told a congressional committee that cutting aid to Turkey would jeopardize moves over Cyprus and that Denktash would be visiting New York for talks with the UN Secretary-General about Famagusta.

mind a five-point plan which included a top-level meeting between Mr Kyprianou and Mr Denktash. In return for what was demanded of the Turkish Cypriot side, the Greek Cypriots would be required not to resort to international forums and to stop rearmament.[70]

The five-point ideas of the Secretary-General, about which there had been press speculation, were later included in his report to the Security Council.[71] The ideas, described as the Secretary-General's 'scenario', were formulated as follows:

To open the door to a high-level meeting and to the resumption of the intercommunal dialogue, the parties will reach an understanding with the Secretary-General to the effect that as long as he is engaged in the present diplomatic effort:

(a) No further step to internationalize the Cyprus problem will be undertaken, and initiatives now under way will not be pursued;

(b) There will be no follow-up to the 15 November 1983 declaration by the Turkish Cypriots, and initiatives now under way will not be pursued;[72]

(c) Both sides will make reciprocal commitments to the Secretary-General not to increase qualitatively or quantitatively the military forces in the island; they will also agree to a system of verification inspections by UNFICYP;

(d) The Turkish Cypriot authorities will transfer the Varosha area, as delineated in their proposals of 5 August 1981, to the Secretary-General, who will place it under interim United Nations administration, as part of the buffer zone controlled by UNFICYP. The transfer will be effected in phases over a period of (6 to 9) months, to be agreed upon between His Excellency, Mr Denktash, and the Secretary-General and announced at the time of a high-level meeting. The transfer will begin with the area east of Dherinia Avenue extending southward to the existing buffer zone, which will be transferred within two weeks of the coming into force of this plan. The Turkish Cypriot authorities will draw up a calendar for the phased transfer of the remaining portion of the Varosha area to be completed within the (6 to 9) month time-limit indicated and will implement that calendar. The area to be administered by the Secretary-General will become therefore part of the buffer zone, which implies that the process of settlement by the Greek Cypriots will be determined by the Secretary-

---

[70] Soysal's art. in Turkish mainland paper *Milliyet* of 24 Mar. 1984.

[71] S/16519 of May 1984, prepared in pursuance of para. 2 of res. 544 (1983).

[72] According to Turkish mainland paper *Milliyet* of 26 June 1984, the UN Secretary-General was informed by the Turkish side that a referendum on the new constitution and elections would be postponed.

General. It is understood that the area will not revert to the jurisdiction of the Greek Cypriots until a final agreement on a settlement of the Cyprus problem has been reached. No armed personnel other than UNFICYP will have access to this area;

(e) The parties will agree to accept a call by the Secretary-General for the holding of a high-level meeting and to the reopening of the intercommunal dialogue.

In Nicosia, Mr Denktash handed to the Secretary-General's Acting Special Representative a letter dated 30 March addressed to the Secretary-General, in which he requested clarification on the first four points of the scenario.[73] In this letter Mr Denktash asked particularly to know the exact scope of the term 'internationalization', whether it was intended to restrict its meaning to cover only recourse to the UN General Assembly and the Security Council or whether it would also include all other activities in the international arena. As to the suggestion concerning Varosha, Mr Denktash expressed the fear that once the area in question was handed over, before the talks were resumed, 'that area would have been lost for no purpose in so far as a final solutin is concerned, in the event that the talks are not resumed or if they are broken off after resumption'.

On 31 March 1984 the Secretary-General's reply was cabled to Mr Denktash.[74]

On 18 April Mr Denktash submitted his side's response to the Secretary-General's scenario.[75] He presented a set of 'concrete ideas' which he hoped would facilitate working out a common ground for the resumption of the negotiating process. The plan contained the following points:

1. The parties, considering that a summit meeting will be held to reaffirm their determination to promote a just and lasting settlement through direct negotiations, on an equal footing and on the mutually agreed basis, agree:

   (a) Not to take any step whatsoever to internationalize the Cyprus question;

   (b) The Turkish Cypriot side agrees to place the sector to the

[73] The text of this letter is an annexe to the Secretary-General's Report referred to in n. 71 above.
[74] The text of this letter is an annexe to the Secretary-General's above-referred Report.
[75] The text of this letter is also annexed to the Secretary-General's above-referred Report.

east of Dherinia road, as defined in the Turkish Cypriot map of 5 August 1981, under interim United Nations administration;

(c) In the event the Secretary-General reports one year after the present agreement has come into force that the parties have complied with (a) above, then the resettlement by Greek Cypriots of the area under UN administration will commence;

(d) Simultaneously with the beginning of the resettlement process, tourists from third countries will be allowed to use both Turkish Cypriot and Greek Cypriot air and sea ports of their own choice.

2. The parties agree to accept a call by the UN Secretary-General for holding a summit meeting.

3. At the summit meeting a decision will be taken on the date of resumption of the negotiating process for a comprehensive settlement on the existing, mutually agreed basis.

4. Greek Cypriot settlement to the sector to the west of Dherinia road of the Varosha area shall be considered simultaneously with the beginning of negotiations for a comprehensive settlement.

5. The Varosha area will not be placed under the jurisdiction of Greek Cypriots until a final agreement on a comprehensive settlement of the Cyprus problem has been reached.

6. Simultaneously with the beginning of the resettlement process in the sector west of Dherinia road the Greek Cypriot side will take practical measures to promote goodwill and shall lift all restrictions on the Turkish Cypriots.

7. In the event that the Greek Cypriot side does not fulfil its commitment under paragraph 6 above, the interim UN administration over Varosha will come to an end.

8. The parties agree in principle to reopening the Nicosia international airport for civilian traffic under UN administration.

9. The present agreement shall expire five years after it will enter into force, should a final comprehensive political settlement on the question of Cyprus not be reached during that period.

Upon announcement that the Turkish Cypriot community intended to hold a constitutional referendum and elections in

August and November 1984 respectively, the UN Secretary-General sent his Special Representative, Ambassador Hugo Gobbi, to Cyprus to contact the two sides concerning his scenario. He saw Mr Kyprianou on 16 April. Later in the day he saw Mr Denktash and delivered to him a letter from the Secretary-General. The Secretary-General wrote that the intended action by the Turkish Cypriots would tend to prejudice an essential part of the scenario. He appealed to Mr Denktash to respond favourably.[76]

On 11 May, the Security Council adopted resolution 550 (1984).[77] After the adoption of that resolution, the Secretary-General held meetings with Mr Kyprianou on 12 May and with Mr Denktash on 14 May. He continued to be in contact with both sides with a view to exploring ways and means of making progress in the search for a solution to the Cyprus problem.

On 15 June 1984 Mr N. M. Ertekün, the Minister for Foreign Affairs and Defence of the Turkish Republic of Northern Cyprus, submitted to the Secretary-General in New York his side's proposals for the resumption of negotiations. According to newspaper leaks[78] the Turkish Cypriot set of ideas comprised the following points:

1. Talks to start about Varosha based on the map presented by the Turkish Cypriot side on 5 August 1981, the Turkish Cypriot proposals of 17 November 1983 and 2 January and 18 April of 1984.

2. The Turkish Cypriot side undertakes not to change unilaterally the status of Varosha.

3. In order to facilitate the good offices mission of the UN Secretary-General and assuming the Greek Cypriots agree to resumption of the talks, the Turkish Cypriots agree not to raise objections to the renewal of the UNFICYP mandate and its continued stationing in the north.[79]

4. The two sides to undertake not to proceed to any further

[76] The text of this letter is also annexed to the Secretary-General's above-referred Report, see n. 71.

[77] See n. 60, above.

[78] Greek Cypriot newspapers *Alithia* and *Agon* of 24 June and *Kyrikas* of 1 July 1984.

[79] By its res. 553 (1984) of 15 June 1984 the Security Council extended the stationing of the force in Cyprus for a further period ending 15 Dec. 1984 and requested the Secretary-General to continue his mission of good offices.

internationalization of the Cyprus problem and in particular to any international forums where there is no representation of both sides.

5. The abolition of the 'embargo' will remove a major obstacle to a solution.

6. Talks should start for the reopening of Nicosia airport under the UN for the benefit of both sides.

7. A settlement of the Cyprus problem must be based on the equality of the two constituent parts. Such equality need not necessarily be numerical but it should give to the Turkish Cypriot side the opportunity to influence certain decisions.

8. As regards the territorial aspect, the talks must start on the basis of the Turkish Cypriot proposals of 5 August 1981 and the guide-lines agreed at the high-level meeting of 1977 (Makarios–Denktash and the Waldheim evaluations of 1981) with margins for further flexibility.

9. After talks resume the Turkish Cypriot side would be ready to submit detailed proposals on the above.

10. Should the UN Secretary-General deem it proper, the Turkish Cypriot side is ready for a new top-level meeting in which the question of negotiations could be considered and defined. Such a meeting could be made without prejudice to the political status which each side claims for itself.

According to Turkish dailies, the Turkish Cypriot 'ideas' involved three proposals:

1. Transfer to Greek Cypriot control, without any interim UN administration, an area of Varosha for settlement by Greek Cypriots (though the area is not specified).

2. Resumption of talks between the Greek Cypriot side and the Turkish Republic of Northern Cyprus.

3. Restoration of the buildings in Varosha with the 250 million-dollar fund proposed by President Reagan[80] and from funds of the UN before any transfer is made.

Mr Denktash was also reported to have said that if the Greek

---

[80] The US President announced on 8 May his intention to establish a 'Cyprus Peace and Reconstruction Fund' to serve as a positive incentive to the two Cypriot communities in their search for solutions to the country's problems. The Turkish Cypriot leaders welcomed this move but the other side expressed reservation and concern.

Cypriots stop their activities against the Turkish Cypriots and sit at the negotiating table by lifting the economic embargo, then he would freeze the initiatives to get recognition for the Turkish Republic of Northern Cyprus. If the intercommunal talks were sustained and if the Greek Cypriots did not resort to international platforms, the referendum on the constitution and the elections would also be postponed.

According to a disclosure published in the Greek Cypriot daily *Alithia* of 24 June, at a meeting held on 23 June with Greek Cypriot journalists, the spokesman for the Greek Cypriot government gave secret instructions to the journalists to start a press campaign with a view to dispelling the positive atmosphere created by the presentation to the UN Secretary-General of the Turkish Cypriot set of ideas for a solution.[81]

In the pursuit of his mission of good offices, the UN Secretary-General held separate talks with the representatives[82] of the two sides, Mr Mavrommatis and Mr Ertekün, in Vienna, where he presented to them his ideas for the resumption of negotiations. Speaking to reporters after his meeting with the Secretary-General on 7 August, the Greek Cypriot representative Mr Mavrommatis said that the Turkish Cypriot unilateral declaration of independence was the main stumbling block to restarting the talks, thus implying that his side was still insisting on revocation of the Turkish Cypriot declaration of independence.

The Secretary-General's ideas presented to the two sides in Vienna were described as 'working points'. These ideas were not

[81] Mr Glafcos Clerides, leader of the Rally party, confirmed the report and openly criticized the Greek Cypriot government for its negative and destructive attitude. The Greek Cypriot side was concerned that creation of a positive atmosphere could thwart moves aimed at cutting US military assistance to Turkey and exerting pressure on Ankara.

[82] There was some confusion as to whether the talks would be between the 'Government of Cyprus' on the one hand, and the Turkish Cypriot community on the other. Eventually the Secretary-General made it clear that he was inviting the *representatives* of the two sides for talks in Vienna. The Greek Cypriot side reacted by sending Mr Mavrommatis, the former Greek Cypriot negotiator at the intercommunal talks, instead of its Foreign Minister as previously announced. The Turkish Cypriot side was represented by Mr Ertekün, Minister of Foreign Affairs and Defence of the Turkish Republic of Northern Cyprus.

made public but details leaked to local and foreign journalists. They envisaged a plan to reunite Cyprus in a federal system acceptable to both communities. According to Athens press reports quoted in local papers,[83] the 'working points' which should be viewed as an integrated whole, contained suggestions under the headings of (1) political confidence building measures, (2) establishment and development of a governmental structure, and (3) territorial adjustments.

The confidence building measures included proposals for the resettlement of the Varosha area under interim UN administration, a complete moratorium on actions tending to prejudice the Secretary-General's efforts, and the reopening of the Nicosia International Airport under UN interim administration.

As regards the setting up of a central government, the Secretary-General said that it would be imperative to find a proper balance between the equal political status of the two communities, the unity of the country and the functional requirements of a government. He suggested the setting up of working groups on technical matters. The transitional government should come into being after the establishment of the executive and legislative branches and after further territorial adjustments had been agreed upon. These adjustments should include an enlarged version of the areas delineated on the Turkish Cypriot map of 5 August 1981.

According to a report in Greek Cypriot *Simerini* of 19 August, the Secretary-General also requested the two sides to answer the following four questions:

1. Do the two sides agree to discuss the 'working points'?
2. If they do, are they prepared to attend proximity talks under his auspices for the purpose of elaborating the points into a preliminary draft agreement?
3. If the proximity talks succeed, are they prepared to attend a joint high level meeting under his auspices?
4. If so, is the first week of September convenient for the start of talks?

Speaking at Dherinia on 16 August 1984, the Greek Cypriot Foreign Minister deplored pressure on the Greek Cypriot side

[83] *Agon* and *Kyrikas* of 12 Aug. 1984.

for concessions, saying that any further concession would mean 'slow death under the illusion of salvation'.[84] Archbishop Chrisostomos also spoke against accepting the Secretary-General's initiative. A Greek Cypriot spokesman stated that the speech by the Foreign Minister did not amount to comment or criticism of the procedure or substance of the new initiative by the Secretary-General, adding that Mr Kyprianou would be meeting party leaders on 21 August to hear their views.[85] He would also be going to Athens to consult the Greek premier.

The leaders of two of the Greek Cypriot political parties, the communist AKEL and the Rally, requested an urgent extraordinary session of the House of Representatives during the summer recess to discuss the UN Secretary-General's 'working points' before the Athens meeting between Mr Kyprianou and the Greek premier on 29 August. However, the president of the House fixed the date for a session after the Athens meeting, thus giving the impression that the crucial decision would be taken in Athens. This decision of the House president was criticized by the communist AKEL party for being taken in abuse of power. According to AKEL, relations between Athens and Nicosia should be based on the principle that 'Cyprus decides and Greece supports' and that it was unacceptable that the Greek Cypriot political leadership should be committed in advance to a line of policy decided in Athens.[86] On the other hand, Mr Kyprianou was accused by AKEL of reluctance to take a position on the Secretary-General's initiative.[87]

The Greek Cypriot daily *Alithia* of 25 August claimed that the UN Secretary-General proposed to come to Cyprus early in September but was dissuaded or discouraged by Mr Kyprianou

---

[84] *Cyprus Mail* of 17 Aug. 1984.

[85] *Cyprus Mail* of 18 Aug. 1984.

[86] It is important to note also that the Greek Cypriot daily *Haravghi* of 27 Aug. argued that Mr Kyprianou is among those who do not support a federal solution. It said, 'there are some, among them President Kyprianou, who have the impression that the majority of the people do not agree with the policy line of 1977'. This is a reference to the policy drafted during the lifetime of Archbishop Makarios which was expressed in the Greek Cypriot proposals of that year and in the Makarios–Denktash guidelines.

[87] Mr Kyprianou relied on the support of the communist AKEL in Parliament under the so-called 'minimum programme' agreement.

from doing so. The latter intimated that he would himself be going to New York to meet the Secretary-General.[88]

On 31 August 1984 both sides gave their 'positive' responses to the UN Secretary-General's initiatives. This meant that they responded favourably to the four questions asked by the Secretary-General with a view to paving the way to 'proximity talks' under his auspices and that they accepted in principle the proposal to discuss the 'working points'. They were not required to accept or reject the 'working points' themselves which would be open to discussion later. Both sides left it to the Secretary-General to decide when and where he would like the 'proximity talks' to take place. It was also learnt that the former Greek Cypriot negotiator at the intercommunal talks, Mr Mavrommatis, made a reservation to the effect that the Greek Cypriot side did not consider itself bound to implement any agreement on individual 'working points' unless a comprehensive solution was reached. It was known that Mr Kyprianou would seek clarifications about certain points in the proposals of the Secretary-General. Among the most controversial issues were the proposals for a transitional government and Nicosia international airport.

The UN Secretary-General expressed satisfaction with the attitude of the parties. However, the Greek premier, Mr Papandreou, said on 30 August 1984 that there could be no solution 'without the withdrawal of Turkish troops occupying the island'.[89] Mr Denktash retorted by saying that the issue of Turkish troops had not been raised at the intercommunal talks, nor was it relevant in the context of the 'working points'.

Mr Kyprianou expressed his views about the forthcoming discussions in New York at a speech at Pakhna village on 1 September. He said that without securing the fundamental conditions which are essential for the survival of the country, no settlement could be considered because this would mean the commencement of new hardships and adventures. He added

---

[88] The same newspaper pointed out in its issue of 28 Aug. that the UN Secretary-General did not request an acceptance or rejection of the 'working points' themselves but of the procedure he proposed, leaving the rest to be decided during the progress of the negotiations.

[89] It is believed that Greece also has troops in south Cyprus supplementing the Greek Cypriot National Guard.

that he would seek a solution that would take into account the interests of the country and of the people, end the 'occupation', secure the freedom of the whole of the country and of the 'people', and restore their rights that had been trampled upon.[90]

The 'proximity talks' started in New York on 10 September. These talks were crucial in determining whether there was enough ground to encourage the Secretary-General to arrange direct talks between Mr Kyprianou and Mr Denktash. The 'proximity talks' were not confined to the four 'working points' but covered general aspects of the Cyprus problem, such as territory, constitution, and fundamental freedoms, in the context of the UN Secretary-General's search for an overall settlement.[91]

[90] He spoke of the 'people' in the singular whereas there are two 'peoples' in Cyprus with conflicting interests.

[91] An account of the so-called 'proximity talks' is given in ch. 11, below.

# The 'Proximity Talks'

## I. THE FIRST ROUND

The first round of the 'proximity talks' began at the United Nations headquarters in New York on 10 September 1984 under the auspices of the UN Secretary-General. This was a device to overcome the difficulty arising from Mr Kyprianou's refusal to negotiate with the Turkish Republic of Northern Cyprus unless the declaration of statehood was withdrawn. The Secretary-General invited the parties to New York for indirect consultations to prepare the ground for direct talks later on. During the 'proximity talks', the two sides sat in separate rooms while the Secretary-General acted as a go-between, thus performing a shuttle diplomacy, talking to both sides separately.

It was understood that the Secretary-General suggested, as a framework for discussion, the three headings listed in the 'working points',[1] namely confidence-building measures, establishment and developing of a governmental structure, and territorial adjustments. The object was to narrow down existing differences and to lay the groundwork for lending substance to the working points. It was also understood that the Secretary-General suggested that both sides should proceed from the agreed basis. This would include a recommitment to the high-level accords of 1977 and 1979 and the points agreed upon in the course of the intercommunal talks, including the common agreement of the parties for a federal solution of the constitutional aspect and a bi-zonal solution of the territorial aspect of the problem.[2] Any agreement reached at the proximity talks would be submitted to a joint high-level meeting.

It was the Secretary-General's wish that the exchange of

[1] See ch. 10, above.
[2] See e.g. Greek Cypriot dailies *Phileleftheros* of 11 Sept. and *Alithia* of 12 Sept. The concept of bi-zonality was accepted six years before both by Mr Denktash and by the late Archbishop Makarios.

views should be kept confidential. However, some information leaked to the Greek Cypriot press. It was understood that under the heading of 'confidence-building measures' the Secretary-General sought to get the parties to talk about some practical steps to ease the situation—such as the reopening of Nicosia international airport with access to both sides[3] and the readmission of Greek Cypriots to the Turkish-controlled city of Famagusta (Varosha), in both cases under UN supervision. According to newspaper reports the substance of the problem was also discussed. Among these were powers and functions to be vested in the central government of the federal republic, its legislature, and territorial adjustments. The setting up of working groups on procedural questions was also suggested.[4] The working groups would consider necessary amendments to the 1960 Constitution and deal with certain matters such as foreign affairs, federal finances, appointment of federal officers, and defence and security. The transitional government would be established at a time to be agreed in the context of the joint high-level meeting. The question of deconfrontation and the three fundamental human rights, i.e. freedom of movement, freedom of settlement, and the right to ownership of property, were also discussed.[5]

---

[3] Greek Cypriot *Simerini* of 12 Sept. reported that the Greek Cypriot side showed hesitation about the proposal for reopening the airport. It was understood that the Greek Cypriot side insisted that its laws would be enforced at the airport and that its courts would be competent to try offences. It seems that the matter related to sovereignty of the Greek Cypriot administration and no visible progress was made.

*Phileleftheros* of 13 Sept. reported that the UN Secretary-General was not inclined to insist upon goodwill measures due to difficulties in reaching an agreement on these issues and attention was focused instead on the substance of the problem.

[4] *Phileleftheros* of 13 Sept. wrote that the working groups would be set up after a summit meeting and not during the proximity talks.

[5] The Greek Cypriot side argues that it is impossible to have a state with internal borders which would entail restriction of these freedoms. The Turkish side concedes these freedoms but believes that for some time restrictions will be necessary because unrestricted movement might permit former combatants of both sides to confront one another again and thus foment renewed hostilities. It is worth noting that in the 1977 Denktash–Makarios guide-lines for negotiations the late Archbishop Makarios recognized 'certain practical difficulties which arise for the Turkish Cypriot community'.

Towards the end of the first week of the proximity talks the Greek Cypriot side expressed pessimism and disappointment in the talks, an attitude reflected in the Greek Cypriot press. In view of this the Secretary-General issued a statement on 14 September to say that in his judgment the talks had been serious, businesslike, and conducted in a constructive spirit and that he had invited both sides to continue the talks for one more week under his auspices.

At the time of the proximity talks the question of United States military aid to Turkey was on the agenda of the appropriate congressional committees and the Greek side seemed apprehensive that signs of success of the talks might tip the balance in favour of Turkey.

It would seem that instead of concentrating on general principles and trying to find common ground for a high-level meeting, the first round of the talks was complicated by over-detailed treatment of government structure and constitutional matters. According to the Greek Cypriot press, on most issues neither side went much beyond outlining its own positions.[6] It was understood that the Greek Cypriot attitude on the Constitution was very similar to that presented in the 'Kyprianou framework' of 11 January 1984.[7] This would mean the maintenance of the presidential system with a Greek Cypriot President and a Turkish Cypriot Vice-President. The President would be elected without regard to community by the people of Cyprus on a common electoral roll.[8] The Council of Ministers would be composed of seven Greek Cypriot ministers and three Turkish Cypriot ministers. The federal tier of government would have substantial authority in such matters as foreign affairs, finance, security, communications, resources, and federal justice, leaving the regional governments responsible for matters of communal interest such as education and social

---

[6] See e.g. *Simerini* of 13 Sept., *Phileleftheros* of 13 Sept., and *Agon* of 16 Sept. *Ta Nea* of 20 Sept. commented that the first round ended in deadlock, and *Phileleftheros* of the same date said that the UN Secretary-General was disappointed. See also *New York Times* of 21 Sept.

[7] *Phileleftheros* of 16 Sept. The 'Kyprianou framework' proposals are dealt with in ch. 10, above.

[8] Under the 1960 Constitution the President was elected by the Greek Cypriot community and the Vice-President by the Turkish Cypriot community respectively, on separate electoral rolls.

services. The Greek Cypriot proposals on the structure of the federal government were based on the assumption that a 'constitutional government' exists and that the strong central government should devolve powers to the components. In other words, the Greek Cypriot side proposed 'devolving' some power from the 'centre' rather than establishing a 'bi-zonal' federation based on the principle that federal authority must evolve from the existing units joining together to form the federation.

On the legislature, the Greek Cypriot side reaffirmed its preference for a uni-cameral system and mentioned the need to discuss the powers and functions of this organ.[9]

On the territorial aspects of the problem the Greek Cypriot side stressed the need to come to an agreement at a high-level meeting and indicated its readiness to discuss during the proximity talks the issue of the number of refugees who would be allowed to return to their homes.[10]

On the question of guarantees the Greek Cypriot side indicated its preference for international guarantees whereby the interested parties would be barred from a guarantee treaty, that is, Security Council guarantees or guarantees given by countries not directly involved.[11]

[9] The 'Kyprianou framework' included an alternative proposal for a lower chamber in which the two communities would be represented according to population and an upper chamber in which representation would depend on the powers and functions of the chamber, a vague proposition.

In the author's view, a uni-cameral federal legislature is not compatible with the concept of 'federation'. Generally speaking, federal legislatures are composed of two houses and the component units have equal representation in the upper house irrespective of the population of the units.

The Waldheim 'evaluation document' also envisaged that the federal legislature would comprise two chambers and that in the upper chamber the two communities would have equal representation.

[10] Greek Cypriot papers indicated that the boundary revision envisaged by the Turkish Cypriot map of 5 Aug. 1981 could result in the accommodation of 34,000 Greek Cypriot refugees, including 16,000 in Varosha. In the Greek Cypriot view an additional 66,000 refugees should be resettled: *Phileleftheros* of 15 and 16 Sept.

[11] The author's view is that discussion of a future guarantee for Cyprus was at that stage premature. It is worth noting that the former UN Secretary-General Dr Waldheim had suggested in his 'evaluation document' that the question of international guarantees in relation to the status of the federal republic of Cyprus should be discussed at the appropriate level after agreement on all other aspects had been reached.

On the other hand, the Turkish Cypriot side insisted that the two sides should proceed from the already 'agreed basis' for negotiation which envisaged the establishment of a bi-communal, bi-zonal federal state in Cyprus.[12]

In the view of the Turkish Cypriot side certain specified powers and functions should be vested in the central government by the federal constitution and residual powers should be given to the federated units. The presidency of the federal republic should rotate among the members of the 'federal council', which was envisaged in the UN 'evaluation document' of 18 November 1981 to be the executive organ of the federal republic.

The Turkish Cypriot view on the constitutional aspect was that the two communities should have 'equal political status' within the framework of a federal state.[13] The Turkish Cypriot side explained that this does not mean a numerical equality between the constituent partners of the federation as regards all organs of the federal state, but equality between the constituent partners as regards effective say and influence arising from the basic principle of political and legal equality.[14]

It was understood that the Turkish Cypriot side expressed the view that territorial issues should be taken up in relation to the constitutional aspect within the framework of substantive negotiations on a final comprehensive settlement. Readmission of Greek Cypriots to Varosha and to 'six additional areas' delineated on the Turkish Cypriot map of 5 August 1981 should be subject to negotiation. The question of territory should not be taken up in terms of percentages or certain proportions but should be considered in terms of the criteria laid down by the Denktash–Markarios agreement of 1977, e.g. economic viability or productivity, land ownership, and security.

[12] The agreed framework comprised the high-level agreements of 1977 and 1979, the 'opening statement' of the former UN Secretary-General of 9 Aug. 1980, which envisages a federal solution of the constitutional aspect and bi-zonal solution of the territorial aspect of the problem, and the Waldheim 'evaluation document'.

[13] Indeed it is impossible to divorce the concept of 'equal political status' from that of a federal state which the two sides are aiming to establish.

[14] Point 5 of the Turkish Cypriot proposals submitted to the UN Secretary-General by Mr Necati M. Ertekün in New York on 15 June: *Hürriyet* (Ankara) of 5 Aug.

The first round ended on 20 September 1984 without any apparent progress, but further discussions were scheduled for 15 October. The UN Secretary-General stated that the talks had been 'thorough and businesslike' with the parties having 'explained their positions on implementing the respective principles'.

Mr Kyprianou expressed dissatisfaction and pessimism about the first round and initiated a series of meetings with the permanent members of the Security Council to urge them to influence Turkey to show more conciliation. He also visited Athens on 4 October for consultations with the Greek government.

The Turkish Cypriot side continued to give a hopeful impression about the outcome of the first round and the prospects for the second. Mr Denktash said that if the situation had been as bad as presented by the other side the two sides would not have been called for a second round.

## 2. THE SECOND ROUND

On 10 October 1984 both Mr Kyprianou and Mr Denktash received a personal message from the UN Secretary-General, Mr Perez de Cuellar, as they were preparing to leave for New York for the second round of the proximity talks. Although both sides said that it simply referred to details about procedure, reliable sources indicated that the message urged the two sides to show more flexibility.

The second round started on 15 October amid reports that the Greek Cypriot side was going to intensify its rearming of the National Guard especially with the acquisition of sophisticated weapons from France. It was also learnt that the Greek Cypriot authorities had signed an agreement with the Soviet organization 'Selkhozpromexport' empowering the latter to undertake the preparation of a feasibility study for the 'Karkotis River Dam Project'[15] which, if implemented, could cause the drying-

---

[15] *Cyprus Mail,* 20 Oct. 1984.

up of the western part of the country under the control of the Turkish Republic of Northern Cyprus.[16]

The second round took place betweeen 10 and 26 October. Mr Cuellar told both sides that, at the end of the second round, he would submit a report to the Security Council informing it of their attitudes. This meant that the parties would be exposed before the Council if they did not co-operate.

On 16 October the UN Secretary-General submitted an 'Agenda for the Second Round of Proximity Talks'. This was a draft document attempting to lay down principles to be agreed upon by the two sides, which could be submitted to a summit meeting. The Secretary-General's aim was to find common ground on the various aspects of the problem.

Even though both sides had been committed to a confidentiality pledge, a version of the 'agenda' appeared in the New York Greek-language newspaper *Proini* on 21 October.[17]

According to newspaper leaks, the agenda recorded first the points acceptable in principle, and second, the points under discussion. The points acceptable in principle included recommitment to the high-level agreements of 1977 and 1979; determination to proceed at the earliest possible date to the establishment of a federal republic that would be independent and non-aligned,[18] bi-communal as regards the federal constitutional aspect, and bi-zonal as regards the territorial aspect; and reaffirmation of acceptance of those introductory constitutional provisions that were agreed upon at the intercommunal talks in 1981–2. According to these provisions the federal republic of Cyprus would have international personality and exercise sovereignty in respect of all of its territories. The people of the federal republic would comprise the people of the provinces or federated states and there would be single citizenship regulated by federal law.

---

[16] Water is a scarce resource in the Turkish Republic of Northern Cyprus. It is feared that the contemplated project may cut off the *ab antiquo* right of Turkish Cypriots to water from Karkotis river and surrounding rivulets.

[17] A translation from the Greek text was also published in the *Cyprus Mail* of 23 Oct.

[18] It may be questioned whether it is right to commit the future federal republic to a policy of non-alignment at such an early stage. The federal republic may, for instance, find that its place is in fact with the Western world.

Under the heading, 'Points under discussion', the powers and functions of the central government of the federal republic were listed. These were: foreign affairs, federal financial affairs, monetary and banking affairs, posts and telecommunications, international transport, natural resources,[19] federal health and veterinary affairs, standard setting,[20] federal judiciary, appointment of federal officers, defence,[21] and security.[22]

The agenda provided that the legislature of the federal republic would be composed of two chambers, the lower chamber with a 70–30 and the upper chamber with a 50–50 representation. Federal legislation would be enacted with regard to federal competence listed in the agenda. Appropriate constitutional safeguards would be incorporated in the federal constitution; approval by both chambers would be needed on those matters which, under the 1960 Constitution, required decisions by separate majority, and on additional matters necessary for the continued functioning of the federal government (for example, on budgetary questions).

The agenda provided that the President and Vice-President would symbolize the unity of the country and the *equal political status* of the two communities.[23] In addition, the executive would reflect the functional requirements of an effective government. This would be achieved either through a system derived from part III of the 1960 Constitution[24] or through the institution of a system of parliamentary responsibility.

A tripartite body[25] with one non-Cypriot member would be

[19] Including water supply and environment.

[20] Weights and measures, patents, trade marks, and copyrights.

[21] To be discussed in connection with international guarantees.

[22] As it pertains to federal responsibility.

[23] The use of the expression 'equal political status' is very important from the Turkish Cypriot point of view, which is that a federation can be established by two equal political units. The principle of political equality also reverses the negative effects of Security Council resolutions 541 (1983) and 550 (1984) which, in considering the declaration of statehood in north Cyprus as 'legally invalid', denied this equality for the northern unit.

[24] Part III of the 1960 Constitution deals with the President and Vice-President of the Republic and the functioning of the Council of Ministers. It is believed that this provision was inserted to emphasize the need to devise a machinery to resolve deadlock in the decision-making process of the cabinet.

[25] This body has been identified with the Constitutional Court which is to be composed of a Greek Cypriot, a Turkish Cypriot, and a non-Cypriot.

set up with the responsibility of ruling on disputes relating to the distribution of powers and functions between the federation and the provinces or federated states and on such matters as may be assigned to it by the parties in accordance with the constitution.

The agenda also provided for the establishment of working groups to consider, *inter alia*, the exercise of the freedom of movement, freedom of settlement, and right to property, and to elaborate territorial adjustments in addition to the areas referred to in the 5 August 1981 Turkish Cypriot proposals. It referred vaguely to a timetable for the withdrawal of non-Cypriot military troops and to the establishment of a transitional government. There were also provisions for the resettlement of Varosha, for a moratorium on actions tending to prejudice the process outlined, and for the reopening of Nicosia international airport under interim United Nations administration.

It is important to note that, in the course of the second round, the agenda text was being revised in the light of comments and views expressed by both sides. It is understood that during the second round both sides elaborated further their already defined positions and attitudes.

It seems that the main points of disagreement that persisted related to the powers and functions of the central government of the future federal republic. The Turkish Cypriot view was that the powers of the central government should be defined and the residue of power should devolve on the federated states. The Greek Cypriot side insisted that the powers of the central government and of the units (provinces) should be listed and the residue of power should devolve on a strong central government.

The Greek Cypriot side rejected the proposal of the other side that the presidency of the federal republic should rotate between the two communities. Another area of contention related to the executive organ. Should the Executive be responsible to Parliament? Should the head of the Executive belong to one community and the deputy head to the other? Should consensus be required on an agreed list of issues? These areas of disagreement remained unsolved during the second round.

On the federal legislature it would seem that the emphasis was on a bi-cameral Parliament. But, should approval by both chambers be needed on all legislation within federal competence, or should approval by both chambers be required only in specified areas of legislation? The Greek Cypriots insisted that a machinery should be devised to resolve deadlock between the two chambers.

On the question of territory, it was believed that the Greek Cypriot side insisted that the Turkish Cypriot province should comprise 25 per cent,[26] as accepted by the late Archbishop Makarios in 1977, whereas the Turkish Cypriot side maintained that the territory under its control should be at least 30 per cent.[27]

At the end of the second round on 26 October, the Secretary-General stated that the positions of the parties had been further clarified but there had not been substantive progress. However, all sides had agreed to hold a final round of high-level proximity talks beginning on 26 November. The Secretary-General added that he considered it essential to undertake further effort before reporting to the Security Council in pursuance of his mission of good offices.[28]

Mr Kyprianou, who faced strong criticism at home from the communist AKEL party and from the leader of the main opposition Rally party of Mr Glafcos Clerides, did not conceal his disappointment at the outcome of the two rounds of proximity talks and blamed the Turkish Cypriot side.[29]

On the other hand, in a statement made on 26 October at the conclusion of the second round, Mr Denktash said that agreement can only be reached if both sides respect each other's existence and equality. His side had done everything possible to help the Secretary-General in his efforts and would continue so to do. He added that in order to conceal their uncompromising attitude, the Greek Cypriots had been trying to deceive the world.

[26] It may be noted that the 'Kyprianou framework' of 11 Jan. 1984 conceded 25 per cent of territory to the north provided Famagusta and Morphou reverted to the Greek administration.

[27] It was understood that the relevant words used were 'thirty per cent plus'. It was not clear whether the buffer zone was included in this calculation.

[28] UN press release: CYP/94/13, Nicosia, 27 Oct. 1984.

[29] *Cyprus Mail*, 27 Oct. ('President not happy') and 8 Nov. ('President's appeal for unity'). In statements made on 7 Nov. after two days of talks in Athens, Mr Kyprianou and premier Papandreou both expressed disappointment at the outcome of the talks. They also denied that differences had cropped up during the Athens meeting with President Karamanlis as alleged by the Greek opposition press.

### 3. THE THIRD ROUND

Mr Kyprianou's ministers tendered their resignations a few days before the third round of the proximity talks was due to begin, amid reports that there would be a cabinet reshuffle.[30] The ministers were asked to stay at their posts until a decision on the matter was taken.[31]

The Greek Cypriot daily *Alithia* of 15 November 1984 wrote that, during a series of consultations Mr Kyprianou had with political parties, it was concluded that the chances of success of the final round were very small and for this reason attention was focused on possible steps to be taken after their failure.

The Turkish side expressed cautious optimism about the talks. On the other hand, in his public statements, Mr Kyprianou declared that the Greek Cypriot side was ready for an 'honourable compromise' but was not prepared to accept partitionist solutions.[32] He added that, based on the experience of the two previous rounds, one could not be hopeful, but he would be most happy to welcome a pleasant surprise.[33]

The third round began in New York on 26 November 1984 under the auspices of the UN Secretary-General. The Secretary-General presented to the parties and discussed with them, as an integrated whole, a preliminary draft[34] for a joint high-level agreement. The package contained elements taken from different positions which could help in bridging the gap which then existed. The discussions moved quickly to the central issues of what could be called the core of a comprehensive solution to the Cyprus problem.[35]

In the form it was presented at the previous round of talks, the

---

[30] The cabinet had been in office since the presidential elections of 1983 following the 'minimum programme' alliance of Mr Kyprianou's ruling Democratic party and the communist AKEL, but there had been differences between the two parties. Mr Kyprianou unilaterally terminated the 'minimum programme' co-operation agreement on 22 Dec. 1984.

[31] There was a cabinet reshuffle on 8 Jan. 1985.

[32] *Cyprus Mail*, 25 Nov. 1984.

[33] *Cyprus Mail*, 27 Nov. 1984.

[34] To be referred to also as the 'agenda', 'draft agreement', 'package proposals' of the Secretary-General or the Secretary-General's 'presentation'.

[35] Secretary-General's Report to the Security Council on the UN operation in Cyprus, S/16858 of 12 Dec. 1984, para. 50.

agenda provided for a 'bi-zonal' federal republic of Cyprus and a bi-cameral legislature, including a senate with equal Greek and Turkish Cypriot representation and a lower house that would be 70 per cent Greek Cypriot.[36] The President and Vice-President of the republic would symbolize the unity of the country and the equal political status of the two communities.

At the third round of the talks the draft agreement was revised by the presentation, in the form of a supplementary paper, of more detailed points on the Executive, Legislature, and safeguards for the Turkish Cypriots.[37]

The supplementary points appended to the package proposals of the Secretary-General provide for a Greek Cypriot President and a Turkish Cypriot Vice-President, as in the 1960 Constitution.[38]

In return for Greek Cypriot acceptance of a bi-zonal federation the Turkish Cypriot side indicated its willingness to retain within the control of the Turkish Cypriot zone territory comprising only just over 29 per cent of the island.

The preliminary draft agreement, as revised on 27 November by inclusion of supplementary points, envisages a Council of Ministers composed of seven Greek Cypriot and three Turkish Cypriot members. The Turkish Cypriot Vice-President of the republic will have the right to veto cabinet decisions on matters specified in the 1960 Constitution[39] plus other matters to be agreed upon. A 'weighted' system of voting is envisaged, which means that cabinet decisions will be taken by simple majority but with at least one Turkish Cypriot member voting in favour.

The President and the Vice-President will also have the right to refer cabinet decisions to the Constitutional Court or return such decisions or laws for reconsideration.

[36] The outlines of the agenda as presented at the second round have been examined earlier.

[37] Looked at from a different angle, the system of 'safeguards' for the Turkish Cypriots have been described as 'deadlock-resolving machinery' in the sense that a procedure has to be devised so that the government and legislature can function without unnecessary impediments.

[38] The Turkish Cypriot side no longer insisted that the presidency of the federal republic should rotate between a Greek Cypriot and a Turkish Cypriot, provided that the Foreign Ministry of the federal republic was entrusted to a Turkish Cypriot.

[39] That is, foreign affairs, defence, and security (art. 57(3) of the 1960 Constitution).

The Legislature will be bi-cameral. The lower house will be composed of 70 per cent Greek Cypriot and 30 per cent Turkish Cypriot members. In the upper house the two component units of the federation will be equally represented. The matters coming within federal competence of legislation will be listed and the residual powers will go to the provinces or federated states. On major matters enumerated in the federal list of powers, legislation will be enacted if approved by separate majorities of Greek Cypriot and Turkish Cypriot members of both houses. On other matters laws will be enacted by simple majority in both houses, but with at least 30 per cent of Turkish Cypriot members in the upper house voting in favour. A conciliation committee composed of three Greek Cypriots and two Turkish Cypriots will be set up to settle differences between the two houses. The concurrence of at least one Turkish member of the committee will be necessary to reach a decision.

The President and Vice-President of the federal republic will have the right to refer laws for the opinion of the Constitutional Court or return laws for reconsideration by the Legislature.[40] The President and Vice-President will also have the right, under certain circumstances, to refer laws and decisions of the cabinet for the opinion of their respective communities by the holding of referendums.

The final point of the preliminary draft agreement for the summit meeting notes the suggestion of the sides as to a special status area adjacent to each other for the purpose of enhancing trust between the sides.[41]

It was announced on 29 November that Mr Denktash, the President of the Turkish Republic of Northern Cyprus, fully agreed with all points of Mr Perez de Cuellar's presentation. The Turkish Cypriot side made final concessions on all issues to help the Secretary-General have his presentation accepted by the other side, on the understanding that the draft agreement would be endorsed and signed without further negotiation at the summit meeting.

---

[40] Under the 1960 Constitution the President and the Vice-President of the Republic, separately or conjointly, had the right of final veto on any law or decision of the House of Representatives relating to foreign affairs, defence, and security (art. 50).

[41] This suggestion is expressed in vague terminology.

Mr Denktash's decision to accept all elements of the Secretary-General's presentation surprised the Greek side. A ten-day recess was announced, and Mr Kyprianou flew home for urgent consultations both with the Greek Cypriot political parties and with Mr Papandreou's government in Greece.

After the ten-day recess the third round of the indirect talks continued in New York between 10 and 12 December. During these talks the Greek side sought unsuccessfully to amend the UN proposal. The Greek press alleged reservations about several points in the draft agreement. It is understood that the Greek side did not accept the draft as a whole. Reservations related particularly to veto powers of the Vice-President and to the Executive. In the opinion of Mr Denktash reservations on a package deal cannot have legal validity.

According to Athens newspaper *Avghi* of 16 December, Mr Kyprianou presented a document to Mr Cuellar on 8 December, giving the Greek Cypriot views on subjects which remained unsettled and were expected to be taken up at the summit meeting in an effort to reach an agreement. The main points of the document, according to the Athens paper were:

1. The composition of the lower house to be 80:20 for the two communities in return for acceptance of a 50:50 representation of the two communities in the upper house.
2. The cabinet to be in the ratio of 7:3 for Greek and Turkish Cypriot ministers.
3. The Turkish-controlled area to be reduced to 25 per cent. Moreover, the Greek Cypriot side considers it important to know how many Greek Cypriots would return to their homes and where.
4. The issue of passports to be in the jurisdiction of the central (federal) government.
5. Airports and ports to be under the control of the central (federal) government.
6. The final agreement should make specific reference to UN resolutions.[42]

[42] The Secretary-General does not, for instance, refer to res. 541 (1983) of the Security Council. The contents of that resolution prejudice the continuation of negotiations by virtue of the categorical censure of the position of the Turkish Cypriots whose co-operation is an indispensable condition for a solution of the problem.

7. The Greek Cypriot side agrees to discuss the assignment of a major ministry to the Turks but it cannot agree that the Foreign Ministry should be permanently reserved for a Turkish Cypriot minister.
8. The Greek Cypriot side accepts 'political equality' for all citizens but not in the sense of equality of the two communities regardless of their numerical strength.
9. The Turkish troop withdrawal should follow the signing of the agreement and in any case be made prior to the setting up of a central government or a transitional government.

The third round ended without a statement being issued. Even though the parties agreed to hold a summit meeting on 17 January 1985, the gap between the two sides remained unbridged.

In his Report to the Security Council of 12 December about the United Nations operation in Cyprus,[43] the Secretary-General stated that it was his assessment that the documentation for a draft agreement could be submitted to a joint high-level meeting. He expected that the interlocutors would, at the high-level meeting, conclude an agreement containing the necessary elements for a comprehensive solution of the problem, aimed at establishing a federal republic of Cyprus. Later on in the same report he said: 'I am confident that both sides will prove at the joint high-level meeting that we have reached a turning point in the development of the question of Cyprus, and that their determination to work together in a Federal Republic will prove strong enough to overcome the remaining difficulties and to dispel existing suspicions.'

During the Security Council debates of 14 December 1984 on the extension of the mandate of the UN peacekeeping force for a further period of six months, most of the speakers expressed their appreciation of the Secretary-General's efforts in promoting a solution to the Cyprus problem. He had succeeded in preparing the ground for a high-level meeting, with agreed parameters, between the leaders of the two communities.[44] Hopes were pinned on the proposed January meeting which might usher in a new era of conciliation and progress.

At the same meeting of the Security Council, the Turkish

[43] S/16585, para. 50.     [44] S/PV 2565.

representative, Mr Kırca, paid tribute to Mr Denktash for showing sufficient courage at the beginning of the third round in indicating total political acceptance of all elements contained in the draft agreement prepared and presented by the Secretary-General.[45]

The two sides seemed however to be approaching the January meeting differently. The Greek side appeared to assume that there would be more negotiating, while the Turkish side indicated that the draft agreement should not be changed and that the only points in abeyance concerned certain dates and blanks left to be filled in during the high-level meeting.

During the first week in January 1985 a preparatory meeting was held in Geneva between one of the UN Secretary-General's aides and the representatives of the two communities[46] to formulate the main principles agreed upon by the two sides during the intercommunal talks in 1981 and 1982. According to Mr Ertekün, the then Minister for Foreign Affairs and Defence of the Turkish Republic of Northern Cyprus, the two sides agreed to include the following five additional points to the draft agreement to be signed in New York:

1. The federal republic of Cyprus to be set up will be independent, non-aligned, bi-zonal, and bi-communal.
2. The territory of the federal republic will comprise the territories of both federated States.
3. Official languages will be Turkish and Greek.
4. In addition to the federal flag, each federated state will have its own flag which may be hoisted on national days.
5. The federated states will have their own constitutions in addition to that of the federation.

### 4. THE SUMMIT

In a press briefing on 12 December, the Secretary-General expressed the view that the convening of a high-level meeting was 'a piece of news which will be considered a very constructive step forward, leading to the overwhelming, comprehensive solution of the Cyprus problem'. Asked what duration he

[45] Ibid. 38.    [46] Messrs Mavrommatis and Ertekün.

envisaged for the high-level meeting, he replied that for him one hour would be enough, but that he would be at the disposal of the two sides for two or three days.

The summit meeting began in New York on 17 January under the auspices of the UN Secretary-General. At the opening session Mr Perez de Cuellar, in whose presence the two leaders met for the first time in six years, said that the joint high-level meeting was a landmark in the complex history for a negotiated, just, and lasting settlement of the Cyprus problem within the framework of the mission of good offices entrusted to him by the Security Council. His expectation was that at that meeting the parties would conclude an agreement containing elements necessary for a comprehensive solution of the problem, aimed at establishing a federal republic of Cyprus. To move from the documentation worked on during the proximity talks to the conclusion of an agreement was the responsibility that had to be faced. He added: 'If you are determined to reach an agreement, a unique chance now exists. If this moment is lost, I am sure you will agree, it may not readily recur.'

The main reason for optimism was that in the third round of the proximity talks, the Turkish Cypriot side had accepted all the elements contained in the Secretary-General's draft agreement consisting of three reaffirmatory paragraphs, fourteen articles, and an incorporated presentation (supplementary paper) consisting of six articles.[47] This documentation envisaged territorial arrangements and laid down the main principles for a new constitution that would establish a two-zone federal republic of Cyprus, with veto powers to protect the rights of the Turkish Cypriots and a deadlock-breaking mechanism to ensure that the government would be able to function. By their favourable reaction the Turkish Cypriots had offered substantial concessions on the constitutional and territorial aspects of the Cyprus problem,[48] on the understanding that what

---

[47] The text of the draft agreement is reproduced as Appendix 5.

[48] During the course of preparations for the third round of the proximity talks the Secretary-General had requested the parties to come to that final round not for bargaining but with their final positions in order to take major political decisions. In taking the crucial political decision to accept the draft agreement the Turkish Cypriot side had complied with the Secretary-General's request.

remained to be done at the high-level meeting was to agree on three dates which had been left blank in articles 9, 11, and 14, decide on the setting up of a working group or groups which would elaborate the details of the agreement, and to endorse, as an integrated whole, the draft agreement.[49]

There is considerable support for the Turkish Cypriot side's understanding of the purpose of the summit. In the first place, the Secretary-General had already indicated that for him one hour would be enough for the conclusion of the summit, even though he would be at the disposal of the two sides for two or three days. Secondly, at the opening session the Secretary-General had expressed his expectation that the parties would, at the joint high-level meeting, 'conclude an agreement', adding: 'We are here to seek an agreement leading to the establishment of a Federal Republic of Cyprus.' Thirdly, the Turkish Cypriot side accepted *in toto* the draft agreement proposed by the Secretary-General on the explicit assurances by him that the draft, representing an *integrated whole*, was the final text to be concluded at the high-level meeting without re-negotiation or any reservations whatsoever, even by way of interpretation.[50]

In his opening address Mr Kyprianou stressed that he came to the high-level meeting with goodwill and a desire that a peaceful solution could be found. He said that he was ready to consider each and every issue in a constructive way in order that a mutual framework could be agreed upon. He believed that this meeting should, in contrast to the 1977 and 1979 high-level meetings, formulate a comprehensive framework. He added that if both sides were after an ideal solution this exercise could not be successful. Therefore an honourable solution that is just and fair should be sought. The republic to be set up should be a workable one. He was ready to co-operate with the Secretary-General, and with Mr Denktash, whom he had not met for a long time. He wished to assure Mr Denktash that he was in favour of an agreed solution. He was ready to listen to everything Mr Denktash had to say. The aim was to create a happy Cyprus.

---

[49] The London *Times* of 1 Dec. wrote that the Turkish Cypriot community had offered important concessions and effectively 'left the ball in the Greek Cypriot court'.

[50] Written statement given to the press by Mr Denktash in New York on 20 Jan. 1985.

The people were waiting anxiously for the outcome of the meeting.

At the same session Mr Denktash voiced the conviction that it was 'perfectly possible for the Turkish Cypriots and Greek Cypriots to live in freedom and security under their own democratic federated states and to administer their joint Republic, as co-founder partners, under the roof of a federation'. He stated that 'as the leaders of the two national communities, it is our historical task to give from here, to our respective peoples, the good news that we have been able to take a major step on the path to a peaceful solution'. Referring to the 'historic opportunity', he said, 'I believe that this opportunity which Mr. Perez de Cueller, the Secretary-General, has brought about is of a historical magnitude. It is our duty not to let this opportunity slip away. I consider this to be the best chance which we have had as yet.' After stating that the high-level draft agreement, which had been prepared after months of hard work, was an enormous leap forward in the search for a negotiated settlement, he concluded: 'Its adoption today by us will mark the beginning of a new era in the relations between our two peoples and we wholeheartedly hope it will lead to the early etablishment of the Republic of Cyprus, which will be a legacy to leave to future generations of Turkish and Greek Cypriots.'

However, by the end of the first day the hopes for the success of the summit were beginning to fade away. Mr Kyprianou made it clear that he came to the summit to negotiate. He insisted that during the meeting there should be discussion on all aspects of the Cyprus problem, and that all that had been proposed in writing or verbally should be on the table.

As from the very first meeting, Mr Kyprianou raised fundamental objections to each and every paragraph of the draft agreement which he described as the 'draft agenda'. He denied the existence of such an agreement.[51] He even questioned basic tenets and principles long since agreed as the inevitable basis of any solution, such as the concept of bi-zonality and the

---

[51] A Greek Cypriot spokesman declared in New York: 'Mr Denktash refuses us the right to negotiate. He wants us to sign a ghost paper' (*New York Times*, 21 Jan. 1985).

equal political status of the two communities, as well as objecting to the agreed legislative, executive, and territorial arrangements. He was not prepared to fill in the blank dates and agree to the establishment of working groups unless a comprehensive framework was first formulated so as not to leave gaps to be filled in by these groups. The Turkish Cypriot side's reply was that the draft agreement could be endorsed at that stage and further high-level meetings could be arranged to resolve differences arising later on.

On the question of withdrawal of non-Cypriot forces Mr Kyprianou put forward demands and views which were incompatible with the relevant provisions of the draft agreement. He insisted that withdrawal of Turkish troops must be completed before the setting up of a transitional or federal government. The Greek Cypriot side was prepared to accept the deployment of an international force so that there would be no security gap. On the question of international guarantees, the Greek Cypriot side referred to a Security Council guarantee but was prepared to consider other formulas provided they excluded Turkey and Greece.[52]

The summit was dominated by confusion and uncertainty as to its purpose.[53] During the meeting in the evening of 17 January, the Greek Cypriot delegation expressed surprise and astonishment when the supplementary points incorporated in the draft agreement were referred to.[54]

---

[52] On this matter the Turkish Cypriot view has always been expressed in very clear terms. The Turkish Cypriots will not accept any treaty or arrangement that does not envisage Turkey's guarantee for their security. Moreover, the Treaty of Establishment and the Treaty of Guarantee, as well as the Treaty of Alliance, are valid and in force and they cannot be changed without the consent of all the parties concerned.

[53] Greek Cypriot daily *Simerini* of 19 Jan. wrote that neither the Secretary-General nor the two leaders seemed to know what was happening. The Secretary-General was not free from blame for not clarifying the issue, the paper alleged.

[54] The supplementary document filled some of the gaps in the draft agreement so that, in the Turkish Cypriot view, the documentation was detailed enough to provide a framework for a settlement. One may ponder why the Greek Cypriot delegation could not readily remember that such a document was presented to the parties in November and that it did in fact exist.

During the second session on 17 January Mr Denktash told Mr Kyprianou that while the Greek Cypriot side still firmly adhered to its old views, Turkish Cypriots had made sacrifices by accepting the draft agreement, and called upon him to make a similar sacrifice and to accept in full the agreement before them. He drew attention to the fact that some of Mr Kyprianou's views were in total contradiction with the draft agreement and that demanding the acceptance of these was tantamount to asking the Turkish Cypriot side to surrender to the Greek Cypriots. He also pointed out that Mr Kyprianou was trying to raise issues which were intended to be left to the working groups. He added that during the summit meeting there would not be enough time to solve issues intended for the working groups and that the draft agreement could not be renegotiated.

During the subsequent meetings held both in private and in formal sessions, Mr Kyprianou continued to reject the existence of an agreement. At one point, he even attempted to deny any knowledge of the very text on which he had based his objections. In the course of these discussions, both the Secretary-General and Mr Denktash made efforts to persuade Mr Kyprianou to accept the existing agreement which the Secretary-General himself had drawn up as an 'honest broker'.

Mr Kyprianou then chose to argue that he had misunderstood the whole exercise and tried to terminate the high-level meeting without accepting the draft agreement. This was designed to keep the Turkish Cypriot side committed to the agreement, while the Greek Cypriot side would be free to extract further concessions. This move was unacceptable to the Turkish Cypriots.

Mr Denktash made it clear that his side could not remain committed to the draft agreement in the absence of acceptance by the other. If everything was to be renegotiated the Turkish Cypriot side would also be entitled to start from 'square one'. In his view, reservations could not be placed on the draft agreement which was to be treated as an integrated whole. He would also have to consult his Parliament and seek the renewal of his mandate by the holding of a presidential election.

Near the end of the summit the Greek Cypriot side intimated that it would agree to the setting up immediately of a working group on the Constitution[55] to report to the high-level meeting. It also suggested that a high-level meeting should be convened on a fixed date for the purpose of discussing the following four issues: a timetable for withdrawal of non-Cypriot troops, external guarantees, three freedoms,[56] and the exact areas the Turkish Cypriots would return as part of their territorial concessions.[57] The Turkish Cypriots maintained that these were matters to be negotiated by working groups as envisaged in the UN plan.

During the final meeting on 20 January, Mr Denktash, in the presence of the UN Secretary-General, told Mr Kyprianou that general elections in the Turkish Republic of Northern Cyprus were inevitable.[58] The Secretary-General remarked that Mr Kyprianou had also said that he himself could face the prospect of an early election.[59]

Despite long efforts the Secretary-General was unable to get the Cypriot leaders to agree on a joint communiqué ending the talks. In a prepared statement he stressed that the Turkish Cypriot side 'fully accepts the draft agreement' while the Greek Cypriot side accepted the same documentation 'as a basis for negotiations in accordance with the integrated whole approach

[55] This offer was made on the understanding that the documentation on the legislature should provide that on major matters there must be separate majorities and on other matters a simple majority in both chambers. In respect of 'other matters' the Greek Cypriot offer deviates from UN proposals on the Legislature, which provide that at least 30% of the Turkish Cypriot members of the upper house must vote in favour of a bill to become law.

[56] Freedom of movement and settlement and the right to own property. There is a contradiction between bi-zonality and completely unfettered freedom of movement, settlement, and ownership, since the latter would theoretically allow Greek Cypriots to flood back into the Turkish zone and take it over.

[57] The *Washington Post* of 21 Jan. and *The Times* of 22 Jan. wrote that on the last day of the conference Mr Kyprianou 'offered to accept the agreement and limit negotiations to four unresolved issues'. In fact, the assertion about acceptance of the agreement is misleading because nearly all of the principal issues would still be left in abeyance.

[58] Under the 1960 Constitution the two communities held their elections on separate electoral rolls. Since 1963 elections have been held separately on both sides.

[59] As reported in the *Cyprus Mail*, 29 Jan. 1985, 'Denktash rules out early talks.' Mr Denktash was of the view that elections would not stand in the way of an agreement.

aiming at a comprehensive and overall solution to the Cyprus problem'.[60]

On 20 January the four-day conference ended in failure without agreement on a framework laying down the principles for a federal solution. In the words of Mr Denktash, 'Mr. Kyprianou was unable, for reasons of his own, to contribute to a successful outcome. He did not want to conclude this agreement.'[61]

The Secretary-General announced that if possible there would be another meeting by the end of February. His belief was that the gap between the two communities had never been narrower. But Mr Denktash expressed surprise at the suggestion of another meeting so soon. 'A new situation has been created by the non-agreement at this summit, and I am not committing myself to any date', he declared, adding that he and Mr Kyprianou should meet in Cyprus.[62]

The Secretary-General was disappointed but maintained an optimistic attitude.

The failure of the talks was disappointing to the United States and other Western governments, which had exerted quiet pressure on both sides and on Greece and Turkey. An agreement on Cyprus would have eased congressional opposition to an increased flow of US arms to Turkey and would have ended the threat to NATO's south-eastern flank that a new Cyprus crisis would have posed.

Each side blamed the other for the failure of the summit. Mr Kyprianou had to face criticism at home. AKEL and the DISI party of Mr Glafcos Clerides accused him of being responsible for the failure of the summit.

According to the *Washington Post* of 21 January, 'UN and western officials said afterward that one motive for Kyprianou's stand was that the Athens government had discouraged an agreement on Cyprus.'[63] The paper referred to a statement by

---

[60] UNFICYP, press release: CYP/85/2, Nicosia.

[61] Written statement made to the press in New York on 20 Jan. 1985.

[62] *New York Times*, 21 Jan. 1985.

[63] 'Negotiations on Cyprus Break Down'. In fact a US congressional committee voted to cut 1988 US aid to Turkey from 913 million to 569 million dollars and link the aid to the Cyprus question. The committee ruled that the aid cannot be used by Turkish troops in the Turkish Cypriot sector of the

Mr Denktash that 'Greece doesn't need a settlement because they use Cyprus to punish Turkey in the U.S. Congress with the help of the Greek lobby.'

### 5. PROSPECTS FOR THE FUTURE

Even though the summit meeting failed to achieve any substantial result, the fact that the two leaders met in direct talks is an achievement in itself.[64]

The UN Secretary-General said that he still hoped for a resumption of negotiations. But he added that he did not know whether the draft agreement for the island's reunification could now remain as the basis for negotiations or whether the whole effort must start afresh. In any case, it would be naïve to deny that failure to agree even on a framework for future negotiations on the creation of a federal state is anything but a severe setback to prospects for a lasting solution to the age-old Cyprus problem.

Mr Denktash expressed scepticism about the usefulness of an early summit. On the other hand, Mr Kyprianou stated that he had requested a meeting with President Reagan in Washington before the second half of February 1985 in order to put his case that further details on issues such as Turkish troop withdrawals and guarantees of a settlement must be negotiated before a draft agreement is signed.

At the end of the summit Mr Denktash said that a political evaluation had to be made in the north, including plans for an election and possibly a constitutional referendum.

As the Turkish Cypriots accepted the UN plan without reservation they should not be blamed for the breakdown of the talks. They felt that they should not shelve indefinitely their plans for consolidating their state.

island. In response Ankara delayed ratification of an agreement to extend to 1990 the Defence and Economic Co-operation Agreement. It was also announced that the planned visit of Turkish President Kenan Evren to the US on 26 May 1987 was being postponed. There has been some speculation as to whether this was for domestic reasons or a snub to congressional moves.

[64] Mr Kyprianou had previously said that he would not talk with the Turkish Cypriots unless the declaration of independence was withdrawn.

# The Constitution of the Turkish Republic of Northern Cyprus

## I. INTRODUCTION

On 15 November 1983 the Turkish Republic of Northern Cyprus was proclaimed by the unanimous vote of the Legislative Assembly of the Turkish Federated State of Cyprus, a democratic representative of the Turkish people of Cyprus.[1] The proclamation emphasized, *inter alia*, that the declaration of statehood was a manifestation of the right to self-determination of the Turkish Cypriot people of Cyprus.[2]

After the failure of the proximity talks and the summit meeting,[3] due to refusal of the Greek side to agree even on a framework for future negotiations on the creation of a federal state, the Turkish Cypriot side intimated that it could no longer shelve plans for a referendum on the constitution of the new Republic and the holding of elections.

The Constitutional Commission composed of a chairman and fourteen members was set up by a decision of the Constituent Assembly taken at its meeting of 23 December 1983.[4]

The Constitutional Commission prepared the draft constitution, which was published in the *Official Gazette* on 8 June 1984 for public notification.

The Constitution was adopted by the Assembly on 12 March 1985 and was again published in the *Official Gazette*. It was approved by a referendum held on 5 May 1985. A vast majority of the people said 'yes' to the Constitution.[5] It was again

---

[1] See ch. 8, above.  [3] See ch. 11, above.
[2] Ch. 9, above.  [4] See ch. 10, s. 4.
[5] Out of 91,810 eligible voters 71,933 cast their votes. Of the 70,459 valid votes 49,447 (70.16%) were in favour of the Constitution and 21,002 (29.82%) were against. The main arguments put forward by those who campaigned for a 'no' vote on the Constitution were that it was not liberal enough, because it did not abolish capital punishment altogether (art. 15, para. 2); that it

published in the *Official Gazette* on 7 May 1985 and became the Constitution of the Turkish Republic of Northern Cyprus.

## 2. CHARACTERISTICS OF THE CONSTITUTION

The Preamble, which article 163 makes part of the Constitution, recites the national struggle and resistance of the Turkish Cypriots and the basic principles and philosophies inherent in the Constitution. Reference is made to the declaration of independence of 15 November 1983, which necessitated the making of the Constitution.

The Constitution has 164 articles and 12 transitional articles.

The 1975 Constitution of the Turkish Federated State of Cyprus formed the basis of the Constitution of the Turkish Republic of Northern Cyprus but there are a number of new provisions regulating the needs of the new Republic.

Article 1 declares that the state is a secular republic based on principles of democracy, social justice, and the supremacy of law.

The Constitution envisages a parliamentary democracy. Sovereignty is vested in the people comprising the citizens of the Turkish Republic of Northern Cyprus. Sovereignty is exercised by authorized organs in the name of the people. No organ or authority shall exercise any state authority which does not emanate from the Constitution. Article 7 provides for the supremacy of the Constitution.

The Constitution provides for the institutional framework of an independent republic with no fetters attached. There is no reference therein to the establishment of a federal republic of Cyprus. But there is a decision of the Constituent Assembly of

sanctioned, as an exception to the right to life, the use of force in defence of a person or in order to effect a lawful arrest or for the purpose of quelling a riot (art. 15, para. 3, which is analogous to art. 2, para. 2 of the European Convention on Human Rights), and that it provided that laws ratifying an international convention or agreement cannot be challenged before the Constitutional Court (art. 90, para. 5).

The left wing did not openly criticize the Constitution for not containing express provisions for a federal solution, but alleged that it was 'oppressive and militaristic' (*Guardian*, 7 May 1985).

12 March 1985[6] which declares that the acceptance of the Constitution of the Republic will not hinder, but facilitate, the establishment, by the two equal peoples, of a federal republic of Cyprus.

Instead of a rigid separation of powers, a flexible system has been preferred and the diffusion of functions and powers has been regulated accordingly. For instance, whereas the Judiciary can control the constitutionality of legislation, the President of the Republic and the Republic's Assembly are to send one representative each to the High Council of Judicature, which is responsible for appointments, promotion, and disciplinary control of judges.

The territory of the Republic and its people is indivisible, the official language is Turkish, and there are provisions as to the flag[7] and national anthem.

### 3. BASIC RIGHTS AND FREEDOMS

Part II incorporates a code of inalienable basic rights and freedoms modelled on the provisions of Part II of the 1975 Constitution of the Turkish Federated State of Cyprus. It is worth noting that the 1975 Constitution itself had adopted the most liberal articles of Part II of the 1960 Constitution and other international instruments on human rights.

The Constitution contains elaborate provisions guaranteeing basic rights and liberties, such as the right to equality; the right to life and corporal integrity; the right to liberty and security of person; the right of access to court; and the right to a fair and public hearing within a reasonable time by independent and impartial courts. Other articles contain a number of economic and social rights. Torture is prohibited. Right to privacy; inviolability of the dwelling house; confidentiality of correspondence; right to free movement and residence; freedom of science and art; freedom of the press; and freedoms of assembly and association are also protected in provisions which reflect the democratic characteristics of the state.

---

[6] Published in Suppl. IV, Part II of the *Official Gazette*, No. 22 of 15 Mar. 1985.

[7] Law No. 15 of 1984.

Citizens have the right to organize unarmed and non-violent assembly or public demonstration without obtaining prior permission. This right may be restricted by law only for safeguarding public order. Unlike the 1982 Constitution of the Republic of Turkey, the Constitution of the Turkish Republic of Northern Cyprus does not itself regulate the right to assembly and demonstration but leaves such matters to be determined by law.

The right to establish trade unions, the rights to collective agreement and to strike are also recognized. These rights may be regulated by law only for the purposes specified in the Constitution itself, such as national security and public order. Public servants can also form trade unions and have the right to strike. Only judges, law officers, members of the armed forces, members of the police, and civil-defence personnel holding key positions have no right to strike. Unlike the 1982 Constitution of the Republic of Turkey, which itself regulates trade-union rights, the Constitution of the Turkish Republic of Northern Cyprus does not prohibit trade unions from furthering a political cause, engaging in political activity, and receiving support from, or giving support to, political parties. Though there is at present a Trade Union Law, in force since 1971, there is no law regulating the right to strike and the corresponding right to enforce a 'lockout'. In very rare cases of strikes affecting essential services only, such as those at sea and air ports, resort has been made to 'Defence Regulations' dating from the British administration, to prohibit strikes for a certain specified period.[8]

Compared with the 1975 Constitution, the 1985 Constitution contains more detailed provisions to protect fundamental human rights and freedoms. For instance, capital punishment for premeditated murder, provided for under the Criminal Code, is abolished by transitional article 13. Article 15 declares that capital punishment can be imposed only by law in cases of treason during wartime, acts of terrorism, piracy *jure gentium*, and repeated murders. Even in these instances no enforcement of capital punishment is possible unless the Legislative Assembly so decides under the provisions of article 78.

New economic and social rights have also been formulated,

[8] In 1986 there were 17 strikes at different places of work in the Turkish Republic of Northern Cyprus, none of which were prohibited.

such as the right to protection from hunger, protection of the unemployed and needy, protection of the consumer, and the development of sports. There are elaborate provisions as to citizenship which also preserve acquired rights.

Restrictions and limitations which may be imposed by law on the exercise of these rights and liberties are set out specifically in each article. Such restrictions can, generally speaking, be imposed by law for purposes of national security, protection of the rights of others, and the maintenance of democratic institutions.

## 4. THE LEGISLATURE

The legislative power of the state is exercised by an Assembly which is composed of 50 deputies elected for a period of five years.

The voting age in the Turkish Republic of Northern Cyprus is 18. Elections are held in accordance with principles of direct secret ballot and universal suffrage. Article 70 provides that political parties shall be formed without prior permission and function freely. Furthermore, political parties, whether in power or in opposition, are the indispensable elements of democratic and political life. The Constitution specifies the principles with which political parties have to comply. Parties which do not comply with these principles may be closed down by the Supreme Court upon application by the Attorney-General. The election system, which is regulated by law, is the proportional representation system. A 'barrier' clause, which requires that in order to be represented in Parliament a party must obtain at least 8 per cent of the total votes cast, was introduced in 1985, just before the last elections. At present four political parties are represented in Parliament. Three other parties that stood for election could not obtain the statutory minimum number of votes required in order to have a seat in Parliament. The constitutionality of this law has been challenged. The Supreme Court, sitting as the Supreme Constitutional Court has ruled that the law is not unconstitutional.

Article 78 provides that the Republic's Assembly will have power to enact laws, to exercise control over the Council of

Ministers and over the ministers themselves, to debate and approve bills in connection with the budget, to give general and special amnesty, and to decide whether death penalties imposed by the courts should be carried out. It also has power to ratify international agreements.

Article 80 declares that the Assembly of the Republic is inviolable. No one may restrict the freedom of the Assembly, act in a manner disturbing its peace, or insult its formal personality. Immunity of the deputies is regulated by article 84. Deputies cannot be held responsible for their votes or statements during parliamentary debates. Where it is alleged that a deputy has committed an offence, he cannot be arrested or prosecuted without the leave of the Assembly, unless in the case of a flagrant offence punishable with death or imprisonment for five years.

The Assembly may, but only by absolute majority of the total number of its members, decide on its dissolution and the holding of general elections. In case of government crises, Article 88 gives the President of the state certain powers. It empowers him to dissolve the Assembly and hold new elections if and when it becomes impossible to appoint a Council of Ministers having the support of the Assembly, within a period of sixty days. If within a period of one year the Council of Ministers cannot obtain a vote of confidence or is defeated three times by a motion of no-confidence the President may dissolve the Assembly and decide to hold elections. The President may, after certain consultations, submit to a referendum the issue of dissolving the Assembly.

Declaration of war and authorization to send armed forces to foreign countries, or to allow foreign armed forces to be stationed in the Turkish Republic of Northern Cyprus, are vested in the Assembly, but if the country is the victim of sudden armed aggression and it is not possible for the Assembly to be convened, the President of the Republic will also be able to decide on the use of the armed forces.

### 5. THE HEAD OF STATE

The President of the Turkish Repubic of Northern Cyprus is elected for a period of five years. He has to be of Cypriot parentage. There is also a five-year residence qualification. He has to be over 35 years of age. He must also be a graduate of an institution of higher education.

Article 102 provides that the President is the head of state; in this capacity he represents the unity and integrity of the state. He is responsible for securing respect for the Constitution, for carrying out public affairs in an impartial, uninterrupted, and orderly manner, and for the continuation of the state. The President of the Republic represents, on behalf of the Assembly, the Commander-in-Chief of the armed forces of the republic. Transitional article 10 provides that legal provisions and all other procedures regarding the armed forces that were in force on the date of the coming into operation of the Constitution shall continue to be in force and implemented. According to legal provisions, the Commander of the security forces is responsible to the Prime Minister in the discharge of his duties. The police force is attached to the Prime Ministry but in the discharge of its duties it is responsible to the Commander of the security forces.

The President may preside over meetings of the Council of Ministers but he does not have a vote. The President will not be responsible for acts committed in the execution of his official functions, but the Prime Minister and ministers may be. The President appoints the Prime Minister from amongst deputies, and he also appoints ministers on the recommendation of the Prime Minister. He can terminate the appointment of any minister at the request of the Prime Minister.

He also has the power either to promulgate by publication in the *Official Gazette,* or to return, laws enacted by the Assembly. He may ask the Supreme Court, sitting as the Constitutional Court, for its opinion as to whether any law or decision of the Assembly is repugnant to or inconsistent with the Constitution.

The Constitution provides that when a state of emergency or martial law is declared, the Council of Ministers, presided over by the President of the Republic, may issue decrees having the force of law on matters made imperative by the state of emergency or martial law. Certain articles of the Constitution may be suspended during a state of emergency or martial law.

The Constitution also provides in article 111 for the establishment of the Republic's Security Council. This body is to be presided over by the President of the Assembly, the Prime Minister, the Ministers of Defence, Interior, and Foreign

Affairs, commanders of the armed forces and police. The Council shall submit to the Council of Ministers its views concerning decisions with regard to the formulation, establishment, and implementation of the security policy of the state and its views on co-ordination. The matters submitted by the Security Council for consideration by the Council of Ministers shall take precedence over other agenda items.[9]

In case of vacancy in the office of President or in case of his temporary absence the President of the Assembly deputizes for him.

## 6. THE EXECUTIVE

Article 106 provides that the Council of Ministers shall be composed of a Prime Minister and ministers. The Prime Minister shall be appointed by the President from amongst deputies. Ministers may be appointed from among persons who are not deputies. Ministers are appointed by the President upon the recommendation of the Prime Minister.

Ministries are to be established by decree, in accordance with the principles laid down by the Constitution, upon the recommendation of the Prime Minister and approval of the President. The number of ministries cannot exceed ten.

The Prime Minister must secure co-ordination between the ministries, formulate the general policy of the Council of Ministers, and see to the observance of the relevant laws. The Prime Minister presides over the meetings of the Council of Ministers. The President may also preside over meetings of the Council, but he cannot vote at such meetings.

A newly formed government has to obtain a vote of confidence before it can be installed in office.

There is no provision in the Constitution as to how the decisions of the Council of Ministers are to be taken. It is submitted that in parliamentary systems like ours there is collective responsibility for the policy decisions of the Council and, therefore, such decisions must be taken by unanimous vote, and not by mere majority.

[9] The Security Council of the Republic has not yet been established.

### 7. THE JUDICIARY

Article 136 provides that judicial power in the Turkish Republic of Northern Cyprus is exercised by independent courts. Appointments, promotions, disciplinary control, and all matters relating to the President and judges of the Supreme Court and to judges of subordinate courts is within the exclusive competence of the Supreme Council of Judicature.

The highest court in the state is the Supreme Court composed of a President and seven judges. When sitting as the Supreme Constitutional Court it is composed of five judges (including the President) and it sits with a quorum of three as the Court of Appeal.

The Supreme Court has jurisdiction to sit as the Supreme Constitutional Court, the Court of Appeal, and as the High Administrative Court.

The Supreme Court, sitting as the Constitutional Court, has exclusive jurisdiction in the following matters:

   (i) to sit as the Supreme Council to hear and determine accusations against the President, Prime Minister, and ministers, as provided by law;

  (ii) as a final adjudicator on any matter relating to any conflict of power or competence arising between the state organs or state authorities;

 (iii) to hear and determine a reference made by the President of the State before promulgation of a law of the Assembly, as to whether such proposed law or any specified provision thereof is repugnant to or inconsistent with any provisions of the Constitution;

  (iv) to hear and determine annulment suits regarding constitutionality of laws or decisions of the Assembly, or of any rules or regulations, which may be instituted by the head of state, political groups, or at least seven deputies and other associations;

   (v) to hear and determine references regarding questions of unconstitutionality of any law or decision, which are reserved by courts for the decision of the Supreme Court, sitting as the Constitutional Court, and

  (vi) to interpret the Constitution.

However, the Supreme Court, sitting as the Supreme Constitutional Court, has no power to adjudicate on an election petition. The Constitution provides for the setting up of election councils to exercise power in relation to elections of the President and of the deputies.

In Cyprus it is possible to challenge the constitutionality of a statute after it has been duly promulgated by publication in the *Official Gazette*. This system was introduced by the 1960 Cyprus Constitution and has been retained both by the Constitution of 1975 and that of 1985.

The Supreme Court, sitting as the High Administrative Court, has exclusive jurisdiction under article 152 of the Constitution to review administrative acts and decisions on the grounds of excess or abuse of power, unconstitutionality, or illegality. This article is analogous to article 146 of the 1960 Constitution, which created exclusive jurisdiction in the Supreme Constitutional Court in the field of administrative law. As this competence is provided to be 'exclusive', no legislation can confer parallel competence on any other court of law. As the text of article 152 of the Constitution is substantially the same as that of article 146 of the 1960 Cyprus Constitution, the case-law which evolved before the intercommunal troubles of December 1963, regarding judicial review of administrative acts in Cyprus, continues to apply in the Turkish Republic of Northern Cyprus today.

## 8. THE OFFICE OF AUDIT

The Office of Audit, which is an organ of financial control, is an independent organ of the Republic. It is not attached to any of the ministries. It has the duty to audit public revenue and expenditure and report its findings to the Assembly. The appointment of the President and members of the Office of Audit and its functions are regulated by law. Its President and members are elected by the Legislative Assembly.

Under article 93 of the Constitution it has a duty to scrutinize bills concerning expenditure accounts of past financial years which are to be submitted to the Assembly for approval within one year from the end of the financial year to which they relate.

## 9. THE ATTORNEY-GENERAL'S OFFICE

The Law Office of the Turkish Republic of Northern Cyprus is an independent office and its head is the Attorney-General. This means that the office of the Attorney-General is not attached to a ministry. The Deputy Attorney-General acts for the Attorney-General in case of his absence.

The Attorney-General is appointed from amongst persons qualified for appointment as a judge of the Supreme Court and holds office under the same terms and conditions as a judge of the Supreme Court. He cannot be removed from office except on similar grounds and in a similar manner as a judge of the Supreme Court.

All matters relating to the appointment, promotion, transfer of, and exercise of disciplinary control over the Attorney-General, the Deputy Attorney-General, and counsel of the Republic (law officers) are within the competence of the Supreme Council of Law Officers. This Council is composed of the Attorney-General as Chairman, a member of the Supreme Court designated for this purpose for a specified period or for a particular meeting, the Deputy Attorney-General, a District Court President who is the most senior in office, a law officer who is the most senior in office among the law officers, and two other law officers selected by secret ballot from amongst the law officers to represent them in the Council. The Supreme Council is an independent body; no other organ or person can issue directives or orders to the Council, or without lawful excuse delay the execution of its decisions.

The Attorney-General is the legal adviser of the state, the Prsident, the Prime Minister, the Council of Ministers, ministers, and other organs of the state. The advisory function of the Attorney-General is similar to that exercised by certain chambers of the Council of State in Turkey. He exercises all such powers and performs all such other functions and duties as are conferred or imposed on him by the Constitution or by law. The powers vested in the Attorney-General are exercised by him in person or by his Deputy or by other counsel in his office.

The Attorney-General's office scrutinizes parliamentary bills from the point of view of constitutionality before they are submitted by the government to the Legislative Assembly. A scrutiny of a similar nature is also carried out by the office before the laws enacted by the Assembly are published in the *Official Gazette*.

The Attorney-General represents the state in all civil cases in which the state is a party, as well as in administrative and constitutional law cases.

In the Turkish Republic of Northern Cyprus the investigation of criminal offences is within the competence of the police authorities, but the institution of criminal proceedings and the carrying out of public prosecutions are within the sole responsibility of the Attorney-General.

### 10. THE PUBLIC SERVICE COMMISSION

Article 121 of the Constitution provides that impartial and independent organs shall be established to exercise power with regard to appointment, confirmation, promotion, transfer, retirement, and disciplinary control of public officers. The establishment and functions of this organ are regulated by law. These powers are now exercised by the Public Service Commission.[10]

The decisions of the Public Service Commission are administrative in nature and are subject to judicial control by the High Administrative Court on an application for review.[11] The grounds for review of administrative acts are, generally speaking, excess or abuse of power, illegality, unconstitutionality, and violation of general principles of administrative law. In disciplinary proceedings against public officers the rules of 'natural justice' must be observed. The Constitution itself lays down strict procedural rules before disciplinary punishment can be given.[12]

The Public Service Commission has no jurisdiction with respect to judges, law officers, the President and members of the

[10] Law No. 53 of 1983. The Public Service Commission was first established by virtue of the provisions of the 1960 Constitution. Such a Commission existed and exercised power in relation to public officers long before Law No. 53/1983 was enacted.

[11] See this author's *Administrative Law* (Nicosia, 1974), 85–97 and 218–73.

[12] Art. 121(4).

Office of Audit, and the police. Other organs exercise powers in respect to these officers. Moreover, there are some specified political offices in the higher echelons of the administration to which appointments are made by an instrument signed by the minister concerned, the Prime Minister, and the President of the Republic.[13] The appointment or termination of appointment of such an officer is a discretionary act but in some instances the High Administrative Court has exercised revisional jurisdiction.

## 11. CONCLUSIONS

The Constitution of the Turkish Republic of Northern Cyprus contains some characteristics of a parliamentary as well as some characteristics of a presidential system.

Legislative control over the Executive is secured by the requirement that the government must obtain a vote of confidence before it can be installed in office and by the procedure of a motion of no-confidence, tabling of questions, and the holding of general debates or investigations. On the other hand, the President is endowed with power, under certain circumstances, to dissolve the Assembly and order the holding of elections.

The Constitution secures the observance of the rule of law. Part II guarantees to the individual certain fundamental rights and liberties which may only be restricted or limited by law for the purposes set out in the Constitution itself. These rights must be respected by the state. Furthermore, the right of access to court is also expressly guaranteed. Article 152 provides for judicial review of executive or administrative acts on the grounds of unconstitutionality, illegality, and excess or abuse of power. The decisions of the High Administrative Court are binding on all organs and authorities in the state. This principle is further amplified by provisions regarding the independence of the courts and tenure of office of judges.

As has been stated by the Supreme Court, a state subject to law is a state that respects human rights and establishes a just order of law whereby these rights are protected and maintained.

---

[13] Art. 121(5) of the Constitution and Law No. 53/1977.

All acts and functions of such a state must be in conformity with the law and the Constitution. In the Turkish Republic of Northern Cyprus an independent judiciary is the guardian of human rights and the upholder of principles that secure respect for law and the Constitution.

# 13

# Statehood and Recognition

## I. STATEHOOD

It is often asserted that the formation of a new state is a matter of fact and not of law.[1] This proposition was thought to follow from the fundamental premise of the so-called 'constitutive' theory of recognition, which held that 'a State is, and becomes an International Person through recognition only and exclusively'.[2]

It is through recognition, which is a matter of law, that such new State becomes subject to International Law. As soon as recognition is given, the new State's territory is recognized as the territory of a subject of International law, and it matters not how this territory is acquired before the recognition.[3]

On the other hand, according to the *declaratory* theory, recognition of new states is a political act which is in principle independent of the existence of the new state as a full subject of international law.[4]

Today most international lawyers subscribe to the declaratory theory that a unit which possesses the criteria of statehood exists as a state independently of recognition, which is nothing else than a declaration of its existence.[5]

... the recognition of a State is not constitutive but merely declaratory.

[1] L. F. L. Oppenheim, *International Law*, i (1st edn., 1905), 624; i (8th edn., ed. Lauterpacht, London, 1955), 544.

[2] Ibid. i (1st edn.), 108 (8th edn.), 125.

[3] Ibid. i (1st edn.), 264 (8th edn.), 514.

[4] See T. C. Chen, *The International Law of Recognition*, ed. L. C. Green (London, 1951), 130, for a full discussion of this proposition.

[5] *Deutsche Continental Gas Gesellschaft* v. *Polish State*, Annual Digest 5 (1929–30) No. 5; Chen, *The International Law of Recognition*; I. Brownlie, *Principles of Public International Law* (2nd edn., Oxford, 1973), 94; O'Connell, *International Law* (London, 1970), i. 123–34; and Brierly, *The Law of Nations*, (6th edn., Oxford, 1963), 139.

The State exists by itself and the recognition is nothing else than a declaration of its existence, recognized by the States from which it emanates.[6]

According to Brownlie,

Recognition, as a public act of State, is an optional and political act and there is no legal duty in this regard. However, in a deeper sense, if an entity bears the marks of statehood, other states put themselves at risk legally if they ignore the basic obligations of State relations.[7]

The criteria of 'statehood' are laid down by international law. Whether these criteria exist in a given case is a matter of fact. Recognition is not in principle constitutive, but only declaratory. Whether a state exists in law is a matter to be decided independently of recognition.[8] In other words, absence of recognition is not tantamount to saying that the state does not exist.

The essential characteristics of statehood in international law are: people, territory, government. The word 'state' is described in the United States case of *Texas* v. *White*[9] in the following terms:

A State, . . . is a political community of free citizens, occupying a territory of defined boundaries, and organized under a government sanctioned and limited by a written constitution, and established by the consent of the governed.

The best-known formulation of the basic criteria for statehood is that laid down in article 1 of the Montevideo Convention, 1933:

The State as a person of international law should possess the following

---

[6] *Deutsche Continental Gas Gesellschaft* v. *Polish State*, Annual Digest, 5 (1929–30) No. 5.

[7] *Principles of Public International Law* (2nd edn. Oxford, 1973), 94; cf. 30–3. O'Connell (*International Law*, i. 123–34) and Brierly (*The Law of Nations*, (6th edn. 1963), 139) are among writers who subscribe to the declaratist view.

[8] *Central and South American Telegraphic Company* v. *Chile, Moore Arbitrations*, 2938; *Tinoco Arbitration* I UNRIAA 369 and Colin Warbrick, 'The New British Policy on Recognition of Governments', ICLQ vol. 30, Part 3, July 1981, 568–92, at 586.

According to *Trendtex Trading Corporation Ltd.* v. *Central Bank of Nigeria* (1977) 1 All ER 881, the rules of customary international law are directly incorporated into English law and the courts may have access to them.

[9] (1868) 74 US (7 Wall.) 700.

qualifications: (a) a permanent population; (b) a defined territory; (c) government; and (d) capacity to enter into relations with other States.[10]

Recognition is subsequent and consequential to the entity possessing these criteria of statehood.

Dealing generally with conditions for recognition, O'Connell on *International Law*[11] says (p. 132):

Recognition is subsequent and consequential, and hence is conditional upon the entity being internally organised in such a way as to be competent to perform an international act. Premature recognition, that is of a community not so organised is an abuse of procedure which constitutes an illicit intervention in the affairs of the mother country from which the community is in the process of breaking away.

O'Connell continues:

However, provided the community is organised in the manner prescribed by international law the parent's consent is not a pre-condition of its statehood—for the parent may be the last to admit hard facts—and therefore the act of recognition is not dependent upon it.

Then on p. 133, he says:

. . . once a community exercises 'independent public authority' over a territory it exists as a state, and is thus recognisable. The qualification should be added, however, that this independence is not likely to be nullified by the mother state.

According to Charles Rousseau, recognition is the acknowledgement of an existing fact; it does not necessarily imply approval. In the long run, political considerations and balances of power are the factors that determine the result. A fact is not nullified by refusal to accept it. Non-recognition, in most cases, is no more than postponement of recognition. What is most important is whether there is a possibility of bringing back the status quo ante by the use of force.[12]

---

[10] *League of Nations Treaty Series*, vol. 165, p. 19. For an incisive analysis of these criteria, see J. Crawford, 'The Criteria for Statehood in International Law', *The British Year Book of International Law* (1975–6), 94–182.

[11] 2nd edn.

[12] *Droit international public*, iii (Paris, 1977), 526.

There is some academic opinion to the effect that a new rule has come into existence, prohibiting entities from claiming statehood if their creation is in violation of an applicable right to self-determination.[13] In Fawcett's words,

. . . to the traditional criteria of the recognition of a regime as a new State must now be added the requirement that it shall not be based upon a systematic denial in its territory of certain civil and political rights, including in particular the right of every citizen to participate in the government of his country, directly or through representatives elected by regular, equal and secret suffrage. This principle was affirmed in the case of Rhodesia by the virtually unanimous condemnation of the unilateral declaration of independence by the world community, and by the universal withholding of recognition of the new regime which was a consequence.

It would follow then that the illegality of the rebellion was not an obstacle to the establishment of Rhodesia as an independent State but that the political basis and objectives of the regime were, and that the declaration of independence was without international effect.[14]

In the above context 'self-determination' denotes the right of the people of an existing state to choose its form of government in a way which makes it possible for the citizens to participate in the government of that state.

The late Sir Hersch Lauterpacht was of the view that in international law there was a legal duty to accord recognition if certain conditions were met.[15] Although most international lawyers would agree that premature recognition of revolutionary authorities may violate international law, many eminent jurists consider all other aspects of recognition to be within a state's absolute political discretion.

[13] See Dr James Crawford, 'The Criteria for Statehood in International Law', *British Year Book of International Law* (1975–6), 149–64, particularly 163–4.

[14] *The British Year Book of International Law*, 41 (1965–8), 103, at 112–13. The Privy Council in *Madzimbamuto* v. *Lardner-Burke* (1968) 3 WLR 1229, at 1250, did not consider this position, arguing instead that Southern Rhodesia was not a state because the legitimate government was still trying to reassert itself. Cf. *In re James* (1977) 2 WLR 1 (CA).

[15] *Recognition in International Law* (London, 1948), at 158–74.

## 2. RECOGNITION OF STATES AND GOVERNMENTS

After the Second World War there was an enormous increase in the number of states which came about largely from decolonization.[16] Some of the newly independent states face special difficulties as they do not have the traditional means to maintain and defend their sovereignty.[17] But the size of a unit is not a factor determining recognition.

In some quarters membership of the United Nations is seen as setting the final seal of approval on a country's independence. The United Nations Charter provides that membership of the organization is open to all peace-loving states which accept the obligations contained in the Charter and, in the judgment of the organization, are able and willing to carry out these obligations. In practice the admission of states to membership is effected more or less automatically by a decision of the General Assembly on the recommendation of the Security Council. Membership of the UN is not obligatory. Switzerland, for instance, has not sought it.

In a recent debate in the House of Lords, Baroness Young explained the criteria which the British government normally apply to the recognition of a state. Such a state 'should have, and seem likely to continue to have, a clearly defined territory—with a population, and a government which is able of itself to exercise effective control of that territory, full internal autonomy, and independence in its external relations'. She went on to say that 'there are, however, exceptional cases where other factors—including relevant United Nations resolutions—may have to be taken into account'.[18]

Recognition of a government is distinguishable from recogni-

---

[16] At the end of the Second World War there were about 70 independent states in the world. Today there are some 170.

[17] Events in the Caribbean island of Grenada in Nov. 1983 highlighted this problem, and it was discussed when the Commonwealth heads of government met in New Delhi later in the month. That meeting requested the Secretary-General of the Commonwealth to undertake a study on the special needs of small states consonant with the right to sovereignty and territorial integrity which they share with all nations.

[18] *Hansard*, House of Lords, 15 Feb. 1984, cols. 318–45, col. 341.

tion of a state. Recognition of government implies recognition of the state; it would be impossible to recognize a government but not the state of which it is the governing body. Conversely, it is possible to recognize a state but not the government of that state. On the other hand, within the territory of a state it is possible to recognize two governments, one of them *de jure* and the other *de facto*.[19]

The traditional view is that there are two kinds of recognition of a government which may be accorded by the executive, i.e. *de jure* and *de facto* recognition.[20] *De jure* recognition implies a definite indication of preparedness for normal diplomatic relations. On the other hand, *de facto* recognition indicates willingness to maintain only limited diplomatic or consular contacts with that government. The latter type of recognition is more tentative than the former. It is not normally accompanied by the establishment of full diplomatic relations. However, there is no consensus of opinion as to the precise legal meanings of these terms.

On 28 April 1980 the British government announced a change in the policy and practice relating to recognition.[21] According to the new policy the formal act of recognition of *governments* is now to be dispensed with. Where a new regime comes to power unconstitutionally the attitude of the British government on the question whether it qualifies to be a government will be left to be inferred from the nature of dealings with it on a normal government-to-government basis. That is to say, without accordance of recognition to such a regime, the

[19] As for the German situation after the Second World War, see *Carl-Zeiss-Stiftung* v. *Rainer and Keeler Ltd.* (1966) 2 All ER 536. Two separate governments within the territory of the German state came into existence after the War.

[20] In some cases the courts have given effect to acts of established governments even though the Executive had not accorded *de facto* or *de jure* recognition: see the author's article, 'Acts of Unrecognised Governments' in the Apr. 1981 issue of the *International and Comparative Law Quarterly*, 388–415.

It was held in *Trendtex Trading Corp.* v. *Central Bank of Nigeria* (1977) 1 All ER 881, that international law confers status on *de facto* governments. The House of Lords has also laid emphasis on the principle of judicial abstention from adjudicating directly on the transactions of foreign sovereign states: *Buttes Gas & Oil Co.* v. *Hammer and others* (1980) 3 All ER 475.

[21] *Hansard,* House of Commons, vol. 985, col. 385.

British government will have dealings at the appropriate level with the new leaders. It should be stressed however that the policy statement makes it clear that British practice in respect of recognition of *statehood* remains unchanged; recognition of *states* continues in accordance with common international doctrine.[22]

### 3. THE TURKISH REPUBLIC OF NORTHERN CYPRUS AND RECOGNITION

When the Turkish Federated State was set up in 1975 no federal structure existed to which it could be federated. The reason behind such a move was to keep the door open for a federation of two federated states. However, in the international field the Turkish Cypriots remained 'stateless' because the Turkish 'Federated' State did not, and could not, ask for international recognition. Paradoxically, the Greek Cypriot administration claimed to be the 'government' of the whole of Cyprus even though its writ has not run in Turkish areas since December 1963, as confirmed by U Thant, the then UN Secretary-General.[23]

All through the process of the intercommunal talks conducted under the auspices of the United Nations since 1975, the Greek Cypriot side assumed, in complete disregard of the present realities, that a unitary 'government of Cyprus' still existed and that the Greek Cypriot administration was that 'government'. This attitude has been a dominant factor especially with respect to the constitutional aspects of the problem and on the matter of practical measures that should be considered by both sides to promote goodwill, mutual confidence, and the return to normal conditions.

The Western powers followed the procedure adopted by the UN in 1964 in recognizing the Greek Cypriot administration as the only government representing Cyprus. Had they treated the

[22] The new British practice seems to have some similarities with the 'Estrada Doctrine' propounded by the Foreign Secretary of Mexico in 1930, to the effect that recognition of governments should not be given because to do so would be a breach of the standard of non-intervention.

[23] Report to the Security Council on UN operation in Cyprus, S/6228 of 11 Mar. 1965.

Greek and Turkish administrations as integral components of one state, in the spirit of the bi-communal provisions of the 1959 Zurich Agreement the trend towards separation could have been contained and the chances of a settlement based on eventual reunification facilitated.[24] The recognition of the Greek Cypriot administration as the only government of Cyprus pushed the Turkish Cypriots into isolation and forced them into increasing dependence on Turkey. Inevitably a *de facto* separate state evolved with the passage of time.

The aim of the Turkish Cypriots in declaring, on 15 November 1983, an independent state, i.e. the Turkish Republic of Northern Cyprus, was to assert their status as co-founders of the future federal republic of Cyprus and to ensure that the sovereignty of the Republic will derive from the existing two states joining together as equals to form the future federal republic. The establishment of the independent state is not a final solution of the Cyprus problem but leaves the door open for a federal solution.

The declaration of statehood made it clear beyond any doubt that the new Turkish Cypriot Republic could ask for international recognition. However, the UN Security Council resolution of 18 November 1983,[25] deplored 'the declaration of the Turkish Cypriot authorities[26] of the purported secession of part of the Republic of Cyprus' and considered the declaration as legally invalid and incompatible with the 1960 Treaty of Establishment[27] of the Republic of Cyprus and the 1960 Treaty of Guarantee, and called for its withdrawal.[28] The Security Council also called upon all states not to recognize any Cypriot state other than the 'Republic of Cyprus'.

---

[24] See ch. 9 n. 71, above.     [25] 541 (1983).

[26] The word 'authorities' denotes legal standing, but leaves the matter undefined.

[27] Art. 10 of this treaty stipulates that any dispute or difficulty concerning the interpretation of the provisions of the treaty be referred to a five-member tribunal consisting of representatives of the government of Cyprus, the three guarantors, and a neutral appointed from the International Court of Justice. *Quaere* whether this adjudicatory procedure should not have been followed before the Security Council passed judgment on the validity of the declaration of 'statehood' in the north.

[28] At the risk of cavilling, one might question the utility of withdrawing a declaration which is purportedly invalid.

The Security Council resolution clearly shows how principles of law can be overshadowed by politics. First, the resolution presupposes wrongly that the 'state of affairs' created by the Treaty of Establishment and guaranteed under the Treaty of Guarantee still exists. The treaties themselves are valid and in force, but the bi-communality of the state, its government, and its organs came to an end in December 1963 when the Turkish Cypriot co-founder partner was ousted by force from all organs of the government and the administration and was deprived of all its constitutional rights as a prelude to changing the 1960 Constitution by unconstitutional means and to establishing a purely Greek Cypriot administration. Moreover, the declaration states that the Turkish Cypriot community considers itself bound by the treaties which gave birth to the Republic of Cyprus and stipulates that the newly created entity will not unite with any other state, except with the southern unit to form a federal republic of Cyprus.[29]

No parallels can be drawn between the 'unilateral declaration of independence' (UDI) in Southern Rhodesia and the declaration of statehood in north Cyprus. A 'secession' or 'UDI' implies a breakaway from an omnipotent exclusive government that exercises effective control over the whole territory under its sovereignty. In Cyprus, with the geographical separation of the two ethnic peoples and their respective governments, there was not a single exclusive government at the material time.

In Rhodesia, the unilateral declaration of independence was condemned by the world community and recognition of the new regime was withheld[30] because it was based upon a systematic denial in its territory of certain civil and political rights, including in particular the right of every citizen to participate in the government of the country, directly or through representatives elected by regular, equal, and secret suffrage.[31] The creation of the Rhodesian regime was in violation of an

[29] The text of the declaration of statehood is included in UN Doc. A/38/586-S/16148 of 16 Nov. 1983.

[30] For the Security Council resolution requiring the non-recognition of the Smith Government of Rhodesia, see SC Res. 211, SCOR, 25th year, Resolutions, 5.

[31] Fawcett, *The British Year Book of International Law*, 41 (1965–6), 103, at 112–13. On *Madzimbamuto v. Larder-Burke*, see above, n. 14.

applicable right to self-determination, which in that context denotes the right of the people of an existing state to choose their form of government in a way that makes it possible for the citizens to participate in the government of the state.[32] While in Rhodesia a section of the population was denied basic human rights and the right to self-determination in choosing a representative government, in Cyprus the Turkish Cypriots, who had been ousted from the bi-communal Republic in 1963 and had been the victims of violations of their human rights, in declaring statehood were themselves making a choice as to their political organization in the exercise of the right to self-determination.

The Turkish Republic of Northern Cyprus has been recognized by Turkey and this is fundamental for its survival. The new republic has, and it will continue to have, relations with other foreign countries for the time being on a limited basis, that is, without the establishment of full diplomatic relations which amount to official recognition.

The Turkish Republic of Northern Cyprus possesses all the criteria of statehood, a clearly defined territory,[33] with a population, and a government which is able of itself to exercise effective and exclusive control of that territory, full internal autonomy, and independence in its external relations, but it has not been accorded universal recognition. According to the above views, this state exists independently of international recognition.

Recognition is not, however, merely a matter of law, it is a

---

[32] James Crawford, *The Creation of States in International Law* (Oxford, 1979), 104.

[33] The contention of the Greek Cypriot side is that the Turkish Republic of Northern Cyprus has no 'territory' of its own because the area in question is part of the territory of the Republic of Cyprus. However, it is a fact that, as a result of evolutionary developments, two separate and exclusive administrations came into being, as is also acknowledged by the Geneva Declaration of 1974 (ch. 4, s. 5), and the territory of the Republic has been effectively divided into two sectors. Either of these administrations cannot by itself represent the Republic of Cyprus.

Moreover, there is some official acknowledgement of the territory under the control of each of these separate administrations. For instance, the Makarios–Denktash guide-lines of 1977 refer to the 'territory under the administration of each community'. It is now generally accepted that the territorial aspect of a future Cyprus settlement will be based on the principle of *bi-zonality*.

matter that has a very high political overtone. The political element is so strong that an entity which possesses all the criteria of statehood may not be recognized as such for political reasons. This is really the obstacle that has hindered the recognition of the Turkish Republic of Northern Cyprus by other states, except Turkey.

The UN Security Council resolution 541 (1983), taken soon after the proclamation of the Turkish Republic of Northern Cyprus, deploring the declaration and decreeing it as legally invalid, may be considered as one of the impediments to recognition. This resolution has considerable effect, especially on non-aligned countries. It can be criticized because it is biased and does not take into consideration the legitimate rights of the Turkish Cypriots.

Since then, however, the success of the policy followed by the Turkish Republic of Northern Cyprus towards the mission of good offices of the UN Secretary-General (such as the success achieved at the 1985 summit[34] and the rejection by the Greek Cypriot side of the 29 March 1986 document[35]) has gradually mitigated the rigour of that resolution. In this way it has been possible to consolidate the state by the acceptance of the Constitution after a referendum[36] and to hold general elections.

Some lawyers also argue that recognition of this Republic may cause complications *vis-à-vis* the international agreements that gave birth to the Republic of Cyprus. This argument is not convincing when one takes into consideration the fact that the state of affairs created by these agreements ceased to exist in December 1963, anyway, as a result of which two separate states and governments have evolved.

## 4. STATES CREATED AS A RESULT OF USE OF FORCE

The prohibition of the threat or use of force in international relations is one of the most fundamental of the rules of international law. It is said therefore that recognition of a state created as a result of illegal use of force is incompatible with the

---

[34] Ch. 11, above.
[35] Ch. 14 s. 2, below.
[36] Ch. 12 s. 1, above.

principles of international law. In such a case the entity owes its existence directly and substantially to illegal intervention—in which case it is unlikely to be, and will be presumed not to be, independent—or it does not, in which case the normal criteria for statehood will presumably apply. This principle is also known as the 'Stimson doctrine' and was invoked during the Manchurian crisis, as the basis for refusal by the United States and the large majority of the League of Nations to recognize the 'State of Manchukuo' that was created in 1932 by illegal Japanese intervention.[37]

According to Charles Rousseau, the 'Stimson doctrine' has not been successfully applied. He says that the basic criterion is whether or not there is a strong will to bring back the status quo ante. If this is not possible, the prohibition against recognizing illegal situations becomes academic. The law has in the long run to keep abreast with the *de facto* situation.[38]

There is also a similar principle known as the 'Hallstein doctrine' formulated after 1945 to discourage the recognition of the German Democratic Republic.[39] According to this doctrine, recognition of the German Democratic Republic would be considered by the Federal Republic of Germany to be an unfriendly act that would entail revision, and suspension, of diplomatic relations between the Federal Republic and the recognizing state. This doctrine was applied in 1957 against Yugoslavia and in 1963 against Cuba. But gradually the Bonn government changed its strict attitude towards recognition of

---

[37] However, since Manchukuo was both illegally created and not independent (in the sense that it was a puppet state) the need in practice to distinguish the two points (creation of the state by use of force and its not being independent) did not really arise: See James Crawford, *Creation of States in International Law*, 59–60.

[38] *Droit international public*, iii (Paris, 1977), 526.

[39] The official text of this doctrine was tabled before the Parliament of the Federal German Republic (Bundestag) on 1 Dec. 1955 by the then Foreign Minister Von Brentano. Its reasoning was formulated as follows: 'There is only one German State; the authority and sovereignty of only one state can exist on the German territory; the so-called "German Democratic Republic" is an illegal and superficial arrangement imposed by the Soviet occupation forces.' It should be noted that the doctrine did not purport to apply to states that had already recognized the German Democratic Republic after its inception (1949) and before the doctrine was enunciated.

the German Democratic Republic, and re-established diplomatic relations with Yugoslavia on 31 January 1968 and with
Cuba on 18 January 1975 respectively. By 1969 the relaxation of
the rule became more apparent. The Federal Republic
protested to, but did not sever relations with, six Afro-Asian
countries (Iraq, Kampuchea, Sudan, Syria, South Yemen, and
Egypt) that recognized the German Democratic Republic. On
18 September 1973 the Federal Republic of Germany and the
German Democratic Republic were admitted without opposition to the United Nations. Both are now widely recognized,
and the once controversial issue of their separate statehood is
now only of academic interest.

According to one learned author, recognition and acquies-
cence cannot purge the illegality of a situation created by the
unlawful use of force.[40] However, Bangladesh has been recognized as an independent state by all the components of the
international community, notwithstanding the fact that it relied
massively on Indian intervention to acquire statehood. The new
Ugandan government which overthrew Amin's regime with the
help of the Tanzanian army was at once recognized by most
states. Had the international community shared the conviction
that the intervening states were in breach of a peremptory norm
of international law, it would have contested the statehood of the
new entity or the representativeness of the new government.[41]

Turning once again to the question of Cyprus, the Turkish
military intervention of 1974 has to be examined in the light of
the principle prohibiting the use of force in international
relations. The recognition of the Greek Cypriot administration
as the 'Government of Cyprus', in spite of the fact that it has lost
control over a substantial territory in north Cyprus, is
sometimes based on the assumption that the situation created as
a result of the Turkish intervention must not be recognized. The
other aspect of this line of thinking is that, as the Turkish
Republic of Northern Cyprus was created as a result of Turkish
military intervention, the same principle prohibits its recognition.

---

[40] I. Brownlie, *Principles of Public International Law* (2nd edn., Oxford, 1973),
514.
[41] Natalino Ronzitti, *Rescuing Nationals Abroad Through Military Coercion and
Intervention on Grounds of Humanity* (Dordrecht, 1985), 133.

As has already been pointed out, the international community has not always been consistent in upholding the twin principles against use of force and non-recognition of the *de facto* situation created in consequence thereof. It is submitted, however, that these principles of international law cannot be applied to the situation in Cyprus for the following basic reasons. First, the Turkish military intervention of 1974, after the crisis that erupted in the island, was not an illegal intervention. It was based on the Treaty of Guarantee under which Turkey, as one of the guarantor powers, had a right, and an obligation, to intervene to re-establish the status quo and to protect the Turkish Cypriots.[42] Secondly, the Turkish Republic of Northern Cyprus was not established as a result of the Turkish intervention of 1974. That state was established on 15 November 1983 (some nine years after the Turkish intervention) by the Turkish people of Cyprus in the exercise of the right to self-determination.[43] The declaration of statehood was the culmination of a process of political and administrative evolution which began in December 1963 when Turkish Cypriots were ejected, by the Greek Cypriot wing of the Cyprus Republic, from all organs of the bi-national state.[44]

Finally, it is important to note that the declaration of statehood in north Cyprus on 15 November 1983 was not a secession from the Republic of Cyprus. The Turkish Cypriots did not secede from a constitutional order. The participation of the two communities in the running of the affairs of the Republic of Cyprus had ceased in December 1963 with the outbreak of communal troubles. Since then, the Greek Cypriot side had assumed the powers and functions of the 'Government of the Republic of Cyprus' and had changed the 'basic articles' of the 1960 Constitution even though this was forbidden by international treaties.[45] This was a matter of international law stemming from the Treaty of Guarantee. In such a situation it was the duty of the guarantor powers (Great Britain, Greece, and Turkey) to refuse to recognize the *de facto* situation created

[42] See ch. 5, above.    [43] Ch. 9, above.    [44] See ch. 2 s. 8, above.
[45] Art. 182 of the Constitution provides that the basic articles thereof, set out in Annexe III thereto, which have been incorporated from the Zurich Agreement of 11 Feb. 1959, cannot be amended, whether by way of variation, addition, or repeal.

as a result of that violation and not to recognize the Greek Cypriot administration as the 'government of Cyprus'. For this reason Turkey refused to recognize the Greek Cypriot government as the 'Government of the Republic of Cyprus', while the two other guarantor powers chose to do so. In spite of such recognition, however, there was no organ in Cyprus that could legitimately represent the Republic of Cyprus as envisaged by the 1960 Constitution, the basic articles of which were entrenched by international treaty. By a process of evolution, the government of the Republic was replaced by two *de facto* autonomous and exclusive administrations (one, of the Greek Cypriot community, and the other, of the Turkish Cypriot community),[46] the existence of which were acknowledged by the three guarantor powers in the Geneva Declaration of 30 July 1974.[47]

Moreover, the overriding principle of respect for territorial integrity of states, as also enunciated in the Declaration of Friendly Relations,[48] is subject to such states being possessed of representative governments. The Republic of Cyprus, as envisaged by the 1960 Constitution, had ceased to be a political association of two communities and therefore did not have a representative government. At the time of the declaration of statehood in north Cyprus the island was already divided into two sectors. Each of these territories had its homogeneous population as a result of implementation, on a voluntary basis, of the agreement for regrouping of populations concluded within the framework of the intercommunal talks.[49]

## 5. INDEPENDENCE

Independence is the central criterion of statehood. A new entity will have to demonstrate substantial independence, both formal and real, before it will be regarded as definitely created.[50]

---

[46] See also John Reddaway, *Burdened with Cyprus* (London, 1986), 179–86.

[47] For the text of the Declaration see HMSO Misc. No. 30 (1974) Cmnd. 5712.

[48] GA res. 2625 (XXV) of 24 Oct. 1970.

[49] See ch. 4 n. 41, above.

[50] James Crawford, *Creation of States in International Law*, 48–71.

It is often asserted by the Greek Cypriot side that 'invasion'[51] and 'continuous occupation' by Turkey nullifies this independence.

The Foreign Affairs Committee of the House of Commons, in their Report of 7 May 1987 on Cyprus, also refer to continued 'military occupation' as a factor precluding recognition.[52] But there is no suggestion that the state does not exist.

The Turkish view is that the Turkish forces are in north Cyprus at the request and with the consent of the ruling authority of the territory.[53] These forces are in north Cyprus for the protection of the Turkish Cypriots and when a solution is found they will be withdrawn,[54] except for those that will stay under a guarantee agreement. The Turkish forces do not exercise governmental authority or control over the territory. One should not lose sight of the fact that there are also mainland Greek troops in south Cyprus.[55]

The best way to demonstrate the absence of Turkish authority in north Cyprus is to show the omnipresence of

[51] As to this aspect of the argument, see section 4 of this chapter.

[52] p. xxxiii, para. 137. As to Turkish mainland troops in north Cyprus, the Report states, on the basis of British and UN sources, that the level of Turkish troops was around 27,500 in Dec. 1986, and that the number of the Turkish Cypriot security force is generally regarded to be about 4,500.

[53] This argument is reinforced by transitional art. 10 of the Constitution, which declares that 'All forces used in providing the external and internal security on the date of the coming into operation of this Constitution, shall continue to be so used . . . and the principles of cooperation accepted . . . in respect of these matters shall continue to be implemented.'

[54] The UN Secretary-General's draft framework agreement of Nov. 1984, which the Turkish Cypriot side accepted, states in s. 7 that 'a timetable for the withdrawal of non-Cypriot military troops and elements, as well as adequate guarantees, will be agreed upon prior to the establishment of the transitional federal government.'

[55] The Foreign Affairs Committee of the House of Commons state in their recent Report on Cyprus (para. 58) that the number of mainland Greek troops is now very much lower than the level reached during the 1964–7 period. The Report says that 'UN estimates, confirmed by British sources, suggest that there remain about 2,500 regular Greek troops (mainly officers and NCOs) in support of a Cypriot National Guard of between 11,000 and 12,000 men. In addition, there are a substantial number of Greek Cypriot reservists, estimated at about 50,000 by the UN and at about 60,000 by the Institute of Strategic Studies.'

Turkish Cypriot authority. The evolutionary stages of administrative and political organization of the Turkish Cypriot
community have been recounted in this work.[56] The separate
status of the two communities was reinforced by the three
guarantor powers' Declaration in Geneva on 30 July 1974,
following the first Turkish intervention, which amongst other
things 'noted the existence in practice in the Republic of Cyprus
of two autonomous administrations'. Although the Greek
Cypriots claim that this Declaration was merely a description of
a temporary situation arising from the 1974 coup and
intervention, and was not reflected in subsequent UN resolutions, it has provided much of the justification for the Turkish
Cypriots' subsequent pursuit of a bi-communal and bi-zonal
federation. With the creation of the Turkish Federated State of
Cyprus in February 1975, the Turkish Cypriots began the
process of creating an independent and autonomous administration in the north, as a prelude to securing agreement with the
Greek Cypriots on the formation of a federal constitution for the
whole island. The setting up of the Turkish Republic of
Northern Cyprus in November 1983 was the culmination of this
gradual process of political and administrative evolution on the
Turkish side.

[56] See ch. 2 s. 8 and ch. 4 s. 8, above.

# 14

# Developments after the Summit of 1985

After the failure of the summit the Turkish Cypriot side proceeded towards consolidation of the independent Republic.[1] The Constitution was adopted by the Assembly on 12 March 1985. A referendum was held on 5 May 1985. The Constitution was published in the *Official Gazette* on 7 May 1985.[2]

On the other side of the 'Green Line', Mr Kyprianou faced strong opposition. The communist AKEL party of Mr Ezekias Papaioannou and the Democratic Rally (DISI) of Mr Glafcos Clerides accused him of being responsible for the failure of the summit. On 22 February 1985, AKEL and DISI parties joined forces in the Greek Cypriot House of Representatives in securing a resolution that censured Mr Kyprianou for his handling of the Cyprus problem and called on him to abide by the views of the majority or else proclaim early presidential elections. The House called upon Mr Kyprianou to inform the UN Secretary-General without further delay of his acceptance of what was agreed at the three rounds of proximity talks, which would be binding only after the pending issues were discussed and agreed upon at the levels and stages stipulated in the draft.

Finally, the House of Representatives voted in late March 1985 by 20 (AKEL and Democratic Rally) to 2 (Socialists), after a walkout by 9 Democratic party deputies, to call for Mr Kyprianou's resignation and the holding of new presidential elections within 45 days. However, Mr Kyprianou resisted the pressures, buttressed by his constitutional position as directly elected 'President' and declared that he would not abide by the

---

[1] The draft constitution was published in the *Official Gazette* on 8 June 1984 for public notification but, in view of the 'proximity talks', the Turkish side delayed the process of final acceptance of the constitution in order not to disrupt the intercommunal negotiations.

[2] See ch, 12 s. 1.

decision of the House and would stay on till the expiry in February 1988 of his current term of office.

In April 1985 the UN Secretary-General, Mr Perez de Cuellar, prepared another document which he submitted to the parties. The document consisted of a 'Statement' of the Secretary-General and a draft 'Agreement'. He stressed that the Agreement was an 'integrated whole', which contained elements for an overall solution of the Cyprus question, to the framework of which the parties would be tied. The parties were expected to negotiate all outstanding issues in good faith and without circumscriptions beyond those contained in the Agreement and the Secretary-General's Statement of 12 April. The overall settlement would be submitted for approval when the working groups completed their work.

On the difficult political issue of Turkish troops and guarantees the Secretary-General stated that 'I understand that the Turkish Cypriot side does not *a priori* exclude any time-table for the withdrawal of non-Cypriot troops and that the Greek Cypriot side does not *a priori* exclude any country as guarantor.'[3]

The Turkish Cypriot side objected to the way the April document was prepared. There was a grave error of procedure in that the Secretary-General had, in the preparation of the document, consulted only the Greek Cypriot side, which, according to the Secretary-General's Statement of 12 April, accepted it.[4] The Turkish Cypriot side, which was then engrossed in constitution making, was not consulted. Apart from some 'cosmetic' changes to the January document, on one or two issues the Secretary-General had made some notable changes to the original document. One of these related to voting in the Upper House. The January document provided that voting should be by separate majorities in both Houses on major matters, and simple majority in both Houses on other matters,

---

[3] Mr Denktash has stated to journalists on 30 Jan. 1986 that the Secretary-General had given an undertaking to the Turkish Cypriot side that any future guarantee agreement would include Turkey's guarantee.

[4] It later appeared that the preparation of the April document and its purported acceptance by the Greek Cypriot side was a tactical move to bring pressure to bear on the Turkish side not to proceed with the acceptance of the constitution and the consolidation of the state. If this was not so, there was no apparent reason why Mr Kyprianou should not have accepted a later presentation by the Secretary-General, i.e. the 29 March 1986 document.

but there was a clause which required the consent of 'at least 30% of Turkish Cypriots in upper house' for a bill to become law. This clause was omitted in the April document. Moreover, the January document stated that residual powers would be vested in the provinces or federated states whereas the April document did not include any such explicit provision.

Presidential elections were held in the Turkish Republic of Northern Cyprus on 9 June 1985. Mr Rauf R. Denktash, who entered his nomination as an independent candidate, received 70 per cent of the votes cast and became the President of the Turkish Republic of Northern Cyprus.

Parliamentary elections were held in the Turkish Republic of Northern Cyprus on 23 June 1985. As a result of the elections the following seats were allocated to the four main political parties which received more than 8 per cent of the total votes cast within the Turkish Republic of Northern Cyprus, and thus qualified to be represented in Parliament:[5]

National Unity party: 24 seats
Republican Turkish party: 12 seats
Communal Liberation party: 10 seats
New Birth party (Renaissance party): 4 seats.

The first government of the Turkish Republic of Northern Cyprus was formed on 19 July 1985. This was a coalition government between the National Unity Party and the Communal Liberation Party. Dr Eroglu of the National Unity Party became the Prime Minister.[6]

The flurry of political and judicial activity in the south in the campaign to remove Mr Kyprianou resulted in a number of references and recourses being made to the Greek Cypriot Supreme Court on such issues as whether a 'vote of no confidence' in the legislature is binding on the 'President' of a presidential regime and whether the voting age could be reduced from 21 to 18 years.

Eventually the Greek Cypriot House dissolved itself to clear

[5] A law passed before the elections provided for a 'barrier' system of 8% of the votes cast. Three of the political parties that entered the elections could not pass the 'barrier' and were not represented in Parliament.

[6] The present government is made up of the National Unity party, supported by an independent.

the way for the holding of parliamentary elections. The House decided that elections should be held on 8 December 1985.[7]

On the eve of the elections, Mr Papandreou, the Greek Prime Minister, urged Greek Cypriots not to accept any solution to the Cyprus problem which would involve a mere time-table for withdrawal of Turkish troops and insisted instead on total withdrawal before any transitional government could be formed.[8]

As a result of the Greek Cypriot elections Mr Clerides's DISI party was allocated 19 seats, Mr Kyprianou's DIKO 16, Mr Papaiannou's AKEL 15, and Mr Lyssarides' EDEK 6 seats in the House. The AKEL party lost its first position in the House and now occupies only third place. The opposition parties, DISI and AKEL, together could not obtain a two-thirds majority, which is necessary to change the Constitution of 1960 relating to some aspects of the presidential regime, and therefore they called off the fight against Mr Kyprianou.

## 2. 29 MARCH 1986 DOCUMENT

The UN Secretary-General, Mr Perez de Cuellar, pursued the mission of good offices entrusted to him by the Security Council in resolution 367 (1975) and contained in subsequent resolutions, most recently in resolution 578 (1985).

The two sides agreed to the procedure the Secretary-General proposed to overcome the remaining differences. This was to hold a series of lower-level talks with representatives of each side before the Secretary-General could present a draft framework agreement simultaneously to both sides. With this in mind, low-level technical talks were held in London on 18–19 November 1985, between Turkish Cypriot representatives and UN officials. Similar talks were held in Geneva between UN officials

[7] A law of the Greek Cypriot House raised the number of deputies from 35 to 56.

[8] This was the position advocated by Mr Kyprianou. Therefore, it may be deduced that Mr Papandreou's speech was made in order to influence the elections in favour of Mr Kyprianou. This view is also supported by a statement made by the Central Committee of the communist AKEL party on 1 Feb. 1986, which was reported in the *Cyprus Mail* the following day.

and Greek Cypriot representatives on 30 November and 1 December. Another round of lower-level talks was held in Geneva on 26 and 27 February 1986 with the Turkish Cypriot side and on 28 February and 1 March with the Greek Cypriot side. This was followed by further discussions with both sides in Nicosia during the week of 3 March. The purpose of these talks was to bring into clearer focus the respective concerns of the two sides on the issues which remained to be resolved and to explore in conceptual terms ways of reconciling them.[9] The Secretary-General stated that these talks revealed many points of convergence and indicated ways of overcoming divergences that remained and of dealing with outstanding issues.[10]

On the basis of discussions with both sides, the Secretary-General prepared a 'Draft Framework Agreement' which preserved all the points on which agreement had been reached since August 1984, suggested solutions to the remaining divergencies, and proposed procedures for negotiation of the outstanding issues which remained to be tackled, including withdrawal of non-Cypriot forces, guarantees, and the three freedoms (i.e. freedom of movement, freedom of settlement, and the right to property). Once again, the draft described the matters therein as an integrated whole whose elements were interrelated, by which it was meant that they constituted a package and that each party's ultimate commitment to an overall solution would depend on their being able to resolve all outstanding issues. On 29 March 1986 he presented this document for consideration to both sides[11] with a letter of presentation.[12]

The Secretary-General presented a copy of the 'Draft Framework Agreement' together with his letter of presentation

[9] The UN Secretary-General had also sent a message to the Conference of Foreign Ministers of Islamic Countries held at Fez in Morocco 6–10 Jan. 1986, urging them not to take any action that could worsen the situation in Cyprus. This conference was also attended by the Foreign Minister of the Turkish Republic of Northern Cyprus. It is believed that the UN Secretary-General's message was intended to deter Islamic countries from giving recognition to the Turkish Republic of Northern Cyprus.

[10] Report by the Secretary-General on the United Nations operation in Cyprus: S/18102/Add. 1, dated 11 June 1986.

[11] For the text of the 'Draft Framework Agreement', see Appendix 6.

[12] Apendix 7.

to the President and members of the Security Council and to the Permanent Representatives of Greece and Turkey.

The Secretary-General's 1986 plan called for the reunification of Cyprus as a bi-national federal republic with a Greek Cypriot President and a Turkish Cypriot Vice-President, each with defined veto powers over a bi-cameral legislature.[13] The proposals would have reduced the land area under Turkish Cypriot control from 35.8 per cent to a little over 29 per cent.

Mr Kyprianou engaged in extensive consultations, both individually and collectively, with the other Greek Cypriot party leaders and the Greek Prime Minister. However, he kept his counsel until 20 April when he submitted his response to the UN Secretary-General.[14] It was brief but did not answer the Secretary-General's proposals. He stated that before the Greek Cypriot side could express its views on the Draft Framework Agreement 'it was necessary that there be agreement on the basic issues of the Cyprus problem as a matter of priority,' namely on 'withdrawal of the Turkish forces of occupation and settlers', as he put it, 'effective international guarantees and the application of the three freedoms, that is freedom of movement, freedom of settlement and the right to property'. Towards that end Mr Kyprianou requested the Secretary-General to convene an international conference to deal with the first two issues or, if this proved impossible, to convene a high-level meeting to deal with all three issues.

For the Greek Prime Minister the Secretary-General's document was one of 'unconditional surrender' for the Greek Cypriots[15] and he told the Greek Parliament:

I want to state categorically that in case the security of Cypriot Hellenism is threatened, the Greek government will respond, exhaust-

[13] The Foreign Affairs Committee of the House of Commons, in para. 104 of their Report on Cyprus, which was released on 2 July 1987, state that, with the wide-ranging veto powers in the executive and legislative fields, the proposed framework for a federal constitution 'provides a recipe for almost immediate deadlock and confrontation between the two ethnic communities'. The Committee observe that the idea of a federal constitution with only two parts has been regarded by political scientists in the past as unworkable. For this reason the Report suggests reviving the idea of a multi-cantonal constitution.

[14] The text of this letter is reproduced as Annexe IV to the Secretary-General's Report to the Security Council, S/18102/Add. 1 of 11 June 1986.

[15] *The Times*, 26 Apr. 1986.

ing all its capabilities to any suitable request by the lawful Cyprus government, within the framework of national, legal, and historical obligations linking us with Cyprus.[16]

The Turkish Cypriot side replied to the UN Secretary-General's initiative on 21 April. In his letter Mr Denktash set out his views and considerations in the light of which he informed the Secretary-General of the Turkish Cypriot acceptance of the 'Draft Framework Agreement'.[17] He stressed that the 'guarantee of Turkey in both law and practice is a *sine qua non* condition for the security and survival of the Turkish Cypriot people'. As for the withdrawal of non-Cypriot troops, he said, 'excluding those that are to remain on the island, there can be no withdrawal until all aspects of the Cyprus problem have been settled, agreed and approved by the two sides, that is, until the Greek Cypriot administration representing exclusively one of the two national communities of Cyprus is actually replaced by the transitional federal government and military troops and elements in the south are disposed of in accordance with the terms of the agreement'. On the question of the 'three freedoms' (i.e. freedoms of settlement and movement and the right to property) Mr Denktash said:

those 'freedoms' should be regulated, as already agreed at the summit meeting of 1977, in such a way as to insure that the security of the Turkish Cypriots would not in any way be endangered and that the agreed basic characteristics of federation (i.e. bi-communality and bi-zonality) are preserved and protected.

Mr Denktash had put some riders to matters to be discussed on the Secretary-General's Draft Framework but he accepted that document on the basis that it was an 'integrated whole', as the Secretary-General had indicated, and that nothing agreed was binding until everything had been agreed. In a further letter dated 27 April, Mr Denktash stated that he was prepared to sign the Draft Framework Agreement *as it was* when the blank dates had been filled in.[18] Moreover, he said that the

[16] *Cyprus Bulletin*, 30 Apr. 1986.
[17] The text of his letter is contained in Annexe V to the Secretary-General's Report to the Security Council, S/18102/Add. 1 of 11 June 1986.
[18] This is included as Annexe V in the Secretary-General's Report to the Security Council, S/18102/Add. 1 of 11 June 1986.

Turkish Cypriot side could not accept any procedure other than that contained in the Draft Framework Agreement.

The Secretary-General had laboriously brought back the parties to a situation similar to that of January 1985, with a Draft Framework Agreement which, according to a UN spokesman 'remained absolutely faithful to what the two sides have agreed to', but once again Mr Kyprianou could not cross the Rubicon.

In view of this the Secretary-General observed in his report to the Security Council that 'since one side is not yet in a position to accept the draft framework agreement of 29 March 1986, the way is not yet open to proceed with the negotiations I have proposed for an overall solution'. He added that he was concerned by the dangers inherent in the present situation.[19]

### 3. SUGGESTIONS FOR AN INTERNATIONAL CONFERENCE

On 21 January 1986 the Soviet Ambassador at the UN, Mr O. Troyanovsky, communicated to the UN Secretary-General and all interested parties a document containing Soviet proposals for a Cyprus settlement.[20] According to a Tass dispatch, the Soviet Union mentioned a set of principles on which a settlement should be based. These included the requirement that the Republic of Cyprus remain an independent, unified nation in which any form of dismemberment is inadmissible and that questions of the state structure, including a federation, must be discussed by the two communities, that an international conference under UN auspices should be held to consider the international aspects, and that international guarantees should be widened. The Republic of Cyprus and all members of the UN Security Council could participate in such a conference. Other countries, particularly those that are non-aligned, could also participate.

Such an international conference should conclude a treaty or

[19] Ibid. para. 19.
[20] The Soviet proposals entitled 'Principles of a Cyprus settlement and ways of achieving it' have been circulated as General Assembly and Security Council docs. A/41/96 and Corr. 1-s/17752 and Corr. 1. They are also referred to in the Secretary-General's report S/18102/Add. 1 of 11 June 1986.

other document stipulating the following integrally interconnected components of the settlement: demilitarization of the island (including withdrawal of all foreign troops), dismantling of all foreign military bases and installations, a system of international guarantees ensuring independence, sovereignty, unity, territorial integrity of the Republic of Cyprus, and respect by all parties for its status as a non-aligned state. The system of international guarantees should exclude the possibility of future outside interference in the affairs of the Republic. The permanent members of the UN Security Council, or all the member states of the Security Council together with Greece and Turkey, as well as some non-aligned countries, might be named as guarantors. Measures towards implementing the guarantees should be taken upon universal consent of all the guarantor states. Cyprus should not be subject to use of force or be threatened by the use of force.

Mr Kyprianou welcomed the Soviet proposals while Mr Denktash expressed misgivings.

According to some observers, the convening of an international conference is not compatible with the good-offices mission of the UN Secretary-General. The views of the Soviet Union as to convening an international conference were known years ago and there is considerable speculation as to its motives and timing.

Mr Perez de Cuellar, in a press briefing for British correspondents on 8 May 1986, said:

The Greek Cypriots have not answered my proposals . . . I don't think and you can quote me, that at this stage either to convene an international conference or to convene a high level meeting are viable . . . I think we have to be realistic. I don't discuss their right to make suggestions. Of course I have given consideration to their suggestions. My first reaction to their suggestions is I said that they are not viable . . . because I don't think that it will be accepted by the other side.

Mr Perez de Cuellar, in his Report of 5 December 1986[21] to the Security Council on the United Nations operation in Cyprus said:

The mission also informed President Kyprianou that my soundings of the members of the Security Council had revealed differing positions

[21] Doc. S/18491.

and lack of agreement at present on his proposal for the convening of an international conference.

In a letter to Mr Kyprianou of 10 April 1987 the Secretary-General repeated that his soundings have revealed 'differing positions and lack of agreement' among the members of the Security Council.[22] He added:

May I nevertheless take this opportunity to reiterate that I am deeply aware of the fundamental importance of the issue of troop withdrawal and international guarantees, and of the need to tackle them expeditiously.

More recently there have been some indications that the Soviet Union itself may have changed its stance on the convening of an international conference. In a statement made on 28 April 1987 the Soviet ambassador said that his country would not reject a Western plan on Cyprus including the old Anglo-American-Canadian plan, merely because of its origin.[23]

However, at a meeting with party leaders[24] on 2 May 1987 which was convened by Mr Kyprianou, it was decided to pursue the recourse on the Cyprus problem at the forthcoming session of the UN General Assembly where the following three issues should be raised: (1) promoting the holding of an international conference, (2) the question of 'strengthening of Turkish troops', and (3) the Famagusta (Varosha) issue. Taking into consideration the 'necessity for constant mobility of the Cyprus problem', it was further decided that parallel to the recourse to the General Assembly preparations should continue for a large scale 'enlightenment campaign'.

This means that the Cyprus problem will, once again, be taken to international forums and the mission of good offices of the Secretary-General will suffer a grave setback or be stalled altogether.

---

[22] The text of this letter was revealed by the Greek Cypriot government on 29 Apr. Mr Cuellar was replying to Mr Kyprianou's letter of 10 Mar. requesting his views on the convening of an internatinal conference under UN auspices: *Cyprus Mail*, 30 Apr. 1987.

[23] *Cyprus Mail*, 30 Apr. 1987. As for the Anglo-American plan, see ch. 6 s. 4, above.

[24] Opposition Rally party leader Mr Clerides boycotted this meeting.

## 4. CYPRUS AND THE EUROPEAN COMMUNITY

It is widely acknowledged that the European Community has a prominent role to play in the future of Cyprus.

The Association Agreement[25] between Cyprus and the European Community was signed in 1972. Despite the political problems of the island the Community acted on the basis that its obligation would be to the two communities of Cyprus as a whole. Both communities were consulted during the negotiations, and articles 4 and 5 of the Agreement prohibited discrimination between the products of Contracting countries, as well as, nationals or companies of Cyprus.

Negotiations for the second stage of the customs union, were, however, conducted between the Community and the Greek Cypriot administration, on behalf of the 'Republic of Cyprus'. These negotiations began in November 1985. The first round was of an exploratory nature. The second round was taken up in February 1986. In December 1987 the European Parliament approved the Agreement for the second stage of the customs union of Cyprus with the Community. This Agreement was also ratified by the Greek Cypriot House of Representatives by 31 votes to 17. The Rally, and the Democratic Party voted in favour, whereas the AKEL and the socialist EDEK voted against the ratification of the Agreement. Under the Agreement the Community will dismantle all customs duties and quotas on Cypriot produce and Cyprus will apply Community customs tariffs to non-Community imports. Most barriers will be dismantled by 1977 after which the two will move towards full customs union over the next four or five years.

The Community allocated £29 million under the second five-year financial protocol for Cyprus, which expired in December 1988. A further financial protocol was agreed in 1989, under which £41 million will be provided over the next five years. However, the Greek Cypriot administration has obtained for southern Cyprus almost all the Community aid allocated for the whole of the island.

[25] Official Journal, 21 May 1973, L. 133. As for the text of the Agreement for the second stage of the customs union, see Official Journal, 31 Dec. 1987, L. 393.

Moreover, the Greeks and Greek Cypriots have succeeded in constructing an international boycott against the Turkish Cypriots. Their own economy has prospered, and they have profited considerably from the economic displacement which has occurred in nearby Lebanon. But the economic embargo is a self-defeating strategy because it causes further widening in the gap between the two components of a future federation.[26]

The Turkish Cypriot view is that the European Community should not exclude the Turkish community from negotiations for a customs union, because, supposing that the Community is relying on the 1960 Constitution, it should not fail to note that the conclusion of international treaties, conventions, and agreements is a matter that, under that Constitution, requires the consent of both communities. Article 50 of that Constitution is explicit on ths issue.[27] So far the Community has disregarded this provision and the realities of Cyprus and dealt with the Greek Cypriot administration as the 'Government of Cyprus'.

A customs union between Cyprus and the Community can be seen clearly as a prelude to full membership. The Community's position is that it recognizes the Greek Cypriot administration as the sole government of Cyprus, but at the same time it should endeavour to ensure that the Turkish Cypriot people are included on an equitable basis in any agreement. Since presently there is no customs union between the north and south sectors of Cyprus a *modus vivendi* has to be found so that the Community will not discriminate between these sectors and that both will benefit from the accords with the Community.

[26] The economic embargo takes diverse forms. For instance, ships that come to the ports of the Turkish Republic of Northern Cyprus are blacklisted and their captains are tried and punished if they later call at a port in south Cyprus. Other methods are also used to hinder trade and communications with north Cyprus. As a countermeasure the Republic of Turkey announced that as from 14 May 1987 it would not allow ships that carry the Greek Cypriot flag to call at Turkish ports. If implemented, this would mean massive loss of trade to Greek Cypriot ships.

[27] Admission of Cyprus to full membership of the Community entails economic association with the Community, particularly with Greece, which is a member of the Community. It is important to note that under article 1 of the Treaty of Guarantee the Republic of Cyprus undertook to ensure maintenance of its independence, territorial integrity, and security, as well

Greece is now a member of the Community and Turkey applied on 14 April 1987 for full membership. Greece is unlikely to accept Turkish membership until the Cyprus issue is resolved to its satisfaction, not to mention the question of the Aegean.[27] But if Greece tries to exercise a veto over Turkish membership, Turkey, likewise, may try to exert a similar hold over Cyprus's membership.

Economically and politically Turkey is important to Europe and therefore the Community is unlikely to accept Cyprus fully into its fold over the objections of either the Turkish Cypriots or Turkey. It seems that membership of Cyprus will be possible only if Greece agrees not to object to Turkish membership when the economic and political conditions are ripe. The full membership of Cyprus should therefore depend on the resolution of the conflict in Cyprus and of that between Greece and Turkey.

## 5. THE AEGEAN DISPUTE

Greece and Turkey have a long-standing dispute over the continental shelf in the Aegean. This dispute relates to the extent of territorial waters in the Aegean and sovereign rights for the purpose of exploring and exploiting its natural resources. Many of the Aegean islands, several hundred miles from the Greek mainland and some of them only a few miles from the Turkish coast, were acquired by Greece at the end of the Second World War—mainly from Italy, which had occupied them in 1912.

During the meeting of the then Prime Ministers of the two countries, Messrs Karamanlis and Demirel, in Brussels on 31

as respect for its constitution. The second paragraph of the same article enjoins the Republic 'not to participate, in whole or in part, in any political or *economic union* with any State whatsoever'. It is doubted whether this clause can be construed as intending to bar the entry of Cyprus into the Community. The Community is a regional arrangement of European states, presently composed of 12 full members. It would seem that the Treaty was intended to bar economic union with another state entailing consequent domination of Cyprus by that state, rather than prohibiting membership of a regional economic arrangement.

May 1975, it was decided that the two countries should resolve their differences by peaceful means and through negotiations and, as regards the continental shelf of the Aegean Sea, by the International Court at the Hague.

Later, however, the Greek government had recourse to the UN Security Council alleging that the Turkish research ship *Sismik 1* had repeatedly violated the Greek continental shelf near the islands of Lemnos and Lesvos. The Security Council adopted resolution 395 (1976) of 25 August 1976 calling upon the two countries to exercise utmost restraint to reduce tension in the area. It also invited the two governments to 'take into account the contribution that appropriate judicial means, in particular the International Court of Justice, are qualified to make to the settlement of any remaining legal differences'.

Greece also invoked the jurisdiction of the International Court of Justice on the basis of the General Act of 1928 and requested from the court an indication of interim measures of protection. The court, in its order of 11 September 1976, found, by twelve votes to one, that the circumstances were not such as to require the court to indicate interim measures of protection, and decided that the written proceedings should first be directed to the question of jurisdiction.[28] Turkey did not appear before the court. In its judgment of 19 December 1978, the court decided, by twelve votes to two, that it was without jurisdiction to entertain the dispute.[29]

When the proceedings before the International Court of Justice were pending the *Procès-verbal* of Berne was agreed upon on 11 November 1976. The two parties thereby decided to continue negotiations with a view to reaching an agreement based on their mutual consent with regard to the delimitation of the continental shelf between themselves. In this respect the two

[28] *Aegean Continental Shelf Case,* ICJ Reports (1976), 3.

[29] ICJ Reports (1978), 3. However, in the 'Fourcade Report' (Doc. 1–234/81 of 27 May 1981) drawn up on behalf of the Committee on External Economic Relations of the European Parliament, which was aimed at defining the customs territory of the Community, it was suggested that the Greek islands should have a continental shelf subject to the method of equidistance (para. 65). Para. 62 of the Report was prejudicial against Turkey in that it was there stated that the Greek islands were indivisible parts of the mainland Greek territories and on the basis of sovereignty could claim a territorial sea of 12 miles, an economic zone of 200 miles, and a continental shelf.

parties agreed to study state practice and international rules, with a view to identifying certain principles and practical criteria which could be useful for the delimitation of the continental shelf.

The Graeco-Turkish relations were further strained early in 1982 due to the announcement of the Greek government that it saw no use in continuing the dialogue with Turkey over the Aegean dispute. An incident of 7 March 1984 in the Aegean, when Turkish warships on exercise allegedly fired against a Greek destroyer, grew into a short-lived crisis. The two countries were again on the brink of war in March 1987 when it was learnt that Greece had granted a licence to the Northern Aegean Petroleum Company,[30] an international consortium, to drill for oil in international waters east of the Greek island of Thassos. The crisis was averted when both sides desisted from the dispute. The Turkish Prime Minister Mr Turgut Özal has repeatedly stated the position of the Turkish government, which is that the matter is political and must be settled through negotiations between the two countries. The Greek Prime Minister Mr Andreas Papandreou has, on the other had, stated categorically that he can accept bilateral talks only to prepare a compromise framework on the basis of which the dispute can be referred to the International Court.[31]

The recent crisis over the Aegean has clearly shown, once again, that the Cyprus dispute cannot easily be solved in isolation from the other long-standing disputes between Greece and Turkey.

## 6. COMMENTS AND CONCLUSIONS

Despite optimistic statements of the UN Secretary-General, the rift between the two sides seems to be greater than ever. The

---

[30] NAPC. Greece later announced that a bill had been submitted to parliament to authorize the Greek government to buy the shares of the Canadian company Denison, a member of NAPC, and thus obtain the majority of NAPC shares.

[31] In a letter addressed to the Security Council (Doc. S/18766 of 27 Mar. 1987) the Greek representative stated that the dispute 'is the delimitation of the Aegean continental shelf and not its partitioning'.

Greek Cypriot side rejects the Secretary-General's proposal for the establishment of a transitional government parallel to the implementation of the timetable for the withdrawal of Turkish troops and is adamant on the question of withdrawal before a transitional government is formed. That side insists on the full and effective implementation of what are called 'three fundamental freedoms' (the freedoms of movement, settlement, and ownership of property which, according to the high-level agreement of 1977, have to be discussed in the light of certain difficulties which may arise for the Turkish Cypriot side) and international guarantees to replace the present guarantee system. Furthermore, that side is pressing for the holding of an international conference, as suggested by the Soviet Union, to discuss the withdrawal of foreign troops and the question of guarantees. On the other hand, the Turkish Cypriot side accepts the formula put forward by the Secretary-General and insists on bi-zonality and political equality and on effective guarantee by Turkey.

The demand of the Greek Cypriot side that the external aspects of the Cyprus problem (withdrawal of non-Cypriot troops and external guarantees) must be given precedence over internal aspects (such as constitution, territory, and goodwill measures) is an attempt to change the very basis of the intercommunal negotiations. It may be recollected that when the negotiations were resumed in September 1980 both sides agreed that the following questions would be entered on the agenda of the intercommunal talks and taken up in rotation.[32] These would be (1) Varosha, (2) practical measures to promote goodwill, mutual confidence, and a return to normal conditions, (3) constitutional aspects, and (4) territory. The Waldheim 'evaluation document' submitted to the parties in November 1981 also suggested that the question of international guarantees in relation to the status of the federal republic of Cyprus should be discussed at the appropriate level after agreement on all other aspects had been reached.[33] This was the understanding that lay at the basis of the intercommunal talks. In insisting, after so many years of arduous negotiations, that external

---

[32] See ch. 6 s. 6, above.
[33] See ch. 6 s. 9, above.

aspects must be discussed first, the Greek Cypriot side is putting the cart before the horse.

The question of future guarantees for Cyprus has not in fact been on the agenda of the intercommunal talks.[34] The interlocutors cannot themselves find an alternative to the 1960 Treaty of Guarantee which is in force. This is a matter primarily for the guarantor powers, without whose consent it is not possible to replace the present guarantee system. Moreover, before a federal republic of Cyprus is established by mutual consent it is not possible to know what in fact will be guaranteed. An international conference on the matter would only be an academic exercise and opinions would be conflicting as to what should be guaranteed or who should be the guarantors.[35]

According to the Greek and Greek Cypriot view, there can be no justification for the continuing presence of Turkish troops on the 'territory of the Cyprus Republic' and even if it were to be argued that there was justification at the time of the intervention, this has long ceased to exist.[36] The Foreign Minister of Greece, addressing the UN General Assembly on 30 September 1982, suggested that Turkey should withdraw its forces from Cyprus immediately and an enlarged UN peacekeeping force should take its place.[37]

The Turkish, as well as Turkish Cypriot, view is that the Turkish troops cannot be withdrawn from Cyprus unless the reason for their presence is removed. The immediate withdrawal of the Turkish troops would push the situation back to the pre-intervention days, which would clear the way for

[34] It is true however that the 8th clause of the 19 May 1979 Denktash–Kyprianou accord says that the island should be guaranteed against union in whole or in part with any other country and against any form of partition or secession, but this is a prospective statement and purports to refer to a guarantee after a federal republic has been established by mutual consent.

[35] It is submitted that the UN cannot really provide an effective guarantee; in any case the majority of the members of the Security Council are non-permanent.

[36] *Cyprus Mail* 17 Apr. 1983, reporting a comment by Mr Kyprianou on a statement of the then Turkish Prime Minister, Mr Ulusu. Mr Kyprianou advocated the reimposition of the US embargo until Turkish troops are withdrawn.

[37] This is hardly any consolation for Turkish Cypriots who have seen how UN authority has been flouted in the past by the Greek Cypriot administration.

intercommunal hostilities. The Turkish government has repeatedly stated officially at the highest level that Turkey would
withdraw her forces from the island once a settlement
acceptable to both communities is found, with the exception of
those that would be mutually agreed upon within the framework of such a settlement.[38]

On the question of troop withdrawals from Cyprus, in a
House of Lords debate Lord Belstead, expressing the view of the
government, said:

Any comprehensive settlement must include the withdrawal of those
[Turkish] troops. We ourselves have voted in the past for appropriate
United Nations resolutions calling for the withdrawal of foreign troops
from the Republic of Cyprus. But there are many other aspects of the
problem, and it really is wrong, I think, to take only one of them in
isolation if ever one hears the matter being argued in that way.[39]

Referring to a suggestion as to the introduction of a United
Nations force to replace the Turkish troops, Lord Belstead
stated:

Here I would simply say that Turkish Cypriot security concerns make
it unlikely that Turkish troops could be withdrawn in advance of
progress towards a settlement, which brings us back to the importance
of the intercommunal talks.[40]

The Turkish Cypriots believe that a future Cyprus settlement
must guarantee their security and not allow a return to the pre-
1974 era. The *Enosis* bugbear has never been dispelled from the
minds of Turkish Cypriots. It is not clear whether this objective
has been abandoned.[41] Nor is it satisfactory to put the blame on

[38] Address of the Turkish Foreign Minister before the UN General
Assembly on 3 Oct. 1978.

[39] Parliamentary Debates (Hansard), House of Lords Official Report, vol.
441, 20 Apr. 1983, 632. It is important to remember that there are also Greek
troops in the south.

[40] Ibid. Dr David Owen, a former British Foreign Secretary, in reply to a
question in the House of Commons said that the conditions in which
withdrawal of Turkish troops may be possible are most likely to be established
within the context of a negotiated settlement in Cyprus (*Cyprus Mail*, 29 March
1979).

[41] Whether the *Enosis* objective has been shelved or abandoned is doubtful.
In a ceremony held on the Greek side of Nicosia on 25 Mar. 1979, which was
attended by Greek Cypriot high-ranking officials, including Mr Kyprianou

the Greek junta alone, because political agitation for *Enosis* began long before the junta came to power in Athens.[42]

One may ask whether there is enough will on the Greek side to accept a federal solution. Mr Kyprianou was quoted by the *New York Times* of 17 November 1983 as having said that while Mr Denktash wants a bi-zonal federation, a *unitary state* is what Cyprus needs. Moreover, the Athens daily *Ethnos* of 24 November 1983 reported the following statement by the premier of Greece, Mr Andreas Papandreou:

Our Cyprus policy can be summarized as follows: we can only negotiate for a *unitary Cyprus*. For us neither federation nor confederation is an acceptable solution. So, what do we propose? Our proposal is for the establishment of a unitary state. We can negotiate on this after the departure of the Turkish soldiers.

The Greek Cypriot daily *Haravgi* of 27 August 1984 asserted that Mr Kyprianou is among those who do not support a federal solution and who believe that the majority of the people do not agree with the policy line of 1977 whereby the two leaders, Archbishop Makarios and President Denktash, recorded their agreement as to an independent, non-aligned, bi-communal, *federal republic*.

and Archbishop Chrisostomos, the Eoka Oath of 7 Mar. 1953 pledging to unite Cyprus with Greece was renewed. The occasion was reported in the local Greek newspaper *Simerini* on 27 Mar. 1979, under the headline: 'We must turn to our National Ideals for the Survival of Cyprus.' Again in an article by Mr Farmakides published by the Greek Cypriot daily *Simerini* of 13 June 1979, it is asserted that the right of self-determination is an undeniable right and cannot be abandoned. The right of self-determination is equated to *Enosis*.

Very recently, in fact soon after the resumption of the sustained intercommunal talks, the 'Pancyprian Fighters Union' on the Greek side issued a proclamation expressing support for the movement of *Enosis* (*Cyprus Mail*, 23 Sept. 1980).

[42] In a speech on 7 Apr. 1983 at a dinner in Athens in honour of Mr Kyprianou, Mr Karamanlis, the Greek President, said: 'It was natural for the Greek people of Cyprus always to have their eyes turned towards Greece and to want to unite with her. This reasonable desire became more intense and bit by bit took on the form of a liberation struggle from the time Greece became an independent state. That struggle passed through many stages, the most critical of them, however, and the most dramatic was the one that began after the Second World War and *continues still*' (ANA News Agency of 11 Apr. 1983; author's italics).

The UN Security Council resolutions 541 (1983) and 550 (1984), adopted at the instigation of the Greek Cypriot side, do not refer to the high-level agreements or to the other agreed framework which are fundamental for a federal solution of the Cyprus problem. The agreed framework comprises principles, such as those enshrined in the 'opening statement' of the UN Secretary-General read at the resumed intercommunal talks on 9 August 1980 as to a federal solution of the constitutional aspect and bi-zonal solution of the territorial aspect of the Cyprus problem, and the Waldheim 'evaluation document'.

In a speech in Athens at a forum sponsored by the 'Independent Movement for Freedom', the Greek Cypriot government's former Foreign Minister, Mr Nicos Rolandis, accused Mr Kyprianou of never wanting a federal solution to the Cyprus problem.[43] According to Mr Rolandis, Mr Kyprianou 'never at heart wanted an agreed basis on which the solution of the Cyprus problem, federation, would be built'. It may be recalled that Mr Rolandis had resigned on 20 September 1983 because of Mr Kyprianou's unwillingness to accept the 'indicators' of the UN Secretary-General.

It is therefore doubtful whether as yet there is enough will on the Greek side for reunification on the basis of a bi-zonal, federal solution. This is why the 'proximity talks' and the summit meeting which followed failed to achieve any substantial results. This is why the Greek side did not accept the recent framework agreement prepared by the UN Secretary-General.

According to Nancy Crawshaw, 'the Western powers must bear some responsibility for the consolidation of partition'.[44] As noted in earlier chapters, two separate administrations emerged, each representing its own people and neither in fact representing the whole of Cyprus as such.

Continued recognition of the Greek Cypriot administration as the 'Government of Cyprus' will continue to hinder the process of the intercommunal talks because that side will go on assuming that it represents the whole of Cyprus and will be most unwilling to give away anything from that sovereignty to which it is wrongfully clinging. In view of this, it may be said that there is now, more than ever, a need for foreign governments and international organizations to look at the facts and the

[43] *Cyprus Mail*, 5 Mar. 1985.
[44] See ch. 9 n. 71 above.

constitutional developments that have taken place and make a reappraisal of the situation. So long as the Greek administration continues to reap the benefits of recognition there will not be much incentive to accept the other side as its partner in a Cyprus federation. Once the process of recognition of the Turkish Republic of Northern Cyprus gets under way it will facilitate the establishment of a federation between two equal states, joining together by their free will. Conversely, de-recognition of the Greek Cypriot side as the government of Cyprus and breathing life into the Geneva Declaration that only two autonomous administrations exist will take the wind out of the sails of Greek Cypriot leaders and the two sides will be able to sit and discuss their problems as equals.[45]

The recent moves of the Greek Cypriot side to internationalize the Cyprus problem and resort to the General Assembly of the United Nations have effectively stalled the good-offices mission of the UN Secretary-General. The opportunities that have been lost by the Greek Cypriot rejection of the Secretary-General's initiatives will not readily recur. The Turkish Cypriot reaction to Greek moves will, in all probability, be twofold: (1) intensification of efforts to bring to the attention of the world that there is no single, or unitary, 'Government of Cyprus' that can represent the 'Republic of Cyprus' and that the Greek Cypriot administration is not that 'Government', (2) commencing the process of recognition of their State, the Turkish Republic of Northern Cyprus. The Turkish Cypriots believe that the future federal republic of Cyprus should derive from the two ethnic peoples of Cyprus that are organized in states or units of their own, exercising on an equal footing their right of self-determination to form such a federation or other association by mutual consent.

### 7. POSTSCRIPT: THE FOREIGN AFFAIRS COMMITTEE REPORT

The Foreign Affairs Committee of the House of Commons published its Report on Cyprus on 2 July 1987. The Report

---

[45] The author has also put forward these views to the Select Committee of the House of Commons on Foreign Affairs during the Committee's visit to Cyprus, Dec. 1986.

deserves careful consideration by all concerned.[46] The general conclusion reached is that the long-term aim of a reunited Cyprus remains a much more desirable proposition than a drift into partition.[47] On the other hand, there would be little advantage to anyone involved if a 'federal solution were to be adopted which was expected from the start to be unlikely to last. There needs to be a more creative examination of all elements which make up a federal solution for the island. But if reunification along the lines of a federal solution proves impossible in the reasonably near future, the next-best option is a 'confederal' solution which will at least keep open the prospect of closer collaboration in the future.[48]

The Committee recommends[49] that the UK government should for the time being support the UN Secretary-General's initiatives but should convey to the parties concerned the alternative constitutional proposals referred to above. The UK government should invite the guarantor powers, Greece and Turkey, to discuss the current situation and possible ways of reaching an enduring settlement. The UK government should review its aid programme to Cyprus so that both communities can benefit equally. While the Committee rejects official recognition of the Turkish Republic of Northern Cyprus, it recommends that Britain should help to facilitate normal trade and contacts between the two communities and the outside world.[50]

The Committee recommends that the two Cypriot administrations should be prepared to make more goodwill gestures to demonstrate their wish for reunification.[51] The Report suggests that the Greek Cypriot government should lift the economic

---

[46] The Greek Cypriot administration, which is referred to as the 'Greek Cypriot Government' in most parts of the Report and not as the Cyprus government, criticized the Report for being pro-Turkish. *The Times* of London, however, in its issue of 6 July 1987 described the Nicosia government's reaction to the Report as 'premature' and 'ill-considered'.

[47] Para. 135.

[48] Ibid. para. 136.

[49] Ibid. para. 139.

[50] Ibid. para. 139.

[51] Ibid. para. 140.

embargo on the north as a step towards preventing *de facto* partition.[52]

The Committee calls upon Turkey to declare formally that it has no territorial claims on Cyprus, to respond positively to proposals by the UK government for future talks between the guarantor powers about the Cyprus problem, and effect substantial reduction in her military forces stationed in Cyprus.[53] The Committee also calls upon Greece to renounce formally any aspirations towards *Enosis*[54] and respond positively to proposals of the UK government for further talks between the guarantor powers about the Cyprus problem and the means for encouraging its resolution.[55]

## 8. WIND OF CHANGE

After many years of stagnation, the Greek and Turkish Prime Ministers, Mr Papandreou and Mr Özal, met at the Swiss resort of Davos on 30–1 January 1988 with the aim of starting a dialogue for friendly settlement of disputes that bedevilled relations between the two NATO neighbours. The Greek premier's decision to meet his Turkish counterpart at Davos marked a change in the socialist premier's attitude; he had been arguing for at least six years that no dialogue was possible until Turkey had pulled its troops out of Cyprus and renounced 'territorial designs' in the Aegean.

The thaw set in immediately after the euphoric meeting between the two Prime Ministers in Davos. There was no breakthrough in solving any of the problems at once, but what was achieved, as Mr Papandreou later put it, was a straight 'no war' deal. The two premiers agreed to set up a crisis telephone

---

[52] Ibid. para. 141. However, *de facto* separation already exists.

[53] Ibid. para. 145.

[54] In para. 94 of the Report the Committee state that the Greek Cypriot leaders had been adamant in rejecting *Enosis*, but that one senior Greek Cypriot leader told them that no politician would risk rejecting *Enosis* in principle, at least in public.

[55] Ibid. para. 144.

link between their capitals and hold a summit once a year to avoid confrontation.

Mr Özal announced his intention of visiting Athens between 5 and 7 June, the first official visit by a Turkish Prime Minister in 35 years.

Speaking to Greek journalists in Istanbul for an unusual seminar on Greek–Turkish relations, Mr Özal proposed joint military manœuvres and meetings between military representatives. Turkey called off three military exercises scheduled for the Aegean region.

Earlier, Turkey repealed a 1964 decree freezing Greek property and assets in Turkey estimated to be worth £200 million. Mr Papandreou responded by saying that, provided the repeal of the decree was made retroactive so that all those who suffered losses were adequately indemnified, Greece would sign the EEC–Turkey association agreement.

Early in February Mr Özal sent the General Secretary of the Foreign Ministry to Athens to negotiate the details of joint committees on defining problem areas and exploring areas of co-operation.

Mr Papandreou and Mr Özal met again in Brussels after the NATO summit meeting early in March.

There have been reports that a proposed visit by President Evren of Turkey to the Turkish Republic of Northern Cyprus, which would have antagonized the Greeks, has been indefinitely postponed, and that Ankara may withdraw 5,000 of its troops deployed on the island.

While Turkey appeared to be moving swiftly to implement what has become known as the 'spirit of Davos', in Athens doubts and questions emerged almost as soon as the applause died down. The conservative opposition alluded to a possible sell-out of Greece's right to veto Turkey's accession to the EEC. But it was not easy for Mr Özal either. Turkish opposition reactions ranged from sceptical to dismissive. The process which the two Prime Ministers inaugurated seemed fragile and volatile, but it could possibly gain its own momentum and lead to a peaceful resolution of problems.

The Greek Prime Minister explained the reasons for his turnabout at an address to the garrison officers of Ioannina, in north-western Greece, in the following words:

For quite some time both Cyprus and Greece fought in terms of a triangle—Greece puts pressure on the Americans, who pressure the Turks to solve our problems. The formula is no longer valid. We must rely on our own resources to establish peace with Turkey through a dialogue on an equal footing.[56]

The political climate in the region improved following the apparent Greek–Turkish *rapprochement*. Even though the impression was given that the Cyprus issue was carefully left out of the discussions at Davos, or only very lightly touched upon, the desire for change was also the dominant theme of the presidential elections which were held in south Cyprus on 14 February 1988. Four candidates contested the presidency. They were the outgoing Greek Cypriot President, Mr Spyros Kyprianou of the Democratic party, Mr Glafcos Clerides of the Democratic Rally party, Dr Vassos Lyssarides of the EDEK Socialist party, and the independent, but communist-backed, Mr George Vasiliou. Mr Clerides won first place with over 33 per cent of the vote while Mr Vasiliou received just over 30 per cent, thanks to the backing of the communist AKEL party. Mr Kyprianou, who lagged in third place with just 27 per cent of the vote, was swept from power after 11 years. Dr Lyssarides, who received only about 9 per cent, was also eliminated.

As none of the candidates received over 50 per cent of the vote in the first round, a second round had to take place on the following Sunday, that is, on 21 February, between the two candidates who received most of the votes.

While the outcome of the second round of the presidential race was still in the balance, Mr George Vasiliou secured a commitment from the small Socialist party. On the other hand, Mr Clerides, who promised an all-party government to secure broader support, made a surprise move on 18 February when he announced that he was resigning as leader of his Democratic Rally party so that he could be a truly non-partisan President.

In the second round of the presidential race, where only a simple majority was enough to win a five-year term, Mr Vasiliou, a 56-year-old economist and millionaire, was elected President in a close run-off with his conservative rival, Mr

[56] Mario Modiano, *The Times*, 23 Feb. 1988, p.8.

Clerides. Mr Vasiliou received over 51 per cent of the vote, while Mr Clerides received just over 48 per cent.[57]

Mr Kyprianou was beaten in the first round mainly because voters rejected his platform of no deal with the Turkish Cypriots before the pull-out of Turkish troops and the mainland settlers from the north of the island. This was in line with the policy of Athens at the time, but brought him into conflict with the opposition. Moreover, the Greek Cypriot voters wanted a change.

Both Mr Vasiliou and Mr Clerides seemed eager to end the stalemate and get the ball rolling again. However Mr Vasiliou added that, 'while we shall pursue our targets relentlessly, we shall be flexible in our methods'. This is believed to have helped more than anything in the defeat of Mr Vasiliou's conservative opponent, Mr Glafcos Clerides, in the second round of voting.

Mr Vasiliou said that his aim is to bring Greek Cypriots and Turkish Cypriots closer together and restore mutual confidence. The President of the Turkish Republic of Northern Cyprus, Mr Rauf Denktash, congratulated Mr Vasiliou on his election and renewed his offer to meet the winner at the United Nations conference room at the Ledra Palace on the 'Green Line' that divides Nicosia. Mr Denktash added that the meeting had to be between equal political entities. Mr Vasiliou responded by saying that this condition was unacceptable. Instead, he proposed to meet Mr Özal. Ankara retorted by saying that Mr Vasiliou's counterpart was Mr Denktash.

[57] Votes cast and the percentages are given below. First round figures are in brackets:

| | Votes | % |
|---|---|---|
| Vasiliou (independent) | 167,834 (100,631) | 51.6 (30.1) |
| Clerides (Democratic Rally) | 157,228 (111,491) | 48.4 (33.3) |
| Kyprianou (Democratic Party) | — (91,262) | — (27.3) |
| Lyssarides (Socialist) | — (30,832) | — (9.2) |

Registered voters 363,740; valid 2nd round votes 325,062; spoiled 17,968.

Mr Vasiliou explained what he meant by a 'just and lasting solution'. It would 'ensure the withdrawal of all Turkish troops and [mainland] settlers, the right of return to their homes for all refugees, and the three basic freedoms [the freedoms of movement, ownership and settlement], and respect for human rights'. Mr Vasiliou added that in the pursuit of these targets, he would be 'flexible' in his methods, but no clear indication is given as to what will be his methods. This cliché is an echo of statements by his predecessor, Mr Spyros Kyprianou.

On 28 February Mr Vasiliou was invested by the House of Representatives before which he made the affirmation set out in article 42 of the 1960 Constitution. The same day he announced his cabinet. He had been saying all along that he would appoint ministers from all parties and the whole spectrum of political life, but Mr Clerides's Rally party charged that Mr Vasiliou did not form a national unity government and that the Rally party could not share responsibility for the formation of a government which would implement Mr Vasiliou's policy declarations.

Mr Perez de Cuellar, the United Nations Secretary-General, stood by for election fever to subside before resuming his initiatives for a settlement. The United Nations Special Representative for Cyprus, Mr Oscar Camilion, met both Mr Vasiliou and Mr Denktash on 2 March. The recent agreement between Greece and Turkey to improve relations is expected to ease his task.

Mr Vasiliou visited Athens on 13 March for consultations on a common strategy.

Lingering doubts about the extent of Mr Vasiliou's commitment to the Moscow-line Progressive party (AKEL) may widen the rift between the right and the left in Cyprus. His insistence on an international conference on Cyprus proposed by Moscow may not be helpful to initiatives to solve the Cyprus problem in the context of the intercommunal talks.

If there is an earnest desire for a negotiated settlement of the Cyprus dispute it is imperative to make an evaluation of the priorities once again. The constitutional aspects of the Cyprus problem should be taken up as a matter of priority and hopes should be pinned on settlement of these issues first. Then the more difficult points can be taken up. But taking up the hot issues first, such as troop withdrawals, the question of guarantees, and the rights of the displaced persons, before there is an agreement of principle on the constitutional and territorial aspects, will not help. If the basic tenets of an agreement for a bi-zonal, federal republic can be worked out, then it is easier to reach a package deal on the other issues.

There is good cause to believe that the *rapprochement* between Greece and Turkey will usher in a new era in Graeco-Turkish relations, which will help towards an agreed and peaceful solution of the Cyprus dispute. The omens for early resumption and progress of the intercommunal talks, have—with qualifications—improved, but the difficulties cannot be underestimated.

It is important to note that if a negotiated settlement can ever be reached within the framework of the intercommunal talks, such a settlement should be submitted to a referendum on both sides, so that the two peoples shall be able to exercise separately their right of self-determination, either in favour or against that settlement. The two leaders cannot impose a settlement on their respective peoples.

# APPENDIX 1

## The Akritas Plan[1]

Recent public statements by Archbishop Markarios have shown the course which our national problem will take in the near future. As we have stressed in the past, national struggles cannot be concluded overnight; nor is it possible to fix definite chronological limits for the conclusion of the various stages of development in national causes. Our national problem must be viewed in the light of developments which take place and conditions that arise from time to time, and the measures to be taken, as well as their implementation and timing, must be in keeping with the internal and external political conditions. The whole process is difficult and must go through various stages because factors which will affect the final conclusion are numerous and different. It is sufficient for everyone to know, however, that every step taken constitutes the result of a study and that at the same time it forms the basis of future measures. Also, it is sufficient to know that every measure now contemplated is a first step and only constitutes a stage towards the final and unalterable national objective which is the full and unconditional application of the right of self-determination.

As the final objective remains unchanged, what must be dwelt upon is the method to be employed towards attaining that objective. This must, of necessity, be divided into internal and external (international) tactics because the methods of the presentation and the handling of our cause within and outside the country are different.

### A. METHOD TO BE USED OUTSIDE

In the closing stages of the (EOKA) struggle, the Cyprus problem had been presented to world public opinion and to diplomatic circles as a demand of the people of Cyprus to exercise the right of self-determination. But the question of the Turkish minority had been introduced in circumstances that are known, inter-communal clashes had taken place and it had been tried to make it accepted that it was impossible for the two communities to live together under a united

---

[1] The full version in Greek was published by S. Papageorghiou in one of three volumes of documents on Cyprus (*Ta Khirisima Dokumenta tou Kypriakou*), vol. A, Athens, 1983, 250–7.

international circles, by the London and Zurich Agreements, which
administration. Finally the problem was solved, in the eyes of many
were shown as solving the problem following negotiations and
agreements between the contending parties.

(a) Consequently our first aim has been to create the impression in
the international field that the Cyprus problem has not been
solved and that it has to be reviewed.

(b) The creation of the following impressions has been accepted as
the primary objective:

(i) that the solution which has been found is not satisfactory
and just;

(ii) that the agreement which has been reached is not the
result of the free will of the contending parties;

(iii) that the demand for the revision of the agreements is not
because of any desire on the part of the Greeks to
dishonour their signature, but an imperative necessity of
survival for them;

(iv) that the co-existence of the two communities is possible,
and

(v) that the Greek majority, and not the Turks, constitute
the strong element on which foreigners must rely.

(c) Although it was most difficult to attain the above objectives,
satisfactory results have been achieved. Many diplomatic
missions have already come to believe strongly that the
Agreements are neither just nor satisfactory, that they were
signed as a result of pressures and intimidations without real
negotiations, and that they were imposed after many threats. It
has been an important trump card in our hands that the
solution brought by the Agreements was not submitted to the
approval of the people; acting wisely in this respect our
leadership avoided holding a referendum. Otherwise, the
people would have definitely approved the Agreements in the
atmosphere that prevailed in 1959. Generally speaking, it has
been shown that so far the administration of Cyprus has been
carried out by the Greeks and that the Turks played only a
negative part acting as a brake.

(d) Having completed the first stage of our activities and objectives
we must materialise the second stage on an international level.
Our objective in this second stage is to show:

(i) that the aim of the Greeks is not to oppress the Turks but
only to remove the unreasonable and unjust provisions
of the administrative mechanism;

(ii) that it is necessary to remove these provisions right away
because tomorrow may be too late;

(iii) that this removal, although reasonable and essential becomes impossible because of the unreasonable stand of the Turks and therefore unilateral action is justified as common and concerted action with the Turks is impossible due to the state of affairs;

(iv) that this question of revision is a domestic issue for Cypriots and does not therefore give the right of intervention to anyone by force or otherwise, and

(v) that the proposed amendments are reasonable and just and safeguard the reasonable rights of the minority.

(e) Generally speaking, it is obvious that today the international opinion is against any form of oppression, and especially against oppression of minorities. The Turks have so far been able to convince world public opinion that the union of Cyprus with Greece will amount to their enslavement. Under the circumstances we stand a good chance of success in influencing world public opinion if we base our struggle not on ENOSIS but on self-determination. But in order to be able to exercise the right of self-determination fully and without hindrance we must first get rid of the Agreements (e.g. the Treaty of Guarantee, the Treaty of Alliance etc.) and of those provisions of the Constitution which inhibit the free and unbridled expression of the will of the people and which carry dangers of external intervention. For this reason our first target has been the Treaty of Guarantee, which is the first Agreement to be cited as not being recognised by the Greek Cypriots.

When the Treaty of Guarantee is removed no legal or moral force will remain to obstruct us in determining our future through a plebiscite.

It will be understood from the above explanations that it is necessary to follow a chain of efforts and developments in order to ensure the success of our Plan. If these efforts and developments failed to materialise, our future actions would be legally unjustified and politically unattainable and we would be exposing Cyprus and its people to grave consequences. Actions to be taken are as follows:

(a) The amendment of the negative elements of the Agreements and the consequent *de facto* nullification of the Treaties of Guarantee and Alliance. This step is essential because the necessity of amending the negative aspects of any Agreement is generally acceptable internationally and is considered reasonable (we can even justify unilateral action) whereas an external intervention to prevent the amendment of such negative provisions is held unjustified and inapplicable.

(b) Once this is achieved the Treaty of Guarantee (the right of intervention) will become legally and substantially inapplicable.

(c) Once those provisions of the Treaties of Guarantee and Alliance which restrict the exercise of the right of self-determination are removed, the people of Cyprus will be able, freely, to express and apply its will.

(d) It will be possible for the Force of the State (the Police Force) and in addition, friendly military Forces, to resist legitimately any intervention internally or from outside, because we will then be completely independent.

It will be seen that it is necessary for actions from (a) to (d) to be carried out in the order indicated.

It is consequently evident that if we ever hope to have any chance of success in the international field, we cannot and should not reveal or proclaim any stage of the struggle before the previous stage is completed. For instance, it is accepted that the above four stages constitute the necessary course to be taken, then it is obvious that it would be senseless for us to speak of amendment (a) if stage (d) is revealed, because it would then be ridiculous for us to seek the amendment of the negative points with the excuse that these amendments are necessary for the functioning of the State and of the Agreements.

The above are the points regarding our targets and aims, and the procedure to be followed in the international field.

### B. THE INTERNAL ASPECT

Our activities in the internal field will be regulated according to their repercussions and to interpretations to be given to them in the world and according to the effect of our actions on our national cause.

1. The only danger that can be described as insurmountable is the possibility of a forceful external intervention. This danger, which could be met partly or wholly by our forces is important because of the political damage that it could do rather than the material losses that it could entail. If intervention took place before stage (c), then such intervention would be legally tenable at least, if not entirely justifiable. This would be very much against us both internationally and at the United Nations. The history of many similar incidents in recent times shows us that in no case of intervention, even if legally inexcusable, has the attacker been removed by either the United Nations or the other powers without significant concessions to the detriment of the attacked party. Even in the case of the attack on Suez by Israel, which was

condemned by almost all members of the United Nations and for which Russia threatened intervention, the Israelis were removed but, as a concession, they continued to keep the port of Eliat in the Red Sea. There are, however, more serious dangers in the case of Cyprus.

If we do our work well and justify the attempt we shall make under stage (*a*) above, we will see, on the one hand, that intervention will not be justified and, on the other hand, we will have every support since, by the Treaty of Guarantee, intervention cannot take place before negotiations take place between the Guarantor Powers, that is Britain, Greece and Turkey. It is at this stage, i.e., at the stage of contacts (before intervention) that we shall need international support. We shall obtain this support if the amendments proposed by us seem reasonable and justified. Therefore, we have to be extremely careful in selecting the amendments that we shall propose.

The first step, therefore, would be to get rid of intervention by proposing amendments in the first stage. Tactic to be followed: Reasonable constitutional amendments after the exhaustion of efforts for common understanding with the Turks. As common agreement is out of question we shall then try to justify unilateral action. At this stage actions (ii) and (iii) of page 2 are to be applied in parallel.

2. It is evident that for intervention to be justified there must be a more serious reason and a more immediate danger than simple Constitutional amendments. Such reasons can be:

(*a*) The declaration of ENOSIS before actions (*a*) to (*c*).
(*b*) Serious intercommunal unrest which may be shown as a massacre of Turks.

The first reason is removed as a result of the Plan drawn up for the first stage and consequently what remains, is the danger of intercommunal strife. As we do not intend to engage, without provocation, in massacre or attack against the Turks, what remains is the possibility, as soon as we proceed with the unilateral amendment of any article of the Constitution, of the Turks reacting strongly and inciting incidents and strife, or falsely staging massacres, clashes or bomb explosions in order to create the impression that the Greeks in fact attacked the Turks and that intervention is imperative for their protection. Tactic to be employed: Our actions for amending the Constitution will not be secret; we would always appear to be ready for peaceful talks and our actions would not take any provocative and violent form. Any incidents that may take place will be met, at the beginning, in a legal fashion by the legal Security Forces, according to a plan. Our actions will have a legal form.

3. Before our right of unilateral amendment of the Constitution is established and accepted, actions and decisions which require positive dynamic action by our side, for instance, the unification of municipalities, should be avoided. Such a decision necessitates for the government to intervene dynamically for the realisation of the unification and the seizure of the municipal property by force, something which makes it probably imperative for the Turks to resort to dynamic reaction. On the contrary, it is easier for us through lawful action to amend, for instance, the provision for 70:30 when it will be the Turks themselves who will need positive dynamic action, whereas for us the act will not be action but 'refusal'. The same for separate majorities relating to taxation. The measures have already been examined and a series of measures have been decided upon for their application. After our right in connection with the unilateral amendment of the Constitution is confirmed *de facto* through such actions, we can then proceed according to our discretion and power, in a more dynamic way.

4. It is, however, naive to believe that it is possible for us to proceed to substantial actions for amending the Constitution, as a first step towards our more general Plan as described above, without expecting the Turks to create or stage incidents and clashes. For this reason the existence and the strengthening of our Organisation is imperative because: (*a*) if, in case of spontaneous resistance by the Turks, our counter attack is not immediate, we run the risk of having a panic created among Greeks, in towns in particular. We will then be in danger of losing vast areas of vital importance to the Turks, while if we show our strength to the Turks immediately and forcefully, then they will probably be brought to their senses and restrict their activities to insignificant, isolated incidents.

(*b*) In case of a planned or unplanned attack by the Turks, whether this be staged or not, it is necessary to suppress this forcefully in the shortest possible time, since, if we manage to become the masters of the situation within a day or two, outside intervention would not be possible, probable or justifiable.

(*c*) The forceful and decisive suppressing of any Turkish effort will greatly facilitate our subsequent actions for further Constitutional amendments, and it should then be possible to apply these without the Turks being able to show any reaction. Because they will learn that it is impossible for them to show any reaction without serious consequences for their Community.

(*d*) In case of the clashes becoming widespread, we must be ready to proceed immediately through actions (*a*) to (*d*), including the immediate declaration of ENOSIS, because, then, there will be no need to wait or to engage in diplomatic activity.

5. In all these stages we must not overlook the factor of enlightening, and of facing the propaganda of those who do not know or cannot be expected to know our plans, as well as of the reactionary elements. It has been shown that our struggle must go through at least four stages and that we are obliged not to reveal our plans and intentions prematurely. It is therefore more than a national duty for everyone to observe full secrecy in the matter. SECRECY IS VITALLY ESSENTIAL FOR OUR SUCCESS AND SURVIVAL.

This, however, does not prevent the reactionaries and irresponsible demagogues from indulging in false patriotic manifestations and provocations. Our Plan would provide them with the possibility of putting forward accusations to the effect that the aims of our leadership are not national and that only the amendment of the Constitution is envisaged. The need for carrying out Constitutional amendments in stages and in accordance with the prevailing conditions, makes our job even more difficult. All this must not, however, be allowed to drag us to irresponsible demagogy, street politics and a race of nationalism. Our deeds will be our undeniable justification. In any case owing to the fact that, for well-known reasons, the above Plan must have been carried out and borne fruit long before the next elections, we must distinguish ourselves with self-restraint and moderation in the short time that we have. Parallel with this, we should not only maintain but reinforce the present unity and discipline of our patriotic forces. We can succeed in this only by properly enlightening our members so that they in turn enlighten the public.

Before anything else we must expose the true identity of the reactionaries. These are petty and irresponsible demagogues and opportunists. Their recent history shows this. They are unsuccessful, negative and anti-progressive elements who attack our leadership like mad dogs but who are unable to put forward any substantive and practical solution of their own. In order to succeed in all our activities we need a strong and stable government, up to the last minute. They are known as clamorous slogan-creators who are good for nothing but speech-making. When it comes to taking definite actions or making sacrifices they are soon shown to be unwilling weaklings. A typical example of this is that even at the present stage they have no better proposal to make than to suggest that we should have recourse to the United Nations. It is therefore necessary that they should be isolated and kept at a distance.

We must enlighten our members about our plans and objectives ONLY VERBALLY. Meetings must be held at the sub-headquarters of the Organisation to enlighten leaders and members so that they are properly equipped to enlighten others. NO WRITTEN EXPLANATION OF

ANY SORT IS ALLOWED. LOSS OR LEAKAGE OF ANY DOCUMENT PERTAINING
TO THE ABOVE IS EQUIVALENT TO HIGH TREASON. There can be no action
that would inflict a heavier blow to our struggle than any revealing of
the contents of the present document or the publication of this by the
opposition.

Outside the verbal enlightenment of our members, all our activities,
and our publications in the press in particular, must be most restrained
and must not divulge any of the above. Only responsible persons will
be allowed to make public speeches and statements and will refer to
this Plan only generally under their personal responsibility and under
the personal responsibility of the Chief of sub-headquarters concerned.
Also, any reference to the written Plan should be done only after the
formal approval of the Chief of the sub-headquarters who will control
the speech or statement. But in any case such speech or statement MUST
NEVER BE ALLOWED TO APPEAR IN THE PRESS OR ANY OTHER
PUBLICATION.

The tactic to be followed: Great effort must be made to enlighten
our members and the public VERBALLY. Every effort must be made to
show ourselves as moderates. Any reference to our plans in writing, or
any reference in the press or in any document is strictly prohibited.
Responsible officials and other responsible persons will continue to
enlighten the public and to increase its morale and fighting spirit
without ever divulging any of our plans through the press or otherwise.

NOTE: The present document should be destroyed by burning under
the personal responsibility of the Chief of the sub-headquarters and in
the presence of all members of the staff within 10 days of its being
received. It is strictly prohibited to make copies of the whole or any
part of this document. Staff members of sub-headquarters may have it
in their possession only under the personal responsibility of the Chief of
sub-headquarters, but in no case is anyone allowed to take it out of the
office of sub-headquarters.

The Chief
AKRITAS

# APPENDIX 2

## Resolution 353 (1974)

ADOPTED BY THE SECURITY COUNCIL ON 20 JULY 1974

**The Security Council.**

**Having considered** the report of the Secretary-General at its 1979th meeting about the recent developments in Cyprus,

**Having heard** the statement made by the President of the Republic of Cyprus and the statements by the representatives of Cyprus, Turkey, Greece and other member countries,

**Having considered** at its present meeting further developments in the island,

**Deeply deploring** the outbreak of violence and continuing bloodshed,

**Gravely concerned** about the situation which led to a serious threat to international peace and security, and which created a most explosive situation in the whole Eastern Mediterranean area,

**Equally concerned** about the necessity to restore the constitutional structure of the Republic of Cyprus, established and guaranteed by international agreement,

**Recalling** Security Council resolution 186 (1964) of 4 March 1964 and subsequent resolutions of the Security Council on this matter,

**Conscious** of its primary responsibility for the maintenance of international peace and security in accordance with Article 24 of the Charter of the United Nations,

1. **Calls upon** all States to respect the sovereignty, independence and territorial integrity of Cyprus;

2. **Calls upon** all parties to the present fighting as a first step to cease all firing and requests all States to exercise the utmost restraint and to refrain from any action which might further aggravate the situation;

3. **Demands** an immediate end to foreign military intervention in the Republic of Cyprus that is in contravention of operative paragraph 1;

4. **Requests** the withdrawal without delay from the Republic of Cyprus of foreign military personnel present otherwise than under the authority of international agreements including those whose withdrawal was requested by the President of the Republic of Cyprus, Archbishop Makarios, in his letter of 2 July 1974;

5. **Calls on** Greece, Turkey and the United Kingdom of Great Britain and Northern Ireland to enter into negotiations without delay for the restoration of peace in the area and constitutional government in Cyprus and to keep the Secretary-General informed;

6. **Calls on** all parties to cooperate fully with UNFICYP to enable it to carry out its mandate;

7. **Decides** to keep the situation under constant review and asks the Secretary-General to report as appropriate with a view to adopting further measures in order to ensure that peaceful conditions are restored as soon as possible.

# APPENDIX 3

## The Geneva Declaration of 30 July, 1974

1. The Foreign Ministers of Greece, Turkey and the United Kingdom of Great Britain and Northern Ireland held negotiations in Geneva from 25–30 July 1974. They recognized the importance of setting in train, as a matter of urgency, measures to adjust and to regularise within a reasonable period of time the situation in the Republic of Cyprus on a lasting basis, having regard to the international agreements signed at Nicosia on 16 August 1960 and to Resolution 353 of the Security Council of the United Nations. They were, however, agreed on the need to decide first on certain immediate measures.

2. The three Foreign Ministers declared that in order to stabilise the situation, the areas in the Republic of Cyprus controlled by opposing armed forces on 30 July 1974 at 22.00 hours Geneva time should not be extended. They called on all forces including irregular forces, to desist from all offensive or hostile activities.

3. The three Foreign Ministers also concluded that the following measures should be put into immediate effect:

(*a*) A security zone of sizes to be determined by Representatives of Greece, Turkey and the United Kingdom in consultation with the United Nations Peace-Keeping Force in Cyprus (UNFICYP) should be established at the limit of the areas occupied by the Turkish Armed Forces at the time specified in paragraph 2 above. This zone should be entered by no forces other than those of UNFICYP, which should supervise the prohibition of entry.

Pending the determination of the size and character of the security zone, the existing area between the two forces should be entered by no forces.

(*b*) All the Turkish enclaves occupied by Greek or Greek Cypriot Forces should be immediately evacuated. These enclaves will continue to be protected by UNFICYP and to have their previous security arrangements.

Other Turkish enclaves outside the area controlled by the Turkish Armed Forces shall continue to be protected by an UNFICYP security zone and may, as before, maintain their own police and security forces.

(*c*) In mixed villages the functions of security and police will be carried out by UNFICYP.

(*d*) Military personnel and civilians detained as a result of the recent hostilities shall be either exchanged or released under the supervision of the International Committee of the Red Cross within the shortest time possible.

4. The three Foreign Ministers, reaffirming that Resolution 353 of the Security Council should be implemented in the shortest possible time, agreed that within the framework of a just and lasting solution acceptable to all the parties concerned and as peace, security and mutual confidence are established in the Republic of Cyprus, measures should be elaborated which will lead to the timely and phased reduction of the number of armed forces and the amounts of armaments, munitions and other war material in the Republic of Cyprus.

5. Deeply conscious of their responsibilities as regards the maintenance of the independence, territorial integrity and security of the Republic of Cyprus, the three Foreign Ministers agreed that negotiations, as provided for in Resolution 353 of the Security Council, should be carried on with the least possible delay to secure (*a*) the restoration of peace in the area and (*b*) the re-establishment of constitutional government in Cyprus. To this end they agreed that further talks should begin on 8 August 1974 at Geneva. They also agreed that representatives of the Greek Cypriot and Turkish Cypriot Communities should at an early stage, participate in the talks relating to the constitution. Among the constitutional questions to be discussed should be that of an immediate return to constitutional legitimacy, the Vice-President assuming the functions provided for under the 1960 Constitution. The Ministers noted the existence in practice in the Republic of Cyprus of two autonomous administrations, that of the Greek Cypriot Community and that of the Turkish Cypriot Community. Without any prejudice to the conclusions to be drawn from this situation the Ministers agreed to consider at their next meeting the problems raised by their existence.

6. The three Foreign Ministers agreed to convey the contents of this declaration to the Secretary-General of the United Nations and to invite him to take appropriate action in the light of it. They also expressed their conviction of the necessity that the fullest cooperation should be extended by all concerned in the Republic of Cyprus in carrying out its terms.

THE TEXT OF THE BRIEF STATEMENT ALSO SIGNED BY THE
BRITISH, GREEK AND TURKISH FOREIGN MINISTERS
CONCERNING THE 1960 CYPRUS INDEPENDENCE TREATY

The Foreign Ministers of Greece, Turkey and the United Kingdom of

Great Britain and Northern Ireland made it clear that the adherence of their Governments to the declaration of today's date in no way prejudiced their respective views on the interpretation or application of the 1960 Treaty of Guarantee or their rights and obligations under that Treaty.

# APPENDIX 4

## Security Council Resolution 541/83 of 18 November 1983

The Security Council,

**Having heard** *the statement of the Foreign Minister of the Government of the Republic of Cyprus,*

**Concerned** *at the declaration by the Turkish Cypriot authorities issued on 15 November 1983 which purports to create an independent state in northern Cyprus,*

**Considering** *that this declaration is incompatible with the 1960 Treaty concerning the establishment of the Republic of Cyprus and the 1960 Treaty of Guarantee,*

**Considering** *therefore that the attempt to create a 'Turkish Republic of Northern Cyprus' is invalid, and will contribute to a worsening of the situation in Cyprus,*

**Reaffirming** *its resolutions 365 (1974) and 367 (1975),*

**Aware of the need** *for a solution of the Cyprus problem based on the mission of good offices undertaken by the Secretary-General,*

**Affirming** *its continuing support for the United Nations Peace-Keeping Force in Cyprus,*

**Taking note** *of the Secretary-General's statement of 17 November 1983,*

1. **Deplores** *the declaration of the Turkish Cypriot authorities of the purported secession of part of the Republic of Cyprus,*

2. **Considers** *the declaration referred to above as legally invalid and calls for its withdrawal,*

3. **Calls for** *the urgent and effective implementation of its resolutions 365 (1974) and 367 (1975),*

4. **Requests** *the Secretary-General to pursue his mission of good offices in order to achieve the earliest possible progress towards a just and lasting settlement in Cyprus,*

5. **Calls upon** *the parties to cooperate fully with the Secretary-General in his mission of good offices,*

6. **Calls upon** *all states to respect the sovereignty, independence, territorial integrity and non-alignment of the Republic of Cyprus,*

7. **Calls upon** *all states not to recognise any Cypriot state other than the Republic of Cyprus,*

8. **Calls upon** *all states and the two communities in Cyprus to refrain from any action which might exacerbate the situation,*

9. **Requests** *the Secretary-General to keep the Security Council fully informed.*

# APPENDIX 5

November 1984

## Agenda for the Third Round of the Secretary-General's Proximity Talks on Cyprus

(preliminary draft for a joint high-level agreement)

Held at United Nations Headquarters,
on      1984

The parties have agreed on the following matters which are to be viewed as an integrated whole:

The Parties:

(*a*) Recommit themselves to the high-level agreements of 1977 and 1979;

(*b*) Indicate their determination to proceed, at the date referred to in paragrah 14 below, to the establishment of a federal republic that will be independent and non-aligned, bi-communal as regards the federal constitutional aspect and bi-zonal as regards the territorial aspect;

(*c*) Reaffirm their acceptance of those introductory constitutional provisions that were agreed upon at the intercommunal talks in 1981–82:

(i) The Federal Republic of Cyprus shall have international personality; the federal government shall exercise sovereignty in respect of all the territory.

(ii) The people of the Federal Republic shall comprise the Greek Cypriot community and the Turkish Cypriot community. There shall be a single citizenship of the Federal Republic of Cyprus regulated by federal law.

(Reference verbatim to the provisions agreed upon during the course of the intercommunal talks are to be annexed to this document. In both cases wording as reproduced in the revision dated 18.5.82 will be used and checked with both parties.)

1. Powers and functions to be vested in the federal government of the Federal Republic shall comprise:

(*a*) Foreign affairs.

(*b*) Federal financial affairs (including federal budget, taxation, customs and excise duties).

(*c*) Monetary and banking affairs.

(*d*) Federal economic affairs (including trade and tourism).

(*e*) Posts and telecommunications.

(*f*) International transport.

(*g*) Natural resources (including water supply, environment).

(*h*) Federal health and veterinary affairs.

(*i*) Standard setting: weights and measures, patents, trademarks, copyrights.

(*j*) Federal judiciary.

(*k*) Appointment of Federal officers.

(*l*) Defence (to be discussed in connection with international guarantees); security (as it pertains to federal responsibility).

Additional powers and functions may be vested in the federal government by common agreement of both sides. Federal legislation may be executed either by authorities of the federal government or by way of co-ordination between the competent authorities of the federal government and the two (provinces or federated states).

2. The legislature of the federal republic is to be composed of two chambers, the lower chamber with a 70–30 representation and the upper chamber with a 50–50 representation. Federal legislation will be enacted with regard to the matters of federal competence referred to in 1 above. Appropriate constitutional safeguards will be incorporated in the federal constitution, including deadlock-resolving machinery and special provisions to facilitate action on matters necessary for the continued functioning of the federal government (for example, on budgetary questions), as follows:

3. The president and the vice-president will symbolize the unity of the country and the equal political status of the two communities. In addition, the executive will reflect the functional requirements of an effective federal government. To this end, the following structure will be adopted:

4. A tripartite body with one non-Cypriot member having a vote will have the responsibility of ruling on disputes relating to the distribution of powers and functions between the federation and the (provinces or federated states) and on such other matters as may be assigned to it by the parties in accordance with the constitution.

5. As regards the freedom of movement, freedom of settlement and

right to property, a working group will be established to discuss the exercise of these rights, including time frames, practical regulations and possible compensation arrangements, taking in account guideline 3 of the 1977 agreement.

6. Territorial adjustments in addition to the areas already referred to in the 5 August 1981 Turkish Cypriot proposals will be agreed upon at the high-level meeting, bearing in mind the criteria contained in the 1977 high-level agreement. The size of that adjustment will be expressed in the high-level agreement in a measurable form and will also be reflected in the number of Greek Cypriot displaced persons to be resettled. Those adjustments will correspond to_____

_____
_____
_____

7. A timetable for the withdrawal of non-Cypriot military troops and elements, as well as adequate guarantees, will be agreed upon prior to the establishment of the transitional federal government. In the meantime, military deconfrontation measures will be pursued by both sides, using the good offices and assistance of UNFICYP.

8. A fund for Development of the Turkish Cypriot (province or federated state) shall be established with a view to achieving an economic equilibrium between the two (provinces or federated states). A fund will also be established to facilitate the resettlement of the Greek Cypriot displaced persons and for the Turkish Cypriot displaced persons as a consequence of the implementation of paragraph 6. The Federal Government shall contribute to these funds. Foreign governments and international organizations shall be invited to contribute to the funds.

9. The Varosha area and the six additional areas delineated in the Turkish Cypriot map of 5 August 1981 will be placed under United Nations interim administration by _____ as part of the UNFICYP buffer zone, for resettlement.

10. Moratorium on actions tending to prejudice the process outlined in this agreement, both on the international scene and internally.

11. The Nicosia international airport to be reopened under interim United Nations administration with free access from both sides. United Nations arrangements to that effect will be concluded no later than _____ months after the day of the high-level meeting.

12. Adequate machinery for the handling of allegations of non-implementation of confidence-building measures will be agreed upon.

13. Working Group(s) may be set up in light of the political decisions agreed upon at the high-level meeting to elaborate the details of the agreements involved.

14. The required working groups having completed their work, the parties agree that the transitional federal government of the Federal Republic of Cyprus will be set up on ____.

ADDITIONAL POINTS

1. Executive (no rotation)

A. Presidential system—VP veto
   Cabinet ——— 7/3

   1960 Constitution +
   weighted voting, i.e.
   simple majority but
   with one Turkish
   Cypriot voting in
   favour

B. Safeguards/deadlock-resolving machinery:

   (i) Constitutional court—referenda
   (ii) President and vice-president have right to send back for reconsiderationa both laws and cabinet decisions.

2. Legislative:

A. Two chambers:

   Lower house 70/30
   Upper house 50/50
                     1

   On major matters (as, for instance, ten of paragraph 1 list)
   voting by separate majorities in both houses

   On other matters:
   Simple majority in both houses, but at least 30% of Turkish Cypriots in upper house.

B. Safeguards/deadlock-resolving machinery:

   (i) Conciliation committee (3 Greek Cypriots and 2 Turkish Cypriots—weighted voting on Turkish Cypriot)
   (ii) Constitutional court
   (iii) Referenda

   3. Three freedoms as per paragraph 5 without reference to articles 13 and 21.
   4. Territory
      29+ (Twenty-nine plus).
   5. Residual powers with provinces.
   6. Both sides to suggest special status area adjacent to each other for the purpose of enchancing trust between sides (respective civilian jurisdiction to remain).

# APPENDIX 6

## Draft Framework Agreement on Cyprus Presented by the UN Secretary-General on 29 March 1986

Recognizing with satisfaction that the initiative of the Secretary-General, which bore in mind the relevant United Nations resolutions and which began in August 1984 in Vienna and continued through the high-level proximity talks from September to December 1984 and the joint high-level meeting of January 1985 held in New York, has now resulted in an important step towards a just and lasting settlement of the Cyprus problem.

The parties agree on the following matters which are to be viewed as an integrated whole:

1.1 The Parties:

(*a*) Recommit themselves to the high-level agreements of 1977 and 1979;

(*b*) Indicate their determination to proceed, at the date referred to in paragraph 15.1 below, to the establishment of a Federal Republic that will be independent and non-aligned, bi-communal as regards the federal constitutional aspect and bi-zonal as regards the territorial aspect;

(*c*) Reaffirm their acceptance of those introductory constitutional provisions that were agreed upon at the intercommunal talks in 1981–1982:

(i) The Federal Republic of Cyprus shall have international personality. The Federal Government shall exercise sovereignty in respect of all of the territory. The attributes of international personality shall be exercised by the Federal Government in accordance with the federal constitution. The provinces or federated States may act in their areas of competence in accordance with the federal constitution and in a manner that would not duplicate the powers and functions of the Federal Government as defined in the federal constitution.

(ii) The people of the Federal Republic shall comprise the Greek Cypriot community and the Turkish Cypriot community.

There shall be a single citizenship of the Federal Republic of Cyprus regulated by federal law.

(iii) The territory of the Federal Republic shall comprise the two provinces or federated States.

(iv) The official languages of the Federal Republic shall be Greek and Turkish. The English language may also be used.

(v) The Federal Republic shall have a neutral flag and anthem to be agreed. Each province or federated State may have its own flag using mainly elements of the federal flag. The federal flag shall be flown on federal buildings and federal locations to the exclusion of any other flag.

(vi) The Federal Government shall observe the holidays of the Federal Republic. Each province or federated State shall observe the federal holidays as well as those established by it.

(vii) The parties reaffirm all other points that were agreed upon during the course of the intercommunal talks as contained in 'revision' dated 18 May 1982 concerning general provisions, part I, fundamental rights and liberties, part II, as well as parts III and IV.

2.1 The powers and functions to be vested in the Federal Government of the Federal Republic shall comprise:

(*a*) Foreign affairs.

(*b*) Federal financial affairs (including federal budget, taxation, customs and excise duties).

(*c*) Monetary and banking affairs.

(*d*) Federal economic affairs (including trade and tourism).

(*e*) Posts and telecommunications.

(*f*) International transport.

(*g*) Natural resources (including water supply, environment).

(*h*) Federal health and veterinary affairs.

(*i*) Standard setting: weights and measures, patents, trademarks, copyrights.

(*j*) Federal judiciary.

(*k*) Appointment of federal officers.

(*l*) Defence (to be discussed also in connection with the treaties of guarantee and of alliance); security (as it pertains to federal responsibility).

2.2 Additional powers and functions may be vested in the Federal Government by common agreement of both sides. Accordingly, the residual powers shall rest with the provinces or federated States. Federal legislation may be executed either by authorities of the

Federal Government or by way of co-ordination between the competent authorities of the Federal Government and of the two provinces or federated States.

3.1 The legislature of the Federal Republic will be composed of two chambers: a lower chamber with a 70–30 Greek Cypriot and Turkish Cypriot representation, and an upper chamber with a 50–50 representation. Federal legislation will be enacted with regard to the matters of federal competence as referred to in paragraph 2.1 above. The adoption of legislation on major matters, as for instance on ten of the twelve functions referred to in paragraph 2.1 above, will require separate majorities in both chambers. The adoption of legislation on other matters will require majorities of the membership in each chamber.

3.2 Appropriate constitutional safeguards and deadlock-resolving machinery including special provisions to facilitate action on matters necessary for the continued functioning of the Federal Government (e.g., on budgetary questions) will be incorporated in the federal constitution. In case of deadlock in the legislature, the proposed legislation may be submitted in the first instance to a conciliation committee of the legislature composed of three Greek Cypriots and two Turkish Cypriots, whose decision will be taken on the basis of majority vote including at least one Turkish Cypriot. If the deadlock persists, the President and Vice-President of the Federal Republic will, upon request, appoint on an *ad hoc* basis one person each, selected for their knowledge of the subject involved, who, with the assistance of experts as needed including from outside the Federal Republic of Cyprus, will advise the legislature on ways the deadlock could be resolved. The matter may also be submitted to a referendum among the population of the community which opposed the draft legislation. Legislation adopted by the legislature may be taken to the Constitutional Court for ruling as to whether it violates the constitution or is discriminatory against either community.

4.1 The Federal Republic will have a presidential system of government. The President and the Vice-President will symbolize the unity of the country and the equal political status of the two communities. In addition, the executive will reflect the functional requirements of an effective federal government.

4.2 The President will be a Greek Cypriot and the Vice-President will be a Turkish Cypriot. The President and the Vice-President will, separately or conjointly, have the right to veto any law or decision of the legislature and the Council of Ministers in areas to be agreed upon, it being understood that the scope will exceed that covered by the 1960 constitution. The President and the Vice-President will have the right, separately or conjointly, to return any law or decision of the legislature or any decision of the Council of Ministers for reconsideration.

4.3 The Council of Ministers will be composed of Greek Cypriot and Turkish Cypriot ministers on a 7 to 3 ratio. One major ministry will be headed by a Turkish Cypriot, it being understood that the parties agree to discuss that the Minister for Foreign Affairs will be a Turkish Cypriot. The Council of Ministers will take decisions by weighted voting, that is a simple majority including at least one Turkish Cypriot minister. It is understood that the parties agree to discuss that weighted voting will apply to all matters of special concern to the Turkish Cypriot community to be agreed upon.

4.4 Appropriate constitutional safeguards and deadlock-resolving machinery related to decisions by the Council of Ministers, including special provisions to facilitate action on matters necessary for the continued functioning of the Federal Government, will be incorporated in the federal constitution. In case of deadlock, the President and Vice-President of the Federal Republic will, upon request, appoint on an *ad hoc* basis one person each, selected for their knowledge of the subject involved, who, with the assistance of experts as needed including from outside the Federal Republic of Cyprus, will advise the Council of Ministers on ways the deadlock could be resolved. The matter may also be submitted to a referendum among the population of the community which opposed the draft decision. A decision by the Council of Ministers may be taken to the Constitutional Court for ruling as to whether it violates the constitution or is discriminatory against either community.

5.1 The Constitutional Court, when ruling on disputes relating to the distribution of powers and functions between the Federal Government and the provinces or federated States and on such other matters as may be assigned to it by the parties in accordance with the federal constitution, will be composed of one Greek Cypriot, one Turkish Cypriot and one non-Cypriot voting member.

6.1 As regards freedom of movement, freedom of settlement and right to property, a working group will discuss the exercise of these rights, including time-frames, practical regulations and possible compensation arrangements, taking into account guideline 3 of the 1977 agreement.

7.1 Territorial adjustments, in addition to the areas already referred to in the 5 August 1981 Turkish Cypriot proposals, will be agreed upon. These territorial adjustments will result in the Turkish Cypriot province or federated State comprising in the order of 29+ per cent of the territory of the Federal Republic. It is understood that when discussing the actual territorial adjustments the two sides will have in mind the 1977 high-level agreement including 'certain practical difficulties which may arise for the Turkish Cypriot community' and the questions related to resettlement. Both sides agree to suggest special status areas adjacent to each other for the purpose of enhancing trust between the sides. These areas will remain under their respective civilian jurisdictions.

8.1 A timetable for the withdrawal of non-Cypriot military troops and elements, as well as adequate guarantees, will be agreed upon prior to the establishment of a transitional Federal Government. In the meantime, military deconfrontation measures will be pursued by both sides, using the good offices and assistance of UNFICYP.

8.2 The two sides undertake to discuss these issues in good faith and to consider each other's concerns on them.

9.1 A fund for development of the Turkish Cypriot province or federated State shall be established with a view to achieving an economic equilibrium between the two provinces or federated States. A fund will also be established to facilitate the resettlement of the Greek Cypriot displaced persons, and for the Turkish Cypriots displaced as a consequence of the implementation of paragraph 7.1. The Federal Government shall contribute to these funds. Foreign Governments and international organizations shall be invited to contribute to the funds.

10.1 The Varosha area and the six additional areas delineated in the Turkish Cypriot map of 5 August 1981 will be placed under United Nations interim administration as part of the UNFICYP buffer zone for resettlement by ____.

11.1 Both parties agree not to take any action tending to prejudice the process outlined in this agreement, both on the international scene and internally.

12.1 The Nicosia international airport will be reopened under interim United Nations administration with free access from both sides. The United Nations will conclude the arrangements to that effect by ____.

13.1 Adequate machinery for considering allegations of non-implementation of confidence-building measures will be agreed upon. The Secretary-General will make appropriate recommendations to both sides in this regard.

14.1 The parties agree to establish working groups to work out the detailed agreements on the matters referred to in this Agreement, whose elements are interrelated and constitute an integrated whole. The working groups will carry out their work under the direction of joint high-level meetings. These joint high-level meetings will take place every three to four months, on the basis of an agenda prepared by the Secretary-General, to discuss the issues which remain to be negotiated under this agreement, to review the work and provide guidance to the working groups. The joint high-level meetings will be convened by the Secretary-General after adequate preparation.

14.2 Each working group will be composed of delegations from the two sides and will be chaired by a representative of the Secretary-General. The working groups will begin their meetings at the United Nations premises in Nicosia on ____. Each working group will prepare a programme of work and will submit it for approval and guidance to the joint high-level meeting which will take place at the United Nations premises in Nicosia on ____.

14.3 The representative of the Secretary-General chairing each working group will every three months prepare an assessment of the progress made by the working group, which will be presented to the next joint high-level meeting together with the views of the Secretary-General.

15.1 The parties agree that, the required working groups having completed their work and having obtained the approval of the two sides, the transitional Federal Government of the Federal Republic of Cyprus will be set up on ____.

16.1 The Secretary-General will remain at the disposal of the parties to assist in the elaboration of this agreement, and, if required, in its interpretation.

# APPENDIX 7

## Letter Dated 29 March 1986 from the Secretary-General Addressed to President Kyprianou and to His Excellency Mr Denktaş, Presenting the Draft Framework Agreement on Cyprus

I wrote to you on 24 January with my assessment of the point we had then reached and my proposals about how we should proceed. I have now carefully studied reports on the discussions that took place with each side during the lower-level meetings. It is evident that both sides have made a real effort to overcome the remaining differences. I would like to take this opportunity to express to you my appreciation for the constructive approach taken by your representatives.

The talks that took place with each side in Geneva and in Nicosia proved most useful in bringing into clearer focus their respective concerns and indicated points of convergence on the substance of the issues which remained to be resolved. This has made it possible to draft a framework agreement which preserves all that has been achieved since August 1984 and endeavours to reconcile the outstanding differences in a manner that protects the interests of both communities.

I am pleased to present to you herewith the draft framework agreement as it has emerged from our joint efforts. When considering this text, I would urge both sides to keep the following in mind:

This framework agreement is an indispensable step in an ongoing process. Both sides have agreed on the matters that will be negotiated after the framework agreement is accepted, and to do so in good faith and with a willingness to consider each other's concerns.

These negotiations will provide each side with ample opportunities to assure itself of the good intentions of the other. While the text commits the two parties to proceed towards an overall solution within an agreed framework, its ultimate implementation will depend on both sides being able to negotiate to their mutual satisfaction the matters on which agreement has yet to be achieved.

Acceptance of the draft framework agreement will allow, for the very first time, all the outstanding issues to be tackled in earnest and in a decisive manner as an integrated whole.

Upon receiving both sides' acceptance of the draft framework agreement, I shall spare no effort to maintain the momentum towards a just and lasting solution of the Cyprus problem. The procedures set out in paragraphs 14.1 to 14.3 of the enclosed draft are designed towards that end.

Both sides have made it clear that they do not wish negotiations to drag on. It is therefore important that these meetings, whether at the high-level or working-level, be carefully prepared. This approach would ensure that all outstanding issues will be thoroughly and expeditiously dealt with.

I hope that the two sides will be able to advise me soon of their acceptance of the draft framework agreement. I propose that thereafter senior members of my staff should visit Nicosia to finalize the dates to be inserted in the framework agreement and to prepare for an early joint high-level meeting, with my personal participation, to formalize the Parties' acceptance of the framework agreement and the steps that follow from it. I propose that this preparatory meeting in Nicosia should take place on 21 April.

Much effort has been expended by the two sides and by the United Nations in our joint endeavour since August 1984. I believe it to be of the greatest importance that we should all now seize the present opportunity to break through to a just and lasting solution of the Cyprus problem. In doing so, we shall not only respond to the wishes of the people of Cyprus; we shall also fulfil our responsibility to relax tensions and promote international peace and security in the region as a whole.

# Select Bibliography

BIRAND, M. A., *30 Hot Days*, K. Rustem & Brother, Oxford (1985).

BUCHHEIT, LEE C., *Secession: The Legitimacy of Self-Determination*, Yale University Press, New Haven and London (1978).

CLERIDES, GLAFKOS, *Cyprus: My Deposition*, Alithia Publishing Co. Ltd., Nicosia (1989), 2 volumes.

CRAWSHAW, NANCY, *The Cyprus Revolt: An Account of the Struggle for Union with Greece*, George Allen & Unwin, London (1978).

DENKTASH, RAUF R., *The Cyprus Triangle*, K. Rustem & Brother and George Allen & Unwin, London (1982 and 1988).

ECEVIT, BÜLENT, *The Cyprus Question*, Turkish Cypriot PIO, Lefkoşa (1984).

EHRLICH, THOMAS, *International Crises and the Role of Law, Cyprus 1958–1967*, Oxford University Press (1974).

ERTEKÜN, NECATI, *The Cyprus Dispute*, K. Rustem & Brother, Oxford (1984).

FOLEY, CHARLES, *Legacy of Strife: Cyprus from Rebellion to Civil War*, Penguin, Baltimore (1964).

GENÇ, ALPER F., *Cyprus Report: From My 1974 Diary*, Lefkoşa (1978).

GIBBONS, SCOTT H., *Peace Without Honour*, ADA Publishing House, Ankara (1969).

HIGGINS, ROSALYN, *United Nations Peacekeeping Documents and Commentary: Europe 1964–1979*, OUP/RIIA, Oxford (1981).

KYRIAKIDES, STANLEY, *Cyprus: Constitutionalism and Crisis Government*, Univ. of Pennsylvania Press, Philadelphia (1968).

OBERLING, PIERRE, *The Road to Bellapais: The Turkish Cypriot Exodus to Northern Cyprus*, Columbia University Press, New York (1982).

PATRIC, RICHARD A., *Political Geography and the Cyprus Conflict 1963–71*, University of Waterloo Publications, Waterloo, Ont. (1976).

POLYVIOU, POLYVIOS G., *Cyprus in Search of a Constitution*, Chr. Nicolaou & Sons Ltd., Nicosia (1976).

PURCELL, H. D., *Cyprus*, Ernest Benn Ltd., London (1969).

REDDAWAY, JOHN, *Burdened with Cyprus: The British Connection*, K. Rustem & Brother and Weidenfeld & Nicolson Ltd., London (1986).

STAVRINIDES, ZENON, *The Cyprus Conflict: National Identity and Statehood*, Loris Stavrinides Press, Nicosia (1975).

STEPHENS, ROBERT, *Cyprus: A Place of Arms*, Pall Mall Press, London (1966).

TORNARITIS, CRITON G., *Cyprus and its Constitutional and Other Legal Problems*, Proodos Ltd., Nicosia (1977).

# Index